Electronic Exchanges

The Elsevier and IIT Stuart
Center for Financial
Markets Press

ILLINOIS INSTITUTE OF TECHNOLOGY

Center for Financial Markets

Series Editor: Michael Gorham

The Elsevier and IIT Stuart Center for Financial Markets Press is a partnership between Elsevier Inc. and the IIT Stuart Center for Financial Markets at the Illinois Institute of Technology's Stuart School of Business. The partnership was created to publish a series of books pertaining to developments in global financial markets. The books explore the markets, institutions, and instruments that are integral to the global financial system. The titles in the series can take a country-specific approach as in *India's Financial Markets*, or an institutional approach across countries as in *Electronic Exchanges*. The goal of the Elsevier and IIT Stuart Center for Financial Markets Press is to provide a deep understanding of the workings of these wonderful and mysterious things called financial markets.

Series Editor Michael Gorham is Industry Professor and Director of the IIT Stuart Center for Financial Markets at Illinois Institute of Technology in Chicago. Mike serves on the board of directors for two exchanges—the CBOE Futures Exchange and the National Commodity and Derivatives Exchange of India. He serves on the Business Conduct Committees of the Chicago Mercantile Exchange and the National Futures Association, the editorial boards of the GARP Risk Review and of *Futures Industry* magazine. He is also regional director of the Global Association of Risk Professionals for Chicago. He served as the first director of the Commodity Futures Trading Commission's new Division of Market Oversight, a division of 100 economists, lawyers, futures trading specialists and others dedicated to the oversight of the nation's 12 futures exchanges. Earlier, he worked for 4 years as an economist at the Federal Reserve Bank of San Francisco and 18 years in various capacities at the Chicago Mercantile Exchange. He holds a BA in English literature from the University of Notre Dame, an MS in food and resource economics from the University of Florida and a Ph.D. in agricultural economics from the University of Wisconsin. He served for two years in the Peace Corps in Malawi, Africa.

Electronic Exchanges
The Global Transformation from Pits to Bits

Michael Gorham
Nidhi Singh

AMSTERDAM • BOSTON • HEIDELBERG • LONDON
NEW YORK • OXFORD • PARIS • SAN DIEGO
SAN FRANCISCO • SINGAPORE • SYDNEY • TOKYO
The Elsevier and IIT Stuart Center for Financial Markets Press

Stuart School of Business
ILLINOIS INSTITUTE OF TECHNOLOGY

Center for Financial Markets

Elsevier Inc.
30 Corporate Drive, Suite 400, Burlington, MA 01803, USA
525 B Street, Suite 1900, San Diego, California 92101-4495, USA
84 Theobald's Road, London WC1X 8RR, UK

This book is printed on acid-free paper. ∞

Library of Congress Cataloging-in-Publication Data
Application Submitted

British Library Cataloguing-in-Publication Data
A catalogue record for this book is available from the British Library.

ISBN: 978-0-12-374252-0

For information on all Elsevier publications
visit our Web site at elsevierdirect.com

Printed in the United States of America
09 10 11 12 13 14   9 8 7 6 5 4 3 2 1

Dedications

This book is dedicated to my parents, Marjorie Jane Cowell and John Orville Gorham, he a wellspring of humor, she a fount of fun, hard work and integrity, who were both determined that I receive a good education, even if they had to make great sacrifices to see that happen. And to my siblings, Linda, Steve, Margaret and Elizabeth, each of whom have followed their own unique paths, and from each of whom I have learned something profound.

Michael Gorham

To the visionaries, innovators and entrepreneurs who dragged financial markets into the future. To my parents, for encouraging me to seek my own path. And to the new dog I am getting when this book is published.

Nidhi Singh

Contents

Acknowledgments

This book would not have existed if two major things hadn't happened. First, Karen Maloney, Economics and Finance Publisher at Academic Press/Elsevier, asked Mike to write a book about the markets. Thanks to Karen for that and also for her patience and guidance along the way. And thanks to Assistant Editor, Stacey Walker, for all her work in making this book a reality. Second, at one of their periodic lunches, Mike told Nidhi about the project and realized how much stronger the book would be with Nidhi's extensive technology background (at OCC, TT and Goldman Sachs). Luckily, Nidhi agreed to join the project.

This book has benefited greatly from the help of others, and we hope that we have properly remembered all of them below, though we sometimes lay awake at night knowing that we have surely forgotten some. Dick Dufour (of the CBOE) helped early on by loaning us articles, books and his time, especially in explaining some of the less known details of the equity options exchanges. His boss (and Mike's former boss), Bill Brodsky, was also very helpful in explaining industry subtleties. David Krell gave us an inside view of the creation of the ISE. Thanks to Gary Lahey for the many hours of discussion over the years on the ins and outs of option trading. Herbie Skeete was incredibly generous in giving us access to his wonderful resource Mondo Visione, which was very helpful when trying to get details on the many exchanges worldwide. Thanks to Rich Heckinger and John McPartland of the Chicago Fed for reading and commenting on early chapters. Thanks to both Gary Ginter and Jim McNulty for conversations on the unfolding of certain aspects of electronic trading. Thanks also to Patti Cone, a thoughtful and attentive editor, for reading many of the chapters. Thanks to Patrick Catania of NCDEX, the only person I know who actually worked for Intex when it unsuccessfully took on the CBOT and CME in 1984, an event few remember. Thanks to Dick Lamm and Meg Austin of the CME for helping us understand the CME's demutualization process. And thanks to Paula Voigt of the CME, who helped in digging out data for the history of CME membership sale prices. We are deeply grateful to Andrea Corcoran, one of the most knowledgeable humans on earth regarding market regulation, for contributing a chapter on same. And thanks to photographer Leon Dimitrios, who allowed us to use a great photograph of the SIMEX floor on the cover of this book. The photo is taken from "Exchanges," a coffee table book about exchanges and trading to be published by Leon and Mike in 2009/2010 (see www.corellapublishing,com for details).

We would like to thank Harris Brumfield, CEO of Trading Technologies, for providing valuable insight in early electronic trading systems at CBOT and Eurex and for always being available to answer questions. Thanks to Diane Saucier of Trading Technologies for helping us understand energy trading. We would also like to thank Krista Dugan of Goldman Sachs whose feedback on our early outlines was tremendously valuable. Thanks also to Raakhee Tharani of Goldman Sachs for her help in distilling the pros and cons of electronic trading. Thanks to Malcolm Kwakye and Bill Herder (even on his vacation!) of Trading Technologies for reading and editing many versions of our chapters and always providing honest criticism. Thanks also to Suzanne Mueller of Stuart School of Business, and Amar Lohana and Karthik Ramanan of Goldman Sachs for brainstorming book and chapter titles.

A number of students at the Stuart School of Business at the Illinois Institute of Technology gave freely of their time to create charts, graphs and dig out data, and I would like to thank Van Pezzello, Director of Student Services for helping me recruit some of these students. The students (by now many are former students toiling in the vineyards of finance) include: Bikram Chandra, Gaithithri Choda, Shekar Gupta, Saideep Janyavula, Poulomi Kundu, Taral Meta, Phil Perkins, Cindy Quendangen (whose special project on electronic equity exchanges was especially helpful), Rajeev Ranjan, Ankit Rambhia, Vikram Sanjeeva, Varun Sareen, Jalpan Shah, Ashmita Tiwari, Falgun Vithalani, Donghui Wang, and Gaohua Zhou. In addition, Stephanie Frang, an MBA student at DePaul with experience in the industry, took on the task of reading the entire manuscript before it was submitted.

Nidhi's special acknowledgment:

I would like to thank Mike for inviting me to join this project, and for his patience, insight, thoughtful criticism, and encouragement. I could not have written this book with anyone else. I would not have written it with anyone else.

Writing a book turned out to be significantly more difficult than I imagined. I am grateful that Pinku Surana hounded me to finish this book. He served as research assistant, copy editor, and personal chef. I could not have finished this book without his help.

1 An Era of Creative Destruction

Executive Summary

This chapter presents a quick history of exchanges, their purpose, and their development. It delves into the process of floor-based trading, the system used for well over a century on exchanges such as the New York Stock Exchange (NYSE) and the Chicago Board of Trade (CBOT). Then it explores the technological innovations that led to the development of electronic exchanges and gives an overview of its process and implications for the future.

Introduction

The book has a primary and a secondary purpose. The primary purpose is to tell the fascinating and important story of how and why those institutions we call exchanges have begun to bear no resemblance to their former selves, of how the stock and derivatives exchanges of the world are being rapidly transformed into institutions that are much more accessible and efficient than their predecessors of the recent past.

The secondary purpose is hidden in the primary one: By telling the story of the transformation and how it is affecting virtually every aspect of the way exchanges function and the way people and institutions trade, the reader will also walk away from the book with a thorough understanding of the organization, role, and function of exchanges today.

The basic story of the transformation is a story of Schumpeter's "creative destruction,"[1] in which old systems, old ways of doing things, and old ways of life are being destroyed as new, more efficient, more transparent systems are taking their place. Old jobs disappear and new jobs are created. The clerks, runners, and price reporters are no longer needed to manage the flow of customer orders as the orders shift from voice to keyboard and as the bids and offers are automatically matched and captured. The staffs of both exchanges and brokerage firms are shifting from those who took care of order entry, trade matching, and trade and price reporting on a physical trading floor to those who take care of the hardware and software of screen-based systems.

The traders themselves are moving from floor jobs, where a strong voice and athletic endurance were important, to desk jobs surrounded by six screens, a keyboard, and a mouse. At the extreme, some traders have become black-box babysitters, merely watching as a sophisticated set of programming code makes all the trading decisions at the speed of light. It's a wonderful thing for a trader to drop all his or her accumulated wisdom into emotionless lines of "if-then" instructions, but it also raises questions about the end game. Will trading still be fun a decade from now? Will humans still be involved? In the short term, the exchanges are continually struggling to improve system architecture and increase bandwidth to keep up with growing volumes and the higher frequency and more complex trading styles made possible by electronic access.

But to tell this story in a meaningful way, it is important to explain what these exchanges do, how they are organized, how they are populated, how they innovate, and how they compete and cooperate. So this is really a book that explains the modern exchange and all its most important features, and that is the secondary purpose of the book.

Trading: Simple Concept, Complex Process

A simple definition of trading is the exchange of goods or services and money between buyers and sellers. Whether it is the exchange of agricultural goods or credit default swaps, the essential idea of trading has not changed. Buyers and sellers must meet, negotiate a price, and exchange goods for money.[2] Though people have traded with each other for thousands of years, recent innovations in technology have led to radical improvements in every step of this simple process. Where people once met every fall to sell their crops, farmers can now enter into contracts with buyers around the world who promise to purchase those crops sometime in the future. Where people once negotiated loans to local businesses, they can now trade debt in companies and countries around the world in the blink of an eye. In fact, they can trade insurance on that debt to lower the risk of default. Where people once met face to face under a tree, in a coffeehouse, or on a large trading floor to trade equity in companies, they can now instantly trade shares for almost any company on any market in the world from a computer at home. Technology enables buyers and sellers anywhere in the world to quickly negotiate a price and reliably exchange any product in mere seconds. It has transformed trading into a system that is global, faster, and more complex, requiring a web of infrastructure and regulations that brings every country, market, and individual closer together.

Long ago, people met in various ad hoc venues, such as weekly markets, churches, coffee shops, or town halls. Individuals were responsible for finding buyers or sellers themselves and negotiating the terms for each trade. However, these multiple and separate meeting places meant the pool of potential trading partners was often fragmented and, therefore, the items were not necessarily traded at the best price. As the demand for trading increased, these gathering places became overcrowded and made it more difficult to conduct trades smoothly. These factors prompted the adoption of a designated place to conduct trades in a structured way. This evolution resulted in the modern exchange.

The Birth of Exchanges

From their humble beginnings as a place for buyers and sellers to gather to trade goods, exchanges have grown into complex organizations critical to the global economy. The introduction of exchanges marked the beginning of the modern financial market structure. The exchange was a novel idea introduced to address some of the inefficiencies in early trading and to protect brokers and dealers who were professionally engaged in handling these assets. It provided people a designated place to meet and trade a suite of products with each other. There were specific exchanges to trade agricultural products, others for trading metals, and still more were formed to trade stocks. The formation of exchanges all across the globe has a very interesting and colorful history.

The New York Stock Exchange (NYSE) was formed by 24 stockbrokers under a buttonwood tree outside of 68 Wall Street. The Buttonwood Agreement of 1792 between these brokers read, in part:

> We the Subscribers, Brokers for the Purchase and Sale of the Public Stock, do hereby solemnly promise and pledge ourselves to each other, that we will not buy or sell from this day for any person whatsoever, any kind of Public Stock, at least than one quarter of one percent Commission on the Specie value and that we will give preference to each other in our Negotiations.[3]

The early formation of exchanges was often spurred by the growing interest in trading. In 17th-century England, informal stock trading began to finance the Muscovy Company and the East India Company, which were attempting to reach China and India, respectively. The companies began selling shares to merchants, giving them the potential to earn a portion of any profits made from the voyage. These people frequently met in coffeehouses in London's famous Change Alley. As interest in these and many other floatations of shares increased and the number of participants outgrew the Alley, they moved to a bigger place of their own in 1773 and called it the Stock Exchange. Similarly, the oldest stock exchange in Asia, the Bombay Stock Exchange (BSE), was also formed by a group of people who regularly met under a banyan tree. When the number of buyers and sellers grew and spilled into the streets, they also agreed to form a designated place for trading by creating an exchange.

Although the history of trading began with agricultural products and metals, trading stocks is mechanically simpler than trading goods because it is merely the exchange of documents entitling the bearer to some fractional ownership of a firm. Commodities, on the other hand, involve the exchange of many head of cattle or bushels of wheat of differing grades, weights and locations. The fluctuation in production caused the prices of these goods to be volatile. To protect themselves from the volatility of prices, farmers, merchants, and agricultural companies began writing and trading contracts for grain to arrive in Chicago on some future date. A *futures contract* is an agreement between two parties to buy or sell a product at a specified date in the future. Without a central counterparty, the onus was on individuals to ensure that the agreement was honored at the specified delivery date. It was not uncommon for the buyer or the seller to back out of the agreement if market conditions changed dramatically before the time of delivery. The commodity exchanges were formed to standardize these contracts, ensure that both parties honored these trades, and establish a structured delivery mechanism for the goods upon settlement.

Chicago, one of the original birthplaces of modern futures trading, was an ideal location for commodities trading due to its close proximity to farmland. Chicago has long boasted two of the world's oldest commodities markets: the Chicago Board of Trade (CBOT), founded in 1848, and the Chicago Mercantile Exchange, CME, originally started as the Chicago Butter and Egg Board in 1898. These markets helped bring together buyers and sellers of commodities in one designated area, thus making it easier to find someone to trade with. Similar markets were created throughout the country to support regional agricultural or other physical commodity products. The New York Mercantile Exchange (currently NYMEX) was one of the largest physical commodity markets, trading everything from butter and cheese to dried fruit, canned goods, and poultry. The Minneapolis Grain Exchange was formed to support the grain farms for the region. Similarly, the London Metal Exchange (LME), the largest and oldest market for metals, had its roots in groups of ship charterers, metal traders, and financiers who would get together in various coffeehouses to trade mostly domestic metal. As demand grew and global trade increased, people began trading metals from regions as far away as South America and Asia. The increasing number of traders and the growing list of metal products prompted the group to form the London Metal Exchange to provide a structured trading location and to better manage the flow of metals traded.

These early stock, commodity, and metal exchanges were formed across the globe to trade a variety of products. They were all formed to eliminate the constant struggle to find a buyer or seller, to provide structure and ensure fairness in trading, and to provide better price discovery. After the birth of these early markets, many exchanges were formed for specific regions or for specific products. For example, there were over 40 exchanges in China at one point, over 20 exchanges in India, and over 250 in the United States. These exchanges served as a designated place, called the *trading floor*, where the buyers and sellers gathered to trade. Floor-based trading, or *pit trading*, has been the foundation of financial markets for well over a century. The exchanges transformed trading into a world of organized chaos, although outsiders who see a trading floor for the first time find it difficult to see *any* order in the chaos. Exchanges eliminated the inefficiencies of locating people to trade with and introduced rules and regulations to ensure fair and orderly trading. They also ensured that products were properly transferred between the two parties after a trade.

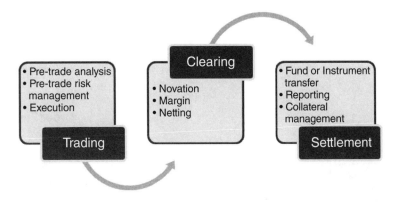

Figure 1.1 The trade cycle.

Though modern exchanges have evolved into complex organizations by adopting new ideas and innovations to improve their overall structure, the physical floor remained the cornerstone of trading. The model worked successfully for centuries, despite the noisy chaos on the floor.

Figure 1.1 shows the major processes that every trade undergoes. Throughout the book we will be discussing these three main processes and the changes happening within each of these processes. However, the basic concept of these three main processes remains the same.

The *trading phase* involves the activities associated with trading. This process generally includes steps that traders take to analyze the market or their strategies (pre-trade analysis). *Pre-trade risk management* is more widely associated with the electronic trading model; it allows risk managers to analyze the risk of a trade before it reaches the exchange. Of course, the trade function also includes the activities of *buying* and *selling* products. *Clearing* and *settlement*, discussed in greater detail later in this chapter, include the final reconciliation of the trades for the day and actual transfer of funds or the instrument that was bought or sold on the exchange. This process continues even as the financial markets shed their century-old floor-trading (open outcry) model and adopt an electronic trading model.

To understand the current transformation, let's first explore how the open outcry model handled these trading functions.

Open Outcry Trading

The uninitiated visitor watching a trading floor sees a place full of chaos, emotion, drama, and excitement. But behind this adrenaline-fueled trading model was a structure and process that worked for over a century. It was a

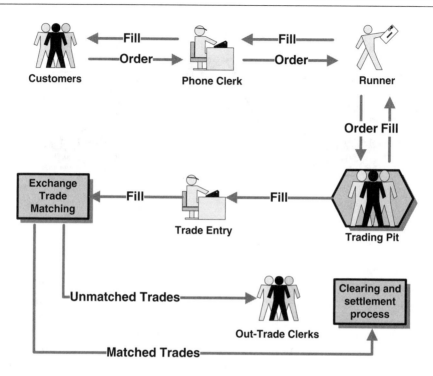

Figure 1.2 The floor-trading model.

tediously manual process requiring hundreds of people on the floor and behind the scenes to ensure that every trade on the floor was accounted for, recorded, executed, cleared, and settled. Trading on the exchange has followed this floor-trading model, also called *open outcry*, as the primary method of trading. Figure 1.2 details the floor-trading model and the various job functions required to process a trade.

As shown in Figure 1.2,[4] the floor-trading model is extremely people-intensive. A trade touches many hands before it is executed between a buyer and seller. The phone clerks take the incoming orders from external customers and write these orders on slips of paper. The runners deliver these orders to the floor brokers, who gather along with floor traders trading for themselves in a *trading pit*, an area of a trading floor assigned for a specific product. These floor traders and the floor brokers have traditionally been members of the exchange and the only people authorized to trade on the trading pit. They scream and shout at each other to indicate their orders. Hand signals are commonly used to indicate the price, buy/sell orders, and additional details about the product, such as expiration month, quantity, and type of order. In addition, the runners run from pit to pit to give the floor brokers the orders received by their firm's clients. All these orders are then recorded on a paper or cardboard *trade card*,[5] including the traders' symbols.[6] These trades eventually reach the *market makers/specialists*.[7] The specialist serves as a human matching engine, posting bid and ask prices, managing limit orders, and executing trades. In the early days, people quickly updated chalkboards with the current bid and ask prices. As the exchanges adopted technology, the prices for products were updated automatically on screens installed throughout the trading floor.

The yelling and screaming continue throughout the trading sessions in the trading pits. As the specialists match the trades, the runners deliver the confirmation back to phone clerks, who notify the customers. The trade clerk enters all the fills for the exchange matching system. By the end of the day, the floor is covered with paper discarded from the day's trading.

As exciting and energetic as floor-trading was, the process for a trade to go from order to settlement was extremely lengthy and cumbersome. The trades often contained an error. The exchange trade-matching process consisted of reconciling all the trades received from the trading pits for the day for the final clearing and settlement process. The process was not pretty. Every day the out-trade clerks would handle numerous out-trades or unmatched trades. The team of out-trade clerks would correct errors made on the floor, such as trades with the wrong price or the wrong quantity ("Fifty" and "Fifteen" often sound the same on a noisy trading floor), and there would be a number of trades that simply could not be corrected. Every morning before entering the trading floor, traders would line up at the out-trade desk to review the list of these error trades. Either these trades would need to be canceled or traders themselves would need to correct the errors. All the matched trades from the end of the day were sent to the clearing and settlement process, the final step in the trade cycle. Generally referred to as *back-office processing*, the clearing and settlement process is both tedious and complex. These processes further required coordination among the various players in financial markets, and it took days before the executed trades were settled.

The Clearing and Settlement Process

An important step within the trade cycle, the clearing and settlement process ensures that executed trades are matched and processed accurately. Every trade executed on the exchange must flow through the clearing process, where the buy and the sell trades are matched, and at contract maturity the settlement process delivers the funds and the product to the trading parties.[8] A simple process on surface, trade matching and clearing comprises a series of complex steps to ensure that the contractual terms of each trade are fulfilled. Prior to the birth of exchanges, people not only had the burden of finding someone to trade with, they also took on the risk that the trades might not be honored by either the buyer or the seller. For example, let's say that the buyer and seller agreed on a contract for wheat at a specific price. Without the clearing and settlement process, trading parties faced substantial credit and/or default risk. In our example of the wheat trade, the buyer faces issues such as not receiving the wheat or receiving a different quality of wheat than agreed on. The seller faces the risk of not getting the payment for the wheat sold. People traded primarily based on trust and always carried substantial risk of the other party not honoring its side of the contractual obligation of the trade.

The creation of exchanges brought the buyers and sellers together to trade, but the credit and default still remained. To ensure that traders had trust and could trade with anyone on the trading floors, *clearing houses* were established. The role of these clearing houses is to provide the trading community with trust that the trade obligations will always be fulfilled. A clearing house fulfills this role by acting as a *central counterparty* (CCP) that serves as the guarantor behind all the trades executed on the exchanges. The CCP takes the burden of the credit and default risk associated with trading. With the CCP as a middleman and as a guarantor of every trade, the trading community can trade on the exchange without the worry of the other party backing out of the trade.

To provide this guarantee, every trade executed on the exchange flows through the clearing and settlement process. Every day millions of trades are executed by trading firms, and every single trade has to go through the complex process at the clearinghouse. The clearing process matches all the trades. All the buy orders for a specific product at a specific price are matched against the matching sell orders.

To minimize the number of trades that flow to the settlement process, clearinghouses perform a process called *netting* during the trade-matching process. The netting process balances all the buys and the sells executed by the same trading firm for the same security and calculates the net difference, which is the delivery requirement for the trading firm. To guarantee the contractual obligation of these trades, the CCP takes the opposite side for every trade. In the process commonly known as *novation*, the CCP guarantees the delivery of the financial instrument to the buyer, and the seller is guaranteed the payment for the financial instrument sold, even if one of the parties defaults or becomes insolvent.

Today all the regulated exchanges[9] around the world have a clearing and settlement process that provides the trust for the trading community to trade with anyone on the trading floor without the worry of credit or default risk. To ensure a smooth post-trading operation and to be a guarantor for every trade, the clearing and settlement process includes functions such as risk management, margining, and collateral management. Although the basic concept of the clearing and settlement process remains the same across asset classes, there are some key differences in both the clearing process as well as the settlement process between the equities and the derivatives asset class.

Equities

The clearing and settlement process in the equities world is simpler than in the derivatives world. The equities trading process involves the trading of corporate stocks, which requires the transfer of ownership between the buyer and the seller. When a stock is traded on an exchange, this is followed by a transfer of ownership of the stock from the buyer to the seller and a transfer of funds from the seller to the buyer. The clearing process ensures that every executed buy order matches an equivalent executed sell order. The clearinghouse serves as a guarantor of the trade and inherits the risk of the seller not having the stock or the buyer not having proper funding for the stock, though the clearinghouse first looks to the clearing broker to ensure or make good on performance. The settlement process ensures that the ownership and the funds are simultaneously transferred between the buyer and the seller. The settlement process in the securities world is generally referred to as T + n, meaning trade date plus the number of days, n, that it takes for the ownership and funds to transfer. In the United States, securities are settled on a T + 3 basis; most securities exchanges around the world perform settlement on a T + 2 basis, and the clearinghouse carries the risk until the settlement process is complete.

Derivatives

Derivatives such as physical commodities, futures, and options follow a similar process of netting and novation as the equities. In equities trading, the clearing and settlement process is completed in two or three days (depending on the T + n requirement), and the ownership and the funds are transferred in full at the time of settlement. Derivatives, however, are contracts that provide the user the right and/or obligation to purchase these underlying instruments at a later date, which could be months or even years in the future. Due to these long settlement dates, the derivatives positions stay open until the time of the settlement date, which means that the actual delivery does not occur until the future date. This poses a prolonged risk exposure for the clearinghouse, since there is a much longer period during which the buyer or seller could default. To mitigate this risk, the CCP requires the settlement process for the derivatives to be completed on the same day. This means that every day the settlement process takes place based on the daily revaluation of the derivatives contracts. This process is called *mark to market*. Every contract is revalued based on the day's settlement price, and the buyers and sellers' accounts are adjusted based on the price changes. This process continues until the expiry date or until the contract is liquidated.

This floor-trading model has been followed globally since the birth of exchanges. There were physical floors around the world to support various asset classes. In addition, the exchanges generally only supported regional or national areas. The exchanges hardly ever had any significant global customer base. For example, at the beginning of the 20th century, there were numerous regional exchanges for the same asset class. For example, the United States and the United Kingdom each had close to 30 different regional stock exchanges.[10] These exchanges seldom competed with each other because there was no way to connect these markets. However, the birth of telecommunications provided an early glimpse at the future of global connectivity. For example, the NYSE earned a larger market share than the Philadelphia Stock Exchange (the first stock exchange in the United States) because it adopted the telegraph, which allowed it to expand by receiving orders from customers not physically located on the trading floor.[11] Later the adoption of the telephone spurred even more competition between exchanges because traders could now get information on other markets via telephone. As telecommunications improved, the floors were filled with telephones to support the increased market participation. More people could now trade by calling in their orders to the trading firms, which would then transmit the orders to the floor brokers. As computer systems were introduced, exchanges adopted them to help specialists store trade data, making it easier to track all the orders received. Although trade volume grew and the number of market participants increased, until the recent technology transformation exchanges functioned in the same manner as before: Traders screaming at each other in open outcry pits.

Technology and Its Impact on Financial Markets

The innovations in computer technology have had a profound and lasting impact on the world. This technology gave rise to the Information Age, which created entire industries that processed data rather than physical goods. From ancient mainframes that filled entire rooms to tiny computers embedded in credit cards, computer technology has rapidly become smaller, cheaper, and more powerful. Computers have been used for decades to store and process massive amounts of data. This eliminated the inefficiency of storing information on paper for people to process manually. Results are obtained quickly and automatically, with fewer errors. Early computers were too large and expensive to be used in many industries, but size and cost were reduced at an astonishing rate. This allowed more industries to employ computers for data processing tasks, culminating in the introduction of the personal computer (PC), which brought this technology to the masses. Today companies and even individuals can easily get access to computers that are as powerful as recent supercomputers. This computing power is now applied to financial markets to react to events in milliseconds and to mine mountains of data for new insights. It is used by exchanges and clearinghouses to process millions of trades per day, as well as by regulators to monitor all those trades. Customers can trade on markets anywhere in the world from their cell phones.

The development of the Internet was required to connect all these computers into a global telecommunications network. Originally developed as a network for military computers, the Internet is like a telephone system for computers, without a central routing authority. Information does not move directly from point A to point B; instead, each message takes its own route through several computers to reach its destination. For this reason, communication on the Internet incurs a small delay, called *latency*, and can be insecure. To avoid these problems, many financial companies have reused the enabling technologies for the Internet to create a private network directly to the exchange. Large investments in global fiber optics have led to a glut of network capacity around the world. Fortunately, this means there is plenty of bandwidth available between global financial centers.

These technology advancements have driven not only the changes in financial markets but the global economy as well. These innovations have connected the world electronically. They have made information access easy, fast, and cheap. The increasing productivity of companies, economies, and governments has widely been attributed to the Information Age. The Internet and PCs have become integral parts of the global economy and people's personal lives. And just as the Internet and the PC have changed the world, they have had a profound impact on the financial markets. In recent years the financial markets have been full of excitement, energy, and drama, except this time it is not on the trading floor. It is the excitement of watching the technological pioneers and early adopters challenging the century-old floor-trading model. It is the energy of witnessing new jobs and new functions being created in the financial markets. It is watching the drama of pessimists defending the old models and the floor-trading. The Information Age is truly revolutionizing the financial industry.

Trading is an information-intensive activity. In addition to the current trading price for the product, information such as economic news, historical prices, analysis, and trends also plays a critical role in making trading decisions. In the past, the financial markets used technology to improve processes and to add efficiency on the floor. For example, in the old days, chalkboards were updated by exchange employees who sprinted throughout the day to provide the latest bids and offers on products. Technology replaced these human workers with electronic bulletin boards installed throughout the trading floor that were updated via keyboard every time a specialist entered a new bid and offer for a product. In former times, external news on the economy or information about products was generally obtained by traders and brokers on the floor by talking to each other or by calling their firms' analysts or customer brokers upstairs. Technology brought computer terminals[12] onto the trading floors, allowing floor traders and brokers to access external news as well as market data.

Technology adoption, however, primarily benefited the floor and the floor-trading process. For the general public, which was far removed from the floor-trading world, the only way to receive market information was by either calling the broker or reading newspapers and trade journals, but the information was limited and stale. Things today have changed dramatically. Anyone with a PC and Internet connectivity can access the market information for exchanges around the globe in real time. The digital revolution has allowed financial markets to access, store, and process more information than they ever could in the floor-trading days. The wealth of information available today has transformed the way financial markets utilize this information. It has allowed trading firms to redefine their trading strategies and trading styles. It has created a level playing field between the trading community and the general public.

The Decade that Changed the Financial World

Much of the 1990s was a prosperous decade for the world economy. More commonly referred to as the *dot-com era*, it was a time of unprecedented growth in technology. Today the term *dot-com* is remembered for the dot-com bust, the eventual collapse of the speculative bubble, but it is the source of many of the positive technological advances that continue to have a profound impact on the world.

The 1980s saw the birth of some well-known companies such as Microsoft, Dell, and Cisco. Companies such as Microsoft and Dell brought personal computers and their operating systems to the general public and the first real glimpse of technology that is part of all of us today. Much of the success of these companies came in the early 1990s, when the Internet made its entrance in the mainstream. The rise of the PC and the Internet created hundreds of companies that went public with simply an idea and a catchy name. Most disappeared when the bubble burst, but they left behind a global electronic network and launched one of the most profound transformations of the global economy.

The dot-coms were businesses created over the Internet, meaning that they conducted most of their business electronically. They challenged the "old economy" to a new one. As the new kids on the block, they did everything differently from the old guard, from business culture to business infrastructure. One of the major business models of many dot-coms was to increase market share first and make money later. Although this proved to be a failed business model, it was partially responsible for the spread of the Information Age. Dot-coms used the Internet to conduct their business. For the first time, people could buy almost anything on the Web. Companies such as Amazon were formed to allow customers to buy everything from books to groceries over the Internet from the comfort of their homes. These new Internet companies relied heavily on technology. Since dot-coms used the Internet to conduct their business, their growth drove the growth in electronic storage, computer processing power, and transferring capacity.

The 1990s brought the general public many new methods of communication. Things such as email, instant messaging, and cell phones, which are embedded in our daily lives today, were in their infancy in early 1990s. The increasing growth in technology saw a dramatic reduction in technology cost. For example, the cost of a three-minute transatlantic phone call dropped from a staggering $245 in the 1930s to $3 by the 1990s and to less than 30 cents by 2007.[13] The cost of storing, transmitting, and processing information dropped 25–30% annually.[14] The dramatic cost reduction, along with the growth of the Internet, brought the people of the world closer together. Communication and information transfers across the globe became easier and cheaper. The growth in technology had a profound impact on almost every industry. Innovation and competition in technology were thriving. Pioneers and new entrants used the new technologies to improve efficiency and processes within their industries. Financial markets, massively dependent on information, began adopting technology to improve their processes. Just as the NYSE took the bold step a century ago to use the telegraph to become the dominant stock exchange, a number of new players began challenging the old model of floor-trading. The rise of technology allowed these new competitors to challenge the status quo and to pave the way for global transformation of the financial markets.

The First Electronic Market

Technology innovation and the growth of computing gave birth to the first all-electronic market: the National Association of Securities Dealers Automated Quotations (Nasdaq).[15] The market did not follow the traditional floor-trading model, and for the first time there was an equities market that had no designated physical space for trading. It used computers and telecommunications to eventually connect the buyers and sellers.[16] Although a novel concept at the time, Nasdaq remained in the limelight for over a decade, slowly improving itself by adopting technology along the way. Originally the home for small companies such as Microsoft that could not afford the NYSE's listing requirements, Nasdaq slowly grew into the second largest equities market in the United States. Technology advancement in the 1990s saw a significant increase in the number of new startups. Nasdaq became the home for these technology companies that were trying to raise capital to continue to innovate in technology areas. These small companies helped propel the Information Age that is now transforming the global financial markets.

Nasdaq and electronic trading would not have been possible without the innovation in telecommunications and the computer industry. The benefits of technology were seen as early as the birth of the telegraph, when the NYSE became the dominant U.S. exchange. Those early changes are all but forgotten in the past 10 years. Exchanges and financial markets today thrive on liquidity and rely on information to make trading decisions. The technology innovation in recent years brought the exchanges and the financial community just that: surges in volume and wealth of information. The current transformation of financial markets generally and of exchanges specifically can be widely attributed to the rapid innovation in technology.

Electronic Communication Networks and U.S. Equity Markets

The U.S. stock market saw the first hints of electronic trading with the birth of Nasdaq and its electronic price quotations in 1971. But it wasn't until the early 1990s that the U.S. stock exchanges saw a real threat to their livelihood. For the first time in history, the "old boy's club" was challenged, and it was largely due to the birth of *electronic communication networks* (ECNs) and discount brokers. ECNs and discount brokers used technology to disseminate trade information and to allow trading without the need for physical space. These newcomers provided trade information to the general public that had been available only to the privileged few on the floor and the brokers. Prior to ECNs and discount brokers, the only way the general public could trade was by calling their brokers to place trades. The information one could get was limited and delayed. Discount brokers and ECNs took the information once only available on the floor and provided it electronically to all their customers. They made trading easier and more accessible. Anyone who wanted to trade stock just needed a personal computer and an Internet connection. ECNs and discount brokers provided this information quickly, efficiently, and at much lower cost. People saw their trade transaction cost dropping from over $100 to just under $10. Along with ECNs and discount brokers,[17] Internet companies such as Yahoo! and Microsoft began providing information such as market data, analytics, historical prices, and company data that people needed to make informed trading decisions. And much of this information was provided at very low prices or at no cost at all. Within just a few years of coming into existence, ECNs began handling over 40% of Nasdaq volume.[18]

Halfway across the world, technology was having a similar impact on a completely different asset class. Europe was undergoing major transformation of its own at a political and economic level. It was the beginning of the formation of the European Union (EU), a community of major countries in Europe that created a legal and economic system to allow the freedom of movement of people, goods, services, and capital. The collaboration between these countries would require information flow at all fronts. Technology provides the ideal platform to provide a fast, efficient, and smooth information flow between the European countries.

Exchanges and financial markets in various European countries began using technology to develop an electronic platform for trading, which would eliminate the physical boundaries of an exchange and connect the financial systems across countries through cyberspace. Markets such as OM[19] began as an electronic trading platform for options in the 1980s. It has since merged with over eight stock exchanges in the Nordic and Baltic countries and is now part of the Nasdaq OMX group. Similarly, technology advancement also led to the very important merger of two electronic exchanges, Deutsche Terminböse (DTB) and the Swiss Options and Futures Exchange (SOFEX), to form Eurex, today one of the largest derivatives exchanges in the world. Around the globe, pioneers began adopting technology to create an electronic trading infrastructure that would give financial markets a facelift.

Technology was being used in financial markets not to simply improve existing processes on the floor but to change the overall architecture of the trading model. Electronic trading leaders such as DTB and Intercontinental Exchange (ICE) began challenging the old model. As we discuss in later chapters, there were plenty of new entrants in electronic trading and, similarly to dot-coms, most of the early ones failed for various reasons, but enough survived to prove the benefits of technology. Technology provided exchanges on a platform that could let them expand their pool of buyers and sellers by shedding their physical boundaries. The merger between ICE and the International Petroleum Exchange (IPE) would never have been a success without the use of technology. DTB's use of an electronic platform showed how an exchange could list its competitor's products, expand its horizon globally, and even steal liquidity away from its competitors.[20] Traditional exchanges with a designated physical space certainly competed with each other by listing competing products in hopes of capturing market share; they could simply never do it as well. Listing new products was limited due to physical space limitations, and connectivity to capture global market share was primitive and mostly confined to telephone orders. Electronic trading models would make it easy for exchanges to list products and expand its market share around the globe. Technology began to transform exchanges around the world, and for the first time in history, began challenging the century-old floor-trading model.

Technology Advances in the Financial Industry

The electronic trading exchanges such as DTB and ICE adopted technology to create electronic trading infrastructure instead of the traditional floor-based exchanges. DTB, for example, was one of the first markets to challenge the old model for trading. Although a recent player, ICE came into the financial markets as simply an OTC market but quickly established itself as an important player in the energy markets. These exchanges took the initiative of defining the initial electronic trading architecture that would allow a successful transformation from floor-based trading model to an electronic trading model. These exchanges, along with the pioneers who took the risk of adopting electronic trading, saw tremendous growth in their exchange volume and significant increase in their market share. In the case of DTB, it became one of the largest derivatives exchanges in the world. In the case of ICE, it was successfully able to complete the acquisition of IPE and establish itself as one of the key markets in energy trading, threatening the survival of the world's largest physical commodities futures[21] exchange, NYMEX. The pioneers laid the foundation for the electronic market structure and forced the established exchanges to wake up to the world of electronic markets.

As the financial markets began their journey toward electronic trading, they brought much-needed competition and innovation to the financial marketplace. The adoption of new technology has forced much of the floor-trading to extinction and brought trading screens that connect traders around the globe. By moving trading off the floor and into the virtual world, the exchanges have been able to position themselves as a global marketplace, making it possible for traders to trade virtually any product anywhere in the world. As the technology improved, the changes in electronic infrastructure accelerated and so did the competition to gain or retain market share. The pioneers have continuously improved their electronic trading architecture to provide a fast, reliable, stable, and globally scalable trading platform. The followers have leveraged the same technology used by the early adopters of electronic trading, hence reducing the time and cost of building an electronic marketplace from scratch and allowing them to catch up in the race to become electronic. New players, new markets, and new products brought an unprecedented level of changes as well as collaboration in the financial industry. New players built applications and tools to provide the financial community access to electronic markets and the trading information required to make robust trading decisions. These players began competing with each other by providing trading screens, analytical tools, risk management applications, and technology to support the electronic infrastructure. The global financial markets, including exchanges around the world, today have tremendous dependency on these new players as well as each other to build and support the electronic trading infrastructure.

The exchanges around the world are shedding their floor-trading models and moving toward electronic trading models (see Figure 1.3). The new electronic trading model has similar processes as the floor-trading model, and it continues to provide the core benefit of the exchange: a designated place where people meet to trade with each other. The electronic trading model provides the meeting place virtually, with far less human intervention.

As the financial markets began embracing technology, many of the processes in the trade cycle were automated. The army of clerks, runners, and other floor personnel are now replaced with computers. Instead of touching many hands, a trade today goes through many computers. In the electronic trading model, orders are entered by traders through trading screens, or computers automatically submit orders. Trading screens utilize programs that allow traders to view the entire market on the computer screen.[22] Black-box applications are

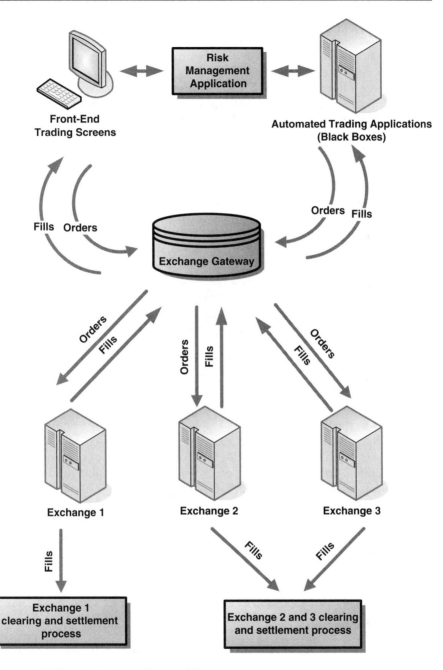

Figure 1.3 The electronic trading model.

programs developed to submit orders without any human intervention. Traders can focus on building their trading models designed to automatically submit orders when triggered by the rules built into the program, such as a price or volume or a particular news event.

These orders flow through risk management applications, which are software programs that allow a risk manager to monitor and reject trades before they reach the exchange. This process allows the trading firms to ensure traders are not taking risky positions or are not trading beyond the limits set for them. The orders then flow to the exchange gateway, which is the connectivity bridge between the trading screen and the exchanges around the globe. The orders reach the electronic infrastructure of the various exchanges through the exchange gateways.[23] The matched orders are electronically transferred to the clearing and settlement process of the exchanges.

The electronic trading model has transformed the trade cycle. Plenty of jobs have been eliminated and plenty of new ones created. The exchanges no longer rely on runners to deliver orders from pit to pit or specialists to match orders. Technology has helped exchanges automate many of these processes. It has also allowed the financial community to adopt new concepts such as risk management, which provides greater control and transparency for the trading community as well as exchanges. Technology has also allowed exchanges to provide more trade information than a specialist could ever track or provide on the floor. The electronic trading model brings greater flexibility for traders to trade more products and for exchanges to reach a far greater number of traders than they could in the floor-trading days.

The electronic trading model has also brought greater dependency among the players in the financial markets. The exchanges today depend on the new players who provide the trading screens and automated trading applications for order routing. The exchanges depend on the technology providers that provide network connectivity to support their electronic trading infrastructure. The financial markets today rely on technology for data transfer between each other. The financial market players, competitors and partners alike, continue to collaborate to standardize processes for data transfer between the players. The new players, in collaboration with exchanges, brokers, and trading firms, have continued to improve on standardization of data transfer.

Standardization

A trade touches many processes from the time a buyer and seller agree to trade. Prior to electronic trading, all these processes were done manually by humans. As the trading continues to migrate toward electronic trading, technology to transfer the trade information between parties, whether clearinghouses, exchanges, or brokers, has also seen significant improvement. The information exchange between these processes requires a common understanding of the trade cycle. During the floor-trading days, when humans processed and transferred the information, the process was standardized because there was a basic understanding of the products traded. The communication used was a common language such as English, French, or German or the hand signals used on the trading floor. When a trader used a hand signal, everyone around him understood what the trader wanted. Similarly, the clerks on the trading floor and in the back office all used an agreed-on terminology when processing the trade.

The electronic trading world is no different except that instead of humans, it is machines that have to understand the information that flows through the trade cycle. The financial market players need to collaborate to define a standardized language for the electronic trading infrastructure, to ensure data transfer and processing is done quickly, efficiently, and accurately. As the adoption of electronic trading grew, so did the standardization of messaging protocols for the trade cycle across systems. As shown in Figure 1.3, a trade passes through multiple systems, from trading screen to clearing and settlement system. Standardization allowed financial markets to define a language commonly understood by computer programs processing the trade flow.

The financial markets have spent a significant amount of time and resources in the past two decades to standardize the financial message flow. As the electronic trading infrastructure evolves, so do the standard protocols used by these electronic systems. Today there are several protocols used by the financial markets to support the full trade cycle. These standard languages are critical to the success of the electronic trading infrastructure. They allow information to flow smoothly, efficiently, and accurately between systems. They allow the financial markets to trade across asset classes around the globe by displaying the market information to a trader in a standard format and processing the order flow seamlessly. The most commonly used standard protocols in the financial industry are:

- *Financial Information eXchange (FIX)*. FIX is a standardized protocol used for financial information processing and transfer. FIX is primarily used for front-end data processing. For example, FIX is commonly used by trading screens and exchange gateways for order flow and market data between the trading community and the exchanges.
- *Financial Information eXchange Markup Language (FIXML)*. FIXML is an extension of FIX that utilizes XML[24] vocabulary for data transfer. The use of XML allows FIX to be flexible and scalable so that it can adapt the constant changes in and additions to the financial market. FIXML allows financial markets to create standard markup protocols for various financial data. For example, Financial Products Markup Language (FpML) allows the financial industry to create standard protocols to define the financial products that are

transferred across systems, or the Market Data Market Language (MDML) that standardizes the format for market data information.

- *Society for Worldwide Interbank Financial Telecommunications Market Language (SWIFT)*. A standard language used primarily for back-end data processing. Predominantly used by clearinghouses and other back-office players, SWIFT provides a secure and standardized protocol to send the clearing and settlement information associated with trades.

The use of these standardized languages allows the systems to have a common understanding of the financial data transfer. Without the standardization, it would be very difficult for systems in the electronic trading model to communicate with each other. The use of standard language helps expedite the transformation of the financial market. The use of standard language makes it easier for financial market players to merge more easily. For example, two exchanges using standard language to handle trade information allows them to merge their technology faster and more smoothly since the same protocol is used to define the financial data. As the dependency on technology grows within the financial markets, it will be critical for the financial markets to agree and use one common standardized language to ensure that the market continues to reap the benefit of electronic trading.

The electronic markets have flourished. The electronic trading has allowed traders to trade in more markets and with more products. The volumes in the electronic marketplace have grown tremendously; the exchanges have added numerous innovative products and are now competing in a global marketplace. As these exchanges expand both in size and through their product listing, they must continually improve their architecture to support the growing volume while maintaining a real-time transparent marketplace. One way to ensure that the exchanges survive in the new competitive world of electronic trading is to continually enhance its electronic infrastructure. The exchange today must provide new products, handle growing volume, and support new trading strategies via its stable electronic infrastructure. The financial markets are using a very common technique that runs across many industries using technology to reform their business: outsourcing.

Outsourcing

The move toward electronic trading has brought an unprecedented amount of innovation, competition, and collaboration in the financial markets. To remain competitive in the financial industry, there is an increasing amount of dependence between exchanges and the new players entering the financial markets. Exchanges globally have used outsourcing to utilize components from a different exchange. It is now common for two competing exchanges to share technology to provide reliable, robust, and scalable exchange architecture for an optimal trading experience for their customer base while keeping the cost low. The following examples illustrate some of the technology interdependences between exchanges:

- The CBOT has utilized the electronic trading platforms of two European exchanges, Eurex and Euronext.liffe.
- NYMEX made a deal with the CME to list its entire product suite on the CME GLOBEX platform to respond to competitive threats from its rival Intercontinental exchange.
- BrokerTec utilized OM's technology platform for electronic trading.
- NYSE will utilize the Archipelago (ARCA) and Euronext technology to move toward electronic trading.
- Mexican Derivatives (MexDer) and the Italian Derivatives exchange both utilize the Spanish MEFF's matching engine.

The transformation so far has been phenomenal. The drama and excitement of the trading floor is certainly not there, but it is replaced by the excitement of transformation that will leave the financial market a different place than what it was a century ago. In the past decade, exchanges around the world have gone through the transformation to arrive at the electronic trading model used today. We share many of these transformations throughout this book, to show the dramatic and unprecedented change the financial industry has undergone. Whether it is the CBOT's journey toward electronic trading by leveraging technology of another exchange or the global competition brought by Eurex US that finally gave the wakeup call to the U.S. futures markets to move to electronic trading if they want to hold onto their market share, or the launch of the International Securities Exchange,[25] which challenged one of the oldest options markets, CBOE, by launching an all-electronic market, the experience has been unique and challenging. So, although we might miss the excitement and camaraderie of floor-trading, it is by no means a boring era for financial markets. The excitement and challenges of the transformation will most certainly keep everyone in the industry occupied for a very long time.

The Transformation of Exchanges: Basic Themes

Though the transformation is multifaceted, there are four major currents to the story: (1) the shift from floors to computer screens, (2) the shift from private clubs to public companies, (3) the shift from local and national to global competition, and (4) the shift from smaller to larger operations. We explore each of these shifts, search for the drivers behind them, and try to look forward to the various implications arising out of them. But to set the stage, let's deal briefly with each of the four trends.

Floor to Screen

For much of the last century, when exchange executives brought their visitors to the window in the exchange visitor's gallery to explain what was going on, their guests stared wide-eyed in amazement that such a teeming mass of humanity yelling at one another actually got the job done. In fact, they got it done only with teams of individuals, known as out-trade clerks, who would try to clear up all the mistakes traders made in their misstating or mishearing the price or quantity of various trades. But an exchange was a business with a big, loud, totally fascinating circus right inside the building.

The shift from floor to screen is the most visible, dramatic, and traumatic of the three shifts. It involves the shutting down of trading floors, many of which have been in use for many decades, and their replacement with computer screens on traders' desks. In some cases, such as China, the screens have been placed on a large trading floor so that participants can walk over and talk to the people on the other end of their transactions, and the public still has something to come and look at. But more commonly, the screens are actually spread over a city, a country, or even the world, as in the case of Eurex or the CME's GLOBEX as exchanges continue to go after a larger share of the global market. It is a shift toward substantially increased efficiency, transparency, and honesty, but it is also a shift away from a system that was more colorful, rowdy, and visually interesting.

In the new world, participants can see all the bids and offers (including order size) as well as prices and quantities on prior transactions to assist in more informed trading decisions. In the new world, the trade is completed and confirmed in milliseconds rather than in minutes or hours. And in the new world, traders can translate their trading strategy into code in a black box that can fire off hundreds of orders per second.

Private Club to Public Company

In most parts of the world, exchanges traditionally emerged as member-owned cooperatives. They were a way to bring buyers and sellers together in one place, to set and enforce rules regarding trading behavior, to disseminate prices, and to create a protocol for the settlement of disputes. These mutually owned entities did a good job for their members and were often enjoyable places to hang out. But member-owned exchanges were very democratic and inefficient. In the new world of stockholder-owned exchanges, especially those that have become public companies, there is a new financial discipline and a new ability to get strategic decisions made in a very timely manner. One of the keys of the success of the National Stock Exchange of India is that it never went through a period of being owned by its members. Because it was stockholder owned, it was nimble. Because it was electronic, it was quick and transparent. Consequently, it ate the competition's lunch.

National to Global Competition

In the old days, exchanges competed with other exchanges a few blocks away or, at most, a few cities away. Until their merger in 2007, the CME and the CBOT had competed with one another for over a century, though they were always less than a few city blocks apart. Because of the regulatory and technical difficulties of trading across borders, the exchanges in other countries were never really viewed as competition.

As telecommunication costs have dropped, as electronic trading systems have made it easier to cross borders, and as regulators have become more accommodative, an exchange in Chicago or New York no longer competes only with other exchanges in its own city or country but now competes with exchanges worldwide. In 2004, both Chicago exchanges found their product lines being directly attacked by exchanges in London and Frankfurt. Mexico and Brazil have faced direct competition from Chicago in dollar/peso, dollar/real, Brady bonds, the Mexican Stock index, and the key Mexican interbank rate, called TIIE.[26] And for some time Japan has found competition from a competitor 3300 miles across the water in the form of the Singapore International Monetary Exchange (or SIMEX, which is now a part of the Singapore Exchange known as SGX).

Smaller to Larger

To grow, an exchange can develop and list its own new products and for years that's exactly what most exchanges did. Of course exchanges occasionally would copy what each other was doing, but it is usually very difficult to be successful by imitating successful products at other exchanges. The other approach is just to buy a product line by acquiring another exchange. Mergers and acquisitions occurred at a very slow pace over most of the 20th century. They have sped up visibly at the beginning of the 21st. In 2007, for example, the Intercontinental Exchange (ICE) acquired futures and options contracts on coffee, sugar, and cocoa along with a large number of currencies by buying the New York Board of Trade (NYBOT) and renaming the subsidiary ICE Futures U.S. The CME suddenly acquired U.S. Treasury notes and bonds as well as grains by buying the CBOT. The NYSE acquired an electronic trading system (and a public listing) by buying Archipelago (ARCA).

These are examples of derivatives exchanges merging with other derivatives exchanges or stock exchanges with other stock exchanges. Increasingly, mergers are going across asset boundaries. So, for example, the stock exchange known as NYSE is merging with a pan-European exchange called Euronext, which combines equities and derivatives trading.

Implications of the Transformation

After we have explored each of these four transformations, we will then examine the effect they are having on the world of exchanges. We will look at how traders can now access markets worldwide on a single screen because of the work of vendors such as Trading Technologies, Pats Systems, and many others. We will examine the concept of the new modular exchange that leases a matching engine, legal services, regulatory services, marketing, product development, and other services from various vendors instead of building all that from scratch. We then turn to the field of regulation with the help of Andrea Corcoran, who has one of the most comprehensive, international understandings of regulatory issues of anyone we know. The shift to screen-based trading has resulted in a virtual explosion of new products, at least on the derivatives side of the street, and we look at how that is playing out. We then turn to an overview of the positives and negatives of these four transformations and finally end with some thoughts about where we are heading in the future.

The journey of electronic trading has not been without its share of challenges. Just like any new idea, it has gone through its ups and downs. It has endured its share of pessimists who firmly believed that the only way to conduct trading was through a floor-trading model. They believed one had to feel the market and its surroundings to make a trade and that trading in a room with just computers cannot provide the same experience. Throughout the transformation, plenty of jobs have been eliminated, plenty of new ideas have failed, and plenty of money has been lost. But the upside has also been remarkable. Electronic trading has brought the financial community closer together than ever before. There is more collaboration and more interaction between the various groups within the financial markets. The upside of the use of technology has led the floor-trading model to extinction. Screams and shouts have been replaced by computer and mouse. Member-owned exchanges are transforming into public companies and becoming global. Floor jobs lost have been replaced by new jobs created to build and support the electronic trading network. Electronic trading brought the transparency long sought by the traders. It has allowed regulators to track orders from front to back. The exchanges have seen tremendous volume increase and expanded their pool of buyers and sellers globally without any physical boundaries. Technology has connected the global financial markets, providing them with a virtual framework that will change the financial markets and the trading world for the coming century.

We will continue to see the new electronic market challenge the old models. We will see how exchanges compete with each other and with their new public company model and how they respond to the electronic platform entering the market. The changes in the exchanges have been pushing the rest of the financial markets to adopt technology to revamp their business models. It is forcing regulators to deal with challenges that are global in nature. The clearing and settlement process is undergoing renovation to keep up with the transformation of exchanges around the world. Trading firms are utilizing technology to not only innovate and improve their electronic market structure but to create and build new trading strategies and develop new trading styles. The past few years have shown the enormous success of electronic trading, and most of the players in the financial markets have accepted, either willingly or reluctantly, that electronic trading is here to stay. It is the future of financial markets. And as one trader sums it up: "Business can't succeed on nostalgia; if it's electronic, so be it."[27]

Endnotes

1. *Capitalism, Socialism and Democracy*, New York: Harper, 1975 [orig. pub. 1942], pp. 82–85.
2. Though we generally refer to all trades as *buying and selling*, the world is a bit more complicated. Many derivatives instruments are actually contracts two parties enter into, committing to do something at some time in the future. For example, a person might say that she bought cattle futures, but this is shorthand to mean that she entered into a contract to buy a truckload of cattle six months from now. She did not *buy* a futures contract; she *entered into* a futures contract. Both parties posted a performance bond (a.k.a. margin), but the buyer made no payment to the seller.
3. Richard J. Teweles, Edward S. Bradley, and Ted M. Teweles (1992), *The Stock Market*, 6th ed., p. 97.
4. The model described here is a generic floor-trading model. There are some variations between exchanges across asset classes. For example, there are no specialists on the futures trading pit, whereas every stock at the New York Stock Exchange traditionally has an assigned specialist who tracks all the orders and matches them based on the time the order was received.
5. Exchanges had slightly different variations on the type of trade cards used. Some were paper and some were cardboard.
6. Each floor trader and floor broker wore a jacket with a badge that indicated a three- or four-letter acronym. These were linked to the trader or broker's full name or full firm name. Badges displayed two pieces of information: trader name and clearing firm number, which were utilized for trade processing.
7. Each pit had one or more specialists who were responsible for matching the orders received from the pit traders and brokers.
8. The actual delivery varies from product to product. Though the delivery might sometimes be arranged through the exchange, often it is handled between the matched buyer and seller, who send evidence of the delivery to the exchange. The exchange becomes involved only if there is a problem. The CME lumber contract is an example where the buyer and seller make arrangements directly with one another.
9. Over-the-counter (OTC) markets are largely unregulated, and the concept of central counterparty clearing does not exist in the OTC trading.
10. "The Stock Market: A Look Back," www.investopedia.com/articles/basics/06/alookback.asp.
11. Nicholas Economides, "The Impact of the Internet on Financial Markets," http://129.3.20.41/eps/fin/papers/0407/0407010.pdf.

12. Bloomberg terminals were installed throughout the floor. These were the first computer applications developed to provide exchange floor market information over computers.
13. "The Stock Market: A Look Back," www.investopedia.com/articles/basics/06/alookback.asp.
14. Technology Transforms the Financial Markets," Tim M. Guildmann, SunGard. World Bank: Sovereign Debt Management Forum, November 2, 1999.
15. Nasdaq started as an OTC market, not as a traditional regulated exchange.
16. At first, Nasdaq served as a bulletin board that showed all the current bids and offers. It connected the buyers and the sellers much later.
17. Discount brokers are generally brokers who offer lower commissions on trades and provide no investment advice. Ameritrade or E*Trade are examples of discount brokers.
18. www.computerworld.com/networkingtopics/networking/story/0,10801,75259,00.html.
19. Optionsmäklarna.
20. As we discuss in detail in later chapter, DTB listed LIFFE's flagship product, Bund, eventually stealing Bund away from LIFFE.
21. www.nymex.com.
22. We explore this concept in greater detail in later chapters. In a simple definition, the computer screens allowed traders to essentially view all products on a single computer screen. The trader could even see all the products across multiple exchanges on a single computer screen. Generally, traders would pick and choose the products they are interested in trading or monitoring, and the front-end trading application would display those products on the traders' computer screens.
23. Chapter 6 discusses details of the electronic infrastructure at the exchanges.
24. Extensible Markup Language (XML) is a computer language that allows users the flexibility to define various elements of financial data that needs to be shared across systems.
25. First electronic options markets.
26. This is the key short-term interbank reference rate known in Spanish as the *Tasa de Interés Interbancaria de Equilibrio,* or interbank equilibrium interest rate.
27. David Barboza, "In Chicago's Trading Pits, This May Be the Final Generation," http://query. nytimes.com/gst/fullpage.html?res=9901E7DD153CF935A3575BC0A9669C8B63&sec=&sp on=&pagewanted=print, August 2000.

Part One

The Four Basic Transformations

2 From Floor to Screen: The Electronic Pioneers

Executive Summary

The most important of all the transformations that exchanges are undergoing is the shift from trading floors to trading screens. The earliest electronic exchanges were not conversions of existing floor-based markets but rather brand-new operations like INTEX, the New Zealand Futures Exchange, OM, SOFFEX, DTB, Nasdaq, and the Chinese exchanges. We tell the stories of these early adopters and look for the lessons. The late arrivals to screens, such as MATIF and LIFFE, had trouble competing and were absorbed by others. The last exchanges to the party were at most risk and at one point had been written off, but one of these has emerged as the world's biggest derivates exchange.

Introduction

Beginning in the 1970s and 1980s, innovations in technology developed to such a point that people began to think about bringing traders together without having them meet up on a trading floor every morning. This was especially relevant when traders from several cities all wanted to be part of the trading crowd. Electronic order routing and matching brought people who were geographically dispersed into a single cyberspace where they could signal to each other what they were willing to do. It promised customers a previously unheard-of transparency and a new, significantly lower cost of trading. These efforts began in several places and with different levels of success.

The names of some of the early pioneers are all but forgotten; others have become wildly successful beyond the imagination of the time. These first efforts to create screen-based trading systems were all *de novo*—new startups. They were not conversions from floor-based exchanges but new exchanges basing themselves on a new electronic model. With no pre-existing structure, there was no baggage and no cost of conversion from floor to screen. The simple question facing the people putting these new exchanges together was how we can best create a new exchange, given our situation and objectives. The choice was between the tried-and-true traditional floor or this relatively untried new approach based on computers and screens. Following the old model was the easiest path. You didn't need to justify it; everyone was doing it. But to deviate required a reason. For Nasdaq, the government made them do it.[1] For INTEX, it was a matter of being fed up with the inefficiencies and abuses on U.S. trading floors. For the Swiss and New Zealanders, it was a way to settle the dispute over where the exchange should be and to avoid the fragmenting of liquidity that would have resulted if multiple exchanges had been created in each country.

But the early adopters of screen-based trading had guts. It was a wonderful experiment, and most often it worked. In some cases, the pioneers were rewarded with spectacular success. In other cases, as in the case of the first real pioneer, the path being blazed came to an unfortunate dead end. We will now visit this first pioneer, a little-known exchange that battled mightily but existed for only a brief period in the mid-1980s. (See the list of derivatives exchanges ranked by the date they became fully electronic in Table 2.1.)

INTEX: The Forgotten First Electronic Derivatives Exchange[2]

The first fully electronic derivatives exchange is one that almost no one remembers today. No one remembers INTEX because it opened for business over a quarter-century ago and because it was a total failure. No one keeps records on failed ventures, especially old ones. However, it is worth recounting the story of INTEX not only because it was first but also because its failure spotlights an important aspect of the shift from floor to screen—namely, that strong forces have shackled the U.S. exchanges to traditional floor-trading while the rest of the world was speeding ahead in the electronic trading race.

INTEX was born of a personal frustration with the trading floors of the 1970s and 1980s. A futures broker named Eugene Grummer had spent a career at Merrill Lynch and was tired of being abused and poorly treated by the floors of the various exchanges. The pit of a trading floor in the 1980s was not very transparent compared to the modern screen-based market. Say a customer wanted to buy July corn futures at the CBOT. She would know two things: She'd know the price of the last transaction, and if she were speaking directly to the floor, which only larger, more active customers could do, she'd know the last bid and offer. Traders were fond of saying that the bid or offer on a floor was good only as long as the breath was warm—in other words, about a second. So, usually the last bid and offer was not a price at which anyone could necessarily trade. Often the price at which an order was executed would seem to be a little worse than the most recent bid or offer.

And then there were the delays. In those days, when orders came in more rapidly than floor brokers could really handle, a "fast market" was declared by the pit committee and many of the obligations of executing brokers were temporarily waived. It could sometimes take two hours before a customer would know whether his order was executed and at what price. In an extreme case during the bull market in precious metals in 1979 and 1980, the main metals exchange, COMEX (which was later absorbed into NYMEX), was

Table 2.1 Derivative Exchanges Become Electronic

	Fully Electronic	Partially Electronic	Exchange
1	10/25/1984	N/A	INTEX
2	1/20/85	N/A	NZ Futures and Options Exchange
3	6/85	N/A	OM
4	4/1/1988	N/A	Tokyo Grain Exchange
5	6/15/1988	N/A	SOFFEX
6	1/26/1990	N/A	DTB
7	1990	10/31/1987	Australian Stock Exchange
8	8/1990	N/A	SAFEX
9	4/1/1991	N/A	Tokyo Commodity Exchange
10	5/28/1993	NA	Zhengzhou Commodity Exchange
11	1997	1990	BOVESPA, Brazil
12	12/1997	N/A	Wiener Boerse AG
13	6/2/1998	4/8/1998	MATIF
14	9/28/1998	NA	Eurex
15	11/1998	N/A	Budapest Stock Exchange
16	1/4/1999	N/A	Tokyo Stock Exchange
17	2/5/1999	1998	OSLO Exchange
18	1999	N/A	Shanghai Futures Exchange
19	7/1999	10/1988	Osaka Securities Exchange
20	7/1999	N/A	Taiwan Futures Exchange
21	10/1999	N/A	Tel Aviv Stock Exchange
22	11/1999	11/1989	Sydney Futures Exchange
23	5/8/2000	N/A	Mexican Derivatives Exchange (MEXDER)
24	5/2000	N/A	International Securities Exchange (ISE)
25	5/8/2000	N/A	Mercado a Termino De Buenos Aires
26	6/12/2000	N/A	National Stock Exchange
27	11/25/2000	11/30/1989	LIFFE
28	1/1/2001	NA	Dalian Commodity Exchange
29	6/2001	N/A	Malaysia Derivative Exchange
30	10/1/2001	1996	Bourse De Montreal
31	11/18/2003	N/A	Multi Commodity Exchange of India
32	12/15/2003	N/A	NCDEX
33	11/2004	N/A	Euronext NV (Amsterdam, Brussels, Paris)

Table 2.1 (*Continued*)

	Fully Electronic	Partially Electronic	Exchange
34	12/20/2004	N/A	Winnipeg Commodity Exchange
35	4/2005	N/A	ICE Futures U.K.
36	7/2006	N/A	Boston Options Exchange
37	10/1/2006	N/A	U.S. Futures Exchange
38	10/2006	11/2004	SIMEX Singapore
39	2/29/2008	1/12/2007	NYBOT (ICE Futures as of Jan 2007)
40	Not yet	6/25/1992	CME
41	Not yet	1994	CBOT
42	Not yet	2001	CBOE
43	Not yet	9/2/2001	London Metal Exchange
44	Not yet	2003	Pacific Exchange
45	Not yet	10/2000	Brazilian Mercantile & Futures Exchange (BM&F)
46	1/14/2008	2004	Kansas City Board of Trade
47	Not yet	6/12/2006	NYMEX
48	12/19/2008	12/2004	Minneapolis Grain Exchange
49	Not yet	Not yet	AMEX

Source: Exchange Websites, emails from exchanges, and assorted news clips.

choking on paper. In some cases, customers did not get confirmations that their orders were filled for several days. There were clearly problems with floor-trading.

So Grummer decided that a transparent electronic marketplace would solve many of these problems he had faced for so long. He first needed money, so he raised venture capital from a Texas oilman named Wallace Sparkman. He needed an experienced person to run the company, so he hired as president Junius (Jay) Peake, who had been a partner at the securities firm Shields and Company. Grummer himself became chairman. INTEX was born in 1981, though it would be several years before the first trade took place.

Grummer and Peak wanted to start the exchange within the United States. That's where they resided and where most of their potential customers lived. So they went to see the federal derivatives regulator, the Commodity Futures Trading Commission (CFTC). The result was not good. They were told informally that an electronic system would likely take years to gain regulatory approval. It wasn't that the CFTC didn't like the idea of electronic trading; on the contrary, they loved it.

The CFTC staff knew that screen-based trading would allow them to know precisely when each trade was entered, received, and executed. They would be better able to see whether, for example, a broker was trading ahead of his customer.[3] It was very difficult to pin down the precise time that a pit trade occurred, since execution consists of a shout and a reply and the only record of the time of execution was the time the floor broker or trader wrote down on an order or trading card. Often the floor guys would execute a number of trades and then, when they had a second to do so, write them down, guessing a little at the precise time each trade took place. In a very busy market, considerable time could elapse between actual execution and the time at which the trade was written down. All this makes it very difficult for either the exchange or the regulator to know whether a broker traded ahead of his customer in a floor-based system. According to someone involved with INTEX at the time, the reason that the CFTC informally advised Grummer and Peak to go offshore was because the big floor-based exchanges in Chicago and New York would do everything they could to slow down the approval and the process would probably take years instead of months.

So, to get up and running more quickly, the INTEX leaders decided to establish the new exchange in Bermuda. Why Bermuda? INTEX had chosen the London Commodity Clearing House (LCCH) to clear the Exchange's trades, and LCCH already had a presence in Bermuda, so it would be relatively quick to get permission to both establish the Exchange and import the state-of-the-art computer equipment into the country. What was state of the art at the beginning of the PC revolution was Tandem computer equipment placed in Bermuda at the INTEX offices and then hardwired via transatlantic cable to DEC 10 computers at member desks in the United States.

Those who wanted to join INTEX had to pay about $36,000—$20,000 for the membership and another $16,000 for the computer. INTEX had 600 memberships available, and by the Fall 1984 launch date, some 285 of the 600 had been sold.

The launch date had been announced and missed a number of times during the period of INTEX's gestation. One participant recalls at least four official launch dates. The problem was the old one of "the perfect being the enemy of the good." The exchange tried to incorporate all the suggestions given by potential participants. During the planning process there had been discussions of listing both gold and U.S. Treasury bonds (T-bonds) on day one, but the Exchange finally decided to put only one egg in the opening basket, and that egg was gold. The idea was to later add T-bonds, freight rate futures, and possibly silver to the contracts available for trading.

So finally, on October 25, 1984, INTEX successfully opened its electronic doors. Opening day was disappointing. The world's first electronic futures exchange saw only 142 gold contracts traded in an abbreviated four-hour session.[4] And things never got much better. INTEX was a failure.

Why did INTEX fail? It was partly the choice of contract. The conventional wisdom is that new contracts have the greatest chance of success in a bull market. They generate more of a buzz and more speculative interest. By the time INTEX launched gold in October 1984, the metal was in anything but a bull market. Gold, with a few reversals, had been in a long bear market since its $850 peak in January 1980 and was just under $340 that Thursday morning in October when INTEX opened its doors. The fact that it was headed down below $290 by March didn't help things.

Even more important, there were strong forces at work to ensure that INTEX would fail, no matter what product it chose. All the floor-based exchanges in Chicago and New York saw INTEX as a threat to their way of life. The several thousand individual members of the CME, CBOT, and COMEX knew how to make a living in a floor-based world. They did not want their exchanges to go electronic, and their elected leaders who ran the exchanges did what they could to maintain the status quo. So, when the big exchanges were given an opportunity to participate in INTEX, they all declined. But they went even further: They made it clear to the brokerage firms that they'd better not support INTEX either. If they did, things could get nasty. We don't know whether any threats were carried out, but we do know that firms were threatened with the loss of prime booth space on the trading floor (that is, near the pit) if they threw any business to INTEX.

So, what happened to INTEX? Four and a half years after the abortive launch of the INTEX exchange, the parent, INTEX Holdings, joined with Telerate, a supplier of financial data, to create an electronic trading system for the London International Financial Futures Exchange (LIFFE).[5] This screen-based system was called APT (for Automated Pit Trading) and became an after-hours electronic system, similar to GLOBEX at the CME, Project A at the CBOT, and Access at NYMEX.

So the first attempt at screen-traded derivatives failed. We now turn to the second attempt, which started in a rather surprising place and which, unlike INTEX, was at least a modest success.

New Zealand and the Wool Guys[6]

It's clear why the first automated exchange was set up in Bermuda: because it would have taken forever to get approval in the United States. It was really a U.S. exchange run by U.S. citizens largely directed to U.S. customers but set up in a place where regulatory approval was possible. But why was the second one set up in New Zealand? The entire country of New Zealand has a population about half the size of Chicago. It has never been considered to be on the frontier of technology. But little New Zealand was absolutely a pioneer in the development of screen-based trading. It's almost like no one ever told them they *couldn't* do it.

It all started with seven wool traders who were spread around four wool-trading centers: Auckland, Wellington, Christchurch, and Napier. They had traded with each other over the telephone and had traded wool futures on the London Wool Terminal Market, a futures market for Australian and New Zealand wool. They decided it was time to set up a local futures market in New Zealand, a market that would reflect local New Zealand prices. But there was a problem: Because they were scattered around the country, they could not all be present for trading on a physical floor in any one of the four wool centers. So they decided that the exchange needed to be computerized.

First, they needed to join forces with some deeper pockets, so they enlisted the support of 10 financial institutions. Together the wool traders and financial institutions would own the exchange. Second, they established a relationship with the International Commodity Clearing House (ICCH), a subsidiary of the London Commodity Clearing House. ICCH became the new exchange's clearinghouse, but just as important, it helped them develop the new automated trading system, cleverly called ATS for, yes, *automated trading system.*

So, on January 20, 1985, the New Zealand Futures Exchange opened its computer screens for trading in three financial contracts: prime commercial paper, 5-year government bonds, and U.S. dollar/New Zealand dollar. The 10 financial institutions wanted to lead off with the financial products. Wool was added a few months later. Volumes were small; 200 contracts was a big trading day. However, due to the 1990 Gulf War, volumes picked up and the system slowed down. So, the system was modified to handle more volume and, more important, to accommodate the individual share options added in 1990. The exchange also added two more words to its name, becoming the New Zealand Futures and Options Exchange (NZFOE). The name no longer exists, since the 17 owners sold the exchange to the Sydney Futures Exchange (SFE) in 1991, which was merged with the Australian Stock Exchange in 2006. The SFE, incidentally, had developed its own electronic system, called SYCOM, which was created not as the primary trade matching system but only as a venue for trading once the pits had closed for the day.

So there are two answers to the question of why New Zealand was the number-two fully automated derivatives exchange in the world. First is that screens solved the logistical problem of traders spread around the country, and second, the exchange was brand new, so there was no painful transition from a floor.

The first electronic exchange, INTEX, failed. The second electronic exchange, NZFOE, survived. But we have to get to number three before we begin to see really spectacular success.

OM: The First Successful Screen-Based Exchange

OM, the abbreviation for a Swedish word[7] meaning *options market,* was founded by Olof Stenhammer in 1985, making it the third electronic exchange in the world, after INTEX and New Zealand, and the first really successful one. Though Stenhammer had an early encounter with options as a New Jersey broker selling options right after the creation of the Chicago Board Options Exchange (CBOE) in the early 1970s, he was mainly an entrepreneur looking for opportunity. When his New Jersey brokerage firm went belly up, he left options for the better part of a decade and returned to Sweden as the CEO of a sporting goods company.

But he couldn't get options out of his head, and he began designing a fully electronic system that would leapfrog the technology of the CBOE, which had in 1984 introduced a system for the automatic execution of small retail orders.[8] A relentless and persuasive marketer, Stenhammer lined up prestigious backers that would immediately put the new Swedish exchange on the map. With the country's largest bank, Enskilda, and its biggest industrial concern, the Wallenberg Group, capitalizing the venture (he kept only 10% of the shares for himself), he began an aggressive campaign, visiting all the institutional investors, banks, and securities firms in the country.[9]

OM was a success from the start. In its first year, when it started with options on six Swedish stocks, it actually made a pretax profit of $24.4 million on revenues of $121.8 million.[10] Two years in, its trading volume averaged 30,000 contracts per day. And this was only options on individual shares; index options would come later.

OM would be challenged and tested while still an infant. OM's success and relatively high fees invited competition. A new Swedish options exchange, called SOFE, opened for business in 1987, when OM was only two years old.[11] SOFE was the opposite of OM. It was nonprofit and floor-based, adopting the model in use worldwide—a perfect test, two new exchanges, one old style, floor based and not for profit, the other new style electronic and stockholder owned. The president of SOFE was Stefan Ingves, a former professor of economics and vice president of a Swedish bank, who would later become the chairman of the Central Bank of Sweden. But despite his later accomplishments, a professor and the old model pitted against an entrepreneur and the new model was no contest, especially given OM's two-year head start. OM stayed and prospered; SOFE disappeared. The advantages of screen-based trading in terms of transparency and cost are generally so great that we will see the outcomes of similar competitions settled in a similar manner. In a case in the 1990s, when a floor-based London exchange had a significant head start over a screen-based Frankfurt exchange, the screen won hands-down again.

This electronic success of OM was a very different outcome from the failure of the first screen-based exchange, INTEX, which had attempted to compete with some of the biggest and oldest futures exchanges in the world. Next, we turn to one last early and unsuccessful pioneer, which made its try also in 1985 and was a neighbor to the wool guys.

Melbourne Tries Screens[12]

There is one other exchange that deserves mention simply to set the historical record right. Sometime in 1985, the Stock Exchange of Melbourne (Australia) set up a futures subsidiary to list futures contracts on individual shares of stock. The venture was born out of a healthy rivalry between Melbourne and the Sydney Stock Exchange, which had built up quite a successful business in equity options. Melbourne hoped to match Sydney's successful voyage into equity options by creating successful equity futures business. The new exchange was called the Australian Financial Futures Market (AFFM) and it was totally electronic. Over the next two years AFFM added both a Dow Jones-type index and an index of gold-mining companies. But the exchange never got traction, and by the early 1990s all trading had dried up. Why? Because commissions for futures were lower and the new contracts were cash-settled instead of resulting in a delivery of stock, so brokers viewed them as competitive and potentially eroding their stock commissions, and thus were not anxious to sell them. In addition, a new futures law separated futures from equities and made it more difficult for the floor brokers on the stock exchange to support them. For those reasons, today this early pioneer is more of an historical footnote.

Next we turn to two markets that were absolutely not footnotes. These are the markets of two countries located in the middle of Europe, a tiny one and a huge one, whose exchanges joined forces to create one of the scariest electronic juggernauts ever seen.

SOFFEX: Unexpectedly Electronic

The Swiss Options and Financial Futures Exchange (SOFFEX) wasn't originally planned as an electronic exchange. Otto Nageli, former CEO of the new Swiss derivatives exchange, called it "an accident caused by federalists."[13] When a group was formed in Switzerland in 1982 to discuss the adoption of financial futures and options in the country, the seven Swiss stock exchanges were floor-based, and the idea was to create a floor-based derivatives exchange with trading posts. But there was a slight problem. The three biggest exchanges at Geneva, Zurich, and Basel all wanted these new products to trade on their floors. An initial decision was made to list options at these biggest three. However, as research and discussions continued, it became clear that maintaining floor operations at all three exchanges would be unnecessarily costly. Having the new exchange in cyberspace seemed to solve both the political and cost problems, so, with a financing commitment from the five major Swiss banks, SOFFEX was founded in December 1986.

Even before the new exchange was up and running, SOFFEX's neighbors to the north, the guys who were putting together the new German exchange, suggested an alliance. Deutsche Terminbörse (DTB) was a couple of years behind SOFFEX, but the two exchanges agreed to cooperate, starting with DTB's agreement to license SOFFEX's software.

Between that first planning meeting in 1982 and the official opening of SOFFEX on May 19, 1988, six years passed. The Swiss achievement needs to be appreciated for the fact that though there were several prior attempts to create electronic exchanges, this was the first time that an exchange was being created with an integrated electronic clearing house. The first stage in development was the creation of systems to broadcast price quotes electronically. The second stage involved adding the ability to actually match trades online. This was achieved by OM. The third stage was to integrate the matching engine with the clearing system. SOFFEX was first to do this.

DTB: The Other Half of the World's Biggest Exchange

Deutsche Terminbörse (DTB), an exchange that no longer exists, will always be known for two things. First, it was the first exchange in modern history to steal a liquid, successful market from another exchange (the German Bund from LIFFE). Second, it was half of the 1998 DTB/SOFFEX partnership that became Eurex, the world's dominant derivatives exchange for almost a decade until the 2007 mega-merger of the two giant Chicago derivatives exchanges, the CME and the CBOT. Both of these achievements were the result of screen-based trading.

The idea of a German futures and options exchange came from some visionaries at the German banks—people like Rolf Breuer at Deutsche Bank, who would later rise to become chairman of the bank as well as chairman of Deutsche Boerse AG, the holding company of all the German exchanges.[14] The group of banks recruited Jorg Franke, then general manager of the Berlin Stock Exchange, to set up the new derivatives venture. The Germans had a problem that was similar to that of the Swiss and the wool guys in New Zealand: The banks putting the exchange together were located in Berlin, Hamburg, Stuttgart, Munich, and Hanover, so locating the exchange at any one of the cities would not allow all the rest of them to have convenient access to the trading floor. The only place that would work for all of them was cyberspace.

But to be electronic, the DTB needed a system, and the banks decided that instead of starting from scratch it was better to buy the system from their Swiss neighbors, who were a full two years ahead. They also hired Andersen Consulting to tweak the SOFFEX software so that it met the trading requirements of the German banks. The banks also needed to get the national Stock Exchange Act amended so that futures were no longer considered gambling and the contracts would consequently become legally binding.

By the end of 1989, everything was mostly in place and a start date of January 29, 1990, was announced. The launch date was met, but not without some glitches. One bank was almost not ready, and there were problems with the celebratory video link with the Chicago Mercantile Exchange. But, according to Dr. Franke, the project came in on budget and on time.[15]

The first test of the system was in August of that first year with the breakout of the first Gulf War and a big wave of trading volume. DTB was not ready for these events, and for several weeks performance slowed considerably. Of course, there were also complaints, but the capacity problem was soon fixed.

One of the most important things the DTB did to ensure its success was to pursue the establishment of remote memberships in Paris, London, and the United States. First came Paris. In 1993, Jorg Franke of DTB began discussions with Gerard Pfauwadel, CEO of Marché A Terme d'Instruments Financiers (MATIF). Franke felt that only MATIF, among all exchanges, really understood the competitive power of an electronic exchange.[16] The two agreed to make their products available to the members of each other's exchanges via the DTB platform, so that MATIF members would be able to electronically trade DTB products on DTB terminals placed in Paris. MATIF would reciprocate by making their products available on the DTB system for DTB members in Germany and Switzerland. Pfauwadel knew that the big benefit for MATIF was that this deal would fast-track the exchange into electronic trading, moving the French MATIF ahead of the British LIFFE, which still restricted electronic trading to the end of the day after regular pit trading hours on its APT system. To accommodate this product agreement, Franke had agreed to allow the DTB platform to be adapted to support the MATIF products and French trading rules.

The adaptation was completed, and in 1995 the DTB products were made available to MATIF members. Then came the runaway bride; Pfauwadel left Franke standing alone at the altar. What neither he nor Franke anticipated was the pushback by the smaller MATIF members concerned about the cost of going electronic. They voted not to move the French products to the screen. As a result, Pfauwadel lost his job; Franke lost half his bonus, and it was quite an embarrassment—except that the French traders still had their DTB terminals, and many of them began using them to trade and add liquidity to the DTB products.

All through the French courtship, DTB was also working on bringing U.S. customers to its screens. Specifically, within a year of launching the exchange, Franke had asked the U.S. federal regulator for permission to place its terminals in the United States to allow U.S. traders to trade DTB products. The CFTC staff did what most regulators do when faced with a novel request with unknown consequences: They thought about it, discussed it, and then focused their attention on other pressing matters that made more sense. Finally, after five years of discussion, on February 19, 1996, the CFTC granted the DTB the historic first permission for a "foreign board of trade" to place its terminals in the United States.[17] Both the CME and CBOT allowed DTB terminals on the floor for use by exchange members. Then trading from the United States began to further build volumes and liquidity in the German products.

Though all this remote trading was good for DTB business generally, it played a key role in a very important competition in which DTB was engaged. In short, it allowed the DTB to steal LIFFE's number-one contract, German Bund futures, and to increase DTB's volume in possibly the most spectacular manner of any exchange ever. When DTB and its new Bund merged with SOFFEX to create Eurex in Fall 1998, the result was the biggest derivatives exchange in the world. (See the box for details.)

The Event That Struck Fear in the Hearts of Floor-Based Exchanges Worldwide

In 1988 the floor-based British exchange, LIFFE, crossed geographical boundaries and became the first exchange to list futures on the very important German bund. At the time futures contracts were legally considered gambling in Germany, and thus no German futures exchange had been created. By the early 1990s the bund had grown to be LIFFE's biggest product. Of course, the Germans believed that futures on Germany's key long-term government bond rightfully belonged on a German exchange, and DTB listed the product in 1990, its first year of trading. But there is a longstanding principle in futures markets that once significant liquidity is entrenched in a product, it is virtually impossible for another exchange to successfully list that product.

All buyers and sellers want to be where they are most likely to find other buyers and sellers and thus will be able to easily enter and exit the market. For several years, the principle seemed to hold as LIFFE maintained a significant lead. But there was a difference here. Usually a competitor exchange fails to get a foothold and will struggle for a few months or years until its clone of the first exchange's liquid product disappears. In its first year, the DTB traded 5 million bund contracts, and it grew virtually every year following, though LIFFE continued to maintain more than a two-thirds market share (see Figure 2.1).

Then, in 1997 and 1998, it all turned. DTB cut fees and made its terminals available for free to foreign participants, at least for a limited period. It got the crowd's attention. With traders from the United States, London, and Paris focusing their attention on the much cheaper-to-trade and more transparent DTB bund, volume shifted dramatically. In 1997 DTB's bund volume doubled. In 1998 it tripled and grabbed almost 90% of the market. By 1999 it was all over; the LIFFE contract was dead. LIFFE's bund volume fell from 14.5 million contracts in 1998 to zero in 1999. DTB's volume rose from 90 to 144 million over the same two years.

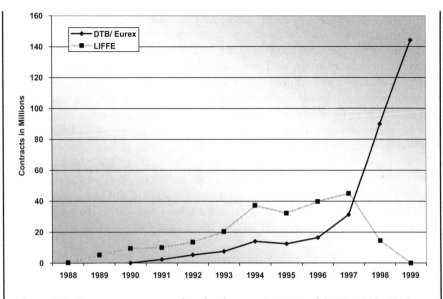

Figure 2.1 German government bond volume at LIFFE and DTB, 1988–1999.

It was an astounding reversal of fortune. LIFFE, which had been number one in Europe and number two in the world, had fallen precipitously from its throne. DTB—or, more accurately, the new Eurex, since DTB and SOFFEX merged into Eurex in September 1998—was now the biggest exchange in the world. Thus the awesome power of screen-based trading struck fear in the hearts of all who were not yet on board.

SOFFEX + DTB = Eurex

The two exchanges formed an alliance and combined their technologies, both of which were at the early stages of launching a fully electronic trading platform. Eurex provided members of both marketplaces a joint platform and clearing services for trading. Eurex focused on building technology to support the full trade cycle and a graphical user interface (GUI) that traders could use to trade. In addition, it built an application that the trading firms could use to manage their risk exposure while trading. As an early adopter of technology, Eurex had no choice but to build these applications itself to ensure that a stable and scalable trading platform was available for its users.

Although in its early years Eurex focused on building applications to support various functions of the trade cycle, it did support new entrants in the marketplace. In 1999, Eurex launched the third version of its software, which provided an open interface that allowed vendors and customers to connect directly to Eurex. Since its launch, Eurex has focused on continued improvement in its technology to grow its market base globally. It provides remote access to allow traders around the globe to connect to Eurex. It has worked closely with vendors and customers to ensure a smooth migration toward electronic trading. Furthermore, it helped bring new independent software vendors (ISVs) into the market. These ISVs built trading screens similar to those built by Eurex. The difference, of course, was that the ISVs connected more than just Eurex markets to their screens. As the electronic trading migration grew and as more exchanges were available electronically, the ISVs built exchange gateways through application programming interfaces (APIs)[18] to connect to these markets.

SAFEX: An Electronic Success from an Unexpected Corner of the World[19]

Some places went electronic just because there was a single entrepreneur who pushed things in that direction. South Africa was one of those places. In January 1985, a bright, driven guy named Russell Loubser and four other guys from a newly constituted Rand Merchant Bank started making a market in bond options. This over-the-counter (OTC) market was the beginning of derivatives markets in South Africa. The market was Nasdaq-like, with prices listed on a screen and deals done via telephone. The big difference was that while Nasdaq had many competing market makers linked together, the new bond options market in South Africa had only one: Rand Merchant Bank. Rand was everyone's counterparty—nice margins, but pretty significant risk for Rand.

Based on the bank's success in bonds, on April 1, 1987, Rand turned its attention to futures on several stock indexes published by the Johannesburg Stock Exchange (JSE). Again Rand was the only market maker. The market-making business was quite profitable, and things were running along nicely until the world market stepped off the cliff known as the crash of October 1987 and the bank got burned badly.[20] Loubser realized that the only way to really grow this market, as well as get out of the job of being South Africa's only market maker, was to get stock index futures listed on a proper futures exchange. So, in August 1990, just seven months following DTB's opening day, the South African Futures Exchange (SAFEX) was created as a screen-based exchange trading many of the same futures that for three years had been traded only OTC.

Loubser became chairman of the new exchange; Stuart Rees became CEO; and a young kid from London named Patrick Birley signed on to do everything else. The exchange grew rapidly during those early years, even though it had fewer than two dozen employees. By 1996, the benchmark All Share Index was trading 1.9 million contracts and the Gold Index another 1.4 million—quite a debut for a tiny exchange in a small, third-world country. A decade later Birley became CEO, and one of his jobs was to assist in the merger of the three South African exchanges (the JSE, SAFEX, and the Bond Market Association) into a single exchange now known as JSE Ltd. Today SAFEX is a division of JSE Ltd., of which Loubser is chairman.

Asian Early Adopters

Japan

The Tokyo Grain Exchange (TGE) was an early innovator, moving its floor system onto screens on April 1, 1988. Though this was almost three years after OM and just a few months before SOFFEX, the TGE has the distinction of being the first floor-based exchange to shift to computer screens. All the exchanges that preceded the TGE into the world of screens—INTEX, New Zealand, OM, and SOFFEX—were new exchanges that were born electronic. The TGE chose to convert from the old method.

Why was the TGE the first exchange to convert from floor to screen? For one thing, it was easier to convert the traditional Japanese trading system to screen than it was to convert the traditional Western system. Here's the difference: In the Western continuous double auction, traders can bid and offer, buy and sell, at any time during a four- to seven-hour trading period, and there might be thousands of transactions at hundreds of different prices during the day, with real-time price feeds sending every bid, offer, and transaction out to a waiting public. In the Japanese single-price auction (known as *Itayose* or session trading), which has been widely used in futures on physical commodities in Japan, there are a small number of trading sessions during the day, in which all interested buyers and sellers are matched at a single price. For example, the Tokyo Grain Exchange has six daily sessions for trading corn futures—9:00, 10:00, and 11:00 a.m. and 1:00, 2:00, and 3:00 p.m. At each of these sessions, the exchange posts a provisional price that it feels represents a balance of potential buy and sell orders. At that price, all members post the number of contracts they and their customers are willing to buy and sell. If there are, for example, more contracts offered for sale than bid on, the provisional price posted is too high and is lowered, and participants again indicate how many contracts they are willing to buy and sell at the new lower price. The process is continued until the number of contracts offered equals the number of contracts bid on. All parties are matched at that price, and the price and quantity transacted for the session are disseminated to the marketplace.

So, beginning on that crisp spring day in Tokyo in 1988, computer terminals were placed directly on the trading floor so that instead of standing and indicating buy and sell orders to exchange representatives via hand signals, the members did the same thing via terminals. As time went on, brokers were allowed to have the terminals in their offices.

Though most Japanese commodities were traded in these single price auctions, in April 1991 the Tokyo Commodities Exchange (TOCOM) converted its precious metals—gold, silver, and platinum—to an electronic version of the continuous double-auction trading system used in the West. This was a more difficult conversion, but technology had advanced by three years since TGE's conversion. Gradually all the Japanese derivatives and securities exchanges converted to an electronic model. The process was completed on September 3, 2007, with the conversion of the final holdout, the Central Commodity Exchange of Japan.

China as an Early Adopter[21]

Chinese futures markets were introduced in the early 1990s, first at the Zhengzhou Commodity Exchange (an overnight train trip west of Beijing), then followed quickly by exchanges in Shenzhen, Suzhou, Dalian, Shanghai, and many other places; by 1993 there were over 40 exchanges in China. But the amazing thing about this rapid proliferation of exchanges is that in a country of cheap labor, where labor-intensive floor exchanges would, at least superficially, seem to have made more sense, virtually all these exchanges were electronic.

So, how did this happen? Initially, in the first couple years of the decade, the exchanges traded cash and forward products and most activity was on a trading floor. At some exchanges, traders wandered around the floor and struck deals one by one. At others, the exchanges would actually hold auctions at which traders would bid. During this period, Zhengzhou sent its president and chief economist to visit exchanges in Europe, Asia, and North America. They came to the conclusion that open outcry was too open and public in that it didn't allow for sufficient anonymity for traders and that the screen system was more orderly. They also figured it was easier to find people who could program than to find people who understood how to make markets on a trading floor. They came back to China and developed a simple electronic trading system for standardized futures, and on May 23, 1993, the Zhengzhou Commodity Exchange, the first true futures exchange in China, traded its first futures contract on a screen. The rest of the exchanges quickly followed suit.

The exception was the Shenzhen Metals Exchange, which created a London Metals Exchange-style trading floor. But it quickly found itself bogged down in errors, misunderstandings, disputes, and defaults, and it too switched to a screen-based system. It concluded that floor-based trading was actually more expensive once you factored in all the problems. For both Shenzhen and all the other exchanges, they were started by and owned by the government in some form, often a municipal government. Even though the initial startup costs were greater for electronic trading, government entities didn't mind and were willing to front the money for these projects. Electronic trading, as even the regulators of the U.S. exchanges knew, was easier to monitor and regulate and would help prevent the cheating of customers.

The Chinese exchanges were electronic, with a twist. All the terminals were located on a trading floor, arranged in circles or in a big U or in two big blocks facing one another, depending on the shape of the trading floor. In a sense it was a hybrid system. Like the exchanges in Chicago, the traders came down to the floor to trade every day. But they sat at terminals on the floor rather than standing in pits waving their hands and yelling out what they wanted to do. In fact, they are still referred to as *pit traders*. Some, called *self-trading members*, trade their own accounts, but the majority, called *agent-trading members*, trade for clients. Order entry and matching are electronic, but entry is handled by these agent-trading members who receive orders over the phone or by fax or email. With all traders sitting in one room, they could get up and wander over to the desks of other traders to discuss a trade, a technical issue, or the latest joke. The arrangement preserved some of the social aspects of the floor. It also had everyone in one room, where they could be more easily monitored by exchange authorities. But the biggest driver for this setup was technical: in the early 1990s in China, it was much easier to connect a trade-matching system to a bunch of computers in one room than to computers spread throughout a building, a city, or a country. The Internet had not really come to China yet.

Both the exchange and the government liked having all the traders in a single room. Since futures—and for that matter, markets generally—were new to China, the exchanges wanted something visual that they could show visitors. This was especially true for potential customers such as grain merchants and others involved in the cash commodity markets. And, since government support was crucial for these new creations, a floor made it much easier to explain to government officials what was going on. Trading floors have always been more interesting than PowerPoint slides. Of course, the government liked having all the traders in one place so it could keep an eye on them. Finally, for purposes of general promotion, there is nothing like a trading floor for the media to take photos of and for the general public to visit, just as they would the Forbidden City, the Great Wall, or the Shaolin Temple.

That was in the beginning. Today upstairs brokers have direct access to the exchange and no longer need to go through the guys on the floor. The floor terminals at China's three existing exchanges have practically all been idled. About 70% of the orders are entered through terminals off the floor, though it is still used as a convenient, though less active, visual representation of the trading process for visitors from all over.

Conclusion

The electronic pioneers were a group of people who saw the world not just as it was but as it could be—in fact, as it should be. Sometimes the screen-based system solved the political problem of which city in a country got to have the exchange, as was the case in New Zealand and Switzerland. But more often it was simply viewed as a faster, cheaper, more transparent way to trade. For those who appreciated the opportunities created by the advance of technology, it was viewed as inevitable. As we've seen, most of the pioneers were setting up new exchanges. It was much easier to adopt this technology in a brand-new business than to radically transform an existing exchange, especially when the member-owners got to vote on whether to stick with the floors they knew or to jump into a world of screens they knew little about.

In the next chapter we examine the second phase of the adoption of electronic trading, where the older floor-based exchanges began to transform themselves.

Endnotes

1. The Securities and Exchange Commission three-volume *Special Study of the Securities Markets* was presented to Congress in 1963 and called for a cleanup of the OTC market to make it more efficient and transparent via the electronic dissemination of quotes and possibly even electronic matching. SEC Chairman William Casey then worked with the National Association of Security Dealers to get the *Special Study's* recommendations implemented. See Mark Ingebretsen, *Nasdaq: A History of the Market That Changed the World*, Roseville, CA: Prima Publishing, 2002, p. 48–61 and 68–71.
2. Unless otherwise indicated, details in this section are taken from Patrick Catania, "Electronic Trading: A Brief History," in Patrick L. Young (editor), *An Intangible Commodity: Defining the Future of Derivatives*, Kent, England, erivatives.com Publishing, 2004, p. 51–55, and from discussions with Patrick Catania, who was an employee of INTEX during the period referenced.
3. Trading ahead of the customer or front running is a violation of the Commodity Exchange Act. A typical example is where a broker receives a very large market order from a customer. Knowing the execution of the order will move the market, the broker first takes a small position for himself, then executes the customer order, which moves the market in a way that favors the broker's position, then offsets his own position to take a personal profit. There are two things wrong with this system. First, the broker was dealing on information known only to him. Second, by taking his own position, the broker got favorable prices that should have gone to his customer.
4. "Electronic Exchange for Futures, Intex, Opens in Slow Trading," *Wall Street Journal*, October 26, 1984, p. 1.
5. "Telerate and Intex Plan Trade System for Commodities," *Wall Street Journal*, March 2, 1989, p. 1.
6. Much of the information in this section relies on a telephone conversation with Greg Boland, currently with Goldman Sachs in New Zealand but a key player in the team that developed the New Zealand Futures Exchange.
7. Optionsmaklarna.

8. In 1984, the CBOE introduced its Retail Automatic Execution System (RAES) for the electronic matching of small retail orders of 10 contracts or fewer in the most active options. CBOE History at www.cboe.com/AboutCBOE/History.aspx.
9. *Wall Street Journal*, November 18, 1988.
10. *Wall Street Journal*, November 18, 1988.
11. *Financial Times*, January 11, 1988, p. 15.
12. Material in this section is largely taken from Edna Carew, *National Market National Interest: The Drive to Unify Australia's Securities Markets*, Crows Nest, Australia: Allen & Unwin, 2007, p. 119–120.
13. Otto E. Nageli, "SOFFEX: How Switzerland Helped Change the World," in Patrick L. Young (ed.), *An Intangible Commodity: Defining the Future of Derivatives*, Kent, England, erivatives. com Publishing, 2004, p. 41. This section draws heavily on Nageli's account of events at SOFFEX.
14. Jorg Franke, "It All Began at Burgenstock," in Patrick L. Young (ed.), *An Intangible Commodity: Defining the Future of Derivatives*, Kent, England, erivatives.com Publishing, 2004, p. 16. This section draws on Franke's account of the creation of DTB.
15. "The Top 10 Financial Technology Innovators of the Decade," *Wall Street Technology*, December 8, 1999.
16. Jorg Franke, p. 18.
17. The process whereby foreign electronic exchanges that wanted access to the U.S. market were given it began with the DTB and continued over the years with a number of other foreign exchanges. It was not exactly a permission, but rather a "no action letter," which was issued by CFTC staff and stated that the staff would take no enforcement action against the petitioning exchange as long as it continued to comply with the guidelines of the program.
18. An API is a set of functions, procedures, methods, classes or protocols that is used by a software program to request another software to perform a task.
19. Information taken from phone conversation with Russell Loubser, CEO, JSE Securities Ltd., May 31, 2007; *Securities Week*, August 28, 1989, p. 10, and a visit to SAFEX in 1994.
20. On October 19, 1987, there was a dramatic crash of stock markets throughout the developed world. The Dow Jones Industrial Average (DJIA) fell 24%—the second largest one-day drop in U.S. history.
21. Information in this section is taken from Xueqin Wang and Michael Gorham, "The Short, Dramatic History of Futures Trading in China," *Journal of Global Financial Markets*, email conversations with Xueqin Wang, Chief Economist, Zhengzhou Commodity Exchange, and Jufeng Zhao, Department of Futures Supervision, China Securities Regulatory Commission.

3 Floor to Screen: The Second Wave

Executive Summary

The late arrivals to the transition to computer screens had advantages and disadvantages. The biggest advantage was that they did not have to build systems from scratch, as did many of the electronic pioneers. An increasing number of vendors, including other exchanges, were happy to sell or lease various modules of the trading system. The disadvantage faced by the latecomers was that they were late and sometimes at a serious competitive disadvantage. Two large European floor-based exchanges, MATIF and LIFFE, had trouble competing and were subsequently absorbed by others. The last exchanges to the party were seemingly at greatest risk, but one of these latecomers has emerged as the world's biggest derivatives exchange.

Introduction

The first pioneers involved in the shift from floors to screens were individuals or groups who were, for the most part, creating new exchanges. They had no legacy problems. The older pre-existing exchanges were universally floor-based, generally owned by their members, and had little appetite for throwing away their floors and sending their sometimes middle-aged members off to fend for themselves in a technological jungle. For most members, floor-trading was a way of life, often handed down by their fathers before them. Though willing to take calculated risks in the market, floor traders were reluctant to take the risk of transforming their institutions into totally different organizations in which they might not be able to effectively compete. They knew how to survive and prosper on the floor; they doubted they could do nearly as well on a screen, especially competing with younger traders who were raised on videogames and had much faster reaction times.

So, the floor-based exchanges, especially those that were member owned, delayed the transition as long as they could. In some cases, as with the French and the British, the delay cost them their independence. They were both absorbed into other exchanges. In fact, as we learned in the last chapter, the British exchange LIFFE (London International Financial Futures Exchange) lost its cornerstone product to an electronic competitor.

Being late to the electronic trading party was not always bad for the exchanges. Most exchanges around the globe found ways to adapt and make the transition. Early adopters had the advantage of defining the exchange architecture, whereas followers had the advantage of avoiding the mistakes and hurdles pioneers went through. They had the chance to see what worked and what did not. They had far greater choices in technology at a lower cost than did the early adopters. The new vendors were developing applications for the electronic infrastructure. Because the pioneer exchanges had already introduced the concept of electronic trading to financial markets, the followers had less of an educational job before them, aside from convincing their memberships to make the move. They simply had to find a way to make the transition. The path of migration varied in terms of both time and choice of technology. The speed of migration depended on the level of threat exchanges faced in their asset class. Along the way there were some memorable migrations that truly represented the success of electronic trading and the pressure it imposed on the global exchanges. The early adopters' success in electronic trading was a wakeup call to the rest of the industry. The industry giants in the marketplace resisted the change, banking on their liquidity and touting the floor-trading model as an efficient way of trading.

The last ones to the electronic party were the U.S. exchanges, especially the derivatives exchanges in Chicago and New York, which as late as January 2009 still had active floors, especially in options. Given that the U.S. exchanges dragged their feet even longer than did the French and the Brits, one might think that many of these exchanges would also disappear. In fact, the CME became electronic enough to both fend off competitors and help NYMEX fend off its electronic competitor by allowing it to list its products on the CME's own electronic platform, GLOBEX. Despite the fact that it took such a long time to become substantially electronic, through a combination of solid, consistent leadership the CME ended up taking over both the CBOT and NYMEX, replacing the electronic giant Eurex as the world's largest derivatives exchange. But let's take a closer look at how this second phase played out.

Late Arrivals Get Absorbed

MATIF

MATIF, the Paris-based derivatives exchange, no longer exists. It opened for business as a traditional floor-based exchange on February 20, 1986. Thirteen years later, in 1999, it was absorbed into a group of French exchanges under the name Paris Bourse. A year later the Paris Bourse was itself absorbed into the pan-European exchange called Euronext NV.[1] During its last year as an independent exchange, MATIF became 100% screen-based.

Unlike its Chicago cousins, which have spent the better part of two decades making the shift, MATIF's transition from floor to screen took just over six weeks. This scared the old floor-based markets to death. But the rapidity of the transition was not just a matter of market participants voting with their fingers.

It was helped along by the peculiar French habit of addressing all problems with a good, old-fashioned strike.

This is what happened: MATIF announced that on April 3, 1998, the floor and new electronic system would run side by side for the interest rate contracts, which dominated business activity. Fees would be the same on both platforms, giving neither one a fee advantage. Participants would have a choice as to whether they placed orders on the floor or in the computer. It was a hybrid system, and it was up to the market how fast the transition from floor to screen would be.

The first strike occurred on February 2, 1998, about a month before the screen system was due to go live. Locals walked off their jobs for four days to protest the requirements they had to meet to participate on the screen. Volumes fell dramatically, and the strike worked because MATIF cut in half the trading requirement locals needed to meet to get free access to the system. Initially the requirement was 250 contracts per day, but this number was renegotiated down to 125 contracts a day.

Then, in early March, the majority of MATIF's locals went out on a second strike, deciding that they wanted even better terms than they had been granted after the first strike. They also wanted lower fees, even though fees had already been cut in January. They were also upset that a special $8 million fund had been set aside to help brokers make the transition to screens, but nothing similar was done for locals. Again, the strike paid off. The exchange offered, for six months, to waive all trading fees, to provide screens at no cost, and to create a $1.6 million bonus pool for locals to share based on the number of contracts each traded. Despite the offer, many locals remained on strike, demanding tens of millions of dollars more.[2]

Because of a hardware problem, there was a five-day delay, and the side-by-side trading of interest rate futures did not begin till April 8. The striking floor locals, through their absence, made it difficult to get trades executed on the floor and made the screen even more attractive than it would have been had the floor been fully open and accessible. By early May, 90% of all interest rate trading was on screen. CAC-40 futures went straight to screen on April 8, and the single stock and CAC-40 options had moved to screen some time before that. In less than seven weeks the market had clearly spoken, and the floor was closed on June 2, 1998. MATIF was now 100% electronic and became the 13th derivatives exchange to become so (see Table 3.1).

The Glitch that Wasn't

There are always glitches in startups, and MATIF had its share, but the exchange got undeservedly bad press for a few weeks that raised concerns on both sides of the Atlantic. On July 23, 1998, the French bond market tumbled when, during a five-minute period, there was a strange series of market sell orders for a total of 10,607 contracts. The Notional bond dropped 149 basis

Table 3.1 Derivatives Exchanges Become Electronic, 1984–2007

	Fully Electronic	Partially Electronic	Exchange
1	10/25/1984	N/A	INTEX
2	1/20/1985	N/A	NZ Futures and Options Exchange
3	6/1985	N/A	OM
4	4/1/1988	N/A	Tokyo Grain Exchange
5	6/15/1988	N/A	SOFFEX
6	1/26/1990	N/A	DTB
7	1990	10/31/1987	Australian Stock Exchange
8	8/1990	N/A	SAFEX
9	4/1/1991	N/A	Tokyo Commodity Exchange
10	5/28/1993	NA	Zhengzhou Commodity Exchange
11	1997	1990	BOVESPA, Brazil
12	12/1997	N/A	Wiener Boerse AG
13	6/2/1998	4/8/1998	MATIF
14	9/28/1998	NA	Eurex
15	11/1998	N/A	Budapest Stock Exchange
16	1/4/1999	N/A	Tokyo Stock Exchange
17	2/5/1999	1998	OSLO Exchange
18	1999	N/A	Shanghai Futures Exchange
19	7/1999	10/1988	Osaka Securities Exchange
20	7/1999	N/A	Taiwan Futures Exchange
21	10/1999	N/A	Tel Aviv Stock Exchange
22	11/1999	11/1989	Sydney Futures Exchange
23	5/8/2000	N/A	Mexican Derivatives Exchange (MEXDER)
24	5/2000	N/A	International Securities Exchange (ISE)
25	5/8/2000	N/A	Mercado a Termino de Buenos Aires
26	6/12/2000	N/A	National Stock Exchange
27	11/25/2000	11/30/1989	LIFFE
28	1/1/2001	NA	Dalian Commodity Exchange
29	6/2001	N/A	Malaysia Derivative Exchange
30	10/1/2001	1996	Bourse de Montreal
31	11/18/2003	N/A	Multi Commodity Exchange of India
32	12/15/2003	N/A	NCDEX
33	11/2004	N/A	Euronext NV (Amsterdam, Brussels, Paris)

Table 3.1 (*Continued*)

	Fully Electronic	Partially Electronic	Exchange
34	12/20/2004	N/A	Winnipeg Commodity Exchange
35	4/2005	N/A	ICE Futures U.K.
36	7/2006	N/A	Boston Options Exchange
37	10/1/2006	N/A	U.S. Futures Exchange
38	10/2006	11/2004	SIMEX Singapore
39	2/29/2008	1/12/2007	NYBOT (ICE Futures as of Jan 2007)
40	Not yet	6/25/1992	CME
41	Not yet	1994	CBOT
42	Not yet	2001	CBOE
43	Not yet	9/2/2001	London Metal Exchange
44	Not yet	2003	Pacific Exchange
45	Not yet	9/2000	Brazilian Mercantile & Futures Exchange (BM&F)
46	1/14/2008	2004	Kansas City Board of Trade
47	Not yet	6/12/2006	NYMEX
48	12/19/2008	12/2004	Minneapolis Grain Exchange
49	Not yet	Not yet	AMEX

Source: Exchange Web sites, emails from exchanges, assorted news clips.

points and then snapped back. All the market orders came from the Salomon Smith Barney office in London. A few trades (for 119 contracts) were busted; most were not.[3]

Salomon Smith Barney was one of MATIF's largest clearing firms, so when the firm claimed this activity was due to a bug in MATIF's NSC software, MATIF hired two independent auditing firms to investigate. This was also a sensitive issue because this same NSC software was the foundation for the new, improved version of CME's GLOBEX system.

Even before the investigation was complete, MATIF implemented three changes to prevent a repeat performance. First, it eliminated the "quick trade" button that allowed traders to trade by pressing a single button. Now a trade would take two buttons pressed simultaneously. Second, it created a temporary freeze feature that would halt the market for two minutes if the bond's price ever fell 25% or more. Third, if a very large, unusual market order came into the system, the market would be halted till the exchange could verify it from the trader. This typically took much less than a minute.

When the two independent auditors, CAP Gemini and Kroll Associates, handed over their reports, it was clear that the problem was not in the NSC system but rather had occurred when the London trader inadvertently leaned against the keyboard, sending a flurry of orders.[4]

LIFFE

In mid-1997, LIFFE was sitting on top of the world. It had just moved up to become the second largest exchange globally, after the Chicago Board of Trade (CBOT) and before the Chicago Mercantile Exchange (CME). It was a teenager, only 15 years old, and had just surpassed the 99-year-old CME, on which it had modeled itself. It had a great product line, the star of which was the German bund. It was also a bit more aggressive about electronic trading than were the U.S. exchanges. It had been the first exchange in the world to create a screen-based after-hours trading system.

However, LIFFE had not been aggressive enough. As mentioned earlier in this book, Frankfurt-based DTB was doing all the right things to ensure that it was able to bring the bund to Germany. It had effectively placed DTB terminals at practically no cost in the United States, France, and right in the heart of London. As a clear sign of what LIFFE was up against, in late March 1998 one of LIFFE's most prominent members dramatically resigned from the LIFFE board. This board member, David Kyte, one of the biggest floor traders in the bund, said he had no confidence in either LIFFE's chairman or its chief executive. He felt that intense competition the exchange was getting from DTB should cause it to immediately throw the bund onto automated pit trading (APT), the electronic system LIFFE had been using for after-hours trading. There wasn't, Kyte felt, enough breathing room to wait and gradually migrate products over to LIFFE Connect over the next 18 months. DTB already had a greater market share than LIFFE and was breathing down LIFFE's neck.

Though he was spot-on in his forecast, Kyte's own business behavior helped DTB prevail. At the time of his resignation, he had already obtained 50 DTB terminals to allow half the hundred traders in his firm to trade the bund in Frankfurt. If even LIFFE board members were abandoning ship, what chance did LIFFE have?[5] Within four months of Kyte's dramatic gesture, both the chairman and the CEO had been sacked or had left the organization.

Despite LIFFE having one of the first after-hours trading systems and despite developing a world-class trading platform in LIFFE Connect, Kyte was right: LIFFE had started too late and got blindsided by DTB. Within nine months of Kyte's resignation from the LIFFE board, DTB had captured 100% of the business in the German bund, LIFFE's flagship product for almost a decade. Three years later, in January 2002, a diminished LIFFE was absorbed by pan-European market Euronext (formed by the merger of the Amsterdam Stock Exchange, Paris Bourse, and the Brussels Stock Exchange).

LIFFE's technology platform, LIFFE Connect, did provide a smooth migration from pit trading to electronic trading. All the markets under Euronext began trading on the LIFFE Connect platform. In addition, the merged Euronext.liffe now sells its technology globally. Today, a number of exchanges utilize LIFFE Connect, such as the Tokyo International Financial Futures Exchange (TIFFE) and, until its 2007 merger with CME, the CBOT.

Last to the Party

The pioneers of electronic trading were almost always new exchanges. There was no cost of or anxiety over conversion. They used screens from day one. And beginning somewhere in the 1990s, all new exchanges adopted the screen-based model. This left the older floor-based, member-owned exchanges, which had put off electronic trading as long as they possibly could. Their embrace of the technology revolution was the most difficult and painful.

The After-Hours Approach

The United States is no technological dwarf. Why, then, did it take so long for the country to get into the screen-based trading game? The answer is simple: U.S. exchanges were owned by their members, by the men and (much less often) women who traded on the exchange floors. The members were making a good living in the old floor system. Why should they throw all this away for a new system that wasn't yet proven and, more importantly, on which they might not be able to compete effectively against a younger generation raised on videogames? The exchanges that would act as pioneers were those without these legacy problems—the new ones, the ones with little to lose.

But the big, member-owned exchanges did put a toe in the electronic waters by adopting limited electronic trading. Specifically, several U.S. and European exchanges, along with the Sydney Futures Exchange, created electronic systems that would be available only after regular trading hours, to solve a different problem and, most important, in a fashion that would not compete directly with their own floors.

This different problem was the need to prevent offshore competition and extend their product monopolies into other time zones as countries in those other zones began to set up their own exchanges. It was an attempt to capture for a given exchange as much of the 24-hour day as possible, or at least the portion of the day in which potential customers were at work. Initially these new exchanges in other time zones would list futures contracts based on their own local equity indexes, their own domestic government debt, and their own commodity products, but there was the chance that they could begin to list U.S. Treasury bonds or Eurodollars or currencies or internationally traded grains or petroleum products and thus compete directly with the big, established U.S. and European exchanges. Even though Japan and other Asian countries were experiencing a financial awakening and were beginning to trade in a big way on the CME, CBOT, LIFFE, and MATIF, these American and European exchanges needed to make their markets accessible during Asian business hours if they expected to maintain this business.

There were at least three ways to extend trading hours and ensure that traders living on the other side of the world would keep trading in Chicago, London, and Paris. The most obvious solution was to simply extend pit trading hours by bringing on a new set of traders to make markets throughout the U.S. or European nights. It was an obvious solution because the physical infrastructure was already there. Just as factories are kept going 24 hours by bringing in three shifts of workers, why not do the same with exchanges? The CBOT actually tried a limited version of this approach with a three-hour evening session for interest rate futures and options in 1987, but it was not successful. The New York Cotton Exchange's (NYCE's) FINEX Division, created for financial instruments, added an evening floor session in 1992, which, amazingly, continued through mid-2007. The problem with night shifts was that not only did the exchange have to attract a new set of fresh traders to the floor, the brokerage firms needed to staff the trading floor booths as well as all other aspects of the trading process. It was a labor-intensive, expensive solution that was ultimately not efficient.

A second approach was to extend trading hours by setting up a trading floor in the targeted time zone. The CME did something close to this in 1984, the same year INTEX set up the world's first fully electronic exchange. It did not actually open its own subsidiary overseas, but it became closely involved with setting up a new exchange in Singapore. Specifically, it established a link with the new Singapore International Monetary Exchange (SIMEX) that tied one of its most important products to an identical product being listed at SIMEX and led to a growth in trading at both exchanges. The product consisted of three-month Eurodollar deposits and the deal, called the Mutual Offset System (or MOS), allowed the CME Eurodollar contract to be traded on the SIMEX floor and then, if the trader wished, his position would be moved to the CME clearinghouse in Chicago and offset on the CME trading floor. In fact, the CME was so committed to establishing a base in the Asian time zone that it actually aided the Monetary Authority of Singapore (MAS) in setting up SIMEX by sending over both staff and traders to train the SIMEX crew.

A more direct attempt to establish a floor in a different time zone was NYCE's attempt to set up a trading floor in Dublin for its FINEX Division's currencies in 1994, which did create a modest amount of business for a number of years. The most recent move in this direction was NYMEX's 2006 creation of a floor-based subsidiary, first in Dublin and later in London, for its energy products. NYMEX's purpose was a little different from NYCE's in that it was attempting to poach some of the experienced traders from a competitor that was replacing its floor with screens. The competitor was the International Petroleum Exchange (IPE), which had been taken over by another closer-to-home competitor, the Atlanta-based Intercontinental Exchange (ICE). Both of NYMEX's attempts to create new European floors failed.

This brings us to the third approach to extending the trading day to protect existing monopolies, and that third approach is after-hours electronic trading. The idea here was to create and use screen-based trading, but only after regular pit trading was done for the day. This avoided any direct screen-to-floor competition and minimized pushback from exchange members currently making their living on the trading floor. So, CME, CBOT and LIFFE products would be available for trading, not only during their own business days, but also during the business days in other time zones. It is worth taking a closer look at some of these after-hours systems.

GLOBEX

Back in the late 1980s both the Chicago Mercantile Exchange and the Chicago Board of Trade viewed the Japanese market as a serious possible threat to Chicago's key contracts. The CBOT, of course, was concerned about its Treasury contracts, and the CME was concerned about its Eurodollar contracts. As mentioned earlier, the CBOT initially took the route of creating a night trading session that began at 6:00 p.m. each evening, right at the beginning of the Japanese business day. The CME took a different route.[6] It made its strategic planning committee's number-one priority the question of how to deal with the broad issue of globalization. Leo Melamed was chairman of the strategic planning committee, and though the CME leader had been, like most U.S. exchange leaders, an outspoken supporter of open outcry against the evils of screen trading, he began to see the value of an electronic solution to the issue of global competition.

The committee developed the idea of extending the trading day, not through an extension of the hours of the physical trading floor but rather via screens that would light up after the pits had closed down. Melamed realized that electronic inroads had been already created in other areas. For example, both the NYSE and the CBOE had established electronic systems for dealing with small retail orders. The London Stock Exchange had undergone the "Big Bang," described later in this chapter, and closed its trading floor, substituting an electronic quotations system called SEAQ. And of course there was Nasdaq, which had been at least partially electronic ever since its 1971 inception.

There were two marketing tasks associated with the CME's creation of an electronic system for after-hours trading. Naturally, Melamed and others needed to convince the world that the CME's electronic system was the platform of choice for after-hours trading, especially since they had decided to invite other exchanges to participate in GLOBEX. But more important, they needed to convince the members of the exchange, the individual owners who made their living every day in the open outcry pits, that this new electronic system not only did not constitute treason but that it was essential to the future of the CME and its members. Without the members' vote, there would be no system.

To convince the members, Melamed did two things. First, he knew that he needed to choose an extremely credible and respectable partner to handle the technology for this system; second, he needed to ensure that members would feel both vested in the new system and confident that it would not destroy their floor-based livelihoods. To create credibility, the CME chose Reuters Holdings PLC as the partner. Reuters was a huge international firm with thousands of terminals on traders' desks all over the world. They had already entered the business of creating markets with the purchase of a company called Instinet, which was an electronic market for stocks traded among large institutions. Reuters had also created a system called Dealing FX, which was an electronic trading system for foreign exchange.

To convince the members that they had nothing to fear, both Leo Melamed and Jack Sandner, then chairman of the CME, promised the members that screen trading would never intrude on regular trading hours without the vote of the membership. To create an incentive for the members and allow them to feel that they were benefiting from the creation of this electronic system, GLOBEX was set up so that a dividend would be paid to the members out of any profits earned by GLOBEX. Specifically, the proposal was that CME members would receive a dividend equal to 70% of the net profits of the operation. The issue of screens was a very sensitive one, and Leo knew that everything had to be just right to gain support from the members. The meeting that was held to unveil the system to the members was preceded by an incredible amount of secrecy. There were to be no leaks. The meeting ended up attracting a huge crowd of more than 1000 members in September 1987.

With presentations from Leo Melamed and Jack Sandner of the CME and Andre Villeneuve and John Hull from Reuters, the members seemed receptive to the idea, and two months later, on October 6, 1987, they approved GLOBEX with a landslide vote. Despite all the good press, it would still take another five years before the electronic trading system was up and running.

It should be noted that GLOBEX was not the first choice of a name for this new system. To emphasize that this was exclusively an after-hours trading system, the name PMT, for Post-Market Trading, was initially chosen. It didn't take long, however, for British friends of the CME to point out that PMT in the United Kingdom had the same meaning as PMS in the United States. Realizing that this would not quite do, the name was changed to GLOBEX, for global exchange.

One thing about GLOBEX was that it strongly emphasized the system being made available to any other exchange that chose to join. Melamed viewed GLOBEX as an industry utility that would have large numbers of exchanges participating in it. The CBOT also sought other exchanges to join its own system, as described shortly. One of the partners that the CME gained was MATIF, the big French exchange.

So after five years of planning and development, the new after-hours system known as GLOBEX finally began on June 25, 1992, with two contracts: the German mark and the Japanese yen. It's always best to start a new system with limited scope so that the financial implications of bugs can be limited and it can be easier to make any repairs that might be needed. A month later, more currencies were added: the British pound, Swiss franc, Australian dollar, and Canadian dollar. In August the CME made its crown jewel, Eurodollar futures and options, available after-hours on GLOBEX. (Eurodollars were three-month deposits of U.S. dollars in banks outside the United States, not to be confused with the currency contract, the Euro FX contract, which was the exchange rate or price of the euro in terms of dollars.)

In February 1997, in a unique technology swap, the CME made a trade with what is now known as Euronext. In this deal, the CME received a state-of-the-art matching engine, known as the Nouveau Système de Cotation (NSC) matching system. It had been developed by the Paris Bourse (the French stock exchange) for MATIF (the French futures exchange that the Paris Bourse had taken over). These two French exchanges had both been absorbed into the pan-European exchange known as Euronext. In return, Euronext received the CME state-of-the-art clearing system known as Clearing 21, which it was able to use to enhance its clearing services.

In that same year, the CME took the first step that would take GLOBEX from a mere after-hours system, accounting for 1–2% of total trading volume, to serving as the platform for virtually all CME trading. Though this full transformation would take over a decade to complete, for the first time in 1997, a contract was launched that would not trade on the floor but would trade only electronically and would be available only during regular trading hours. That contract was the E-mini S&P 500 stock index futures. It was a small version (one fifth the size) of the S&P 500, the mother of all stock index futures contracts.[7]

The floor was still nervous about this, and the launch was done with a compromise that orders for trading in the E-mini could not exceed six contracts. This would prevent big traders from shifting their business away from the floor and to the screen. Though the product was a big success and volumes were large, the number of contracts per trade was small, so it was clear that the product was attracting small retail traders. Therefore, the limit on number of contracts per trade was eventually lifted. Two years later, in July 1999, the CME listed its biggest contract, euro dollars, on the screen during regular trading hours, side by side with trading in the pit.

The other thing that the CME did was to make GLOBEX available to other exchanges to list their products. For example, in June 2002, GLOBEX began carrying the e-miniNY crude oil and natural gas futures for NYMEX. Five months later, the single stock futures venture known as OneChicago began using the GLOBEX platform.[8] In 2006, NYMEX began listing its COMEX Division's gold and silver contracts on GLOBEX, to help it defend itself from an attack by the CBOT with its electronic metals trading. Of course, when the CME bought the CBOT in 2007, the agreement required moving all CBOT electronic trading from LIFFE Connect to GLOBEX.

Though GLOBEX was the most ambitious and ultimately the most successful of the after-hours systems, it took a major competitive event to stimulate the rapid migration of Chicago's trading activity away from the floor and onto the screen, an event we will turn to shortly.

CBOT Can't Make Up Its Mind

Leo Melamed says CBOT chairman Karsten Mahlman described GLOBEX as "an H-bomb that threatened the life of open outcry."[9] Needless to say, the CBOT was not happy with GLOBEX. But to stay competitive, the CBOT gathered some impressive partners and went to work on its own after-hours system that would be very different from GLOBEX. The CBOT's "GLOBEX killer" was unveiled on March 16, 1989, at the annual Futures Industry Association Conference in Boca Raton, Florida. The CBOT claimed to be setting new standards for the industry with a system developed by a team made up of Apple Computer Inc., Texas Instruments (TI), and Tandem Computer. The new system, called Aurora, would—with a combination of colorful Macintosh icons contributed by Apple, artificial intelligence contributed by TI, and raw processing power contributed by Tandem—replicate the feel of the floor.[10] Whereas GLOBEX was a system for international brokers, Aurora was a system for pit traders. It was visually much more attractive than GLOBEX. To sweeten the Aurora choice, the CBOT claimed that it would price Aurora at $1 per round turn, compared to GLOBEX's $4 charge. It should be noted that though Aurora was cosmetically superior, the basic idea of having the screen-based system replicate the floor was already under development at LIFFE in its after-hours system known as APT, for automated pit trading. LIFFE started using APT in November 1989.

Then the CBOT's second reaction to GLOBEX was to join it, or at least to join the CME in discussions about the possibility of combining the two systems for after-hours trading. Actually, the CME made the first move. Leo Melamed and Jack Sandner (CME executive committee chairman and board chairman, respectively) invited Karsten Mahlman and Tom Donovan (CBOT chairman and president) to a private meeting. To keep things quiet, the meeting was held not at the exchange but in the conference room of Melamed's brokerage firm. The CME had a major advantage over the CBOT.[11] The CME's partner, Reuters, was footing the entire bill for building a trading system, which likely cost Reuters about $100 million. The CBOT was paying for Aurora itself, and the costs were mounting. The CME offered to make the CBOT an equal partner in GLOBEX. Remember that at that time the CBOT was still the largest exchange in the world. The offer was good enough for a handshake and a year and a half of discussion leading up to a signed agreement between the CME, CBOT, MATIF and Reuters.

While both exchanges were very ambivalent over this shift to electronic trading, even though it was initially restricted to after-pit hours, the CBOT was the most conflicted. In fact, some on the CME side felt that the CBOT's purpose in joining GLOBEX was to slow it down and kill it.[12] True or not, in April 1994 the CBOT withdrew from the GLOBEX agreement, leaving the CME and Reuters to go it alone. The CBOT exit was also related to an increasing lack of trust and an escalation of competition between the two exchanges. At the same time, the CBOT announced its own new system, which it called Project A. However, Project A, like its predecessor Aurora, would show a trading pit instead of the traditional best bids and offers shown in a ladder format. It was designed to make the floor trader comfortable in the new electronic environment.

In GLOBEX and other systems, matching is done by what is referred to as *price/time priority*, or *first in/first out* (FIFO). It's a widespread system because it is logical and fair. When a market order to buy comes into the system and there are a number of offers to sell available for matching, the first ones matched are the best or lowest offers. And within the best offers, whoever put the orders in first gets matched first—the old tradition of first come, first served.

In Project A, the market order still got the best available prices, but the order would be proportionately allocated to all the offers currently available at that best price. The time at which these offers were made was irrelevant. This was consistent with common pit practice, whereby if four locals offer to take the opposite side of an incoming order, each of them receives 25% of the order. There was one way for the online locals to get a bigger share of trades. Anyone who narrowed the spread by putting in a higher bid or lower offer than the best ones currently present would have their entire bid or offer filled before any of the order was allocated to other traders. This feature was included to encourage aggressive bids and offers.

The downside to Project A, just as with the first generation of GLOBEX, was that the trader was chained to expensive Project A hardware. It attracted some business but would have attracted much more had it opened up its architecture. One of the reasons the CBOT did not make huge investments in Project A was likely due to its on-and-off discussions with Eurex that eventually resulted in the CBOT's shift from Project A to a joint CBOT-Eurex platform in August 2000. The new platform carried one of the more awkward names devised for a technology platform: a/c/e, for Alliance/CBOT/Eurex, but people simply called it *ace*. Luckily the name didn't last long, for in 2003 the CBOT entered into an agreement with LIFFE to license LIFFE Connect for five years. This switch was understandable since EUREX had decided to set up a Chicago subsidiary to compete directly with the CBOT.

Chicago: The Final Push

For almost two decades, the Chicago exchanges, along with NYMEX in New York, walked the difficult path of trying to adapt to the modern world but at the same time protect the livelihoods of their floor-bound members. In other words, the exchanges continued to add technology, but only on the periphery of trading. There were technological improvements in getting orders to the floor, clearing matched trades, and bringing fundamental information and analytical systems to the trading floor. But the execution of trades continued to be done by human beings yelling at one another. That ultimate right of exchange members to execute orders, make markets, and trade against orders, and to do so via hand signals and voice, continued to be preserved as much as possible. Even as electronic trading began to make its way out of the after-hours closet and into regular trading hours, the costs of electronic trades were kept high or speed bumps were constructed to prevent electronic trading from looking too attractive.

But everything changed in the summer of 2003. Eurex, then the biggest exchange in the world, announced that it had plans to open a subsidiary exchange in Chicago, and it began to seek regulatory approval to do so. The Chicago exchanges were scared to death. The smart money was on Eurex. Everyone remembered the battle of the bund, the battle to the death between Eurex[13] and the LIFFE. The London-based LIFFE lost the German government bond to the quick, cheap, transparent, screen-based Eurex. And everyone thought that this would be repeated as screen-based Eurex came into Chicago and took on the floor-based CBOT head to head. Now, it's true that the CBOT had its own after-hours electronic system that it had even started to expand to side-by-side simultaneous floor and screen trading, but the overwhelming bulk of trading on the CBOT was still floor-based. In addition, even though the initial attack was to be on the CBOT products—that is, the Treasury futures and options—the CME felt no less threatened. In fact, its fear was well founded, since after an initial sustained attack on CBOT Treasuries, Eurex U.S. did turn its attention to CME currencies.

So together, the Chicago exchanges launched a counterattack. The first thing they did was to throw up every regulatory barrier they could. For example, they ensured that Congressional hearings were held, given the fact that this foreign board of trade, this German exchange, intended to trade in futures and options based on the sacred and precious government securities of the United States. They also did everything they could to slow down the approval process at the Commodity Futures Trading Commission by questioning every single aspect of the application made by Eurex for the new exchange. Second, since what Eurex had going for it was a transparent, electronic, relatively inexpensive system, the Chicago exchanges needed to replicate that as quickly as they could. So the CBOT lowered its fees practically to zero, to match the low fees being charged by Eurex U.S. And both the CBOT and the CME did everything they could to improve their electronic systems and to encourage existing traders to move their business out of the pits and onto the screens so that by the time that Eurex opened its new exchange it would be competing with largely electronic exchanges and not with floor exchanges.

So, while Eurex was dealing with the regulatory hurdles created by the Chicago exchanges, the exchanges took advantage of the breathing room to significantly upgrade their systems. The CBOT had been using a/c/e, a version of Eurex's own system, but was able to migrate its products onto the superior LIFFE Connect platform, so by the time Eurex U.S. was able to open its doors it was at a technological disadvantage. Those who worked on the CBOT and CME upgrades were impressed with the military precision with which both exchanges stuck to their timelines. They had to be on time because the Eurex U.S. launch was imminent. The CBOT completed its migration on January 2, 2004. Eurex U.S. turned on its screens on February 8, 2004, a little over a month later.

It was impossible to become a totally electronic exchange overnight, but a substantial amount of CBOT business was moved onto the screen before Eurex U.S. opened its doors for trading in early 2004. In fact, to the amazement of many observers, the strategy worked. Eurex failed to achieve any substantial share of the U.S. Treasury futures market. The CBOT was able to hang onto its monopoly. When it was clear to Eurex that the attack against the CBOT was going to be unsuccessful, it switched its attention to the CME currencies. Again, the CME had been able to shift such a large portion of its currency trading to the screen that Eurex did not have the advantage that it once had when it stole the German government bond from LIFFE in London.

Though Eurex failed in its attempt to make inroads into the U.S. derivatives space, the competitive threat did wonderful things for the industry. It caused the exchanges to lower their fees. It caused the exchanges to substantially increase the percentage of their trading that was done on screen. So, after almost two decades of playing around with technology on the periphery, the Chicago exchanges moved toward screens in a big way, pushed mainly by one of the biggest competitive threats that they had ever faced in their entire histories. Eurex had done a big favor for Chicago, even though it failed miserably at establishing its own beachhead and had to retreat to Frankfurt with nothing but a lot of bills for the abortive attack.

New York: The Final Push

Chicago has been an electronic backwater compared to the rest of the world, but one good thing that can be said about the city is that it was way ahead of New York. There have been many derivatives exchanges in New York, but in the past decade they were all merged into two: the New York Mercantile Exchange (NYMEX) and the New York Board of Trade (NYBOT).

NYBOT was a bit of a contradiction. When the World Trade Center was attacked on September 11, 2001, NYBOT was the only exchange that had a physical backup location, and it reopened its trading floor at this Long Island location three days after the attack. However, for an exchange with internationally oriented contracts, NYBOT was surprisingly backward when it came to technology. In fact, it was the only one of the top four U.S. exchanges that had not even set up an after-hours electronic system. It had planned well for a physical disaster but had planned poorly for a competitive disaster. The lesson of an electronic exchange stealing the best product from a floor-based exchange was known to all from the DTB-LIFFE competition we've already explored. NYBOT was very much at risk of a screen-based exchange such as ICE, Eurex, Euronext, or the increasingly electronic CME or CBOT picking off its best products.

ICE was the one that made the play for the NYBOT contracts, but it didn't just list coffee, sugar, and cocoa and use marketing and various incentives to win over customers. Instead, ICE bought the products, customers, and liquidity by purchasing NYBOT outright. In this case, it was more than just the products. ICE had been outsourcing clearing, and with the NYBOT purchase, overnight it had its own clearinghouse. It wasn't too bad a deal for the NYBOT members; on the day they voted 93% in favor of the deal, it was worth $1.57 billion ($400 million cash and 10.297 million ICE shares). Divided among the 970 memberships, that came out to $1.6 million per seat, roughly twice the value of four months prior.[14]

But NYBOT's failure to create its own electronic platform did result in the virtual disappearance of NYBOT as a brand as its products and clearinghouse were simply absorbed into ICE Futures, ICE's futures subsidiary. It could have been both better and worse. It could have been better if NYBOT had created a viable electronic platform several years before and benefited from the additional trading and revenue that electronic access seems to bring about because of the rise of algorithmic trading. Had NYBOT shifted to screens, demutualized, and launched an initial public offering (IPO), the value created for members could have been much better than what they actually ended up with.

But NYBOT's fate certainly could have been worse. If ICE or another exchange had simply listed the NYBOT products and successfully won the business away from NYBOT, the exchange and its members would have been left with virtually nothing except for a clearinghouse they could sell. So NYBOT should probably consider itself lucky, or more accurately, the former NYBOT members should consider themselves lucky, since there is no longer any NYBOT to consider anything.

NYMEX had moved much further down the electronic path than NYBOT. It first created an after-hours system called ACCESS back in the 1990s. It then upgraded that to a better system called Clearport in 2002, and it had begun using the system during the day for a number of products. But NYMEX had two problems. First, the system was not sufficiently robust to be the workhorse for all of NYMEX's products. Second, NYMEX squandered a lot of time and resources on pursuing a floor-based path in 2005 and 2006. This quixotic venture involved setting up, as previously mentioned, trading floors in both Dublin and London. The original plan for its new exchange in Dubai had it as a floor-based exchange, and it also planned to launch trading on the abandoned SIMEX floor in Singapore.

Having an inadequate electronic system and an unfortunate diversion of management attention devoted to pushing a floor-based expansion into Europe, the Middle East, and Asia left NYMEX highly vulnerable to attack from an electronic exchange. The first such attack came from the most logical place— ICE Futures Europe, the former International Petroleum Exchange, which had arguably become a U.S. exchange, even though it was still regulated in the United Kingdom. ICE Europe, like all the ICE subsidiaries, was lean, mean, innovative, and able to under-price. In February 2006, ICE listed a cash-settled clone of NYMEX's cornerstone product, West Texas Intermediate (WTI) crude oil. To add insult to injury, the cash settlement price ICE chose to use for settling its contract was the most liquid one around: the NYMEX futures price. So ICE didn't really want to kill the NYMEX contract, or at least not do so too quickly. It needed that NYMEX price in the same way that a parasite needs its host. If the host dies, the parasite is out of business.

Things did not look good—and then they got much worse. As ICE's market share for WTI crude oil edged up toward 30%, ICE also launched clones of NYMEX's gasoline and heating oil contracts. Then the CME announced that it was developing its own energy contracts. The born-again largely electronic CBOT decided to launch electronic gold and silver contracts, the major products in NYMEX's metals division. NYMEX's very survival was at stake. NYMEX saved itself only by jumping into the arms of one of its potential competitors—the CME. NYMEX's only choice was to become electronic immediately. LIFFE had lost the bund eight years earlier, in part, because it took too long to move to the screen, and by the time it did, DTB had 100% market share. The only way to become immediately electronic (that is, within a few months) was to outsource, and the only viable quick outsource vendor was the CME's GLOBEX. While the price of renting space on GLOBEX was not made public, NYMEX was not in much of a position to bargain, and it surely paid the price for not being ready with its own system.

Once it was up and running on GLOBEX, NYMEX was able to start taking market share back from ICE on energy and from the CBOT on metals. To help matters, when the CME acquired the CBOT in 2007, it was not able to bring CBOT's gold and silver onto GLOBEX along with the other CBOT products because of CME's commitment to NYMEX. So, NYMEX was pulled back from extinction by the CME, but as explained later in this book, the exchange ended up being acquired by that very same protector.

Stock Exchanges Move to Screens

We have told, in great detail, the story of the derivatives exchanges' gradual shift to screen-based trading. And we did that first because the first electronic derivatives exchange appeared in 1984. Screen-based stock exchanges consistently began appearing a half decade later, in 1989; by that time four electronic derivatives exchanges had already been established. But once the trend started on the equity side of the street, it continued with force. Over the next 20 years (see Figure 3.1), between one and four electronic stock exchanges appeared on the scene each and every year. The peak was from 1995 to 2001, when five to 10 exchanges became electronic each year. After 2001, the number of stock exchanges lighting up screens began to fall off. There was a little pop in 2007 when six exchanges became electronic, including two in Dubai. In August 2008, a rapidly growing ECN called BATS was granted exchange status by the SEC, thus becoming the newest U.S. electronic stock exchange.

Table 3.2 lists all the exchanges we could find that were either born as or converted to electronic exchanges. We found 85. As mentioned earlier, screen-based stock exchanges began in earnest in 1989, but there was a lone outlier pioneer not shown in Figure 3.1. Nine years earlier, in 1980, the little Cincinnati Stock Exchange closed its floor and became the world's first fully electronic stock exchange. Because virtual exchanges can be anywhere, the exchange is today headquartered in Chicago and since 2003 has been called the National Stock Exchange.

Though most exchanges listed in Table 3.2 (about 80%) are floor-based exchanges that converted to screen-based markets, the remainder (20%) represent exchanges that were created as electronic exchanges. In fact, after the Cincinnati Stock Exchange, which was a conversion from a floor, the second

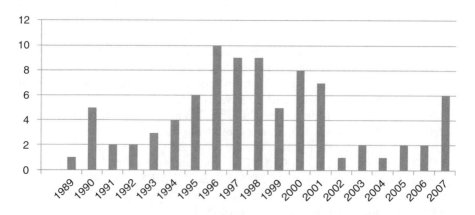

Figure 3.1 Number of stock exchanges becoming fully electronic, 1989–2007.

Table 3.2 Chronology of Stock Exchanges Adopting Electronic Trading, 1980–2007

	Exchange	Established	Fully Electronic	Location
1	National Stock Exchange*	1885	1980	Chicago, United States
2	Bolsa Electrónica de Chile	November 1989	November 1989	Santiago, Chile
3	OMX Nordic Exchange in Helsinki	1912	April 1990	Helsinki, Finland
4	Saudi Stock Exchange (TADAWUL)	1930	April 8, 1990	Riyadh, Saudi Arabia
5	OMX Nordic Exchange in Stockholm	1863	1990	Stockholm, Sweden
6	Australian Stock Exchange (ASX)	1861	October 1990	Australia
7	Shanghai Stock Exchange	November 1990	December 19, 1990	Shanghai, China
8	Warsaw Stock Exchange	1817	1991	Warsaw, Poland
9	Stock Exchange of Thailand	May 20, 1974	1991	Bangkok, Thailand
10	New Zealand Exchange (NZX)	1915	August 1992	Wellington, New Zealand
11	Shenzhen Stock Exchange	December 1, 1990	1992	Shenzhen, China
12	Prague Stock Exchange	1850s	April 1993	Prague, Czech Republic
13	Vilnius Stock Exchange	September 1992	September 14, 1993	Vilnius, Lithuania
14	HKEx	1891	November 1993	Central, Hong Kong
15	National Stock Exchange of India	1992	June 1994	Mumbai, India
16	Tehran Stock Exchange	1936	September 1, 1994	Tehran, Iran
17	Istanbul Stock Exchange	October 1984	November 1994	Istanbul, Turkey
18	Borsa Italiana	1808	1994	Milan, Italy
19	Indonesia Stock Exchange	1912	May 1995	Jakarta, Indonesia
20	Lima Stock Exchange	December 31, 1860	August 1995	Lima, Peru

Table 3.2 (*Continued*)

	Exchange	Established	Fully Electronic	Location
21	Moldova Stock Exchange	December 1994	October 1995	Chisinau, Moldova
22	Ljubljana Stock Exchange	1924	December 14, 1995	Ljubljana, Slovenia
23	Bombay Stock Exchange	1875	1995	Mumbai, India
24	Pune Stock Exchange	1982	1995	Pune, India
25	SWX Swiss Exchange	1850	1996	Zurich, Switzerland
26	Cyprus Stock Exchange	March 29, 1996	March 29, 1996	Nicosia, Cyprus
27	JSE Limited: SAFEX	September 1998	May 1996	Sandton, Republic of South Africa
28	OMX: Tallinn Stock Exchange	April 1995	May 31, 1996	Tallinn, Estonia
29	JSE	November 1887	June 1996	Sandton, Republic of South Africa
30	Bangalore Stock Exchange	1963	July 29, 1996	Bangalore, India
31	Mexican Stock Exchange	1894	August 1996	Mexico City, Mexico
32	Tunis Stock Exchange	1969	October 1996	Tunis, Tunisia
33	Ludhiana Stock Exchange Assoc.	1981	November 1996	Ludhiana, India
34	Ahmedabad Stock Exchange	1894	December 12, 1996	Ahmedabad, India
35	Hyderabad Stock Exchange	November 14, 1943	February 1997	Hyderabad, India
36	Cayman Islands Stock Exchange	June 1997	June 1997	George Town, Grand Cayman
37	Delhi Stock Exchange Association	June 1947	August 1997	New Delhi, India
38	Korea Exchange	March 3, 1956	September 1, 1997	Busan, Korea
39	Osaka Securities Exchange	1878	December 8, 1997	Osaka, Japan
40	Bhubaneswar Stock Exchange Assoc.	1989	1997	Bhubaneswar, India
41	PFTS Stock Exchange	1997	1997	Kiev, Ukraine

Table 3.2 (*Continued*)

	Exchange	Established	Fully Electronic	Location
42	TSX Group	1852	1997	Toronto, Canada
43	Tel-Aviv Stock Exchange	1935	1997	Tel Aviv, Israel
44	Chittagong Stock Exchange	April 1, 1995	June 1998	Chittagong, Bangladesh
45	Dhaka Stock Exchange	April 28, 1954	August 1998	Dhaka, Bangladesh
46	Regional Stock Exchange West Africa	1974	September 16, 1998	Abidjan, Ivory Coast
47	Channel Islands Stock Exchange	March 1998	October 27, 1998	Guernsey, Channel Islands
48	Budapest Stock Exchange	June 1990	November 1998	Budapest, Hungary
49	Bermuda Stock Exchange	1971	Late 1998	Hamilton, Bermuda
50	Kuwait Stock Exchange	1983	1998	Kuwait City, Kuwait
51	Muscat Securities Market	1989	1998	Ruwi, Oman
52	Namibian Stock Exchange	September 1992	1998	Windhoek, Namibia
53	Inter-Connected Stock Exch. of India	February 1999	February 26, 1999	Maharashtra, India
54	Tokyo Stock Exchange	1878	April 1999	Tokyo, Japan
55	Nigerian Stock Exchange	1960s	April 27, 1999	Lagos, Nigeria
56	TSX Venture Exchange	November 1999	November 1999	Alberta, Canada
57	Athens Exchange	1876	1999	Athens, Greece
58	Jamaica Stock Exchange	1961	February 2000	Kingston, Jamaica
59	Amman Stock Exchange	March 11, 1999	March 2000	Amman, Jordan
60	Dubai Financial Market	March 26, 2000	March 26, 2000	Dubai, United Arab Emirates

Table 3.2 (*Continued*)

	Exchange	Established	Fully Electronic	Location
61	Bahamas Intl. Securities Exchange	September 1999	May 2000	Nassau, Bahamas
62	Irish Stock Exchange	1793	June 2000	Dublin, Ireland
63	Bulgarian Stock Exchange—Sofia	November 1991	October 2000	Sofia, Bulgaria
64	Luxembourg Stock Exchange	1928	November 2000	L-2227, Luxembourg
65	National Stock Exchange of Australia	March 2000	December 5, 2000	Newcastle, Australia
66	SWX Europe (formerly virt-x)	2001	2001	London, United Kingdom
67	Malta Stock Exchange	January 1992	2001	Valletta, Malta
68	Macedonian Stock Exchange	September 1995	April 2001	Skopje, Macedonia
69	Egyptian Exchange	1883	May 2001	Cairo, Egypt
70	Stock Exchange of Mauritius	March 30, 1989	June 29, 2001	Port Louis, Republic of Mauritius
71	Armenian Stock Exchange	February 2001	July 2001	Yerevan, Armenia
72	Nasdaq Stock Market	February 8, 1971	July 2001	New York, United States
73	Oslo Børs	March 1, 1881	May 2002	Oslo, Norway
74	Kyrgyz Stock Exchange	1994	May 2003	Bishkek, Kyrgyz Republic
75	TLX	September 2003	September 2003	Milan, Italy
76	Belgrade Stock Exchange	1894	February 11, 2004	Belgrade, Serbia
77	Trinidad and Tobago Stock Exchange	1981	March 2005	Port of Spain, Trinidad
78	São Paulo Stock Exchange	August 23, 1890	2005	Sao Paulo, Brazil
79	Boston Stock Exchange	October 1834	December 2006	Boston, United States
80	Philadelphia Stock Exchange	1790	December 15, 2006	Philadelphia, United States
81	Chicago Stock Exchange	1882	February 2007	Chicago, United States

Table 3.2 (*Continued*)

	Exchange	Established	Fully Electronic	Location
82	Dubai International Financial Exchange	September 2004	August 2007	Dubai, United Arab Emirates
83	Borse Dubai	August 7, 2007	August 7, 2007	Dubai, United Arab Emirates
84	Börse Berlin	1685	November 2007	Berlin, Germany
85	Zagreb Stock Exchange	1918	November 23, 2007	Zagreb, Croatia

*Originally the Cincinnati Stock Exchange.
Source: Mondo Visione, exchange Web sites, communications with exchanges.

screen-based stock exchange was a new 1989 electronic exchange in Chile, called just that—the Electronic Exchange of Chile (Bolsa Electrónica de Chile). The Shanghai Stock Exchange began as an electronic exchange in 1990. Likewise, the Vilnius Stock Exchange in Lithuania and the National Stock Exchange of India were created as screen-based exchanges out of the box.[15] The Moldova Stock Exchange, the Cyprus Stock Exchange, the Cayman Islands Stock Exchange, and nine others were also begun as electronic exchanges.

Nasdaq: Early, But Not All the Way

The first stock market to move in the direction of screen-based trading was not one of the richer, more sophisticated exchanges such as the New York Stock Exchange or the Tokyo Stock Exchange or the London Stock Exchange but rather the relatively disorganized OTC market in the United States.

The OTC market, of course, was the marketplace for stocks that did not meet the listing standards of the exchanges. It was a dealer market, where from one to 10 or more dealers would make a two-sided market in OTC stocks. Each dealer would quote a price at which he was willing to buy and a price at which he was willing to sell. If a customer told her broker she wanted to buy 1000 shares of a specific OTC stock, the broker would call several dealers to get their quotes and then chose the lowest offer of the three dealers.

Of course, shifting the OTC stock market to screens didn't simply happen but rather was instigated by Congress. It all started because the SEC became concerned about pricing abuses in the OTC market. Because there were a number of brokers trading OTC stocks, there were always different bid-ask spreads available in the market from different brokers for the same stock, and it was virtually impossible, or at least very difficult, for investors to know the best price for a given OTC stock. So the SEC decided to conduct a *Special Study of the Securities Market*, which it delivered to Congress in 1963. The study argued that the best way to improve price in the OTC market was through automation, and it charged the National Association of Securities Dealers (NASD) to solve the problem by building an automated quotation system whereby its market makers or dealers would post their bids and offers.

The new system, which went live in 1971, was called the National Association of Securities Dealers Automatic Quotation System, or Nasdaq. And it was what its name said—simply a quotation system. To actually buy or sell required a phone call. The only thing automated was the quotes. But this was a positive shift in transparency. Initially only the median bid and offer was displayed for 2500 OTC stocks. It actually took till 1980 before the best bid and offer was displayed on the screen. That was huge and resulted in a significant narrowing of spreads. Now all dealers and brokers could see the best dealer quotes for each OTC stock.

Actual electronic matching began in 1984 with the Computer Assisted Execution System (CAES) but leapt forward the following year with the 1984 introduction of the Small Order Execution System (SOES). However, this was still a dealer market, so SOES was not matching incoming customer orders with each other but rather with the dealer offering the best quote. Furthermore, SOES was not automatic—dealers had the option of responding or not. So, during the crash of October 1987, many small customer orders delivered via SOES were not accepted and went unexecuted. As a result, SOES participation became mandatory for dealers in 1988. Then came a long list of improvements at Nasdaq, including SuperSoes in 2001, which, among many other things, lifted the minimum size of a SOES order to 999,999 shares, and SuperMontage, a system that displayed and allowed execution against the best five bids and offers for every Nasdaq stock on a single screen. The ECNs played a very important role in stimulating this market improvement. Because they were competing with Nasdaq and with each other for order flow, the ECNs were continually improving their systems.

The situation was really Nasdaq's fault. The ECNs were mostly created after the SEC wrote new order-handling rules in 1997. And why did the SEC write new order-handling rules? Because a couple of academic economists, William Christie and Paul Schultz, published a clever article in the *Journal of Finance*[16] (but released the results to the press prior to publication) essentially pointing out that Nasdaq market makers were colluding to earn bigger bid-ask spreads. There were none of the usual tools used to uncover cheating and collusion—no hidden wires, no bugs on phones, no subpoenaed emails—just statistics. Christie and Schultz showed that though the Nasdaq market traded in eighths of a dollar, an archaic thing to begin with in a largely decimalized world, most quotes and trades were done on the even eights, that is, 2/8, 4/8, 6/8, and 8/8 (i.e., a dollar even). If quotes and prices were random, you'd expect about the same percentage of quotes and trades to occur on the odd eights, but the dealers avoided the odd eights like a plague. The effect was to preserve wide 25-cent bid-ask spreads. To put this in the context of today, there are many stocks with bid-ask spreads of 1 cent, so the Nasdaq dealers were engineering spreads 25 times the size of those today. Both the U.S. Justice Department and the SEC got on the case, and the SEC wrote new order-handling rules, which essentially gave birth to the ECN craze and brought a new level of competition to the market. As part of the settlement, Nasdaq agreed to new order-handling rules and to integrate with other ECNs (also known as alternative trading systems). Thus the ECNs played a major role in bringing electronic trading to the equities market in the United States.

In the mid-1990s, the SEC gave ECNs the status of alternative trading systems and permission to integrate with Nasdaq's system. A number of ECNs, such as Instinet, Archipelago, Brut, and Island, entered the equities market-place. ECNs provided market data (Level 1 and Level 2[17]) to the marketplace beyond traders and market makers at NYSE and Nasdaq. Boosted by the Internet and technological advances in the 1990s, the ECNs evolved into real competition for the two exchange giants. They brought transparency, efficiency, and anonymity to the equities markets and forced the NYSE and Nasdaq to reinvent themselves. By forming partnerships with various discount brokers and investments banks, ECNs made it easier and cheaper for the general public to trade equities. ECNs partnered with online brokerage houses such as E*Trade and Charles Schwab to generate liquidity. By partnering with other ECNs, they linked their order books to provide consolidated liquidity for the whole market. They challenged the rules[18] of the primary exchanges and forced the NYSE and Nasdaq to rethink their traditional trading model for the first time. These markets, cognizant of the threat of ECNs, evaluated their option of demutualization,[19] a trend that was already common in European equities market and even in U.S. futures markets. Most ECNs today have been acquired by one of the primary exchanges or by large investment banks, but their innovation and persistence forced the NYSE and Nasdaq to grudgingly plan their survival for the next century.

The competition for electronic trading really heated up with the emergence of ECNs. The competition from ECNs such as Instinet, Island, and Archipelago forced NYSE and Nasdaq, the two dominant U.S. equity exchanges, to rethink their business models. The ECNs challenged the roles of Nasdaq dealers and NYSE specialists, who served as the middlemen for trade matching. Instead, ECNs matched trades automatically on their systems. The ECNs brought anonymity, lower execution costs, and detailed market data to the trading community. Anonymity, for example, has attracted more institutional traders to ECNs. On the floor of the NYSE and in the Nasdaq dealer community there was always a risk of word leaking out about a large order coming in, which could cause the NYSE floor traders or Nasdaq dealers to drive up the price. These leakages do not happen on a computer screen of ECNs where buyer and seller orders are matched by the system. ECNs' lower execution fees, for example, saved institutional investors 1–1.5% on their trades. So, on a $100,000 trade they would save $1000 to $1500.[20] The two market giants looked to purchase the ECNs to maintain their grip on market liquidity. Most ECNs were eventually purchased by these exchanges[21] and by some of the larger investment banks. With the acquisition of the ECNs, the exchanges were able to adopt just enough technology to improve their floor-trading but not eliminate the trading flow.

The major transformation of the U.S. equities markets did not occur until recently and only when faced with global competitors and the success of markets in Europe. Nasdaq used the infrastructure acquired from ECNs to provide an electronic trading platform to its customer base.[22] However, the NYSE continued to resist the full transformation to electronic trading. It acquired Archipelago on March 7, 2006, and became a public company. Similarly to CBOE's response to the ISE threat, the NYSE rolled out its hybrid system in October 2006 to quell the pressure of electronic trading. The hybrid system would allow electronic trading to exist in parallel to floor-based trading at the NYSE—and it fared well for a while. According to the exchange, the number of trades executing electronically tripled after the launch of the hybrid system.[23]

However, a year later, the exchange once again was facing challenges. The hybrid system in October 2007 was only matching 40% of NYSE listed volume, significantly lower than in the past.[24] New waves of competition from new upstarts such as BATS and Direct Edge as well as from its old rival Nasdaq have continued to challenge the NYSE with their high-speed trading systems and has forced the NYSE to rethink its strategy once again. Today, Nasdaq has expanded globally, with the recent mergers with OMX, the Nordic exchange, and a deal to cooperate with Borse Dubai. The NYSE also merged with Euronext, creating the first transatlantic exchange, and continues to face pressures to complete its migration from floor to screen.

But as we can see from Table 3.2, though Nasdaq was an early adopter of technology, it took 30 years before it gave up the telephones altogether and replaced them with an electronic matching engine for all shares. In fact, the pattern with stock exchanges is similar to that with derivatives exchanges; the exchanges that converted early to full electronic trading were not in the world's financial capitals but rather in more out-of-the-way places like Busan, Santiago, Helsinki, Shanghai, and Riyadh. Furthermore, as in the case of the derivatives exchanges, U.S. exchanges were not leaders but rather laggards when it came to a full adoption of electronic trading.

Toronto

There were other early pioneers, even though they didn't go fully electronic for some time. An important early player in the shift from floors to screens was the Toronto Stock Exchange (TSE). In 1977, it developed a system called CATS, a nice acronym for the more prosaic Computer-Assisted Trading System. CATS was first used for less liquid stocks. It was not uncommon to use electronic matching for marginal situations, such as less liquid stocks in Toronto and Tokyo, or for after-hours trading in derivatives at the CME, CBOT, NYMEX, and LIFFE, or for small orders, as in the DOT and Super DOT system at the NYSE. The TSE has since become a part of a larger exchange group called the TSE Group and uses a new platform, TSX Quantum; in 2008 it announced a new separate order book, TSX Infinity, for high-velocity traders.

Australia

The Australian Stock Exchange, which was created as an association of six different stock exchanges in Australia, was also an early adopter. In 1985 a committee from the exchange took a two-week tour of North American exchanges and came away most impressed with Toronto's CATS system.[25] They came home wanting to use CATS as a model but to build something much faster and more advanced. They spent $1.5 million over the next few years developing the system they called SEATS, for Stock Exchange Automated Trading System.

From a regulatory point of view, it was clear that screen-based trading was highly superior. It created a very transparent audit trail. For example, one of the scams that existed on the Australian floors was something known as the *top pocket account*. The broker would execute a trade and then put the executed order in his pocket for later allocation. If the market moved up in a significant way, he would execute another trade on behalf of the customer and allocate the first trade to his own account, thereby earning a tidy profit. SEATS would prevent that from happening.

But the exchange got huge pushback from the floor traders, who feared they would lose their edge by no longer being able to make eye contact and read body language. The exchange engaged the members, gave a demonstration of the new system, took some 400 suggestions for changes, made the appropriate changes, held roughly 100 meetings to demonstrate the new system, and then was ready for final rollout. The exchange chose October 19, 1987, as the launch date for the new system for a portion of the listed shares. Yes, *that* October 19. Of course, on that day all the press the exchange invited to view the wonderful new system became suddenly uninterested in the clever technology. They wanted to find out why the market was dropping like a rock. It was much worse on Tuesday, when the major index, the All Ordinaries, fell 25%.

But the system passed the test, and the exchange stayed open even though neighbor Hong Kong closed both its stock and futures exchanges as a result of the crash. SEATS traded a limited list of stocks side by side with the floor for the next three years. In September 1990 all stocks began to trade side by side. By the end of the month, all six exchanges that make up the Australian Stock

Exchange had closed their floors. The system did so well that soon after, the Swiss purchased Australia's system.

London's Big Bang

In some cases the transition was not directly from floor to screen but rather from floor to telephone to screen. When the London markets experienced—or suffered, as might be said by the thousands of workers who lost jobs—the Big Bang of 1986, the London Stock Exchange went electronic in a Nasdaq sort of way. In fact, its electronic system was called SEAQ, for Stock Exchange Automated Quotations system, and was, as its name suggests, a network allowing competitive market makers to post bids and offers on a screen. Because there was no electronic matching system, the actual trades were done via telephone. In principle, the trades could also be done on the floor, but the floor was quickly abandoned and all trading moved to the telephone, just as on Nasdaq at that time. So, in a relatively short period of time, one of the major exchanges of the world essentially became an OTC market.[26]

Despite the fact that the new system did not involve electronic trade matching, the combination of the new system along with other market changes resulted in a large increase in trading volume. The other changes included the removal of barriers to entry to the brokerage business from banks and foreigners and the elimination of fixed commissions. Institutional commissions quickly fell 50%, but turnover increased sufficiently to overcome that drop and give the LSE firms an actual increase in income.[27]

Just over a decade later, in 1997, the LSE brought in a new electronic platform called SETS (Stock Exchange Electronic Trading Service). And, having developed the habit of making a big change every 10 years, in 2007 it was time for the newest LSE system, called TradElect. In fact, today TradElect manages everything, and within TradeElect is a series of different trading services that utilize the earlier two systems, SEAQ and SETS, as well as some new ones, including an International Order Book for depository receipts. The 20-year-old system, SEAQ, is used for fixed income and stocks on smaller companies and is still a quotation system with no electronic matching.

Conclusion

For well over a century, the physical trading floor was the only venue available to securities and derivatives traders. Technology finally became good enough that the physical location of the trader began not to matter, because everyone could have access to a cyber trading floor. We have come a very long way from 1984, when the first pioneer INTEX opened with fixed lines and dedicated terminals and then closed after a few months. Today there are few exchanges that are still purely floor-based. Most are totally or at least partially electronic.

Though we still have a lot to do, as explained in later chapters, there is no doubt that this first major transformation we've explored in this chapter is a net good for the customers of exchanges. They now live in a much more transparent world than their predecessors. They live in a world where it is much cheaper to trade and where it is much less likely that they will be taken advantage of by an intermediary like an unscrupulous floor broker. But, as much as any of the transformations we describe in this book, the floor-to-screen shift is also painful, disruptive, and destructive of jobs and old ways of doing things.

We turn now to the structural and ownership transition that exchanges have often gone through before they were able to make the floor-to-screen transition. We now explore the shift from private club to public company.

Endnotes

1. Limited liability corporate entities use different designations in different countries—Inc. in the United States, Ltd. in the United Kingdom, SA in Spanish-speaking countries, and NV in the Netherlands, where Euronext is incorporated.
2. Silvia Ascareli, "France's MATIF Adds Electronic Market in Derivatives to Its Open-Outcry Pits," *Wall Street Journal,* April 7, 1998, p. 1.
3. "MATIF Probes July Glitch," *Futures,* September 1998, p. 12.
4. "Not My Fault," *Futures,* December 1998, p. 12.
5. "Departure of David Kyte Signals Shakeup at LIFFE," *Financial Times,* March 30, 1998, p. 24.
6. Unless otherwise noted, the details of the GLOBEX story are taken from Leo Melamed with Bob Tamarkin, *Leo Melamed: Escape to the Futures,* New York: John Wiley, 1996, p. 331–339, and from one of this book's author's observations during his time at the CME.
7. "Mother" in the sense that it was the biggest, capturing over 90% of all stock index futures trading in the United States. The first stock index futures contract was actually the Value Line index at the Kansas City Board of Trade, which started a few months before the S&P 500, in 1982.
8. It helped that the CME was one of the three owners on OneChicago, along with the CBOT and the CBOE.
9. Leo Melamed, *Escape to the Futures,* p. 339.
10. Howard Simon, "CBT Computer System Seen Setting Standards," *Journal of Commerce,* March 17, 1989, p. 9A.
11. Leo Melamed, *Escape to the Futures,* p. 411–412.
12. Leo Melamed in *Escape to the Futures,* p. 412, says no, but others involved in the process have privately said yes.
13. Technically, the competition was between LIFFE and Frankfurt-based DTB, which later merged with Swiss-based SOFFEX and changed its name to Eurex.
14. "NYBOT Members Approve Deal," *Wall Street Journal,* New York, December 12, 2006.
15. Small time gaps between the establishment of an exchange and start of total screen-based trading should not necessarily be interpreted as cases where the exchange started with a floor, then converted. It is typical to first start and register the exchange and then go to work building the systems to support the trading. There can be a gap of months or years between the founding date and first trading date. For example, the National Stock Exchange of India was

legally established in 1992 but did not see its first trading till 1994, and that trading was screen-based out of the box.

16. William Christie and Paul Schultz, "Why Do Nasdaq Market Makers Avoid Odd-Eighth Quotes?" *Journal of Finance*, Vol. 49, No. 5, December 1994.

17. The Level 1 screen shows only the highest bid and lowest ask for a stock. Level 2 shows all the bids and asks for a stock. Level 2 also shows the recently executed orders.

18. One of the most significant challenges was NYSE Rule 390, which prevented NYSE members from routing their order flow to ECNs and other alternative trading systems.

19. Demutualization of the exchange referred to the move from member-owned organizations to stockholder-owned, for-profit corporations.

20. Hamilton, "New Electronic Networks Push Big Changes at NYSE, Nasdaq," http://articles. latimes.com/1999/jul/30/business/fi-60957, July 30, 1999.

21. Nasdaq currently owns INET (merger of Instinet and Island) and Brut. The NYSE acquired Archipelago, one of the largest ECNs.

22. Nasdaq purchased the Instinet electronic trading platform. The Instinet's brokerage division was bought by Silver Lake Partners, and Instinet's institutional trading division was purchased by the Bank of New York. Matthew Goldstein, "Nasdaq Grabs Instinet ECN," www.thestreet. com/markets/matthewgoldstein/10219371.html, April 22, 2005.

23. "NYSE Gets Regulatory Approval for Hybrid Expansion," www.finextra.com/fullstory. asp?id=16238, December 6, 2006.

24. "NYSE Can Forget the Hybrid," www.nypost.com/seven/10282007/business/nyse_can_forget_ the_hybrid.html, October 28, 2007.

25. This section is drawn from Edna Carew's book on the building of a national Australian exchange out of six regional exchanges: *National Market National Interest*, Crow's Nest, Australia, 2007, Chapter 10.

26. U.S. Congress, Office of Technology Assessment, "Trading Around the Clock: Global Securities Markets and Information Technology," OTA-BP-CIT-66, July 1990, p. 44.

27. U.S. Congress, Office of Technology Assessment, "Trading Around the Clock: Global Securities Markets and Information Technology," OTA-BP-CIT-66, July 1990, p. 44.

4 Floors to Screens: Nuts and Bolts

Executive Summary

This chapter explores the architecture of electronic trading. We discuss the components of the trade cycle for electronic trading and the history of its development, with examples of some key new players in the industry. It's not just time/price any more; we explore the various alternative matching algorithms in use today. We then dig deeply into the technical structure of electronic exchanges, from client applications to exchanges to clearing services.

Traders can now trade markets from anywhere in the world as long as they have a computer and network connection. The movement toward electronic trading has forced the rest of the industry to transform itself. The entire financial markets have seen unprecedented growth and collaboration between industry players to solidify the infrastructure and trading model while competing with each other with new products and ideas. These changes have enabled the creation of more new products, new trading styles, and new trading strategies that have given a facelift to the static world of floor-trading. The benefits of electronic trading have been tremendous.

Although the concept of buying and selling products still remains the crux of trading, the electronic trading model does differ significantly from the old floor-trading model. To appreciate this transformation fully and to further analyze the future path for financial markets, it is important to understand the high-level trade cycle, the electronic architecture built to support this trade cycle, and the roles of the new players in the markets.

The Financial Trade Cycle

A trade touches many hands as it makes its way through the system. The simple act of buying or selling a financial instrument goes through a number of components to ensure that trades are executed, cleared, settled, and reported properly. The functions remain the same; however, a trade requires far less manual processing by humans than it did in floor-trading days. The trade cycle from execution to settlement takes much less time than it did before; in fact, for derivatives it is done in real time, without any manual processing. The electronic infrastructure can be divided into three major sections required to complete the trade cycle: front office, middle office, and back office.

Front Office

The front office is where traders buy and sell financial instruments. It is a virtual trading floor created and accessed by software applications. The front-end application is a major component that allows traders to trade on a number of exchanges around the world. These virtual trading floors have all but eliminated the traditional, physical trading floors. In addition, the front office has seen tremendous growth in innovation. New software companies offer traders tools to help their trading needs. These new players have built platforms to support trading functions and provide analytical tools to study trading styles and adjust their strategies based on numerous parameters such as economic data, market events, and historical trends. The front-end application also provides pre-trade risk management and portfolio management applications to provide a consolidated view of traders' portfolios.

Middle Office

The middle office is the area of trading where every trade undergoes risk management. Every trader has an assigned risk limit based on the amount of money available to trade and the limitations imposed by regulatory bodies and exchanges. In electronic trading, there are systems built to automatically check every trade against the risk limits set for each trader. Risk management has improved significantly over the years compared with the more manual process on the trading floor. Risk management on the floor varied for members who owned a seat on the exchange. Since the membership itself was worth a significant amount, firms allowed members to margin their own account. Traders on the floor who leased the membership generally were risk-managed more. There were rules that required all trade cards to be collected every half hour to an hour for clearing firms to review the trades. Personnel from clearing firms were on the floor, watching the traders throughout the trading day.

Risk management is now far more automated, and there is an enormous amount of tracking and checking that can be implemented by risk management applications. Trades are efficiently managed throughout the trading day while providing risk managers a complete real-time view of all the firm's traders. In addition, the middle office also handles numerous other functions, including reporting and allocations of trades to appropriate accounts, and generally serves as the bridge between the front office and back office.

Back Office

The back office is the area where buys and sells are matched and trades are reconciled. The back office has two major functions: clearing and settlement. As discussed in Chapter 1, these functions are an integral part of financial markets. They ensure that a trade that took place on the exchange is processed accurately. The clearing function covers tasks such as post trading and analyzing credit exposure risk and ensures trades meet all the market rules tied to the trade. Trading firms rely on brokers to clear their trades. In addition, exchanges' clearing arms serve as the CCP. All trades ultimately are cleared through the CCP for the exchanges.

The clearing and settlement process is a significant step in the trade cycle and is generally the longest process in it. The process involves significant coordination between exchanges, brokers, trading firms, and depository firms to ensure post-trade process is completed smoothly. Post-trade processing involves final trade allocations, trade reconciliation, fund and instrument transfer, and reporting. The back-office function also involves reporting between players and the regulatory bodies such as CFTC and SEC.

Electronic Trading Architecture

The early adopters started developing their electronic exchange architecture to bring the electronic trading model as the replacement for floor-based trading. These early exchanges have gone through numerous iterations of their technology platforms to continually improve the stability and reliability of their architecture. They now rely on their hardware and software to gain access to exchanges worldwide.

As adoption of electronic trading by the financial community increased, the trading architecture continued to evolve. New players, whom we will discuss shortly, entered the financial markets to provide application and services for the trade cycle. These new players serve a vital role in this overall trading architecture. Today there are players for every component of the trade cycle. There are front-end trading screen providers, exchange connectivity providers, market data providers, and network connectivity providers. All these players, along with exchanges, must work harmoniously to build an infrastructure that can move trade from the front office to back office with much less human intervention than in the past.

Traders no longer rely on their loud voices and tall statures to buy and sell products on only a single exchange. For the floor-trading model, all one needed to trade was membership on an exchange, a knowledge of hand signals to communicate with others on the floor, and the ability to deal with stress on volatile trading days. For electronic trading, the trader might need membership on some exchanges to gain direct access, but virtually direct access is available to nonmembers at many exchanges. Of course, the trader still needs the ability to deal with stress. Additionally, today the traders need to understand how to use a computer that provides them with market access. Instead of feeling the market on the floor, traders today must understand the wealth of information blasted on their trading screens. They must learn to adapt to the speed of trading on the electronic trading floor. The trader must learn the complex order types and trading strategies available through the vendors to gain an edge in a market that is transparent.

The trading firms must also understand technology and the trading architecture to ensure that they build an electronic trading infrastructure that is fast, reliable, and stable. Today trading firms need to have technical staff who can analyze the pros and cons of the new players offering the trading screens, exchange connectivity through gateways, risk management applications, and tools to help meet regulatory requirements. In addition, they must understand the network details in depth to ensure that they have the hardware capacity to handle the message traffic and telecommunications setup to provide the fastest connection to the exchange.

Therefore, understanding the overall architecture of the electronic trading infrastructure is critical to the success of a trading firm as well as the exchange. An in-depth understanding of the electronic infrastructure will also allow the players to understand who provides software applications for the components as well as the connectivity details that take a trade from the front-end trading screen to the clearing and settlement process. The exchanges and trading firms today must understand this architecture (see Figure 4.1) and the players involved to build and improve their own electronic trading infrastructure.

As we explored in Chapter 1, trades must flow through numerous components of the trade cycle. These components consist of individual applications such as the trading screen, exchange gateway, risk management, and the clearing and settlement process. In the electronic trading model, buyers and sellers submit their orders through the front-end trading systems. These systems are software applications that are installed on traders' computers. The front-end trading systems are also known as *graphical user interfaces* (GUIs) or *trading screens,* since they are windows through which traders can view the market(s) across the globe. The front-end trading systems display the market information from multiple exchanges and route the trader's submitted orders to the exchange gateways. The financial markets have the choice of building these trading screens in house or buying them from third-party vendors. Today there is significant competition among the front-end trading screen vendors. These companies specialize in tools for traders to employ more sophisticated strategies and provide better visualizations across markets as well as charting tools to help analyze market movements. As electronic trading matured, so did the technology of independent software vendors (ISVs). Today companies such as Trading Technologies, RTS, GLTrade, Actant, and many others all provide trading firms access to multiple exchanges through their trading screens.

Today the trades can also be submitted by automated trading engines, also known as *black boxes.* These are software applications that run on computers and submit orders without any human intervention. The trading firms can simply create rules based on their trading strategies and allow the computer to automatically submit orders around the clock. The use of these applications has grown significantly in recent years. For example, an estimated half of the

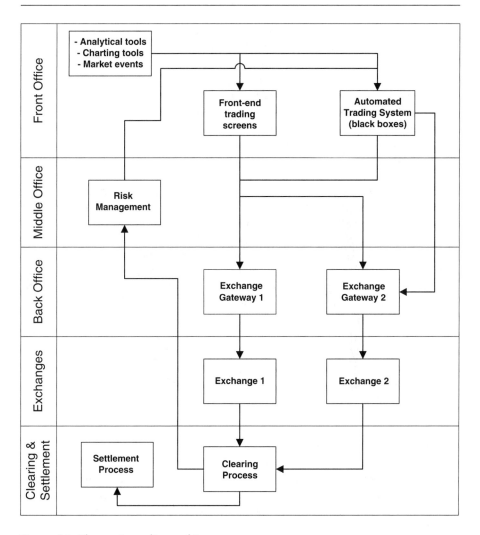

Figure 4.1 Electronic trading architecture.

U.S. stock trades flow through black boxes. They allow trading firms to trade more products across multiple exchanges and to do so at a speed that could not be matched by the fastest human trader.

A number of vendors, such as SmartQuant and Strategy Runner, provide automated trading applications that can be modified to meet individual traders' needs. The large trading firms also spend significant amounts of time and money to build black boxes. For example, the hedge fund giant Man Group's $16 billion assets are traded through its black-box application, called AHL. Built by three analysts with physics degrees from Oxford and Cambridge universities, the AHL black box is the backbone of the hedge fund's trading operations. AHL monitors markets across asset classes, analyzes market direction based on historical data, and every five minutes spits out trading decisions that are executed by a small number of traders.[1]

As the orders are entered by traders in the front-end application or through black boxes, they are also checked by risk management applications. These applications verify the limits set for traders. The risk management application provides controls to meet the risk parameters set by the risk managers of the trading firm. The risk management application also provides risk managers a full view of the trading activity for all the traders within the firm. These risk management applications' monitoring capabilities allow a firm to monitor trading activity in real time. Vendors such as GlobalRisk specialize in risk management applications to provide trading firms with software applications that help the firms manage risk of their individual traders as well as the entire firm. For example, GlobalRisk's FirmRisk application calculates real-time profit and loss, volatility, and equity for traders and an entire firm. The application also provides trading firms with the ability to calculate "what-if" scenarios to determine hypothetical market movements' impact on firms' portfolios.[2]

Once passed through the risk checks, the orders flow to the exchange gateway. A gateway is the bridge between the financial community and the exchanges and must keep pace with the rapidly evolving exchanges as well as the trading needs of the financial community. These are complex applications that perform many different functions to ensure that data flows among the front-end applications, exchanges, and the reporting applications utilized by clearing and back-office systems. Gateways are the software applications that connect to an exchange through the application programming interface (API; see sidebar). Although the design of gateways can vary by asset classes or vendors, their major processes are to route orders to the exchange, disseminate market data to the trading screen, manage order execution, and handle administrative functions such as authenticating the traders and providing audit trails of trading activity. The gateway generally is developed with the following processes:

- *Order server.* This process manages the flow of orders that are sent from the front-end application. Orders from multiple trading screens flow through the order server process. The order server manages and routes orders to the exchange's electronic trading system, where they are processed and matched.
- *Price server.* This process provides real-time market data information to the front-end application. The price server process fetches the market data from the exchange system and publishes these prices in real time on the front-end trading screens. The market data feed contains a significant amount of information, such as the opening price, last traded prices, closing prices, and settlement prices, that traders use to make their trading decisions.
- *Fill server.* As the exchange matches orders, it sends the executed orders back to the gateways. The fill server process receives these executed orders and updates the

trader's order book. It provides confirmation to the traders of all the orders that were filled, along with the quantity of the fill. This is a complex process that tracks the fills for all the traders whose orders flow through the gateway. The process keeps each trader's order book updated as the fills are received from the exchange(s).

- *Administrative process.* The administrative process serves as a gatekeeper process between the trading screens and the exchange. Every exchange has various parameters that are used to validate the traders. This process manages the authentication process for the traders across exchanges. For example, the trader on the front end can only view and trade markets that have passed the validation process in the exchange gateway. In addition, the administrative process tracks other details that are passed between the trading screen and exchange, such as account information, clearing firm code, order IDs, and timestamps for orders and fills flowing between the exchange and the trading screen. It maintains and stores the audit trail of traders' activity.

The gateway sends the orders to the exchange trading system. Via networks, the exchange trading system receives orders from gateways from the trading firms located around the world. The exchange trading system processes these orders through its matching engine (see sidebar). Although the details of the various exchanges' architectures might vary, they all perform the same primary functions: publish market data, match the buys and sells, and send confirmations back to the traders for their filled orders. The exchange trading system also sends the executed orders to the clearing and settlement system for the final processing of the trade. The process involves trade allocations and reconciliation, final margin calculation, fees and charges for the trades, and reports to meet compliance requirements. For example, an application such as GL RIMS[3] processes trades to calculate the fees associated with the trades, create reports for the regulatory bodies, and process settlement instructions for the depository agencies.[4]

The Application Programming Interface

Early exchanges such as Eurex built the electronic infrastructure, including the graphical user interface,[5] or the trading screen, to allow traders to trade on their markets. As the popularity of electronic trading increased, new independent software vendors (ISV) entered the markets. These ISVs developed trading screens that would display the market information and route orders to the exchange. The connectivity between the front-end application and exchanges could not be possible if the exchanges did not provide the API for development. Programmers use the API to develop gateways that fetch price data, submit buy and sell orders, check the volume, and much more. An API is the way you communicate with another system. It contains detailed specifications that allow a programmer to understand the requirements of a particular exchange. For example, the API provides the detailed market data the exchange provides. It is the API that tells the programmers the order types the exchange supports or that the information exchange requires on every trade to validate an order.

The API can either be closed or open; no matter which it is, the API's function is the same: to allow connectivity between the trading screen and the exchange trading system. The difference between closed and open APIs is that an open API such as LIFFE Connect would allow any developer to connect to the LIFFE Connect platform, whereas a closed API would be limited to a select few developers. Today the majority of the exchanges have open APIs.

An open API plays a significant role in the success of electronic trading. It also allows exchanges to essentially outsource the connectivity and user interface development to third-party vendors or customers. As the exchanges made the migration from floor to screen, the competition among the ISVs increased significantly. This competition generated innovative ideas in front-end trading systems as well as spurring improvements in the speed and efficiency of the exchange gateway. Companies such as Pats, GLTrade, and Trading Technologies are some of the well-known ISVs that connect to exchanges around the world using APIs. They connected these gateways to their trading screens to provide the trading community access to exchanges around the world on a single screen.

The ISVs work closely with exchanges to build gateways. As bridges between the financial community and exchanges, they provide the exchanges with valuable insights into their customers' needs. The ISVs also help educate the user community about electronic trading and the functionality offered by the individual exchanges. For example, during CBOT's migration from the Eurex platform to LIFFE Connect, there was a close coordination between the exchanges as well numerous ISVs that were developing the gateway to support CBOT on the LIFFE Connect platform. The CBOT and LIFFE relied on the ISVs to bridge the functionality gap between the LIFFE Connect and Eurex platforms. For example, when CBOT used the Eurex platform for its electronic trading infrastructure, stop orders were supported by the exchange. The LIFFE Connect platform did not support the stop orders. The ISVs developing the exchange gateway developed the functionality to synthetically support the stop orders. The traders were able to continue to send the stop orders through their trading screens, and the exchange gateway would manage the stop order synthetically.

A stop order is an order that is triggered when the specified price is reached (the stop price). So, for a stop market order, an order will be in the order book as a stop order and will convert into a market order when the stop prices are reached in the market. As a synthetic order, the ISV holds the stop order in its exchange gateway and submits the order when the specified price is reached on the exchange.

Both CBOT and LIFFE worked closely with these ISVs to ensure that they were ready for the launch, helping them throughout their development cycle as well as in their testing phases. They knew that for the launch to be successful, the ISVs would need to be ready with their connectivity; otherwise, traders would not be able to trade and the exchange would have no volume.

Side-by-Side and Hybrid Systems

Most floor-based exchanges made the transition to electronic trading in a gradual fashion. Some, like the CME, CBOT, NYMEX, and LIFFE, started with after-hours systems, as described in Chapter 3. But the majority started with what are called *side-by-side arrangements,* whereby the trading floor and the screens were made available during regular trading hours. In such systems, the two markets were two separate pools of liquidity, and customers could choose whichever they preferred. Prices were kept more or less equal via the activity of arbitrageurs. The securities exchanges in the United States would have liked to also follow a side-by-side approach, but the SEC would not allow futures-style side-by-side trading, because customers might sometimes not get the better price available on the other system. Equity and options exchanges could either go all electronic or stay floor based. The CBOE created a "hybrid" system that blended the two markets. And then some years later, the NYSE modeled its own hybrid system on that of the CBOE.

The CBOE's Hybrid System[6]

The CBOE had been exploring electronic trading since at least 1988 when senior exchange officials (Gary Lahey, Dick Dufour, and Kruno Huitzingh) went to visit the pioneer electronic exchanges of Europe—including OM and SOFFEX. Over the subsequent years, the exchange put together a plan, a design, and actually built an electronic trading system. But because the CBOE was member owned, like all other member-owned exchanges, there was a deep aversion to electronic trading and even though the exchange had completed the development of an electronic trading system as early as 1999, there was neither member interest nor SEC willingness to allow electronic trading to proceed side-by-side with floor-trading. Just as important, there was a belief that options trading just would not work well on a screen. So when ISE opened its virtual doors in 2000, the initially light trading volume confirmed the views of those who believed screen trading would not work and the threat level moved back toward green. However, after about a year and a half of trying, ISE gained real traction, volumes started rising, and the ISE became viewed as a real threat to the CBOE and it was clear to the membership that CBOE had to become part of this new world.

While a side-by-side arrangement, where traders could choose, would have been the best and quickest way to get in the game, the SEC had blocked this option by requiring all floor or all screen. The CBOE felt that neither of these extremes was viable. It had already created an electronic system, and it decided to create a hybrid system that would integrate both screen and floor-based trading and thus satisfy the SEC's concern that customers would always get the best available price. The CBOE spent just under a year melding its floor and electronic trading platform into a single, linked system called the Hybrid Trading System.

CBOE received SEC approval to launch its Hybrid Trading System on May 30, 2003. The Hybrid system was launched on June 12, 2003, with Harmony Gold options as the first product.[7] Today CBOE's Hybrid Trading System incorporates electronic and open-outcry trading, enabling customers to choose their trading method. The electronic side of Hybrid is CBOE*direct*, an electronic platform that also supports the CBOE Futures Exchange (CFE), CBOE Stock Exchange (CBSX) and OneChicago. Over 15 ISVs provide connectivity to the trading community to one or more of the CBOE markets.

With its launch of CBOE*direct*, the trade engine behind the hybrid system, the exchange is able to grow and compete with the ISE and subsequent screen-based option exchanges, both domestically and internationally. CBOE*direct* allows firms to trade electronically and still provides the flexibility for them to trade on the floor, if they choose. CBOE*direct* supports an open interface and provides multiple connectivity options. It allows ISVs to connect to CBOE*direct* via its own proprietary interface, CMi, through industry-standard protocol FIX, or through the CMS-based COMPASS. CBOE*direct* allows its customers to trade its options via ISV trading screens through its Hybrid Trading System Terminal (HyTS) and the option to continue to trade on the floor. HyTS provides market access and order routing to all U.S. equity options from a single screen. Similarly, ISVs also provide customers the ability to trade multiple markets through a single screen.[8]

The Hybrid system has turned out to be a reasonable compromise, given the SEC's refusal to allow side-by-side. Options are different from equities and futures, both of which lend themselves to straight buy and sell positions or at least relatively simple spreads. Because there are so many options for any given stock, many transactions often involve the purchase and sale of a number of puts and calls at different strikes. Combining this with the fact that market makers don't always post the best price at which they would buy or sell, because they have to watch so many different options and thus build in a protective cushion in the bid-ask spread, a lot of customers still prefer to negotiate trades on the floor to get better prices. Therefore, worldwide, options have been the financial product most difficult to migrate to the screen. And even on screen-based systems, the options transaction is often negotiated prior the execution on the screen.

Matching Algorithms

One of the key components of trading involves matching bids and offers. In electronic trading, these matches occur based on various formulas called *matching algorithms*. There are several matching algorithms that are utilized by the exchanges. Within a given exchange there are different algorithms depending on the asset class, the trading style, and liquidity of the product. Before we dive into the reasons that a specific algorithm is used for matching, let's explore the various matching algorithms that are currently used. The following four matching algorithms are used in the global derivatives trading world:

- *First-in/first-out (FIFO)*. This is one of the most commonly used algorithms, also known as *price/time priority matching*. Trades are matched in the order in which they arrive into the matching engine.
- *Pro rata*. Often used in illiquid products where the trade with the best price above a specified volume is given the highest priority.
- *Lead market maker (LMM) allocation*. Another algorithm to enhance liquidity, where the market maker who provides a two-sided market is guaranteed a certain percentage of the order.
- *Work-up*. Markets such as BrokerTec and eSpeed have used a work-up model for fixed income trading. The work-up model gives a trader, at a given price, the right to execute all trades within a specified time (generally two to three seconds). This model is considered the least efficient because it gives a trader control over the market for a specific period of time.

Matching algorithms are a critical part of an exchange's architecture. Two critical requirements are to enhance liquidity and to efficiently match trades while maintaining the anonymity of the traders. An early attempt to provide complex matching algorithms was by an upstart, OptiMark. Introduced in the early 1990s, it was an innovative electronic matching algorithm that would match large orders anonymously.[9] If successful, it would have allowed large institutional funds to effectively trade their large orders fully electronically. OptiMark built a proprietary algorithm that would match trades in cycles. The system would match orders in five-minute intervals.[10] In equities trading the "dark books"[11] could have been eliminated if the OptiMark idea was successful. In the futures industry, it would have allowed traders to trade their large block orders anonymously instead of in prearranged deals with human intervention. At the time of its introduction, the concept was well received by the industry. At its peak, it matched close to 3 million trades.[12] However, the complex algorithms and radical new way of trading, at a time when electronic trading was still in its infancy, were too cumbersome for traders to use. Many industry leaders agreed that OptiMark might have been too innovative too early.

The financial market landscape has changed drastically in the last few years. The traders have been able to adapt to the technology, the trading styles have become more complex, and there is a gradual rise in algorithmic trading. The fate of OptiMark could have been much different in the current marketplace. In recent years, large investment banks such as JP Morgan Chase and Banc of America Securities (BAS) introduced new matching algorithms with names such as Aqua, Arid, and Ambush to "stealthily trade stocks on dark books."[13] The innovation in new matching algorithms will continue to efficiently match large institutional orders while maintaining the anonymity of the trader.

New Players Solidifying the Single-Screen Concept

The growth of electronic trading broke the traditional floor-trading model. The early exchanges used technology to design the electronic infrastructure. And, as they opened their APIs, technology vendors entered the markets with fresh new ideas and new concepts in the financial markets. These new players helped shape the direction for the new model and are now an integral part of bringing the trading world onto a single screen. Today, there are client-side application vendors that provide trading screens, charting tools, risk management, and analytical tools. There are vendors that specialize as market data providers. There are vendors that provide applications for the post-trade processing for clearing and settlement processes. And there are players that provide maintenance and support services for the trading infrastructure. These vendors introduced the concept of single-screen trading. They have allowed the financial market players to pick and choose applications to build the electronic trading infrastructure that allows traders access to markets from around the world in real time and analyze market movements against historical data, and, with the help of black boxes, they can trade around the clock.

Endnotes

1. Heather Timmons, "A London Hedge Fund That Opts for Engineers, Not M.B.A.'s," www. nytimes.com/2006/08/18/business/worldbusiness/18man.html?ex=1313553600&en=b2fee1b4 1c85af15&ei=5088&partner=rssnyt&emc=rss (August 18, 2006).

2. "GlobalRisk Firm Risk," www.globalrisk.com/firmrisk.
3. Developed by GL Trade, the majority interest of which is owned by SunGard.
4. Developed by GL Trades, the majority interest of which is owned by SunGard, GL RIMS, www.sungard.com/financialsystems/brands/glrims.aspx.
5. Generally referred to as *green screen*.
6. "CBOE Hybrid®, The Hybrid Trading System," https://www.cboe.org/hybrid/default.aspx.
7. "CBOE Receives SEC Approval to Launch CBOEdirect HyTS, The Hybrid Trading System," www.cboe.com/AboutCBOE/ShowDocument.aspx?FILE=06-02-2003.doc&DIR=ACNews& HEAD=CBOE+News+Releases&SEC=7 (June 12).
8. HyTS provides access to only U.S. equity options, whereas the ISVs' single screen could provide access to markets around the globe.
9. On the floor there is no such thing as anonymity. For example, if a trader wants to trade a large order, others will find out and increase the price; therefore the buyer would not get the best price.
10. At the time, matching at the exchange was continuous, and orders were matched as they were submitted.
11. Dark books, also called *dark liquidity* or *dark pools,* are trading networks used by large institutional investors for their large orders. This is also known as the *upstairs market.*
12. The Industry Standard, http://findarticles.com/p/articles/mi_m0HWW/is_42_3/ai_66672877.
13. "JP Morgan Launches 'Dark Book' Algorithms," www.finextra.com/fullstory.asp?id=15828 (September 8, 2006).

5 From Private Club to Public Company

Executive Summary

Member-owned exchanges were the standard model for many years and did a fairly good job. However, an exchange owned by members meant that members often took precedence over customers. In this chapter we explain what a membership is and how those memberships were transformed into a trading right and a bucket of common stock under a process called *demutualization,* and we review case studies of the CME, CBOT, CBOE, NYMEX, and NYSE. We also explain the drivers behind this important transformation.

Introduction

In this chapter we explore the second of the four basic transformations of the exchanges: the conversion of member-owned exchanges into publicly traded companies. There are really two steps in this process. The first is to convert the exchange from a not-for-profit, member-owned exchange, also called a *mutually owned exchange*, to a for-profit, stockholder-owned exchange. This process is called *demutualization.* The second step is to convert the stockholder-owned company into a publicly traded company by issuing shares to the public in a process known as an *initial public offering* (IPO) and listing the exchange on some stock exchange. Sometimes the exchange even lists itself on itself.

But before we describe the process by which these exchanges became demutualized and publicly traded, we should first take a look at the old form of organization: the member-owned exchange.

The Member-Owned Exchange: The Good, the Bad, and the Ugly

No exchange is born as a public company. Some are born as joint stock companies, but the majority of exchanges (virtually all those in the United States, Canada, the United Kingdom, and Japan, for example) got their start as member-owned mutual organizations. This was an extremely logical choice, given the way exchanges evolved historically. Groups of men (women didn't trade in those days) who traded company stocks or futures-type contracts for corn and wheat wanted to move in from the cold or from the pub or coffee-house to a more professional trading room. The idea was that the members would own the entity that operated the physical trading room, the blackboards, the telephones, the processing and clearing systems. The exchange would operate as a mutually owned, not-for-profit entity that supported the profit-making objectives of the traders.

Good for the Members

How did the members benefit from the creation of these original member-owned exchanges? The members made their income in three different ways. First, some members acted as floor brokers, and any order coming to the floor had to be executed by one of these floor broker members, for which the member would receive a commission. These floor brokers also benefited if their exchange allowed them to trade for their own account in addition to executing customer orders. While they were not allowed to trade in front of an order they received for one of their customers, knowing the orders in their deck, especially if they handled a lot of orders, gave them an information advantage over traders outside the exchange and even over other floor traders who were not also brokers. Dual traders, especially those with a number of customers or a few large customers, knew a lot more about the potential buying and selling pressure that would arise as the market moved up and down, triggering "price orders" and "stop orders." (See box, "Market Orders, Limit Orders, Stop Orders.") U.S. futures exchanges allowed floor brokers to trade for themselves as well as executing orders for customers (a practice known as *dual trading*), based on the argument that this created more liquidity in the pit. This was true and helpful, especially in smaller pits with a handful of brokers. The only exception to this practice in the futures world was the CME, which prohibited dual trading in liquid markets. While the CBOE earlier allowed its market makers to dual trade, it now also prohibits dual trading.

Market Orders, Limit Orders, Stop Orders and What Floor Brokers Know

In floor-based markets, all orders must generally be executed by floor brokers. Though a number of order types are available for use in floor-trading, there are three basic types of orders used in these markets. First is the *market order*, which instructs the broker to buy the specified quantity at the best price currently available in the market. This order is used when the trader is mainly concerned about ensuring that the trade is done and is not willing to wait for a possibly better price. Because these orders must be executed immediately, the information they convey to the brokers who fill them is useful for only a matter of seconds. And though a broker might know that a particular order he has received is large enough to move the market when it is executed, it is a violation of exchange rules, CFTC regulations, and the Commodity Exchange Act for brokers to trade for themselves in front of a customer order.

Second is the *limit order*, which instructs the broker to buy the specified quantity (or as much of it as possible) at a price no higher than the limit specified on the order or to sell no lower than the price specified on the order. Limit orders allow customers to get better prices, but the orders will be executed only if the market rises or falls to the level of the price specified. Floor brokers with big order books thus know something about how much buying there will be if prices fall and how much selling there will be if prices go up. They don't see the whole market, only the orders they are holding, which can still be valuable information.

The third type of order is the *stop order*. These orders allow traders to specify buy prices above the current market and sell prices below the current market. This type of order is used to get out of the market if it moves too far against a trader. It stops losses from getting any worse. For example, a trader may buy at 10, hoping the market goes to 15, but to ensure that he doesn't lose too much if he's wrong, he may enter a sell stop at 8, meaning that if the market falls to 8, his sell stop gets executed and the most he would lose would be about 2. Though limit orders have the effect of stabilizing the market—if the market starts to fall, the buy limit orders tend to stop the fall by accommodating sellers who come in—stop orders destabilize the market. If the market falls and triggers a sell stop, the sell order joins the other market sell orders flowing in and tends to push down the price even more quickly. So, knowledge of large stop orders can tell a broker quite a bit about how the market will behave if the market rises or falls enough to trigger them.

Second, some members operated as market makers, though they were more commonly called *scalpers* or *locals*. What this meant was that they would stand in the pit ready to take the opposite side of incoming orders. If someone wanted to buy, the scalper would sell to them a bit above the last transaction price. If someone wanted to sell, the scalper would buy from them a bit below the last transaction price. The prices at which the market maker would buy and sell were known as the *bid* and the *offer* (or the *bid* and the *ask*). The difference between these two prices was referred to as the *bid-ask spread*. The bid-ask spread was the profit made by the scalper for the service of making a market.[1] These scalpers typically would make very small profits on each transaction, since they would be buying slightly lower than the price at which they would be selling, but of course they would experience losses when markets moved unexpectedly. On a traditional floor-based futures exchange, these scalpers did not have an obligation to make a market; they did so as a profit-making business. When things got volatile, they might widen the bid-ask spread to protect themselves or even withdraw temporarily. But the point here is that making markets as scalpers was another way that exchange members could earn revenue.

Third, members often took positions for their own accounts, speculating as to whether the price of some stock or commodity would rise or fall. Being on the floor gave the members an information advantage compared to speculators who were operating from outside the exchange. Floor traders could hear things being said and could see things that traders away from the floor could not. By knowing that an independent floor broker usually did business for a particular large customer, a floor trader could surmise what that customer might be doing. Being on the floor allowed a trader to read the faces of others, to see anxiety, to see panic when a fellow trader or broker was about to offset a huge position that was losing money. In addition, for individuals who traded frequently, the lower exchange fees available to members resulted in significant savings. For example, throughout the 1990s the fees paid by CME members were only one-tenth the level paid by nonmembers (7 cents vs. 70 cents per side). Today the fee structure is more complex and higher than it used to be for members, and the percentage discount for members is smaller, but for frequent traders, there is still a substantial advantage to being a member. For example, to trade indexes on screen at the CME (each product group has its own fee level) a member pays 70 cents a side and a nonmember pays $2.28.

There were, of course, other, less important benefits. For example, the exchange floor provided a certain degree of camaraderie for the members. Compared to the modern world in which isolated traders might be sitting at terminals in disparate places all over the world, the trading floor was the place that the trader went every day, saw the same people, and developed deep and lasting friendships. When a lot of orders were coming onto the floor, life was intense, stressful, and generally profitable. When there were lags in order flow, traders would swap jokes, stories, and news about things both international and personal. For many, it was a fun place to be.

And for most, the trading floor was a much better place to be than an office of a large corporation. The trading floor was populated by essentially independent entrepreneurs. Traders had no bosses. How well they did was a function not of office politics but rather was based on the hard numbers that showed how much money they made or lost at the end of each day. They determined their own destiny, based on their trading skills. And in a larger sense, they determined their own destiny as a group because they owned and controlled the exchange, the place where they worked every day. The mutually owned exchange was a very democratic place. Members elected a board of directors and often the chairman of the exchange as well.[2] The elected board, in turn, created committees of members to handle all sorts of decisions. There were committees for changing the contract specifications of each separate commodity or commodity group. There were committees that dealt with disputes among members. There were committees that dealt with marketing, finance, new products, and even deciding the appropriate clothing for the trading floor.

Managing Regulators

In terms of controlling and protecting the destiny of the exchange and thus protecting the incomes of the members, exchanges would employ lobbyists to attempt to both move forward the agenda of the exchange and prevent damaging actions by central, state, or local governments. These actions would often involve a proposal for a tax of some sort on the transactions conducted at the exchange. It was not uncommon, for example, that the city of Chicago, in its efforts to find new sources of revenue, would talk about taxing transactions on the CBOT and the CME. But typically a combination of strong lobbying and threats to move the exchange elsewhere prevented the imposition of such taxes. On the national level, donations were often made to elected officials, if not by exchanges directly, which is prohibited in some countries like the United States, then from special funds created as member associations and funded by individual members.

The strong relationship between the Chicago exchanges and Congress came in very handy when the exchanges wanted to slow the approval of a Chicago subsidiary of Frankfurt-based Eurex. This event is dealt with in more detail in Chapters 2 and 6, but because of the relationships that had been created between the Chicago exchanges and various members of Congress, Congress decided to hold hearings on Eurex's application to the Commodity Futures Trading Commission (CFTC) to set up shop in Chicago. This was a very unusual move—it was the first time in history that Congress held a hearing on an exchange application—but it had the intended effect of delaying the Eurex approval until the Chicago exchanges could better position themselves to fend off a competitive attack. And it worked. The Eurex subsidiary was approved with a significant delay, and it failed miserably.

One political risk faced by derivatives exchanges and their lobbyists is the outright banning of trading in certain products by central governments. In some cases, spot market trade groups might try to shut down trading in a product. For example, onion producers were able to successfully have Congress ban the trading of onions at the CME (and everywhere else in the United States) in 1958 after a manipulation and such a deep crash in prices that the sellers couldn't even recover the cost of the bags the onions were delivered in. The CME fought the ban with a temporary restraining order, even after the President of the United States signed the bill. The exchange eventually gave up, and onions became the only futures contract ever banned by the U.S. Congress.

Almost three decades later, the CME was again faced with an industry-led movement to ban trading in another futures contract, the contract on Live Cattle.[3] In 1984, after years of a government program to support dairy prices by purchasing butter and cheese when their prices fell below a certain critical level, the federal government found itself owning mountains of butter and cheese. It wisely decided to attack the problem at its source: there were simply too many dairy cattle. So the U.S. Department of Agriculture launched the "Whole Herd Dairy Buy Out" and offered to pay dairy farmers who agreed to leave the business and either slaughter or export their entire herds. Market analysts predicted that about a third of a million cattle would be put into the program. When the numbers were finally tallied, a million cattle, three times the predicted amount, were signed up to go to slaughter, significantly increasing the supply of beef (especially hamburger-type ground beef) coming to market and sending prices that were already historically low into a tailspin. Live Cattle futures prices fell by the maximum allowed (called the *daily price limit*) at the CME for four of the next five trading sessions.

This time the CME tried to work closely with the industry, putting an official from the National Cattlemen's Association on the CME Board, sending CME members and staff to meet with groups of cattlemen all over the country, commissioning studies of the situation, and generally being open to industry ideas to correct any problems. The conciliatory approach with the cattlemen worked. Though the cattlemen were still angry, the CME made enough concessions that they backed off from pushing for a ban on cattle futures. So the exchange, working on behalf of its members, successfully prevented the loss of one of the exchange's most important contracts, again protecting member incomes.

Not all exchanges fare as well in deflecting negative government actions. In India, for example, four commodity futures contracts (wheat, rice, urad, and tur[4]) were banned in early 2007 and another four (potatoes, soybean oil, rubber, and chana) in early 2008 as a result of a rapid increase in domestic food prices.[5] The fact that this was simply a part of a demand-driven global rise in the prices of physical commodities during that period did not slow down the political decision to ban. Nor did a government report that found that the elimination of futures contracts in 2007 did not halt the continued rise in the spot prices of the banned commodities. So the ban was a visible political action that appealed to people's suspicions that speculative capital had played a role in the price rise.[6] It was intended to show people that the party in power was concerned about the toll that food price inflation was taking on voters all over the country. Part of what this illustrates is that exchanges in India have much less political influence than exchanges in the United States.

One of the other benefits of owning a seat on one of these exchanges was the fact that as business increased, increasing the commission flow to the floor as well as market-making and speculative opportunities, the membership or seat value of the exchange could appreciate significantly. This is because typically the number of seats or memberships at an exchange was fixed. If an outsider wanted to become an exchange member, the only way to do so was to purchase a seat from an existing member.[7] In fact, for some members, their seat value could become a significant portion of their net worth, and retiring members would often retain their seats and lease them for some retirement income.

Member-owned exchanges do have some other advantages. Because the owners were in the building and on the trading floor, they could keep an eye on management, thus minimizing the traditional principal/agent problem,[8] the misalignment of interests between the owners and managers and owners' lack of information about what management is doing. But as exchanges close their floors and as the member-owners disperse to more comfortable and more interesting places to live, this watchdog effect is largely lost.

Jawboning Liquidity for New Markets

A mutual organization was also important in starting markets for new futures contracts. One of the many obstacles in starting new contracts is to get someone to make liquid markets; otherwise the farmers or bankers or oil companies or hedge funds won't come and play. In the old days, this meant having traders who were making a good living in an established pit to come over and lose money in the new pit, at least for short periods of time. Since a successful new contract pushes up membership prices, owner-members know that sacrifices made today may well be repaid several times over.

Of course it helped to have charismatic leaders remind traders of this fact as they escorted them by their elbows over to the new pit to donate 15 minutes of their time to a new market. This was precisely how the CME got the S&P 500 stock index futures started in 1982. Each member was expected to leave his regular pit and walk over to spend 15 minutes in the S&P pit, and members would be reminded of this by visits from executive committee chairman Leo Melamed and exchange chairman Jack Sandner. The public address system would also remind traders of their obligation with periodic interjections of "Fifteen minutes please, fifteen minutes please."

Over time this "sacrifice now for the future" approach became harder to sell as exchange floors became increasingly populated by mere renters rather than owners. The problem was created by retiring exchange members who often chose to retain and lease their memberships rather than sell them and face huge capital gains taxes. As any apartment manager knows, renters never take care of places the way owners do, and naturally lessee floor traders were pretty uninterested in making sacrifices to build up new markets that would inflate seat prices and thus the rents they would have to pay. In addition, this technique worked via peer pressure on trading floors. In a screen-based environment, it becomes much less compelling. Exchanges now pay electronic market makers to kick-start new contracts.

Was It Good for the Customers?

Was the nonprofit, member-owned structure a good one? The fact that many of these exchanges have lasted for many decades, some even for centuries, suggests that to a reasonable extent they satisfied both the members and the public customers. But make no mistake: When people join together into associations, they do so to protect their own interests. Exchanges were no different. Exchanges were associations of brokers and traders who wanted to protect and enhance their incomes. And exchanges often provided a good living for multiple generations of families. Fathers would purchase seats for or pass their own seats on to their children when they came of age. One will observe cases where the chairman of an exchange was the son or grandson of a former chairman.

Both stock and derivatives exchanges have generally been regulated by a national (as in the United States, the United Kingdom, and most other countries) and/or regional (as in Germany and Canada) government body to ensure that they don't abuse customers in the pursuit of their own self-interest.[9] In addition, in some countries exchanges are required by law to regulate themselves. This means that the exchange must monitor its members to be sure that they are not taking advantage of their customers. What this means is that members would monitor members and would investigate, charge, and discipline themselves when needed.

Though self-regulation can play an important role, if it really worked well, the CFTC and the Federal Bureau of Investigation (FBI) would not have felt it necessary to conduct a sting operation on the floors of the CBOT and the CME during the late 1980s. The seeds of this FBI sting were planted in late 1984, when Dwayne Andreas, the chairman of the giant Archer Daniels Midland Corporation (ADM), complained, through his director of security, to the CFTC in Chicago about abuses on the floor of the CBOT.[10] The CFTC referred the case to the Chicago office of the FBI, which was much better equipped to investigate the alleged abuses. Both the CFTC and ADM helped train four FBI undercover agents on the ins and outs of futures trading. The agents then purchased memberships and spent a couple of years both floor-trading and socializing with traders, wearing hidden recording devices the whole time. During this time, the four FBI agents gathered enough information to charge 48 traders in the soybean, Treasury bond, Japanese yen, and Swiss franc pits at the two exchanges.

The abuses existed for two reasons. First, the open-outcry method of trading is sufficiently nontransparent that it is difficult for those outside the pit to see the cheating occur. Customers, like the chairman of ADM, may suspect they are being cheated, but they really have no way to prove it. Even exchange employees and CFTC staffers are unable to know the instant each trade takes place and whether a particular trade relies on inside information regarding an incoming order.

The second reason customer abuses were going on was that in member-owned exchanges, committees that charged traders with violations and committees that decided penalties for those violations were made up of other members. Though it is true that members better understand floor activities and floor violations than outsiders, they would have an understandable inclination to favor their fellow floor traders over outside customers they don't know. But even if the disciplinary committees conducted their business with pure objectivity,[11] there was still the basic problem that members would have to turn in fellow members whom they saw violating rules—a difficult task in any social group.

Problems with Mutual Exchanges in India: The Government Creates a Demutualized Competitor

This phenomenon of mutually owned exchanges looking mainly after their own members' interests is not exclusive to the United States. It is the very nature of member-owned business associations to put the interests of their members first. A great example of this tendency and its dangers takes us back to the early 1990s in Indian equity markets. At that time, there were 22 stock exchanges in India, mostly small regional exchanges in places such as Delhi and Kolkata (then called Calcutta). And then there was the Bombay Stock Exchange, more affectionately known as the BSE.

Mumbai (officially renamed from Bombay in 1995) is the financial center of India and is home to all the major financial institutions. Given its Mumbai location, the BSE would naturally capture the bulk of the business; it held a 75% market share, to be exact. Asia's oldest exchange was for years a well-functioning club that produced comfortable results for its members but perhaps less than exceptional service to investors. Commissions were high and transactions anything but transparent. And until the creation of the Securities and Exchange Board of India (SEBI) in 1988, the BSE was an unregulated market. In 1992 and 1993, SEBI asked for two very modest reforms—first, to have the BSE brokers register with SEBI, and second, to unbundle commissions from the prices of securities instead of embedding the commission in the price of the security the way OTC dealers do. The brokers balked and went out on strike—not a smart move.

Some visionary leaders within the government decided that the best way to deal with the conflict of interest within mutually owned exchanges was to build a new exchange. It was a bold decision. It was intended to serve as a model for the whole country. And it could create competitive pressure for the BSE to reform itself. To Western free-market ears, this sort of government intervention sounds like a prescription for failure, but the new exchange, the National Stock Exchange of India (NSE), actually turned into a raging success, surpassing the BSE in turnover within its first year. The new start-from-scratch exchange dominated the oldest exchange in Asia in less than 12 months. This success was driven by the following objectives and features[12]:

- Increase transparency by trading via an electronic limit order book. (BSE was open outcry with market makers.)
- Increase breadth of the market by allowing trading from all over India via satellite technology. (BSE brokers had to be present on the floor of the BSE.)
- Reduce costs (specifically the bid-ask spread) by setting a small and uniform tick size of .05 rupees, about a tenth of a cent. (BSE ticks were 5 to 25 times larger.)
- Reduce investor/broker conflicts of interest by eliminating brokers from governing the exchange. The NSE would be initially owned by public-sector financial institutions, and brokers would not be allowed on the board of directors. (In contrast, BSE brokerage firms owned and ran the BSE.)

A good business plan is not enough. There are thousands that fail. People make the difference. The crack team of five-star performers seconded from the Industrial Development Bank of India, the major public-sector shareholder, did make the difference. They were young, bright, and naive and devoted untold hours and creative energy to making the NSE a success.

Through lower fees, smaller ticks, greater transparency, and truly national reach, the NSE significantly expanded the investor base and the level of trading activity. All the new business initially went to the NSE while the BSE languished. The BSE quickly got the message and embarked on a road of significant reform. The BSE is now also an electronic exchange and has been growing again during the past several years. So the Ministry of Finance's plan worked. The BSE's instinct for self-preservation spurred it to reform itself. It was brilliant.

Cracks in the System: Drivers of Demutualization

The case we just examined was one in which a government created an electronic, for-profit, stockholder-owned exchange as a model to induce other exchanges to demutualize and switch to screens, but most demutualizations across the world are made without any government involvement. There are three main drivers of demutualization. The first is to streamline decision making to better deal with global competition. The second is to allow the exchange to more effectively participate in the mergers and acquisition process by having its own stock to play with. The third is to raise capital and unlock value for the members. Sometimes, in addition, the regulator itself drives demutualization, or I should say requires that exchanges are created as stockholder-owned as opposed to member-owned entities. This was the case when the Indian government decided to set up the stockholder-owned National Stock Exchange in the early 1990s and later required the new national, electronic, multi-commodity exchanges created for trading derivatives on physical commodities to be stockholder-owned. Hong Kong and Singapore authorities each instructed their stock and derivatives exchanges to demutualize and merge.

Democracies have certain advantages. Efficiency, however, is not one of them. Since these mutually owned exchanges needed to include members in the decision-making process, at a minimum they needed to have boards of directors and a chairman who were drawn from and elected by the members. In addition, as exchanges grew, they needed to appoint committees made up of members that would deal with various aspects of the exchange business. For example, there would be a committee for each major product or product group, for facilities, overseeing the behavior of members on the floor, for auditing, for market data services, for marketing, for new product development, and for any number of other issues and tasks that needed to be dealt with. In 1997, the CME had 207 committees, one of which was called the Committee on Committees. In the old days when all exchanges were mutually owned and when competition was local, or at most national, it wasn't such a disadvantage to be a mutually owned exchange. However, as competition moved to the global level and other exchanges became more nimble as stockholder-owned entities, it became a disadvantage to be burdened by an elaborate democratic decision-making process in which large numbers of members were involved.

Another source of inefficiency in the member-owned exchange lay in the fact that decisions were often guided by politics and the desire by board members and chairmen to be reelected. For example, if two or three members out of the whole body of several thousand members were making their living off one small-volume product that was losing money for the exchange, that product would generally not be dropped. The reason, of course, is that these two or three people whose livelihoods depended on the small illiquid market were voters and had many friends on the floor who were voters, and there would be serious complaints if their contracts were pulled out from under them. In other words, the board preserved pockets of inefficiency to keep members happy. Of course, one of the best examples of this is the fact that the floor-based systems were preserved much longer than would have been the case had the exchanges been operated as for-profit stockholder-owned organizations.

In the mergers and acquisitions arena, there is a huge advantage to being stockholder-owned. A member-owned exchange that wanted to acquire another exchange, and this was occasionally done,[13] generally needed cash to pay the members of the target exchange for giving up their ownership rights. But if the acquiring exchange owned stock and could use its stock to purchase another exchange or another business of any kind, it became a much easier task. For one, it is easier to value a for-profit exchange whose stock is traded in the market every day. For another, it's handy to be able to use one's own stock rather than finance a purchase with bank loans.

But demutualization also helps pave the way for electronic trading. Back in the early 1990s, Gerrard Pfauwadel, then Chairman of the Paris-based MATIF, was speaking to a Chicago audience and described their new deal with the then DTB (which would a few years later merge with a Swiss exchange to become Eurex, which was for almost a decade the biggest exchange in the world). The

DTB was going to put some of its terminals on the MATIF trading floor and make a couple of DTB products directly accessible to MATIF members. Within a year or so, the MATIF was going to create its own electronic trading system based on the DTB platform. It would then take two of its top products off its trading floor and roll them onto the electronic system to be available to the DTB members.

The audience was incredulous. If the CME or CBOT board took a product away from its members on the trading floor, it would suffer a fate more gruesome than anything seen in the French Revolution, not to mention losing the next election. Mr. Pfauwadel was asked how he could possibly do such a thing and still keep his job. He noted that the MATIF was a corporation owned by a group of banks and that this gave him the flexibility to make decisions that were in the best interest of the exchange. He didn't have to worry about members and floor politics. If the CME and the CBOT were ever going to go fully electronic, it seemed that they would have to first demutualize and pay off the existing members with tradable shares. Though the CME did demutualize and do its IPO before seriously ramping up the screen-based volume, the CBOT was forced to shift much trading to the screen before it demutualized. It was pushed by an even more powerful force: fear of extinction and a direct attack by a major European competitor, the 2004 creation of EurexUS.

First Step: Demutualization

The first step in taking a traditional member-owned exchange to public company status is to demutualize it. *Demutualization* means the conversion of a mutual, member-owned, not-for-profit organization into a for-profit corporation. So a demutualized exchange is one that was formerly mutually owned but is now stockholder owned. It may or may not have taken the additional step of doing an IPO and becoming publicly traded. An exchange that was originally established as a stockholder-owned one is not demutualized, because it was never mutually owned to begin with, though some observers use the term this way.

The trend was solidly in place by the late 1990s (see Table 5.1). A very interesting poll was conducted during the November 1999 FIBV Bangkok meeting of the world's stock exchanges.[14] Representatives of 50 exchanges were asked if they had already demutualized, had started the demutualization process, or were at least seriously considering the issue. Forty-four, almost 90%, were in one of these three stages.

But U.S. exchanges have been considerably behind the rest of the world in this new trend. As with many other things, the Northern Europeans were the first to jump on the demutualization bandwagon, and from 1993 to 1997, exchange demutualization was almost exclusively a European phenomenon. The first exchange to demutualize was the Stockholm Stock Exchange, in 1993. Stockholm split its shares between its members and its listed companies. Part of the deal was that the government rescinded the exchange's monopoly on

Table 5.1 Financial Exchanges: Demutualization and IPO Chronology

	Founded	Demutualized	IPO and Listing
Stock Exchanges			
OMX Group	1985	1987	1993
Borsa Italiana	1997	1997	None
Amsterdam Stock Exchange	1602	1997	*
Australian Stock Exchange	1987	1998	1998
Singapore Exchange Ltd	1999	1999	2000
Nasdaq Stock Market, INC	1971	2000	2002
Toronto Stock Exchange	1861	2000	2005
Montreal Stock Exchange	1874	2000	**
London Stock Exchange	1801	2000	2001
Euronext Stock Exchange (Paris)	2000	2000	2001
Deutsche Börse	1993	2000	2001
Hong Kong Exchanges and Clearing	1947	2000	2000
Tokyo Stock Exchange, INC	1878	2001	2006
Osaka Stock Exchange	1878	2001	2004
Oslo Stock Exchange	1819	2001	2001
BME Spanish Exchanges	1995	2001	2006
Philippine Stock Exchange, Inc	1992	2001	2003
SWX Swiss Exchange	1993	2002	*None*
New Zealand Exchange Ltd	1915	2002	2003
Bursa Malaysia	1930	2004	2005
Chicago Stock Exchange	1882	2005	*None*
Dubai Financial Market	2000	2005	2007
New York Stock Exchange	1817	2006	2006
American Stock Exchange	1921	***	
Bovespa Holding S.A.	1890		2007
Derivatives Exchanges			
Athens Exchange (Hellenic Exchange)	1876	1999	2000
Singapore Exchange Ltd.	1999	1999	2000
London Metals Exchange	1877	2000	None
CME	1898	2000	2002
Sydney Futures	1972	2000	2003
Intercontinental Exchange	2000	2000	2005

Table 5.1 (*Continued*)

	Founded	Demutualized	IPO and Listing
Bursa Malaysia	1930	2004	2005
New York Mercantile Exchange	1872	—	2006
BM&F	1985	2007	2007
CBOT	1848	2005	2005

*Acquired by Euronext.
**Acquired by Toronto Stock Exchange.
***Acquired by NYSE Euronext.
Source: Bloomberg and exchange Web sites.

share trading. Seven years later, on July 1, 1999, the Stockholm Stock Exchange merged with OM Stockholm, the Swedish derivatives exchange, creating the one-stop-shopping OM Stockholm Exchange. The second exchange to demutualize was the Helsinki Stock Exchange in 1995, followed in 1996 by the Copenhagen Stock Exchange and the next year by the Amsterdam Stock Exchange and the Borsa Italiana. The year after that, jumping down to the other hemisphere, the Australian exchange joined suit. In 2000, the Toronto, Hong Kong, and London Stock Exchanges all demutualized.

Another milestone was set by the Australian Stock Exchange, which demutualized on October 13, 1998, and then on the following day became the first stock exchange in the world to list itself on itself. The next year it attempted a merger with the Sydney Futures Exchange (SFE) by offering to exchange $220 million, including $70 million worth of its own shares, for ownership of the SFE. Neither the SFE nor the regulator ultimately thought it was a very good idea, so the deal died, at least for a while. Eight years later, in July 2006, the two exchanges did merge to form the Australian Securities Exchange.

U.S. stock markets lagged behind both their European and Asian cousins. By the time Nasdaq went public in July 2002, most of the major European stock exchanges had already done so: the Swedes, the Greeks, the Norwegians, the Germans, the French, and the English (in that order). And by the time the NYSE went public in March 2006, almost all the major stock exchanges worldwide had already done so. The major exceptions were the stock exchanges of Korea, Taiwan, Spain, Italy, and Switzerland, though the latter three had demutualized.

But why change now? Why did exchanges with their roots going back to the 1800s suddenly find demutualization to be such a cool idea? Why were exchanges like LIFFE, the IPE, the CME, the CBOT, and the NYSE finding the for-profit stockholder model so compelling?

Perhaps there are some clues in the insurance industry, which has been experiencing a strong trend toward demutualization since the early 1990s. Like exchanges, insurance companies often grew out of associations of people with mutual interests. Thus during the Middle Ages, some European guilds began to protect guild members and their families from the economic consequences of the illness or death of the breadwinner. In the countryside, German farmers formed mutual associations to protect themselves from losses due to hail, storms, and fires.

Not only were such mutual insurance associations a natural evolution, they also had an advantage over for-profit corporations. First, neighbors, who deal with each other on a daily basis are not as likely to cheat their mutual association with false claims as they might cheat a for-profit company. Second, with things like life insurance, a policyholder is more likely to trust that his family will be cared for by his guild mates or fellow farmers than by a distant entity that could well go bankrupt before his demise.

And bankruptcy was a real risk. Of all the stock insurance companies operating in the United States in 1868, well over half (61%) had failed by 1905—not very comforting for those who paid monthly premiums for years to protect their families. A New York State commission was set up in 1905 to study these and other scandals of the insurance industry and recommended, among other things, that stock companies convert back to the mutual form of earlier years. Prudential, Metropolitan Life, and the Equitable did just that.

The world is a different place today. Many of these same companies are now reverting to the stock corporation model. The Equitable demutualized and was acquired by the AXA Group in 1992. Metropolitan Life demutualized in 2000. Prudential demutualized and went public in 2001, and a number of other mutual insurers in the United States, Canada, Europe, Australia, South Africa, and Japan have either demutualized or begun the process.

Why are they doing this now? The main motivation seems to be to provide a competitive advantage during a period of industry consolidation. If you want to acquire a competitor or even a financial company in a different line of business, using stock is often better than cash, especially when the stock market is overpriced. When buying an overpriced company, it's much better to pay for it with your own overpriced stock than to use scarce cash. In addition, the owners of the acquired company are able to retain an interest in the new combination and to avoid the taxes associated with a cash sale. As both insurance companies and exchanges saw the mergers and acquisitions begin to take place, they knew that to compete in this game they needed a war chest full of their own stock—the ideal currency for acquisition.

There is a danger in this path. Demutualization is a double-edged sword. The managements of most insurance companies and exchanges typically view themselves as the acquirer. In fact, many of them will turn out to be the acquired. A stock corporation is much easier to take over than a mutual company. In fact, hostile takeovers are virtually impossible with mutually owned companies. It should be noted that "in the public interest," governments have put restrictions on ownership, especially foreign ownership, of exchanges. The Australian government decided it was not in the public interest to allow any single entity to control the stock exchange and put a 5% limit on ownership by any single person or entity, though the limit was later raised to 15%.[15] The government of India has placed a similar restriction on ownership of Indian exchanges, with 5% limits applying to foreign ownership.

The Demutualization Process

As we said earlier, the demutualization process consists of converting the structure of the organization from one in which the entity is owned by the members to one in which the entity is owned by stockholders and initially those stockholders are the members. After demutualization, the members, or the traders, have trading rights, but they may no longer have any equity rights in the exchange. Different exchanges have taken different routes when implementing this process. However, the key to each of these transactions is that the members give up the old bundle of equity and trading rights and receive in exchange unbundled equity and trading rights. Sometimes the equity rights, as in the case of the planned CBOE demutualization, are completely unbundled, and there is no vestige of an equity right remaining with the trading right. However, in other cases all the members must own equity rights. This can be done, as in the case of the LME, by simply requiring that every member own an equity right in the exchange. The LME requires that each member own a number of class B shares, where that number depends on the class of membership. It can also be done, as in the case of the CME, by literally stapling an equity right to each trading right. In this case, no membership or trading right can be sold without the attached B share, and no B share can be sold without the attached membership or trading right.

The nature of the special equity right in the exchange differs from one place to another. For example, at the CME the B share, which must be attached to every membership, allows one to both receive the same dividends that class A shareholders receive and also gives them much stronger voting rights than A shares do. At the same time, at the London-based LME, the B shares convey neither rights to receive dividends nor rights to vote.

In most cases, demutualization involves the creation of a new entity, a holding company that owns the entity formerly known as the exchange. So CME Group Inc. (formerly CME Holdings Ltd.) owns the CME. Likewise, LSE Holdings Ltd., NYMEX Holdings Inc., and Bovespa Holding S.A. were each the holding company for the associated exchange.

What Is an Exchange Membership?

Traditionally, most exchanges have been structured as mutually owned or membership organizations. Until 2000, almost all U.S. futures exchanges had been owned by their members.[16] These members owned the exchange, and only they could enter the trading floor to trade for customers or trade on their own behalf. In addition, only members received significant discounts off regular rates when trading for themselves. Customers paid much higher rates (as mentioned earlier, the CME charged 7 cents a side to members and 70 cents a side to customers). So a membership was essentially a bundle of two rights: a trading right (a right to be on the floor and trade for their own account or broker trades for others and to receive a fee discount for their own trades) and an ownership right (a partial ownership of the business and the right to vote for the exchange's board of directors, vote in referenda, and serve on committees).

When members got sufficiently old or sufficiently wealthy that they decided to stop trading, they would often hold onto their membership as they would a stock. Like a stock, the membership price would fluctuate in value. And like a stock generating a revenue flow in the form of dividends, the membership generated a revenue flow in the form of lease fees from renting the seat out to individuals who wanted access to the trading floor. In fact, in the process of leasing out a seat, the member was really leasing only the trading right. The ownership right remained with the original member. As mentioned, seat price appreciation has been substantial, and thus this practice of holding onto seats and leasing them out has usually proved a good investment. In fact, in the spring of 1997, 35% of all CME members, 35% of all the International Monetary Market (IMM) members, and 49% of the Index and Option Market (IOM) members were leasing their seats to others.[17]

Demutualization and the Transformation of a Membership

The critical question in any demutualization is: how do you divide the value among various participants? It's clear that the member-owners of exchanges and of mutual life insurance companies must be the major beneficiaries of the demutualization, since they were the owners to begin with. But how do you decide how many shares of stock go to each of these participants? In the case of the mutual life insurance companies, the value to be distributed was divided into a fixed component and a variable component. The fixed component was divided among all policyholders on an equal basis. The variable component was divided among the policyholders based on certain attributes of those policies, such as the cash value. The fixed component typically was between 15% and 30% of the total value, and the variable component was the remainder. But international practice varies, and an Australian company put the fixed component at 50% and a U.K. Building Society put it at 100%.

In the case of exchanges, there was a difference between stock exchanges and derivatives exchanges. Stock exchanges have listed companies and members, whereas futures exchanges have only members and listed products; therefore, in some cases, the stock exchanges gave a portion of the shares to the companies that had chosen to list on that stock exchange and a portion of the shares to

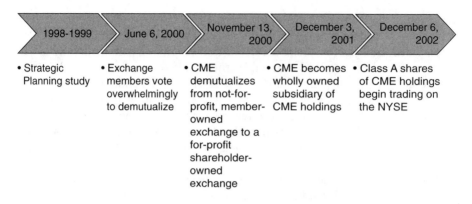

Figure 5.1 CME's steps toward becoming a publicly traded company, 1998–2002.

the members. In the case of the futures exchanges, generally all the shares went to the members in the demutualization. Of course, when the exchange went IPO, the members' ownership was diluted by the issue of new shares to a new group of investors.

Many exchanges have multiple classes of memberships, each class allowing the members to trade specific groups of products. Because of the different rights associated with each of these memberships, each of the memberships carried a different price or value in the marketplace. So when issuing stock to the members, these different rights and values had to be taken into consideration. In other words, some membership classes received more shares than other membership classes.

Case Study: CME Demutualizes

The CME started thinking seriously about converting itself into a for-profit, stockholder-owned exchange back in 1998, when it conducted a strategic planning study on the issue (see Figure 5.1). It decided to move down this path and became the first U.S. financial exchange to "demutualize" ownership (on November 13, 2000) as well as the first U.S. financial exchange to do an IPO and become publicly traded (on December 6, 2002), when it was listed under the ticker symbol CME on the New York Stock Exchange.

The CME's listing history is not a simple one. Two and a half years after its initial listing on NYSE, it decided to also list on Nasdaq. So, beginning May 2005, the CME was dually listed on Nasdaq and the NYSE. It remained dually listed for about three years. Then on July 14, 2008, it dropped its NYSE listing and became exclusively listed on Nasdaq. Why? The CME June 30, 2008, press release on the topic suggested that dropping the NYSE was due to the fact that Nasdaq was experiencing greater volume in CME shares than was NYSE.

However, it is also the case that the NYSE, where the CME had carried its original listing, was about to be designated by the CFTC as a futures exchange[18] and would become a potential competitor for the CME. In addition, the CME and Nasdaq had another business relationship. The CME leased the right to offer futures and options trading in certain Nasdaq stock indexes and agreed to extend the expiration of the existing contract from 2012 to 2019.[19]

The demutualization at the CME involved having members turn in their old memberships and receive new memberships plus a bucket of shares in the exchange. So, the CME memberships were transformed. The old CME membership was a combination of a trading right and an ownership right. Each of the exchange memberships had specific trading rights. For example, the CME seat allowed its holder to trade anything on the floor of the exchange. The IMM seat allowed its holder to trade any financial product at the exchange. The IOM allowed the holder to trade any index or options product. Whatever trading rights existed in the old membership were transferred into the new membership that replaced the old.

Though the CME's new memberships retained the old trading rights, they had virtually all the ownership rights pulled out of them and transferred into the exchange's common stock, called CME A shares. These A shares were given to the members to compensate them for the ownership rights that had been stripped out of the memberships. So before demutualization, the memberships had the traditional bundle of trading rights and ownership rights. After demutualization the memberships had only trading rights and a tiny sliver of ownership rights in the form of one B share. Though the B share paid the same dividends as an A share, its real purpose was to ensure that members still had a significant say in the direction of the exchange (they would elect 30% of the board after demutualization), especially because that direction had an impact on issues critical to members, as we explain in a moment.

The number of shares received depended on the membership class. CME members each got 18,000 shares; IMM members each received 12,000 shares; IOM members each got 1000 shares; and members of the newest and smallest division, the GEM, got a token 100 shares.[20] For each member, all shares but one were A shares. The other was a B share. For example, of 18,000 shares CME members received, 17,999 shares were A shares and could eventually be sold in the marketplace.[21] The remaining share was a B share and remained attached to the CME membership. If a CME membership were sold, the single B share would go with it and the remaining 17,999 shares would remain with the former member, who could retain or sell these shares. This meant that a membership was technically still a bundle of two rights, but the ownership right had become a tiny, tiny fraction of its former self, since most of it had been spun off in the form of A shares. To put this in value terms, at a price of $500 per share, the CME member now had an ownership stake valued at $9 million, of which $500 was still attached to the seat and $8,999,500 was in the form of A shares that could be sold off to interested investors. And as shown in

Table 5.2 CME Demutualization Creation of A Shares*

	Seats	A Shares	Total A Shares
CME	625	17,999	11,249,375
IMM	813	11,999	9,755,187
IOM	1,287	5,999	7,720,713
GEM	413	99	40,887
Total	3,138		28,766,162

*As of 1-17-03 following initial demutualization and later conversion into CME Holdings.

Table 5.2, members of the four divisions of the Chicago Mercantile Exchange were given a total of just under 28.8 million A shares and precisely 3,138 B shares (one for each member).[22]

The CME did at least four things to make a demutualized and publicly traded CME attractive for members. First, members were given both common stock and trading rights so that they would now have the choice of continuing to be owner-traders, just owners, or just traders. Second, the members, via their class B shares, were given the right to elect six of the 19 board members. The other 13 board members were elected jointly by both class A and class B shareholders on a share-equivalent basis. Third, the members, also via their class B shares, would be the only ones who would be able to vote on core rights. The core rights included which products could be traded by each membership division, the trading floor access rights and privileges for members, any change in the number of authorized and issued class B shares, and finally, the eligibility requirements for members.[23] And fourth, the members were given a commitment that as long as there were liquid markets on the trading floor, the trading floor would be preserved and supported.

The Economic Value of Demutualized Membership

So, how did things turn out for CME members? They were able to protect themselves from adverse changes to their core rights. They were able to elect 30% of the directors on the CME board. But how did they do financially? Figure 5.2 gives a clue. The chart displays the value of a membership from January 1994 to May 2008. Specifically, it shows the value of a CME membership or seat on the exchange until November 2002, and then beginning in December 2002, the month of the IPO, it shows the value of the membership plus the value of the shares that a CME member received during demutualization. (See Table 5.3 for the relative values of other memberships.) The idea is

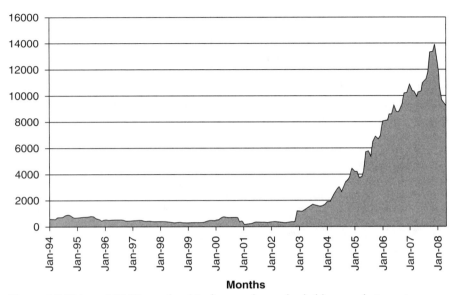

Figure 5.2 Value of CME membership for members who held on to their equity, January 1994–January 2008.

to show a continuous series reflecting the two rights that members had: a trading right and an equity right. Until demutualization, the two were combined in a seat or membership. After demutualization, membership was essentially a trading right and the equity had been spun off into 17,999 A shares. So the chart shows the sum of the market value of the A shares and the market value of the membership trading right from the IPO on.

Let's first look at membership price alone, which is fully shown in Figure 5.2 until the December 2002 IPO. After that it is hidden in the chart as a component of the total value of membership. The mid-1990s was good for CME members. Their seat value hit $925,000 in August 1994. Then seat values slid gradually until they hit a low of $295,000 in December 1998, showing a 68% drop in four years. Prices started rising again and hit another high of $825,000 in April of 2000. They settled back into the mid-700,000s up to demutualization in November 2000, and then they dropped down to $430,000. Even after demutualization, prices slid a bit further to the point that there was a sale in January 2001 for a mere $188,000. Prices then doubled the next year to year and a half and stayed around $400,000 until the IPO in December 2002. Prices then bounced around in the $300,000 to $400,000 range until the summer of 2006, when they started a new rise. In April 2006 there was a sale for $370,000, and then prices rose consistently for the next 20 months until they hit a new peak of $1,550,000 in December 2007, an astounding increase of 319%. So, seat

Table 5.3 Membership Division of the CME

Division	Start	Share Given in Demutualization*	Market Price**	Members Can Trade***
CME	1919	18,000	$1,525,000	Everything
IMM	1972	12,000	$800,000	All financial products
IOM	1982	1,000	$525,000	Index futures, all options
GEM	1994	100	$52,000	Emerging markets and other products

*Class A & B shares in CME Holdings given November 2000 to existing members. One share of number shown was a B share attached to the trading right; the remainder were A shares, which could eventually be sold in the market. For example, IMM members got 11,999 A shares and one B share.
**Transaction dates range from 1/07 to 1/18/2008. 2/16/07.
***With variation, such as IOM trades lumber, GEM trades, GSCI and Russell.

prices can be just as volatile as the prices of the financial instruments traded on the exchange.

Though seat prices had been rising since January 2001, it is the shares that have contributed most to the value of being a CME member. At the CME IPO launch price of $35 a share, the 17,999 shares received by CME members had a market value of $629,965. Over the next five years, the market continued to climb with ups and downs to the point that in December 2007, one share of CME stock went for $686, giving members who still held the shares they received at demutualization a value of $12.3 million and a total value (seat plus shares) of $13.9 million. Even though by May 2008 the stock price had fallen substantially on news that the Justice Department was thinking that the CME and other exchanges should reduce their monopoly power by spinning off their clearing functions, the CME members were still up 47 times from that $188,000 low. The effect of demutualization and the public listing of CME shares has been wildly successful for CME members.

Demutualization and listing its shares on the NYSE and later on Nasdaq was a brilliant move to unlock the value of the ownership portion of exchange memberships. Because the CME could now run as a profit-making enterprise and the audience wanting to own the CME stock was so large, members could sell off the ownership value imbedded in their memberships at very attractive prices and then continue to use the trading rights. Even at a price of $400 per share, a CME member could sell off the ownership rights that were pulled out of his CME membership and imbedded in the 17,999 A shares he was given for $7.2 million and still be left with his transformed membership, worth $1.35 million in May 2008.

CME Demutualization Nuts and Bolts

The CME's demutualization process actually involved two steps. Step one was to merge the existing CME, which was an Illinois not-for-profit membership corporation, into a transitory Delaware non-stock corporation called CME Transitory Co. This step moved the non-stock company known as the CME from Illinois to Delaware. Existing CME memberships were converted into memberships in this new Delaware company. In the second step, which occurred simultaneously with the first step, the Delaware non-stock corporation was merged into a for-profit Delaware stock corporation known as the Chicago Mercantile Exchange Inc. At the same time the memberships in the CME Transitory Co. were converted into shares of common stock in CME Inc. Two classes of shares were issued to members: Class A shares and Class B shares. The initial idea was that Class A shares would be ordinary common stock, and Class B shares would contain both equity and trading rights. This was later changed so that instead of the B share containing the trading and equity right, a new membership was created that contained a trading right with the same privileges as the old membership as well as a single B share, which paid the same dividend as an A share, though it had much stronger voting rights and could never be separated from the membership.

CBOE: An Interesting Speed Bump

The Chicago Board Options Exchange (CBOE) will be the last Chicago exchange to demutualize, as the process was held up for several years by a dispute between the CBOE and CBOT members. The dispute grew out of an ambiguous promise made at the birth of the CBOE. Because the idea for and the founding of this first U.S. options exchange was generated by the CBOT, the 1402 full CBOT members were granted the right to trade on the CBOE without acquiring a separate CBOE membership, though they still had to register and pass a test to be able to do so. These rights, which were included in the CBOE's Certificate of Incorporation, were called Exercise Rights (ER), and many CBOT members did exercise those rights. Though it was clear that the CBOT members had the right to trade, what was less clear was whether they had any equity stake in the CBOE. For many years this was a nonissue. But as the world began to change and exchanges began to demutualize, it became an interesting and economically important problem. In a demutualization, the exchange gives stock to its members in exchange for their membership, though sometimes a new more limited membership is also given. If the CBOE demutualized, would it have to give stock to the 1402 full CBOT members in addition to its own members? If yes, this would create a nice windfall for the CBOT members and significantly dilute the value of the shares received by the CBOE members. Naturally the CBOT felt there was clearly an equity right implicit in the ER and the CBOE argued there wasn't. The CBOE contended that the CBOT's merger with the CME extinguished any exercise right eligibility and even if it had not, the nature and extent of any equity right would have to be determined.

In July 2006, the CBOE set up a special committee to look into this issue and propose a decision as to whether the CBOT members had zero equity rights, full equity rights, or something in between. The CBOT members subsequently sued the CBOE in Delaware court, claiming that they were entitled to equal treatment with the members of the CBOE, should there be a demutualization. However, before the Committee had a chance to complete its work, the CME in 2006 began pursuing a merger with the CBOT, completing it in the summer of 2007. After learning of the merger, the CBOE determined that the merger of the CBOT into the CME essentially eliminated the traditional CBOT memberships and, therefore, no CBOT member would qualify for the Exercise Right. If there were no longer any CBOT members, how could there be any Exercise Rights?

When the CBOT demutualized, it gave three things to former full members of the CBOT: a trading right, some shares, and an exercise right privilege, to allow the holder to trade at the CBOE. In the view of the CBOT, an individual who held all three of these was entitled to receive equity in the CBOE when it demutualized.

The SEC in January 2008 agreed with the CBOE's contention that the CME/CBOT merger effectively eliminated exercise right eligibility. However, there was still the issue of whether other property rights under state law should survive the merger. That issue was referred to the Delaware court, which would convene in June. But before the court could hear either side, in June 2008, the CBOE board reached a settlement agreement with the plaintiff class members and the CME Group, which was now the owner of the CBOT. The agreement included a finding that there were no longer any members of the CBOT eligible to become CBOE members. In return a payment would be made to the class members. In the aggregate, these CBOT members would receive about $1 billion in cash and CBOE stock. Specifically, each class member would receive $300 million in cash, and some would also receive 18% ownership of the CBOE upon demutualization. So the Exercise Right issue was once and for all almost settled. It still needs the blessing of the Delaware court, expected in the first quarter of 2009.

When it comes to the actual demutualization, the CBOE has a somewhat different plan than that of the CME and the CBOT that came before it. The plan will not be implemented until around the time this book is published, so these details are subject to change. The CME, for example, gave its members stock, a trading right, and special voting rights, the latter two preserving their member status very much as it had always been. The CBOE current plan is to give its members only stock—no trading right, no special voting rights. The former members would have to lease a trading right like anyone else if they wanted to trade, and the revenues from the trading rights would become part of the CBOE revenues.

How did the CBOE get away with giving members so much less than the CME did? It may be that the CBOE members have actually chosen a wiser path. The big difference is that about 80% of the CBOE seat holders had leased their seats out to other people who used them to trade on the floor. The members thought of themselves more as equity owners than as floor traders and wanted to ensure that they continued to have a good investment. They were more concerned about returns than preserving their political power. They didn't care about their ability to gain access to the trading floor or about having seats to lease out; they cared mainly about having a good stream of dividends flowing from a well-run, for-profit exchange. And they were convinced that by allowing the exchange itself to manage the number of trading rights as well as the fee for leasing the trading rights, this would be much better than preserving the old system in which each member continued to own the trading right and lease it out for whatever the market would give at that time. In the end, the CBOE would look much more like a modern for-profit exchange, and the CME would look like a mixed corporate structure where the members still exerted significant influence.

CBOT

Though the CME was the first U.S. exchange to demutualize in November 2000, the CBOT was making plans and attempting to get member buy-in for those plans much earlier in the year. Then Chairman David Brennan unveiled an interesting plan to deal with both demutualization and electronic trading simultaneously. The idea was to split the CBOT into two for-profit shareholder-owned companies, one based in the pits and the other based on the screens. The screen-based exchange would utilize the Eurex matching engine that the CBOT had been using. Brennan argued that having separate companies, one of which would be an open-outcry company, would help preserve the open-outcry system for many years to come.

There were a couple of problems with the idea. The first, which would be true for any demutualization, was that there were four classes of CBOT members, and one class in particular, the financial members, who were called associate members, accounted for most of the trading volume but had only a 1/6 vote, compared to a full vote by full CBOT members, who were the guys trading the agricultural products with which the CBOT started. The second problem was that several members felt that a floor-based exchange could not compete with an electronic exchange; therefore, this was simply a trick to convince CBOT members to vote for the plan, which would essentially result in a switch to electronic trading. The plan passed at the board level with a 22-to-1 vote. When a demutualization plan was finally offered to the members, it initially proposed that 88% of exchange ownership be given to full members and 12% be given to the other members; the other members protested and filed suit. They said 12% was too small, given that minority members contribute 60% of exchange volume generated by members.[24] The lawsuit was settled, with the full member share dropping to just under 78% and the other members' share rising to just over 22%.

The Energy Giant Demutualizes

NYMEX, the world's largest physical commodity exchange, demutualized quite early for an American exchange; in fact, it missed being number one by only four days. The CME demutualized on November 13, 2000, and NYMEX demutualized on November 17, 2000. The old NYMEX was converted from a not-for-profit, member-owned exchange into a Delaware for-profit corporation, wholly owned by NYMEX Holdings, a Delaware for-profit stock corporation. NYMEX initially gave each full NYMEX member two things: a class A membership in the NYMEX exchange (essentially a trading right) and one share of common stock in the newly created NYMEX Holdings (an equity right).[25]

Though the CME took only two years before moving to an IPO, NYMEX took six years. Some interesting things occurred during those six years. For example, as NYMEX pursued its quixotic quest to establish unsuccessful floor-based trading venues in Dublin and London, it did so under NYMEX Europe Exchange Holdings Ltd., created in August 2004, which was a wholly owned subsidiary of NYMEX Holdings. This was certainly a money loser for the stockholders. Then in June 2005, NYMEX Holdings entered into a joint venture with Tatweer Dubai LLC to create DME Holdings LLC to launch the Dubai Mercantile Exchange (DME) Ltd. The jury is still out on this venture.

But before going IPO, NYMEX agreed to add a major shareholder. In November 2005, the private equity firm General Atlantic signed a definitive agreement to invest $135 million to acquire 10% of NYMEX Holdings. Though there were other suitors, such as Battery Ventures, NYMEX felt that General Atlantic would best help them prepare for their planned 2006 IPO. The investment was distributed to the 816 NYMEX members, netting each about $165,000. Part of the agreement was to streamline the board, reducing it from 25 to 15 and including General Atlantic President William Ford on the new board.

The NYSE Buys Public Company Status

The NYSE never did an IPO. Instead, it bought Archipelago, which was a publicly traded company at the time, and it used that as a means for making the NYSE a public company. This is how it worked: On March 7, 2006, the NYSE merged with publicly traded Archipelago Holdings Inc. to form the NYSE Group, which began trading publicly the next day. Archipelago, known as Arca in the trading community, was one of the original ECNs, had been a publicly traded company since August 2004, and had acquired a regional stock exchange, the Pacific Exchange, in 2005. The structure was that there was a holding company called NYSE Group Inc. and under the holding company was the New York Stock Exchange LLC, a wholly owned subsidiary, which included the newly merged Archipelago Holdings.

The Last Step: The IPO

The last step in the transition from "private clubs to public companies," the step that actually takes a company public, is the initial public offering listing on an exchange. The IPOs for exchanges are essentially the same as the IPOs for any other company. Filings must be made with the regulatory body, an underwriter or group of underwriters must be established, the exchange takes its senior officials on a road show to talk to potential investors in the company, the underwriters find investors for the initial offering, an IPO price is established based on the discussions with potential investors, and, on the day following the distribution of shares to these early, often lucky, investors, the company is listed on an established stock exchange and the public can buy and sell the stock for the first time.

The amount by which the new stock closes on the first day of trading above its offering price the night before is a sign of demand for the stock as well as a measure of how underpriced the IPO was. Some first-day moves have been dramatic. For example, when NYMEX went public on November 17, 2006, its stock increased 125% by the close of trading on the first day. That represented a jump from a $59 IPO price to a first-day closing price of $132.99. It was the biggest one-day jump of the year.[26] By contrast, but during the period following the tech bust, the very first financial exchange to go public, the CME, saw a jump of only 23% ($35 to $42.90).

Sometime before the IPO, the underwriters give a range for the IPO price. Sometimes that range is adjusted upward and sometimes downward as the IPO approaches, depending on circumstances. For example, as the Chicago Board of Trade prepared for its IPO in mid-September 2005, it raised the estimated price range for the IPO from the $33 to $36 range, set three months earlier, to a new range of $45–49 for one Class A share. This upward adjustment in the CBOT price appears to have been driven by two things. First, investors were still bullish, given the relatively spectacular rise of the price of the Chicago Mercantile Exchange. In addition, the CBOT had revealed that it had received inquiries regarding a possible merger, and there were rumors that the potential merger partners had suggested bid prices that exceeded the original IPO price range.[27] And when the offering is finally priced, the price is not always inside the estimated range. The CME, for example, had an estimated range of $31 to $34 but priced its IPO at $35.

When shares are sold in an IPO, some shares come from existing owners (generally exchange members who have received common shares in the demutualization in the case of exchange IPOs), whereas others come from stock that has been authorized but not yet issued. For example, when the NYMEX did its IPO in November 2006, 1.1 million shares came from existing owners, including member firms Bear Stearns, Calyon Financial, and Man Group. The remainder of the 6-million-share IPO came from 4.9 million shares that had been authorized but previously unissued. Four years earlier, when the CME went public, over a third of the shares offered were by existing owners. Specifically, 1.75 million shares of the total 4.75 million shares sold by CME came from existing owners.[28]

The difference, of course, was that the CME did the very first demutualization and IPO in the United States, so things were less certain. In fact, it was the CME's incredible success, including the fact that the price of CME common stock rose to almost 20 times its initial offering price, that made participants in subsequent demutualizations and IPOs reluctant to part with their shares during the public offering phase. The CME IPO took place less than two years following the technology stock crash in the United States; IPOs had been relatively infrequent ever since the crash.

Because the overwhelming majority of existing owners do not sell their stock, the IPO represents generally a small portion of the total ownership of the firm. For example, NYMEX sold 7% of the company in its IPO.

Conclusion

Like the other trends described in this book, demutualization and public listing have become the norm for financial exchanges worldwide. Those exchanges that have not demutualized typically have been slowed down by some difficult rock in the road, such as the CBOE's dispute with the CBOT over what rights CBOT members continue to have after the CBOT merged with the CME. But these obstacles are gradually being resolved, and within a few years, just as virtually all exchanges will be electronic, virtually all exchanges will also be for-profit, stockholder-owned exchanges.

Endnotes

1. *Making a market* means standing ready to buy and sell at a bid price and ask price for a specific number of contracts or shares. On traditional floor-based exchanges, scalpers did this

voluntarily to earn the profit, which was the difference between the bid and the ask. On stock exchanges with specialists, these specialists were required to make a market. On the NYSE, each stock had a single specialist whose job was to maintain an orderly market in that stock. On the Nasdaq, each stock typically had several competing market makers, obligated to post bids and offers. And as the derivatives exchanges grew larger and especially as they became electronic, the exchanges would engage firms as market makers who would either be paid or receive discounts on fees as compensation for making markets. The CME, CBOT, LIFFE, Eurex, and many other derivatives exchanges have had official market markers who were compensated for their services. The options exchanges had designated market makers for each option.

2. Before demutualization, the members of the CBOT directly elected their chairman, whereas the members of the CME elected the board, which in turn elected the chairman.

3. Live Cattle futures began in 1964 and received the name because the contract required delivery of live animals. Until that time there had been futures contracts on dead animals (such as iced chickens) or animal products such as butter, cheese, and pork bellies, but never on live animals.

4. Urad and tur are lentils, a staple in India.

5. At the time of the second ban, which was to tentatively last four months, unless there was a vote to extend the ban, the four products banned earlier remained under the ban.

6. Two days before the 2008 ban, Finance Minister P. Chidambaram said, "If rightly or wrongly people perceive that commodities-futures trading is contributing to a speculation-driven rise in prices, then in a democracy you will have to heed that voice," in an interview with Bloomberg Television in Madrid, May 4, 2008. He added, "The pressure is to suspend a few more food articles." www.bloomberg.com/apps/news?pid=20601080&sid=aZMFidg5paZI&refer= asia.

7. To become a member of one of these member-owned exchanges, a person must do two things: first, purchase a seat from an existing member. Each exchange operates a market in its seats, posting bid and offer prices, and there are almost always people willing to sell a seat. Second, apply to the exchange to become a member and the exchange will decide whether the applicant is worthy to join. At the CME, this was done via a vetting by the Membership Committee and a recommendation from this committee to the board, which had to approve all new members. Rule 102 of the CME Rulebook, for example, allows that "any adult of good moral character, reputation and business integrity, with adequate financial resources and credit to assume the responsibilities and privileges of membership is eligible for membership in the Exchange."

8. The *principal/agent problem*, a term from political science and economics, refers to the problem in corporations and other organizations that when principals (owners) hire agents (managers and staff), the interests of both are not aligned, and it is sometimes difficult for the principals to know what the agents are really doing. With the members working in the same building with exchange staff, it's much easier to keep an eye on them.

9. The national regulators include the SEC (securities) and CFTC (futures and options on futures) in the United States and the SFA in the United Kingdom. Canadian markets are largely regulated by the province in which they reside, and German exchanges by the state in which they reside. So the Autorité des marchés financiers (AMF) in Quebec regulates the Montréal Exchange, and Eurex is regulated by the German State of Hesse.

10. An extensive treatment of this unfortunate episode can be found in David Greising and Laurie Morse, *Brokers, Bagmen and Moles: Fraud and Corruption in the Chicago Futures Markets*, John Wiley and Sons, 1991.

11. Some exchanges have been putting some non-members on disciplinary committees for decades.

12. Ajay Shah and Susan Thomas, "David and Goliath: Displacing a Primary Market," *Journal of Global Financial Markets*, 1(1): pp. 14–21 (Spring 2000c).

13. For example, NYMEX acquired COMEX; the CBOT acquired the MidAmerica Exchange and the New Orleans Rice and Cotton Exchange; and a group of exchanges combined to form the Coffee, Sugar, and Cocoa Exchange, which later became NYBOT.

14. FIBV is Federation Internationale des Bourses de Valeurs, a world association of stock exchanges.

15. On October 2000, the Minister for Financial Services and Regulation raised the ownership limit on the Australian Stock Exchange to 15%, noting that any investor wanting to acquire more than 15% would have to apply to the minister and might be approved if such a share was deemed to be in the national interest: www.treasurer.gov.au/DisplayDocs. aspx?doc=pressreleases/2000/065.htm&pageID=003&min=jbh&Year=2000&DocType=0).

16. There is at least one exception. In March 2000, the CFTC approved a proposed cattle futures and options market called FutureCom, which was owned by a single Texas oilman in Amarillo. The exchange never opened for business. In some cases the ownership was indirect. For example, when the Coffee, Sugar, and Cocoa Exchange (CSCE) was combined with the New York Cotton Exchange (NYCE) to create NYBOT, the members of the two exchanges owned NYBOT, which in turn owned CSCE and NYCE. The currently inactive exchange known as the Cantor Fitzgerald Futures Exchange (CFFE) was wholly owned by an entity called CFFE Regulatory Services, which in turn was owned 10% by the NYCE and 90% by NYCE members. And because there have been a lot of exchanges historically on which we don't have ownership information or even names of all of them, we can't be certain that all were member-owned. Thanks to Riva Adriance at the CFTC for this clarification.

17. These are the three major membership divisions of the Chicago Mercantile Exchange. CME stands for Chicago Mercantile Exchange, IMM for International Monetary Market, and IOM for Index and Options Market. Each of these allows trading in fewer products than the one preceding it. Percentage of seats leased taken from a letter to Paul O'Kelly, General Counsel of the CME, from the Federal Elections Commission Advisory Opinion Number 1997-5, May 16, 1997; http://herndon1.sdrdc.com/ao/no/970005.html.

18. Technically, the term is a designated contract market, or DCM, when the CFTC accepts an entity's application to become a full-fledged traditional futures exchange. There are also more lightly regulated versions of exchanges, but trading on the lesser regulated exchanges is restricted to large sophisticated participants.

19. Doug Cameron, "CME to List Solely with Nasdaq," *Wall Street Journal*, July 1, 2001. http:// online.wsj.com/article/SB121485998670417207.html.

20. The Growth and Emerging Market (GEM) Division was created to trade a group of contracts based on the currencies, stock indices, and debt instruments of the major emerging markets around the world. The project was controversial and the contracts have been relatively unsuccessful. The GEM member is allowed to trade only five relatively low-volume contracts (three currencies and two indexes): the Mexican peso, Brazilian real, South African rand, and GSCI and Russell indexes.

21. At the time of demutualization, there was a waiting period before shares could be sold.

22. Four different Class B shares were created: Class B1, Class B2, Class B3, and Class B4, which differed from each other only in voting rights because they were associated respectively with the four membership divisions: the CME, the IMM, IOM, and the GEM.

23. "Amended and Restated Certificate of Incorporation of Chicago Mercantile Exchange Holdings Inc." April 19, 2002, p. 12. Not all members are equal, so when voting on changes to core rights, each CME member gets three votes, each IMM member gets two votes, each IOM member gets one vote, and each GEM member gets 1/6 of a vote. And when voting for directors, of the 20 board members, CME members elect three, IMM members elect two, IOM members elect one, and GEM members elect none. So the members, who might hold nothing other than the single B share associated with their membership, elect 30% of the directors, a pretty heavy influence.

24. *Securities Industry News*, March 29, 2004.

25. United States Securities and Exchange Commission, NYMEX Holdings, Inc., Form 10-K, for the Fiscal Year Ended December 31, 2005.

26. Lynn Cowan, "The Buzz: NYMEZ More Than Doubles in Its Opening Day of Trading," *Wall Street Journal,* November 18, 2006.

27. Christine Marie Nielsen, "CBOT Raises Price Range for IPO, Move Sparks Optimism About Potential Success of Deal," *Wall Street Journal,* September 17, 2005.

28. Raymond Hennessey, "Commodities Report: Chicago Merc's IPO Hits This Week—As First Major US Market to Go Public, the Exchange Beats NASDAQ and NYSE," *Wall Street Journal,* December 2, 2002.

6 From National to Global Competition

Executive Summary

There was a time when there were 250 stock exchanges in the United States and not too long ago when there were 23 in India. Competition in those days was, at best, local. Improved communications and falling communications costs brought competition to the national level, and the number of stock exchanges fell dramatically in most multi-exchange countries. Recently, with the shift to screens and the need to build volume to lower per-trade costs, exchanges have begun competing on a global level. This competition has been most successful when the attacker is electronic and the target still floor based—a diminishing opportunity.

Before we explore the shift from national to global competition, we must first clarify what we mean by competition among exchanges. Exchanges, like most business organizations, want to grow. Stockholder-owned exchanges want to grow to increase profits, to benefit their stockholders. Even older member-owned exchanges want to grow to offer increased trading and order-filling opportunities to their members. In both cases the objective is to benefit the owners of the exchange, who traditionally were members and increasingly today are stockholders.

This growth can either be competitive growth or noncompetitive growth. Competitive growth occurs at the expense of other exchanges; noncompetitive growth occurs without any impact on other exchanges. What we are concerned about in this chapter is competitive growth—growth that occurs to the detriment of another exchange and often growth that results from a deliberate attack on a product of another exchange. We are not concerned here about noncompetitive growth, such as where an exchange starts a new product for which there is no close substitute at any existing exchanges within the same political or geographical realm. In other words, *noncompetitive growth* refers to growth at an exchange that results from the development of new business, not from attracting customers away from other exchanges. For example, in the past, when there were significant barriers to sending trades into Brazil, the rapid growth of the BM&F could be viewed as noncompetitive growth because it occurred without any negative impact on the growth of other exchanges in the world. So it is not necessarily the case that one exchange's increase in total market share occurs at the expense of any other exchange, since this increase in market share could arise from new business that would not have gone anywhere else.

But our focus here is on competitive growth, or more accurately, on competition between two or more exchanges in which each exchange is attempting to grow and will do so, at least partially at the expense of competing exchanges. There are actually two types of competition, one obvious and the other more subtle. They are:

- Direct competition, where two (or more) exchanges compete for the same product:
  - An exchange lists a product that is already established on another exchange.
  - Two (or more) exchanges list the same new product at roughly the same time.
- Indirect competition, where two exchanges with non-identical products compete for the same speculative capital

This requires some elaboration. A case where an exchange lists a product that has already been listed and has developed a significant amount of liquidity on another exchange is a clear case of direct competition. Generally the newly listing exchange will succeed only if it is able to draw market share away from the product that already exists at the other exchange. And as has been mentioned elsewhere in this book, the principle of liquidity-driven monopoly generally guarantees that all the liquidity, all the trading, will be eventually resident on only one of the two competing exchanges. Because of this principle that recognizes that traders are attracted by liquidity and will not generally leave a liquid market with lots of buyers and sellers to trade at a new illiquid market with few buyers and sellers, most such attacks on the liquidity of existing products result in failure. The only exceptions are when the attacking exchange has some very significant advantage, and the only cases in which we have seen attacks on liquid markets succeed have been cases of electronic exchanges attacking floor-based exchanges. Examples of failures of such attacks on entrenched products include the case where the CME and the CBOT in the 1980s attempted to draw liquidity away from NYMEX energy products by listing their own energy products. The attempt failed miserably.

Another example is where a number of brokerage firms came to the CME and asked it to list a gold contract in the mid-1980s, after the then dominant COMEX was unable to efficiently process the paperwork during periods of significant gold trading. The CME had already lost an earlier competition over gold with the COMEX, and its contract had been dormant for a couple of years. Based on the requests from the firms and the belief that its systems would do a better job than COMEX in keeping up with the avalanche of paper from a hyperactive market, it resurrected its gold contract. In 1987 it traded 261,000 contracts, a solid first-year number but representing only 2% of the two exchanges' combined volume. COMEX was able to clean up its act and beat back the CME, whose gold volume fell back to zero before the end of the next year. So, like most other cases, the liquidity-driven monopoly prevailed and the CME's attack was a failure.

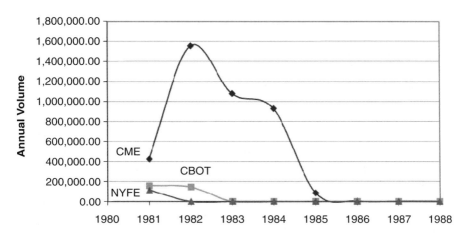

Figure 6.1 Three-way competition for Bank CD futures, 1980–1988.
Compiled from FIA Volume Reports.

On the other hand, the most famous example of a successful attack on entrenched liquidity came when the all-electronic DTB exchange (later to merge with Swiss-based SOFFEX and be renamed Eurex) successfully stole the German government bond futures from the floor-based LIFFE in 1998. This, as we mentioned, was a case where the attacking exchange had a substantial advantage; specifically it was fully electronic, whereas LIFFE was still stuck in the world of trading pits. This also was an early case of global competition in that it was a German-Swiss exchange attacking a British exchange.

A second type of direct competition whereby two or more exchanges list the same or closely related products at roughly the same time is also a clear case of direct competition; typically one exchange is the winner, and given the liquidity-driven monopoly effect, the winner takes all. Back in 1981, the CME, the CBOT, and NYFE[1] (the New York Futures Exchange) all listed negotiable certificate of deposit (CD) futures at roughly the same time (see Figure 6.1). For a few months volumes grew at all exchanges, but within a relatively short period of time, the CME surged ahead, and before the end of 1982, volumes at the other two exchanges had shrunk to zero. This was because the CME already had a liquid short-term interest rate contract, the three-month Treasury bill contract, which allowed spread trades with the newly listed three-month CD contract, a quick way to build liquidity. So the CME won the three-way competition. Usually, winning a competition assured the victor of a contract that would continue for some time.

In this case, however, there were two events that conspired to cut short the life of the CD contract.[2] First, the CME started a new short-term interest rate contract based on U.S. dollar deposits offshore, called three-month Eurodollars.

The contract's value moved with the average LIBOR rate based on a survey of London banks. This was to eventually become the biggest futures contract in the world. The second event was a delivery problem that scared traders away from CD futures. There was a list of banks whose CDs were deliverable on the contract. One of these banks was Continental Illinois National Bank, which had made a number of oil and gas and developing-country loans that started looking very risky. In 1982, analysts began downgrading Continental's earnings estimates, and the rating agencies began downgrading its debt.[3] Even before the bank actually went into bankruptcy, buyers of CD futures began to fear getting a delivery of Continental CDs and started shifting their positions to the Eurodollar futures contract. The result was that all the liquidity in the CD contract eventually moved to the Eurodollar contract, which became the benchmark for short-term, U.S. dollar interest rates. The CD contract had a short, sweet life and was dead within five years.

Another example of two exchanges listing the same product at roughly the same time occurred when the CME and CBOT both listed OTC stock indexes in the mid-1980s. The CBOT listed the Nasdaq 100, and the CME listed the S&P OTC index because it had a relationship with the S&P Corporation. Both exchanges saw some volume, both in 1985 and 1986, and the CBOT's Nasdaq 100 contract did about 50% more volume, but by 1987 both contracts were dead. This was a case of a product whose time had not yet come; despite spending about $1 million each on marketing their products, both exchanges failed to establish a successful contract. Ironically, the CME obtained listing rights from Nasdaq and successfully relisted the Nasdaq 100 a decade later, in 1996.

Measuring Volume at Futures Markets

Comparing futures contracts and exchanges to one another is a tricky thing because the measurement of trading activity differs by country and the method used can give very different results. There are essentially two ways to measure the volume of trading at a futures exchange; the method chosen depends on the way exchanges and brokerage firms in a country charge fees. In places like the United States, Canada, and Europe, fees are based on the number of contracts traded, so exchange volumes are reported as the number of contracts that change hands during a specific period of time, typically a day, a month, or a year. In countries like China and India, on the other hand, fees are based on the nominal value of a trade, so in those countries, volume is measured by the nominal value of the contracts traded.

Using the American-European method, a Eurodollar contract and a cattle contract both count as one contract. Using the Chinese-Indian method, a Eurodollar contract would count for 25 times that of a cattle contract because a Eurodollar contract has a nominal value 25 times that of a cattle contract—$1 million for each Eurodollar contract vs. about $40,000 for one cattle contract (assuming cattle were selling for $1 per pound for the 40,000-pound contract).

So, if 100,000 Eurodollar contracts were traded and 50,000 live cattle contracts were traded on a given day, together that would be a volume of 150,000 contracts using the American-European method, or $100,002,000,000 using the Indian-Chinese method. It's not that one method is superior; each has its own logic driven by local fee customs. One could debate the issue of which fee custom makes the most sense, but we will not do that here. But because the Washington, DC-based Futures Industry Association (FIA) publishes American-style volume numbers for all exchanges that report to them, and because most exchanges want to be included in these monthly reports, increasingly those exchanges that report locally on a nominal value basis also report the number of contracts traded to the FIA.

Indirect competition is a bit more subtle. Usually when we think of competition we think of the case where two or more exchanges are listing the same or very similar contracts. The logic here is that participants in the industry in which the underlying asset is traded can logically go to either one of the competing exchanges to manage the risk associated with the underlying asset. However, there is another side of this equation, and that is not only do these markets attract individuals and firms involved in the production, processing, or merchandising of the underlying asset or commodity, they also attract speculative capital. And speculative capital can go anywhere but is most interested in markets that are liquid and have sufficient volatility to offer trading opportunities. So a hedge fund or managed futures fund can trade cattle, corn, or a stock index as long as the market is liquid and the fund can build a successful trading strategy for that market. In this sense the corn contract at one exchange is competing with the cattle contract at a second exchange and a stock index contract at a third exchange. So, as long as the same hedge funds, swap dealers, managed futures funds, investment banks, and individuals have access to a group of different exchanges, all those exchanges and their products are competing for the same speculative capital.

Bragging Rights Competition

Exchanges tend to compete for bragging rights. So, at one level, exchanges are competing to be able to say that they are the biggest, the most rapidly growing, or the exchange with the largest product in some specific asset class. This was more important in the days before exchanges became for-profit, stockholder entities, focused on the bottom line. Exchanges were still owned by their members. Then, being the biggest, or at least moving toward the top of the heap, was the goal of many exchanges. It was little different from the competition among sports teams from different cities or universities. For example, for decades the Chicago Mercantile Exchange and the Chicago Board of Trade engaged in a sort of schoolboy rivalry as to which exchange was the biggest. Size among exchanges generally refers to the level of trading volume that occurs at those exchanges. But when the CME was still the number-two exchange in terms of trading volume in 1993, it opened a new trading floor that had more square feet than the CBOT, and it immediately created commemorative T-shirts and hats that read "NOW THE WORLD'S LARGEST EXCHANGE." Of course, a short time later the CBOT opened a new, larger trading floor and regained the square footage crown. Not to be outdone, the CME began reworking the definition of "trading volume" and decided to begin using a measure that included options exercises and other things that made the CME look larger than it was under the conventional definition. The Futures Industry Association, the entity that publishes exchange volume, balked at the unilateral definitional change; no other exchange adopted the CME approach, and the CME eventually backed down. Schoolboy bragging doesn't disappear but becomes much less important as exchanges move from the member-ownership to the stockholder-ownership model, where everyone has their eyes on profits and stock prices.

Securities vs. Derivatives Exchanges: Fees and Revenues

All exchanges compete by making products available for trading and attracting traders to trade those products at their exchanges. But there is a difference between the securities and derivatives exchanges' approaches to this competitive activity. First, a securities exchange's products are mainly stocks of companies that have agreed to list on them. So, product development involves seeking these company listings. The exchanges may also allow trading in companies that have listed elsewhere, or developed equity- or bond-based products such as exchange-traded funds (ETFs) or exchange-traded notes (ETNs) to offer investors tailored exposures not efficiently obtainable from individual equities or bonds.

Securities exchanges receive listing fees from public companies that list with them.[4] They do not receive listing fees from companies in which they allow trading but do not formally list. They also do not receive listing fees for products they create that are based on indexes published by others. On the contrary, the exchanges must pay for the rights to use these indexes. AMEX, now part of NYSE Euronext, for example, must pay fees to Standard and Poor's for the very popular ETF, Spider (SPDR), listed there.

Derivatives exchanges never receive fees from anyone for listing products, and, like stock exchanges, they sometimes even pay fees for the privilege of listing a product that utilizes the intellectual property of another company, such as the indexes of Standard and Poor's, Dow Jones, Wilshire, or Russell. At the risk of overgeneralizing, derivatives exchanges compete by creating new products and winning customers for these new products, whereas securities exchanges (within a single country) compete by listing the same products and enticing customers to their markets via a combination of strategies, including liquidity enhancement and actually paying for order flow. There is a difference here between stock exchanges and derivatives exchanges.

Local to Regional Competition

There was a time when competition among exchanges was local and regional. And, as regional victors became established, countries were peppered with a number of regional stock exchanges. The United States still has stock exchanges over 100 years old in New York, Boston, Philadelphia, Chicago, and Los Angeles, but there were once a great deal more. The Chicago Stock Exchange, for example, was the result of a merger of exchanges based in St. Louis, Cleveland, Minneapolis-St. Paul, and New Orleans. In fact, during the 19th century there were roughly 250 stock exchanges operating in the United States.[5]

As late as the 1990s, India had 22 regional exchanges in addition to the main exchange in the financial center of Bombay. England once had 20 stock exchanges and today has only the LSE and a few small competitors. In all these cases you needed regional exchanges to trade regional stocks because it was too costly, difficult, and slow to communicate and deliver stock certificates, even across a country as small as England.

But as communication became cheaper and faster, regional exchanges began trading national products. The regional stock exchanges in the United States have almost totally abandoned any notion of regional stocks. All stocks are now national. And all the regional exchanges compete for trades in the same stocks. The same is true in India. The 23 regional exchanges began competing in the same stocks and were eventually unable to match the financial might of Mumbai (known until recently as Bombay, when a nationalistic Hindu party began throwing out the old British names and restoring the original Hindu names of many cities). Therefore, business tended to migrate to the financial center and the regional exchanges either got absorbed, converted themselves into brokerage firms, or simply dried up and blew away. So, all that's left in England is the London Stock Exchange and a handful of niche players. Most of the Indian regionals—New Delhi, Kolkata, Chennai, and so on—no longer see any real trading. And in the United States, a system mandated by the SEC that connects all regional U.S. exchanges to the New York Stock Exchange has saved them by ensuring that as long as they offer competitive prices they will continue to get a piece of the action. However, over the past few years the number of independent regional exchanges has fallen from five to two (the Boston Stock Exchange and the Chicago Stock Exchange), with the others (Philadelphia, Pacific, and Cincinnati) being absorbed into Nasdaq, the NYSE, and the CBOE, respectively.

Competition and Clearing

The relationship that an exchange has with its clearinghouse is a very important factor when we look at an exchange's ability to compete. There are really three possible relationships between an exchange and a clearinghouse:

- The clearinghouse can be internal to the exchange.
- The clearinghouse can be an external, independent entity or at the extreme.
- The clearinghouse can be an external, independent entity that commonly clears multiple exchanges that have identical, fungible contracts, allowing a position to be put on at one exchange and offset at another.

From the point of view of the exchange, particularly an exchange that is an aggressive innovator or "first mover," one that tends to be the first to market with new products, the internal clearinghouse is the best, and this is the model that futures exchanges have generally chosen for themselves. Since the internal clearinghouse is totally controlled by the exchange, its priorities can be changed quickly to deal with a shifting competitive environment. For example, if the exchange has a new product that it needs to launch very quickly, it can tell the clearinghouse to devote all necessary resources to prepare for this new contract and put other projects on the back burner. This is difficult to do with an external clearinghouse. There, the exchange's new product must take its proper place in the queue behind other products from other exchanges and wait its turn.

Though there are efficiency advantages to having several exchanges clear their products on a single common clearing system, competitive problems can sometimes arise. One of the best examples of problems with an external clearinghouse was that of the Board of Trade Clearing Corporation (BOTCC) and the exchange that created BOTCC, the CBOT. In 2003, the then largest futures exchange in the world, Eurex, decided to create a Chicago subsidiary to compete directly with the cornerstone products listed at the CBOT. At that time, BOTCC was and had been the entity that cleared all CBOT trades for the past 70 years. But because the BOTCC was an external, independent clearing entity, when Eurex approached BOTCC to clear its Treasury products and offered an attractive deal for doing so, BOTCC jumped at the chance. One of the motivations for BOTCC to agree to clear the products of its long-time partner's major competitor was that BOTCC feared that Eurex would be successful and the revenues from its then major client, the CBOT, would disappear. So, it took a calculated risk and decided to clear the products of the Eurex Chicago subsidiary.

Quite naturally, the CBOT decided to sever its relationship with BOTCC, and it asked the CME to take over the clearing of CBOT contracts. The CME agreed to do this because none of the CBOT products were competitive with its own products and it represented the chance that this could lead to a closer relationship between the two exchanges as they did battle against the rest of the world. In fact, as is mentioned elsewhere in this book, the two exchanges grew close enough that they actually merged in the summer of 2007.

The third model of several exchanges commonly clearing identical, fungible contracts is both the best and the worst of all models. It is difficult to imagine a group of competitive exchanges choosing this model, and thus it would most likely exist when imposed by a regulatory entity, as it was when the SEC mandated it for the securities options industry in the United States.

Back in 1973, the CBOE was founded by the CBOT to allow trading of options on individual shares of stocks, and this involved the creation of a captive clearinghouse. The CBOE was successful, and naturally a number of the existing equity exchanges decided that they too would like to list options, a logical product extension for them. The SEC, which regulates all U.S. securities, including options on securities, required that the CBOE spin off its internal clearinghouse and make it available to all other options exchanges in the United States. So, in 1975 the CBOE clearinghouse was spun off and renamed the Options Clearing Corporation (OCC). The SEC further required fungibility of products so that not only would the now independent clearinghouse clear the products of all options exchanges, it also would allow an option that was listed on more than one exchange to be purchased on one exchange and then be sold on the other options exchange cleared by the OCC. This allowed positions to be put on at any U.S. options exchange and offset at the same or any other U.S. options exchange. What this meant was that if one exchange had a successful product, and another exchange decided that it wanted to list that same product, traders knew that if they took a position at the new relatively illiquid exchange, they could always offset the position at the more liquid exchange, if they needed to do so. This basically gave a helping hand to any exchanges that wanted to compete with a product that was already successfully listed at an exchange. The SEC felt that this would create price competition among the various options exchanges and keep transaction fees low. From this point of view, it actually was the best of the models because it encouraged vigorous price competition. However, from the point of view of an individual exchange, especially an exchange that had worked hard to develop liquidity in some new product, this was the worst of all systems because it gave the least protection to the new product.

This third model has been exclusively applied to securities options in the United States. However, there have been proposals to also apply this model to U.S. futures. The brokerage firms, which are always concerned about the fees being charged to them by the exchanges, lobbied in 2003 through their trade association, the Futures Industry Association (FIA), for the CFTC or Congress to impose an SEC-type model on the futures industry. The closest that futures markets came to "real interexchange competition," said John Damgard, FIA president, was the "single stock futures exchanges where U.S. law has mandated fungible contracts [and a single clearing entity]."[6] Damgard was referring to the new futures on individual stocks, which Congress insisted be regulated jointly by the SEC and CFTC and follow the fungible contract model of single stock options. Damgard went on to say that if Congress continues to pay attention to consumer and user concerns, then fungibility would spread to traditional futures as well.

Of course, the futures exchanges have argued that futures contracts are the intellectual property of exchanges and they should be able to protect and not be forced to share this property with every latecomer who stumbles into the party. In addition, they argue, forced fungibility would actually harm the users because the new competition would fragment liquidity into several smaller pools, each with a bid/ask spread that would be wider than the ones in the existing monopolistic pools. So, even if competition did drive down exchange fees, this savings could be more than offset by the cost of wider bid/ask spreads.[7]

While the debate raged between the brokerage firms and users, who wanted product fungibility and common clearing, and the exchanges, who felt these were an invention of the Devil, the federal futures regulator stayed neutral. CFTC Chairman James Newsome made it clear that he wanted the industry members to work it out among themselves; he even had his staff facilitate meetings between the exchanges and FIA members. He also held a formal roundtable discussion on the issue.

Government neutrality was pushed aside when the U.S. Department of Justice (DOJ) dropped a bombshell. In late 2007, the DOJ requested comments from other agencies regarding a possible revamping of financial regulations in the United States. The DOJ responded by arguing in a January 31, 2008, 22-page letter that product fungibility and common clearing should be imposed on the futures exchanges. The DOJ maintained that because futures exchanges in the United States have captive clearing organizations, competitors are not able to tap into the existing liquidity at the exchange that first listed the product. The letter noted that futures exchanges, when they compete for new products, find themselves in a winner-take-all situation. The network liquidity effects,[8] which is to say the fact that buyers and sellers all want to be in the market with the greatest liquidity, result in buyers and sellers congregating eventually at a single exchange when two exchanges compete. And the DOJ maintains that if the futures industry followed the model of the securities industry, specifically the equity market and the equity options market, this would significantly enhance competition among the exchanges, resulting in lower costs of doing business and greater innovation.

It was interesting to note that this DOJ comment letter had such a chilling effect on the industry—and specifically on the CME, which was in the process of trying to acquire NYMEX—that the stock price of both the CME and NYMEX dropped like a rock.[9] The DOJ had gone along with the CME's first big merger with the CBOT in the summer of 2007, but the question now was, would it go along with the proposed CME merger with NYMEX and would it require a restructuring of the industry as the price the CME had to pay for the approval?

Competition in Options

In the beginning there was only the Chicago Board Options Exchange (CBOE). The CBOE, which was conceived by a group of traders at the CBOT, was the first exchange in the world to list options on equities. It was an idea whose time had come. In fact, a number of stock exchanges around the country (like the AMEX, the Philadelphia Stock Exchange, and the Pacific Exchange) saw the CBOE's initial success and felt that the idea was sufficiently powerful that they also began to list options on individual stocks. Initially, the exchanges did not compete directly over identical products, and in a manner similar to basketball or football drafts, the options exchanges would take turns picking stocks on which they would list options. One exchange would choose first, then another exchange, then a third exchange, and so on. Unlike the basketball and football drafts, which are held annually, the options sessions were done a number of times each year. While this was convenient for the exchanges to each have monopolies on the various stock options, the SEC actually wanted it this way. The problem was that had there been multiple listings of each option, for example, both CBOE and AMEX listing IBM, there was not a practical way to ensure that a customer wanting to buy a specific IBM call would have his order filled at the exchange offering the best price. Communication systems were simply not good and fast enough to have exchanges communicate with each other on every order for every one of the many strikes and expirations being offered. The bandwidth of the 1970s was simply not sufficient. So it was best, the SEC thought, to have each company option at a single exchange.

Though the SEC formally eliminated the practice of listing new options only on a single exchange in 1990, each options exchange still chose not to list those options in which significant liquidity had been established at another exchange.

Enter the ISE

Back in 1996, William Porter, who had already founded the online brokerage firm called E*TRADE, and Marty Averbuch wanted to figure out a way to reduce the relatively high transactions costs associated with options so that E*TRADE customers could affordably begin trading these options.[10] They believed that this monopolistic structure in the options market, where each exchange had its own set of options that the other exchanges respected and would not list themselves, was a significant obstacle to lowering options trading costs. Porter realized that the only way to reduce the costs of trading would be to create a new registered options exchange, and he enlisted the support of a consortium of broker-dealers who were also interested in reducing the cost of trading options.

The first thing they did was to hire a small research group called K-Squared Research, founded by David Krell and Gary Katz, both of whom had been managers of the options division of the New York Stock Exchange. The initial task was to produce a feasibility study on the creation of a new options exchange. Krell and Katz came back with the recommendation that a new all-electronic options exchange be created.

The consortium decided to move forward with the new exchange, and the International Securities Exchange (ISE) was founded in September 1997, with Porter as chairman and Krell as CEO. The decision was made to use the technology supplied by OM, the Swedish exchange that had supplied a matching engine to exchanges around the world.

Still, a year and a half away from actual product launch, the ISE announced in November 1998 that it intended to list the 600 highest-volume options trading at other exchanges. The impending launch of the ISE had already created some anxiety for the existing options exchanges, but the explicit announcement that it intended to directly compete with the highest-volume contracts at all the existing exchanges destroyed the comfortable era of noncompetition, and within nine months there was an all-out listing war in the options markets. Both CBOE and AMEX listed Dell options that until then had been a monopoly product of the Philadelphia Stock Exchange. Philadelphia, in turn, listed Apple, a monopoly product of AMEX, and IBM, Coca-Cola, and Johnson & Johnson, all monopoly products of the CBOE. By the end of 2001, virtually every important product had multiple listings at several exchanges.

When the ISE actually went live on May 26, 2000, it started with a very modest listing of options on only three stocks. Once it was clear that the system worked well, it began adding 25 new names every month. By the end of 2001 the ISE had listed options on 458 of the most actively traded options contracts in the United States. Though there was an increase in trading overall, there was no question that the ISE was taking volume away from the existing exchanges, especially the CBOE. Between 2000 and 2001, the CBOEs net income fell 35%, from $10.9 million to $7.1 million.[11]

Table 6.1 U.S. Options Volume* and Market Share, 2007

	Share (%)	Total	Equities	Indexes
CBOE	33.0	944	714	230.5
ISE	28.1	804	788	16.4
PHLX	14.3	408	399	8.8
NYSE RCA	11.7	336	336	0.3
AMEX	8.4	240	227	13.8
BOX	4.5	130	129	0.8
Total	100.0	2862	2593	270.6

*Volume in millions of contracts traded.
Note: AMEX is now part of NYSE Euronext, and PHLX is now part of Nasdaq OMX.
Source: Options Clearing Corp. Annual Report 2007.

So, what is the state of the options industry today? The first dimension to grasp is the dramatic growth in trading activity. In the United States, all stock options and stock index options trades are cleared in a single place, the Options Clearing Corporation.[12] Between 2005 and 2007, the number of options contracts cleared at the OCC essentially doubled, from 1.5 billion to 2.9 billion.[13] At the same time, the OCC dropped its clearing fees by 50%, from 3.4 cents per contract in 2005 down to 1.7 cents per contract in 2007. Because the OCC is a utility owned by all the options exchanges, this drop in fees is not due to competition but rather to the reduction in the average cost of clearing a trade in an increasingly electronic world amid rapidly increasing volume.

The mix of trading in all OCC cleared options is about 90% options on individual equities and about 10% options on indexes (see Table 6.1). The CBOE was the market leader and major innovator. Not only was it the first to introduce exchange-traded stock options, it was also the first securities exchange to introduce stock index options.[14] As a result, it was able to negotiate exclusive trading rights on the major indexes early on (the S&P 100[15] and S&P 500 in 1983 and the Dow Jones Industrial Average in 1997) and consequently has 85% of the index business. So, index options account for a full 25% of its total options volume, with the other 75% in options on individual equities. Its closest index competitor is AMEX, which has recently been taken over by the New York Stock Exchange and has 5.7% of its total volume in index options. All the other exchanges have 2% or less of their volume in index options.

Even though index options represent a small share of total volume, they are an attractive asset for an exchange. First, exchange fees are higher for customer trades in index options—from 18 to 44 cents per contract compared to 0 to 18 cents per contract for equity options trades.[16] This is not all gravy, since an undisclosed portion of the per-contract fee charged to the customer must be passed on to the index provider. Second, index trades are larger, so the average index trade generates more revenue for the exchange. The average index options trade involves over twice as many options contracts as does the average equity options trade: 44.2 options per index trade compared to 18.9 options per equity trade in 2007. Third, because premiums on index contracts average five times higher—$1,731.30 vs. $332.50 for equity options contracts on single companies—market makers likely earn significantly higher bid-ask spreads, since spreads tend to increase as the value of the option increases.

The Battle over Index Options

Given the attractiveness of the index option product, even though the ISE had passed the CBOE in options volume on individual stocks (Figure 6.1), it knew that somehow it needed to break the CBOE's hold on trading in stock index options. For several years the ISE simply complained about the CBOT's exclusive right to trade options on the most popular indexes, the S&P 500 and the DJIA. In fact, it adopted the slogan "Free the SPX," referring to the trading symbol for the S&P 500 option. The CBOE responded with its own slogan imprinted on buttons worn by the members: "Innovation not Litigation." The CBOE felt that it had created this new class of products called index options, it had made the effort and paid the price to obtain the right to use the trademarked premier brands of the index publishing industry, and it had worked to successfully build the liquidity in these contracts—and here was a newcomer trying to free-ride on all this effort.

But on November 2, 2006, the ISE raised the ante by actually filing a lawsuit on the matter. This was a little less aggressive than the last time the ISE had seen a seemingly proprietary product that it wanted. In 2005, it listed options on two of the most popular exchange-traded funds,[17] SPDRs (based on the S&P 500) and DIAMONDs (based on the DJIA), without obtaining a license from the owners of these two indexes, McGraw-Hill and Dow Jones, respectively. The two indexing companies sued the ISE, but the ISE actually won the lawsuit.[18] There is a difference, though, between an option on an ETF and an option on an index. The CBOE has filed its own suit on the matter against the ISE. To keep things messy, the ISE responded by filing another lawsuit against the CBOE on an unrelated matter. It claims that the CBOE's hybrid trading system, which combines floor and screen-based trading, infringes on ISE patents for its own system.

Global Competition: The Past

SIMEX Was Born Global

There are new forces driving global competition to new heights, but competition across country borders has actually been around for some time. For example, a new financial futures exchange was opened in Singapore back in 1984. Named SIMEX, for Singapore International Monetary Exchange, it began with a handful of products, almost all of which were based on other countries' markets—not a surprise for an exchange located in a tiny city-state with relatively tiny underlying financial markets. In the same sense that Singapore's economy was based on foreign trade, the products of its futures exchange were based on foreign markets. SIMEX listed four products in its first year: the German mark, the three-month Eurodollar deposit,[19] gold, and the Japanese yen. Even though the German mark and Eurodollars were SIMEX's largest-volume products in some of the early years, Japanese futures would be its bread and butter over the long haul. In those days, the Japanese financial markets were heavily government controlled and were somewhat insular. So the Japanese exchanges were somewhat slow at listing new products, and when they did, it wasn't always the easiest thing in the world for foreigners to gain access to those products. In 1986, before any Japanese exchange had attempted a stock index futures contract, SIMEX filled the gap by listing the Nikkei 225.

The next year, the Japanese government allowed the Osaka Securities Exchange (OSE) to list the first stock index futures contract in Japan, but instead of listing the Nikkei 225, the best-known and most widely followed index of the Japanese markets, the OSE listed a newly made-up (and thus totally unknown) index called the OSF 50, for Osaka Stock Futures. The contract was a short-term solution to a fundamental problem. At the time, Japanese law required that futures contracts result in physical delivery of those contracts not offset prior to maturity, and it thus prohibited the cash settlement of futures contracts.[20] This was not a problem for corn, wheat, or soybeans, which can easily be delivered on a futures contract, but it was a problem for stock indexes, which are very difficult and costly to deliver. Stock indexes are baskets of stocks, and the Nikkei 225 in particular is a basket of 225 different stocks. Because it would require a large number of odd-sized transactions to put together a delivery basket, making it very cumbersome and costly, stock index futures universally use a settlement system known as cash settlement at the expiration of each contract.[21]

Without the cash settlement alternative, the Japanese chose the OSF 50 because 50 different stocks would be much cheaper to deliver than 225 stocks. The contract never amounted to much and died within four years. Only 248 contracts of the OSF 50 changed hands in 1987, compared to 586,921 contracts of the cash-settled Nikkei 225 at SIMEX. In the next year, 1988, the law was changed to allow cash settlement, and OSE listed its own cash-settled Nikkei 225. From the very beginning of 1988, the Nikkei 225 at the OSE traded significantly higher volumes than were traded at SIMEX. But SIMEX stayed in the game and was able to increase its trading volume each year until the whole Japanese economy turned south and caused a decline in trading volumes in all Japanese products. Twenty years later, the Nikkei 225 is still the most important product at both SIMEX and the OSE.

Table 6.2 The Nikkei Stock Index Competition: Osaka vs. Singapore vs. Chicago Trading Volume, January–June 2008

	Osaka	SIMEX	CME
Nikkei 225 yen	16,753,295	11,326,855	1,933,757
Nikkei 225 mini	41,314,078	31,125	—
Nikkei 225 USD	—	2,759	2,089,702
Nikkei 300	23,616	—	

Source: FIA Volume Report, June 2008.

Why didn't all the business flow to Osaka, since it had greater liquidity? For one thing, Japan had a system of fixed high commissions—several times the level of SIMEX commissions. Japan's first attempt to fix the high fixed commission problem was unbalanced but logical. The Japanese institutions and individuals were a captive audience, and Japanese brokers didn't want to get rid of that gravy train. But they knew they needed to do something to entice the foreign capital from SIMEX to Osaka, so they kept high fixed commissions for locals but allowed them to be negotiable only for foreigners. Still, there were enough other rigidities and costs in the Japanese system that SIMEX could continue to make a good living by offering an easier, generally cheaper alternative to the Japanese system.

The mid-2008 status of the competition for the Nikkei stock index can be seen in Table 6.2. There has been an extension of the competition between SIMEX and Osaka as each have created several variations on the original product, but there has also been the entry of a new competitor, the Chicago Mercantile Exchange. The CME listed a USD-denominated version of the Nikkei 225 back in 1990 with the thought that a Nikkei based in Chicago with a dollar multiplier would appeal to at least some portion of U.S. investors. It then added a yen-denominated version in 2003, which, as of mid-2008, was doing about the same level of business as the 18-year-old dollar-denominated contract. A number of exchanges have found success in offering smaller retail-sized versions of stock index contracts. In July 2006, the OSE tried the same with the Nikkei 225 mini, which is one-tenth the size of the regular Nikkei 225. Two years later it was trading over twice as many contracts as the full-sized Nikkei (which is, of course, only a quarter of the full-sized contract in nominal traded value). The other thing to note is that in 1994, the Japanese government insisted that a new, better-constructed Nikkei be designed and traded by the Japanese exchange. This was the Nikkei 300, which had 75 more stocks and was capitalization weighted, a generally better way of weighting an index to prevent manipulation.[22] All three exchanges—the OSE, the CME, and

SIMEX—listed the 300 just in case it became the new benchmark. The marketplace did not embrace the Nikkei 300 (it preferred the old Nikkei 225 it was used to), and the Nikkei 300 ceased trading at both the CME and SIMEX, but some small degree of volume does persist at the OSE.

About a decade later a similar opportunity presented itself to SIMEX. There had been a growing interest in the Taiwan market, and several exchanges started thinking about listing a Taiwan stock index. The Taiwan regulator had not yet given permission for the local Taiwan exchange to list stock index futures, and neither the stock exchange nor the regulator was keen on allowing an international exchange to list futures on the local TAIEX index. There were, however, other indexes of the Taiwan market aside from the local TAIEX index. The most popular international index of Taiwan stocks was the MSCI Taiwan Index, and both the CME and SIMEX began independently (and unknown to each other) discussing a license with MSCI.[23] After several months of discussion and negotiation, MSCI informed the CME that SIMEX actually had the right of first refusal on any Asian MSCI indexes and had decided to exercise this right with respect to the Taiwan Index. So SIMEX licensed and listed the MSCI Taiwan Index in 1997. The CME was determined to list a futures contract on the Taiwan market, so it turned to Dow Jones, which had its own set of international indexes, though they were not as widely followed. It quickly negotiated a licensing agreement and listed the Dow Jones Stock Index, also in 1997. With two international competitors leaving the gate, the Taiwan regulator allowed the Taiwan Futures Exchange to list its own Taiwan index the following year.

The CME's contract based on the less well-known Dow Jones index lasted only a few months. The real competition was between the Taiwan Futures Exchange and SIMEX. Perhaps because of its one-year head start with an internationally popular index, the Singapore exchange actually outpaced the home market during six of the next eight years (Figure 6.2). In fact, in the most recent data available, the two exchanges traded virtually the same volumes in the regular Taiwan index contract, about 8.3 million contracts in the first half of 2008. The Taiwan Futures Exchange, however, has pulled out ahead, first by adding a mini futures contract, which traded 3.4 million contracts during that same period. But the product extension that really moved the Taiwan Futures Exchange into first place was the option on this index. In a phenomenon that has been observed only in one other market (Korea), the local retail population went crazy over the option on this local stock index. So, during the first half of 2008, there were 46.8 million TAIEX options traded—almost six times the number of regular TAIEX futures. By comparison, SIMEX traded only 137 MSCI Taiwan Index options during that same period.

But SIMEX remains an example of an exchange founded and sustained on the principle of international competition, an exchange that has always derived the overwhelming bulk of its business from international traders trading international products. During the first half of 2008, for example, 92% of SIMEX's

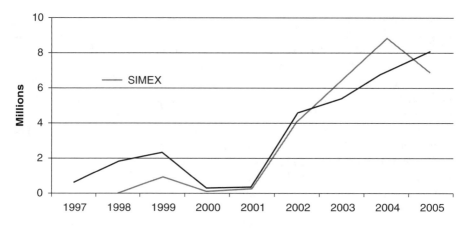

Figure 6.2 Competition for the Taiwan Stock Index (Annual Volume), 1997–2005

futures volume came from products whose underlying assets were tied to other countries, mainly Japan, Taiwan, and India (Table 6.3). Though it also lists Chinese and Pan-Asian indexes, the volumes are inconsequential.

Global Competition in Equities Via the Depository Receipt

Global competition in equities has actually been going on for over 80 years. It began in 1927, when J. P. Morgan created the first American Depository Receipt (ADR) for Selfridge's, the big British retailer. What this meant was that Americans who wanted to buy or sell Selfridge's shares no longer had to convert dollars to British pounds and go through a British broker on the London Stock Exchange; rather, they could trade Selfridge's shares denominated in dollars in New York. An ADR allows a non-U.S. company to list its shares for trading in the United States. The way this happens is that a broker in the home country will purchase shares and place them in a local custodial bank that acts as a custodian for an international depository bank, and the broker then instructs the depository bank to issue depository receipts in the United States. These depository receipts, which represent the deposit of domestic shares at the custodial bank in the home country, may be listed and traded on the NYSE, Nasdaq, or any other U.S. exchange, or they may simply be traded in the OTC market. When depository receipts are issued in Europe, they may be traded at a number of different European exchanges as well.

This is an unusual kind of competition because it is not the same as two exchanges listing precisely the same product and going head to head to see

Table 6.3 SIMEX's Dependence on Various Products, 2008

Product	Volume*	Share (%)
Offshore Products		
Nikkei 225 Futures	11,326,855	38.9
MSCI Taiwan Index	8,358,263	28.7
S&P CNX Nifty Index	6,173,470	21.2
MSCI Singapore Index**	2,335,789	8.0
Mini Japanese government bond	458,333	1.6
Euroyen Tibor	386,112	1.3
Mini Nikkei 225	31,125	0.1
FTSE/China A50 Index	26,224	0.1
MSCI Asia APEX 50 Index	2,846	0.0
USD Nikkei 225	2,759	0.0
Straits Times Index**	78	0.0
Total futures	29,101,854	
% of volume based on domestic products		8.0
% of volume based on international products		92.0

*Volume January–June 2008
**Domestic products
Source: Futures Industry Association International Volume Report, June 2008.

which one is able to develop the liquidity. In this case, you have a depository bank, which is essentially transforming a product, the shares issued on a foreign stock market, into something that is more accessible to U.S. and European investors. The domestic shares don't disappear; they are simply transformed into receipts issued in the United States or Europe. Most of the trading that takes place in depository receipts would likely not occur on the home market, whether China, India, Mexico, Brazil, or Australia. This is because the shares on those markets have been transformed into dollar-denominated securities traded under the well-known rules of U.S. or European exchanges, often with greater liquidity than is available in the home market. So, to a large extent, depository receipts really represent the creation of new customers. However, to the extent that some U.S. and European investors would have gone to the trouble to trade these foreign stocks on the foreign home markets, but now choose the convenience of trading the depository receipts on these stocks in the American and European markets, this does represent competition for stock markets worldwide.

The New Global Competition—Kill the Competitor

We explained earlier in this book how technology has been a fundamental driver in the morphing of exchanges during the current era. We also explained how all exchanges are trying to make their way down this steeply falling cost curve, to minimize the cost per share or the cost per contract traded. And, of course, the only way to move down the cost curve is to have more shares or contracts traded at an exchange. Aside from increasing business in existing products and listing new products, the only way to bring more trades to an exchange's platform is to capture business from other exchanges. And there are really two ways to do that. You can capture business by essentially attracting an existing exchange's business to your own exchange, essentially killing the other exchange in the process. Alternatively, you can purchase that business from the other exchange via a merger or acquisition. We turn to the issue of expanding business through mergers and acquisitions in the next chapter.

When pursuing the "kill the competitor" approach, exchanges first tend to go after other exchanges within the same country. Only after that approach has been exhausted do exchanges tend to jump borders and attempt to capture business from exchanges in other countries. And the kill-the-competitor approach works best when the attacking exchange is electronic, and the target exchange is still floor-based. So there's a relatively brief transitional period in the history of exchanges where this approach could work, and that is where electronic and floor-based exchanges exist side by side.

The new global competition has been more prevalent in derivatives than on the equity side of the street. So we start with global competition in derivatives.

Eurex Tries to Kill the Chicago Exchanges

Eurex didn't originally set out to destroy the Chicago Board of Trade. It actually started in October 1999 with a joint venture that was going to help the CBOT move into the electronic age and would help Eurex gain access to U.S. customers. The original deal was called a/c/e, for alliance/CBOT/Eurex, and had the main advantage to the CBOT of replacing the unsuccessful Project A with a first-class electronic trading system. In fact, within a year, on August 28, 2000, the system was up, and the CBOT had, for the first time in its history, both electronic and open-outcry side-by-side trading, allowing customers to choose between the screen and the pit during regular trading hours. Less than two years later, in July 2002, the bloom was off and the two parties announced that they were going to end their alliance in 2004, a full four years before the original 2008 contract expiration. The claim was that the contract was too inflexible and put a damper on contract innovation. Specifically, Eurex was prevented from offering any U.S. dollar-denominated products, and the CBOT was prohibited from listing any European-currency-denominated products. But the CBOT noted at the time of the announcement that Eurex would continue to be a software provider to the CBOT.

Things turned nasty only six months later, on January 9, 2003, when the CBOT announced that it was going to end its relationship with Eurex, dump the Eurex electronic platform, and replace it with the platform offered by Eurex's main European rival, Euronext.liffe. Literally within hours, Eurex chief executive Rudolph Ferscha announced that Eurex planned to go it alone and create an American-based derivatives exchange when its alliance with the CBOT expired at the end of 2003. The exchange would compete directly with the CBOT and CME with futures and options based on bonds, stock indexes, and individual stocks. "Hell hath no fury like a derivatives exchange scorned," quipped *The Economist*, and it warned, "if Eurex is even partly successful, there will be more pressure on the Chicago exchanges to give up their mutual structures, merge—and turn their trading floors into museums." [24] This turned out to be a prescient statement.

Eurex actually had two basic options: It could buy or build. Some thought that the quickest way to enter the U.S. market would be by buying an existing exchange with a valid operating license or merging with one. Eurex didn't need a trading platform; it already had a great one that it was using in Frankfurt. And the new law that was passed in 2000, called the Commodity Futures Modernization Act, had streamlined many things, including the process of being designated as an exchange, technically as a Designated Contract Market (DCM). Still, clearing was an issue, and if it bought an exchange, it would need one with a clearing system as robust as the CBOT's external clearing agent, the independent Board or Trade Clearing Corporation (BOTCC). This was because if Eurex was successful, it would soon be doing the same volume as the CBOT and CME combined, since it planned to steal the volume of both. In fact, Eurex decided to build rather than buy an exchange, and it approached BOTCC about clearing for the new exchange.

It is important to remember that Eurex was the exchange that in 1998 essentially captured all the liquidity of the number-one contract traded at the London International Financial Futures Exchange (LIFFE). It was able to do this because it was electronic, transparent, and cheap, whereas LIFFE still engaged in non-transparent, inefficient, and expensive floor-trading. So when Eurex set its sights on Chicago, many people thought this was going to be the end of the CBOT and the CME, which, despite its electronic trading systems, still had significant floor business. So Eurex felt that if it could partner with BOTCC for clearing, get a fast-track approval to be a registered exchange with the Commodity Futures Trading Commission, and train and incent new participants to trade on Eurex in Chicago, its attack on Chicago had a high probability of success. And a number of people in Chicago agreed. Why else would BOTCC have been willing to risk the abandonment of its major client, the CBOT, by agreeing to clear for our Eurex? In fact, BOTCC may have thought it was taking very little risk. BOTCC is controlled by clearing members, who are always looking for ways to reduce the costs of trading. Some competition from a new player could help. And where else could the CBOT go for clearing? Given that three separate attempts to have the CBOT and CME commonly clear their products in one place had failed miserably, BOTCC likely reasoned that while the CBOT wouldn't like BOTCC clearing a new competitor, they would probably stay put. And this would be the best of all worlds for the clearing firms.[25]

On September 16, 2003, Eurex held a press conference in Chicago and announced that its Chicago-based subsidiary would be called Eurex US and would initially list the same U.S. Treasury contracts that were listed at the CBOT. Now Chicago was not sitting still. In fact, despite the fact that many observers thought the CBOT would not be able to withstand the Eurex attack, just as LIFFE had not been able to withstand the Eurex attack five years earlier, both the CME and CBOT did everything they could to slow down the opening of Eurex US. They put Eurex's application to the CFTC under a microscope, questioning every possible aspect of the proposal. The advantage of this was that each question required an answer and each answer took time. Because the two Chicago exchanges had courted and funded members of Congress for several decades, the exchanges had access and were able to convince Congressional members to hold hearings on the application. *Business Week* was more colorful when it noted that despite the exchanges' usual affirmations of belief in competition and free markets, "Like any favor-seeking sugar grower or steelmaker, the Chicago boys rushed to Washington to sling as much mud as possible at Eurex. Buttonholing such powerful home state pols [politicians] as House Speaker J. Dennis Hastert, they got a hearing on Nov. 6 [2003] before the influential House Agriculture Committee, where they warned that Eurex could threaten everything from open markets to U.S. national interests."[26]

As the Chicago exchanges took the battle to Congress, Eurex decided to take the battle to the courts. On October 14, 2003, Eurex filed a lawsuit against the CME and the CBOT for violating antitrust laws. The suit, which was filed in federal court in Washington, D.C., but was later moved to the District Court of Northern Illinois in Chicago, alleged that two exchanges offered shareholders of the BOTCC over $100 million to vote against a restructuring plan that was required for Eurex to be able to clear its products at BOTCC. The suit was amended in December, adding the claim that the two Chicago exchanges' testimony at congressional hearings was aimed at delaying the launch of Eurex. The suit was further amended in April 2005, over a year after Eurex US listed its first product, to include the claim that the CBOT engaged in predatory pricing by dropping its fees up to 70% only four days prior to the launch of Eurex US. Eurex further alleged that two exchanges had conspired to prevent or delay an important global clearing link between the Clearing Corporation (CCorp) and Eurex clearing in Frankfurt that would have allowed traders to establish a position at Eurex Frankfurt and offset it at Eurex US, or vice versa.[27] When the two Chicago exchanges tried to have the lawsuit dismissed, Judge James Zagel of the U.S. District Court for the Northern District of Illinois stated, "the Defendants' [CBOT and CME's] description of Plaintiffs' Second Amended Complaint bears so little resemblance to the Complaint itself that I paused to consider whether Defendants have actually read the Complaint. Assuming that they have, the characterizations made in Defendants' briefs are as close to the border of being misrepresentations to this Court as it is possible to come without crossing it."[28] In other words, the judge refused to dismiss the suit.

But the delaying tactics worked. On October 14, 2003, the CFTC announced that it was removing Eurex's application from the 60-day fast track for approval, which would have resulted in a November 15 approval. Moving the application from fast track to normal approval process meant that the CFTC now had until March 16, 2004, to complete the review of the application.[29] Finally, on February 4, 2004, the CFTC approved Eurex US as a Designated Contract Market. Four days later, on February 8, 2004, Eurex US opened its virtual doors for trading.

What did Eurex US have going for it at that time? It had signed up two important Chicago institutions to support it. First, it finally was able to strike an agreement with the Clearing Corporation (formerly known as BOTCC) to clear all Eurex US trades. Second, it enlisted the assistance of the National Futures Association to handle regulatory services for Eurex US. It had in place 36 market makers for the various contracts that it intended to list. And it trained over 100 customers on its electronic trading system.

And what had the two Chicago exchanges been able to do to help fend off the attack? By the time of the Eurex US opening, the CBOT had moved 90% of its Treasury futures trading to the screen and the CME had moved an even greater percentage of its Eurodollar futures trading to the screen. The CBOT had lowered its fees to 30 cents per side for nonmembers on a temporary basis. Since Eurex fees were in the 20 to 30 cents per-contract range, this took away a major part of the fee advantage that Eurex thought it would have going into battle. In addition, the Chicago exchanges had delayed the Eurex launch long enough that the CBOT was able to complete its transition from the Eurex electronic platform to the platform owned by Euronext.liffe, which many observers considered equal to if not better than the Eurex platform. This meant that instead of going to battle with an obsolete, high-priced, nontransparent, floor-based system, Eurex found itself facing an electronic, transparent, low-priced competitor.

Eurex had an uphill battle. By June, Eurex had a very small market share and was not making much forward progress. So it sweetened the pot. On June 22, 2004, Eurex announced that first it would eliminate all fees for trading U.S. Treasury contracts at Eurex US from July 12 through the end of the year; second, it would share up to $40 million in rebates to frequent traders. The plan, which also included stipends paid to market makers to help pay for technology development and free iPods for participating traders, was called X Factor, and it did have an effect. Daily average volume jumped from 2768 contracts in June to 23,922 contracts in July, an impressive 764% increase, but still trivial in terms of market share. At an FIA lunch in Chicago, Eurex US CEO Satish Nandapurkar pleaded with the crowd: "The industry, FCMs and end customers have all been asking for competition ... Credible competitive markets exist. But you have to support them. If you do, you send a message. If you don't, you send a message ... Your destiny is in your own hands."[30]

Over the following months, Eurex tried other things, other incentives and other products, including going after the CME foreign exchange futures, but ultimately the attack failed and Eurex ended up selling 70% of the exchange to Man Group plc for $23.2 million in cash, with Man promising to make a further capital injection of $35 million into the exchange. Despite further injections of cash, by July 2008 Eurex US, renamed USFE, short for U.S. Futures Exchange, was trading only 117 contracts per day, mainly in a dollar-based Indian stock index. The CME, which had absorbed the CBOT and become the CME Group, was trading 990,379 contracts per day—about 8400 times as much. It could have been the other way round.

ICE Tries to Kill NYMEX

Before we describe the battle between ICE and NYMEX, we must first understand what ICE is. Originally, the Atlanta-based Intercontinental Exchange (ICE) opened its doors in 2000 as an OTC energy market for big commercial players.[31] Its founding owners were four investment banks and three big energy companies. From a regulatory point of view, the market was considered an Exempt Commercial Market under the extremely light regulation of the CFTC. When the new futures law was passed in 2000 in the United States, it expanded the types of exchanges that could be created and specifically allowed for several types of very lightly regulated exchanges, which were lightly regulated because only large sophisticated players could participate on them. The Exempt Commercial Market was one of these new exchange types. Over time, ICE acquired futures exchanges in Europe, Canada, and the United States. ICE acquired the London-based International Petroleum Exchange in 2001 and eventually renamed it ICE Europe. In 2007 it acquired both the Winnipeg Commodity Exchange, which it renamed ICE Futures Canada, and the New York Board of Trade, which it renamed ICE Futures US. The original OTC energy business was renamed ICE OTC. So there are four ICE markets: the three futures markets based in Europe, the United States, and Canada and the original ICE OTC market.[32]

There was some initial friction between the original ICE OTC market and NYMEX in that some of the business on ICE could have been drawn away from NYMEX and the fact that the ICE used NYMEX futures settlement prices to cash-settle some of its own contracts. NYMEX sued ICE to prevent it from using without permission the intellectual property of NYMEX, but it was unsuccessful because the court ruled that the settlement prices of an exchange are in the public domain.

But the real competition began on February 3, 2006, when London-based ICE Futures (today called ICE Futures Europe) launched a frontal attack by listing a clone of NYMEX's most successful contract—Light Sweet Crude Oil (AKA West Texas Intermediate). NYMEX had frittered away its resources on establishing trading floors in Dublin and London and had plans to do the same in Singapore and Dubai. In the meantime, it had not done much to upgrade its own electronic trading system, mainly used for after-hours trading. This made it very vulnerable to attack from three quarters. First, its energy products would be very attractive to ICE Futures, which was a renamed acquisition by ICE, called the International Petroleum Exchange (IPE). Second, the CME was anxious to diversify into energy contracts and saw NYMEX's business as quite attractive. Third, the now largely electronic CBOT had listed screen-based gold and silver and was eating into NYMEX's gold and silver business on its COMEX division.

The ICE attack was technically cross-border competition because it was a London-based exchange attempting to directly compete with a U.S.-based exchange. At least that is what it looked like on the surface, but the reality was more complex. It is true that ICE Futures was once a British bricks-and-mortar entity, but it had undergone some changes. It switched from being a traditional member-owned exchange and was now a subsidiary of an American, Atlanta-based parent, the IntercontinentalExchange. It also switched trade matching from a trading floor in London to servers in Atlanta. And, with listing WTI crude, virtually identical to the one listed on NYMEX, it now had a U.S.-based product. With American owners, American servers, and American products, to a number of people it was starting to look like an American exchange. Of course, to the Financial Services Authority, the British regulator of all things financial, ICE futures was still a British exchange because the management of the exchange was based in London.

So when NYMEX complained that the competition from ICE was possibly unfair because ICE was subject to different and in some ways lighter oversight than NYMEX, some information-sharing accommodations were made between the two regulators that allowed both regulators to get a much better picture of large traders on both sides of the Atlantic.

But there were two factors that ultimately prevented ICE from killing NYMEX. The major one was that once the CME announced that it also was going to enter the energy business and compete directly with both NYMEX and ICE, NYMEX knew its days were numbered. It was sitting naked with an inadequate electronic platform facing attacks by two aggressive exchanges with well-honed platforms, and ICE had been able to gain a 30% share in a matter of months. One of the three would win this competition, and it wasn't going to be NYMEX, no matter how hard NYMEX members wanted to believe in floor-based trading.

NYMEX had no choice. To survive, it had to make a deal. The immediate deal it made was to move its energy products onto GLOBEX, CME's electronic platform, in return for CME backing down on its plan to list its own energy products. There was a cost—NYMEX had to pay the CME (a fee that is not publicly known), but in making this deal, NYMEX got rid of one competitor and got a first-class electronic platform to use to fight off the other competitor. And it worked. Once GLOBEX became the NYMEX platform, ICE was not able to make further inroads into NYMEX's market share of the WTI market. In fact, the ICE share declined slightly, from 30% to 28%, for the first nine months of 2008, compared with the same period a year earlier.

The second, rather unusual reason that ICE didn't kill NYMEX, is that by doing so it would have been cutting its own throat. The ICE contract does not involve physical delivery, as does the NYMEX contract, but rather is cash-settled. And the price that ICE uses to cash-settle its contract is actually the price established in the NYMEX contract. So if the NYMEX contract disappeared, the ICE contract, as currently structured, could not be settled and would disappear as well. It's not clear how ICE would have kept NYMEX alive had the momentum continued in its favor and the CME not stepped in to save it.

The New Global Competition in Equities

Aside from the ADRs described earlier, there has been little global competition in equities in the United States. Yes, for a number of years New York has been considered a premier place to list stock for companies located all over the world. And these companies sometimes did an IPO and direct listing of its shares in the United States, rather than merely an ADR listing. But unlike the considerable international competition in derivatives allowed by the CFTC, the SEC has allowed foreign exchanges to set up operations in the United States.

In August 2007, for the first time in its long history, the SEC began working on regulations that could allow U.S. investors access to securities traded off-shore.[33] The model under consideration is referred to as a *mutual recognition model*, in which the SEC would allow both broker-dealers and exchanges in other jurisdictions to forgo the registration requirements with the SEC as long as the securities laws, oversight and enforcement powers in their own jurisdiction were comparable to those in the United States. So, instead of complying with SEC regulations, the foreign broker-dealers and exchanges would simply have to comply with the regulations in their own countries, which would be deemed essentially equivalent to complying with SEC regulations. U.S. exchanges insist that if this were to be allowed, the U.S. exchanges themselves should be allowed to list those same foreign products so that investors would have a choice between trading the foreign products on U.S. markets or on the foreign markets. The mutual recognition model had not been implemented at the time this manuscript was submitted for publication, but the fact that the SEC was considering such a bold step suggests that the equity markets may begin to see the same type of global competition that had already begun in the exchange-traded derivatives markets.

The most active cross-border competition in equities has occurred in Europe, which makes sense because Europe makes up the most politically and economically integrated collection of countries on earth. When the European Parliament issued EU Directive 2004/39/EC on markets in financial instruments, it required that a market in financial instruments organize itself in one of two ways: as a regulated market or as a multilateral trading facility. Regulated markets are more like traditional exchanges (think the London Stock Exchange or the Frankfurt Stock Exchange), whereas MTFs are more like the ECNs that started in the 1990s in the United States (think Island, Archipelago, or Instinet, or more recently, BATS Trading or Direct Edge). In fact, just as in the United States, the entry of these new ECNs/MTFs has created a lively competition among platforms for trading the stocks of various European countries, and trading fees at the major exchanges have fallen. Specifically, the price pressure has been due to the entry of such new MTFs as Chi-x, Turquoise, and BATS Trading Europe.

Among the MTFs in Europe, Turquoise announced first in November 2006, but Chi-x Europe started first, in March 2007. Chi-X's speed in getting to market is said to be due to the focus provided by a single dominant shareholder (Instinet).[34] With only the exchanges as competition, Chi-X has absolutely been the low-cost provider of trading services in Europe. This all changed in 2008. Turquoise opened its virtual doors in February 2008. By the time BATS Trading Europe opened in October 2008, Chi-X had a 6.1% share and Turquoise a 1.5% share, all trading in European stocks. BATS got off to a strong start in Europe and may duplicate its performance in the United States. The London Stock Exchange had 19.3%, Deutsche Börse 17.5%, and NYSE Euronext 15.5%. This makes CHI-X the fourth biggest market for European stocks. To add to the competition, NYSE Euronect announced in August 2008 that it would be starting its own MTF for pan-European blue-chip stocks before the end of the year. It planned to use the very fast technology developed by Arca, an ECN converted to an exchange and acquired by the NYSE, and to include SmartPool, a pan-European dark pool for trading large blocks.

The success of the MTFs has been helped by their ownership and business models. Turquoise, for example, is owned by nine investment banks, which made a commitment to provide liquidity for six months. BATS is owned by 10 investment banks and brokers, five of whom are also Turquoise owners.[35] In other words, these two operations are owned by their customers, who have an incentive to drive liquidity to the platform they own. The bottom line is that Europe will continue to see significant intermarket competition for some time, and this cross-border competition should continue to shower benefits on the users of these markets.

Conclusion

As we have seen, there has been some global competition in the equities market going back to 1927, when the first ADR was created, and in the derivatives markets going back to 1984, when SIMEX was founded on products from other jurisdictions. But the pace has quickened as we have moved into an era of electronic trading, and the need to expand the scale has been heightened. The big attempt at cross-border competition in derivatives failed (the Eurex subsidiary in Chicago), but the event did drive the Chicago exchanges to swiftly shift their trading to screens, resulting in some pretty low exchange fees, at least for a while. The very active cross-border competition in European equities should continue to heat up for a few years, pushing down trading fees in Europe just as they have been pushed down in the United States.

Endnotes

1. The New York Futures Exchange was a wholly owned subsidiary of the New York Stock Exchange and was the NYSE's first attempt to get into futures. Though this attempt was unsuccessful and the exchange was sold to NYBOT, the NYSE eventually (in 2007) merged with Euronext, which had already acquired the big London-based futures exchange known as LIFFE, so the NYSE finally had a successful futures business.
2. This explanation is based on discussions with Galen Burghardt, Rick Kilcollin, and Steve Youngren, all of whom were at the CME at the time, though if there are any errors, they are my own.
3. Federal Deposit Insurance Corporation, "Managing the Crisis: The FDIC and RTC Experience 1980–1994," Washington, D.C., August 1998, p. 547, www.fdic.gov/bank/historical/managing/history2-04.pdf.
4. The NYSE, for example, as of the end of 2008 charged between $150,000 and $250,000 to list a new company.
5. R. C. Michie, *The London and New York Stock Exchanges, 1850–1914*, HarperCollins, 1987, p. 167, quoted in John C. Coffee, Jr., "Racing Towards the Top; The Impact of Cross Listings and Stock Market Competition in International Corporate Governance," *Columbia Law Review*, Vol. 102, pp. 1757–1831.
6. Natasha de Teran, "Fungible Contracts Back on the Agenda," Dow Jones Online Financial News, June 16, 2003.
7. CBOT member Dan Brophy commenting on FIA president John Damgard's letter on fungibility to the *Wall Street Journal*; in the John Lothian Newsletter Blog, April 30, 2007, http://johnlothiannewsletter.com/phpbb/viewtopic.php?p=571.
8. *Network effects* is a term used by economists to refer to those situations in which the value of one person being connected to a network (such as a telephone exchange, a social network Web site, or a market, for example) grows as more members join the group. Elsewhere in this book, we also refer to the end game of this effect as *liquidity-driven monopoly*.
9. The CME experienced a one-day drop of 6%, from $619 on Monday, February 4, 2008, to $588 the following day. While other factors, especially declining confidence in all financial companies, began to affect the stock price, the decline continued down to $461 by early March, $378 by early June, $295 by early July, and $251 by late October.
10. Information on the creation of the ISE is taken from conversations with David Krell and the following Harvard Business School Case Study: George Chacko and Eli Peter Strict, "The

International Securities Exchange: New Ground in Options Markets," Harvard Business School, 9-203-063, June 6, 2003.

11. CBOE Annual Report, 2001.

12. Options on U.S. futures contracts are traded at U.S. futures exchanges, which generally have their own clearinghouses. So, options on S&P 500 futures contracts are traded at the CME and cleared by CME Clearing, whereas options on the S&P 500 stock index are traded at the CBOE and cleared at the OCC.

13. Unless otherwise stated, all statistics in this paragraph are taken from the *Options Clearing Corporation Annual Report*, 2007, p. 14.

14. Several futures exchanges had introduced index options earlier.

15. The CBOE first created its own index, the CBOE 100, which was renamed in late 1983 the S&P 100.

16. Chicago Board Options Exchange, Incorporated Fees Schedule, August 1, 2008. The fees are quite complicated and depend on both product and type of trader. In addition, exchanges must pay index providers a fee for the use of their product, so the cost of offering an index product is greater, though because the deals are private the amount of the payment is not public.

17. An exchange-traded fund, or ETF, is an instrument that trades like a stock but is a basket of stocks that tracks some index. The first U.S. ETF was the Spider (SPDR) listed at the American Stock Exchange.

18. Mark Longo, "Tussle over Index Options: ISE Challenges CBOE's Proprietary Index Offerings in Lawsuit," *Traders Magazine*, January 1, 2007.

19. The CME and SIMEX developed a mutual offset system whereby for Eurodollar futures, a position could be put on at SIMEX, then offset later on the CME. This system lent liquidity to SIMEX's market.

20. Thanks to Nick Ronalds, currently Managing Director, FIA Asia, and President, Rho Financial, and former Director of CME's office in Tokyo, for clarification on Japanese regulations.

21. Cash settlement avoids the physical delivery of the underlying asset in the case of futures contracts. It is poorly named because it suggests that one party is giving the other one a big wad of cash in lieu of handing over the physical commodity. In fact, cash settlement is best understood by starting with the fact that in futures markets, at the end of every day, all contracts are *marked to market*, meaning that based on the closing price in the futures market for that day, all accounts that have lost money have funds transferred into all the accounts that made money. This marking to market occurs every single day, based on the closing, or *settlement*, price in the futures market. When contracts such as stock index contracts are cash settled, this simply means that on the last day of trading there is one additional and final settlement of accounts, based this time not on a futures price but on the cash price in the marketplace. This technique is used whenever physical delivery is impossible or very expensive.

22. Most stock indexes are capitalization weighted, which means that the effect of a change in a stock's price depends on the market capitalization of that stock. For example, a 10% increase in Microsoft has a bigger effect on the S&P 500 than a 10% increase of the stock in a much smaller company, because the S&P 500 is capitalization weighted. The Dow Jones Industrial Average and the Nikkei 225 are simple averages, sometimes called *price-weighted indexes*, where company size doesn't matter. In the price-weighted index, a 10% increase in a stock price will have a greater effect on the index the higher the stock price is, even if the company is a small one.

23. MSCI used to stand for Morgan Stanley Capital International but is now known as MSCI Barra. It has been publishing indexes for over 35 years and has had strong brand recognition.

24. "Ferscha's Leap," *The Economist*, January 18, 2003.

25. Thanks to John McPartland for clarifying this.

26. Joseph Weber, "Chicago, Afraid of a Little Competition?" *Business Week*, November 24, 2003, p. 111.

27. Sarah Rudolph, "Eurex US Files Second Complaint Alleging Chicago Exchanges Continue to Monopolize Market," *Securities Week*, April 4, 2005, p. 6.

28. Sarah Rudolph, "Court Denies CBOT/CME Motion to Dismiss Eurex US Antitrust Suit," *Securities Week*, August 29, 2005, p. 1.

29. Peter A. McKay, "Futures Exchanges Are Sued by Eurex on Antitrust Claims," *Wall Street Journal*, October 15, 2003, p. C1.

30. Satish Nandapurkur, Speech at FIA Chicago Luncheon, July 29, 2004, www.futuresindustry. org/downloads/divisions/chicago/EurexUS_Speech_July-29-04.pdf.

31. In fact, the first trades were in cash and derivatives contracts based on precious metals.

32. ICE also has ICE Services and ICE Data, but these are not relevant to the story of the ICE-NYMEX competition.

33. Nina Metha, "SEC Weighs Access to Foreign Marts," *Traders Magazine*, August 2007, p. 26.

34. Luke Jeffs and Tom Fairless, "Turquoise pioneer relishes the competition," Dow Jones Financial News Online, Nov. 17, 2008, www.efinancialnews.com/assetmanagement/pensionfunds/content/3352490930.

35. Citigroup, Credit Suisse, Deutsche Bank, Merrill Lynch, and Morgan Stanley.

7 Smaller to Larger: Through Organic Growth and M&A

Executive Summary

Exchanges have gotten larger. The driver is a hugely compelling need to move down the steeply declining average cost curve that now exists for exchanges because of the shift to screens. Only by continuing to reduce the average cost of a trade can exchanges remain competitive. Exchanges can grow in two ways: (1) organically, by attracting more trading in existing products and developing attractive new products, or (2) acquiring or merging with other exchanges. Even before electronic exchanges, there were mergers, usually cases of healthy exchanges taking over struggling exchanges, sometimes with the participation of the government. But the pace of M&A has accelerated as exchanges have become electronic. We explore a number of case studies of both the old and new era M&A activity.

In this chapter we explore the last of the four basic transformations of the exchanges: the growth from smaller to larger. Exchanges, like other organizations in capitalist economies, want to grow and prosper. This is true whether the exchange is owned by its members and it wants to grow to increase member opportunity or if it is stockholder-owned and it wants to grow to create opportunity for its stockholders. Members are pleased if they have greater market-making or brokerage opportunities or if their seat values increase. Stockholders are pleased if growth drives up the value of either their stocks, dividends, or both.

Organic Growth: New Contracts

Given that growth is a beneficial thing, how does an exchange go about doing it? Over the years, most exchanges have grown organically, that is via the creation of new products and the search for new customers for existing products. This is in contrast to growth via mergers and acquisitions, to which we will turn shortly. Let's first look at the derivatives exchanges. In 1955, there were precisely 61 different futures contracts listed for trading on U.S. futures exchanges and a lesser number elsewhere in the world, mainly in Japan. In Tables 7.1 and 7.2, we have listed the top 20 derivatives contracts traded globally in 1955 and then 52 years later, in 2007.

Table 7.1 Top 20 Global Futures and Options Contracts, 1955

	Exchange	Contract	Volume
1	CBOT	Soybeans	849,392
2	CBOT	Wheat	680,179
3	Osaka Sanpin Exchange	Cotton Thread #20	570,187
4	CBOT	Corn	491,074
5	Osaka Chem Textile Exch	Synthetic Silk Thread	436,043
6	CME	Eggs	400,545
7	Tokyo Grain Exchange	Azuki Bean	399,519
8	NYCE	Cotton	342,870
9	Tokyo Textile Exchange	Synthetic Silk Thread	249,878
10	Osaka Chem Textile Exch	Wool	202,675
11	Osaka Sugar Exchange	Refined Sugar	202,409
12	Osaka Sanpin Exchange	Cotton Thread #30	197,781
13	Tokyo Rubber Exchange	Rubber RSS #3	182,603
14	Osaka Grain Exchange	Azuki Bean	154,157
15	CME	Onions	147,792
16	Tokyo Sugar Exchange	Refined Sugar	142,579
17	CBOT	Oats	131,852
18	CBOT	Rye	130,994
19	NYMEX	Potatoes	124,617
20	NOCE	Cotton	121,490
	Total		6,158,636

Source: Futures Industry Association Volume Reports and Tokyo Grain Exchange.

A comparison of these two charts makes it clear that organic growth, via new product development and expansion of demand for existing products, has been a major feature of the global derivatives market. Specifically,

- Product innovation over the 52-year period had been sufficiently strong that not one single contract that was in the top 20 list in 1955 was still in the top 20 list in 2007. And none of the top 20 contracts of 2007 even existed in 1955.
- The number-one derivatives contract in 1955 was the Chicago Board of Trade soybean contract, with an annual turnover or volume of 849,000 contracts. The number-one derivatives contract in 2007 was the Korea Exchange's KOSPI 200 option contract, with a turnover of 2.6 billion contracts, about 3000 times as large.
- The total turnover of the top 20 contracts in 1955 was 6 million. The turnover in 2007 was 7.3 billion, about 1000 times as large.

Table 7.2 Top 20 Global Futures and Options Contracts, 2007

	Exchange	Contract	Volume
1	KRX	KOSPI 200 (Options)	2,642,675,246
2	CME	Eurodollars	621,470,328
3	CME	E-mini S&P 500	415,348,228
4	CME (CBOT)	10-yr Treasury Notes	349,229,371
5	Eurex	Euro-Bund	338,319,416
6	EUREX	DJ Euro Stoxx 50	327,034,149
7	CME	Eurodollar (Options)	313,032,264
8	EUREX	DJ Euro Stoxx 50 (Options)	251,438,870
9	BM&F	1-Day Inter-Bank Deposits	221,627,417
10	LIFFE (NYSE Euronext)	Three-Month Euribor	221,411,485
11	MEXDER	TIIE 28	220,608,024
12	Multiple US	Powershares QQQ ETF (Options)	185,807,535
13	EUREX	Euro-Schatz	181,101,310
14	EUREX	Euro-Bobl	170,909,055
15	CME	Five-Year Treasury Notes	166,207,391
16	CBOE	S&P 500 (Options)	158,084,691
17	Multiple US	iShares Russell 2000 ETF (Options)	154,059,054
18	Multiple US	SPDR S&P 500 ETF (Options)	141,614,736
19	NSE India	S&P CNX Nifty	138,794,235
20	NYMEX	Light, Sweet Crude Oil	121,525,967
	Total		7,340,298,772

Source: Futures Industry Association Volume Reports.

- Though not portrayed in the two charts, if we compare the volume of the top three CBOT contracts in 1955 to their volume in 2008, we find:[1]
  - Soybean volume was 46 times greater in 2008.
  - Wheat volume was 32 times greater in 2008.
  - Corn volume was 136 times greater in 2008.

Comparing the Top 20 Contracts in 1955 with the Top 20 in 2007

- Japan dominated half of the top 20 list in 1955 but was totally absent in 2007.
- Every single contract in 1955 was a physical commodity contract, whereas by 2007 the top 19 were all financial (10 interest rate, 9 equity index), with crude oil in 20th place.

- Cotton was still such a sufficiently important product in 1955 that four (20%) of the top 20 contracts were related to cotton (raw cotton in the United States and cotton thread in Japan).
- Though the top 20 contracts of 1955 represented only two countries, the United States and Japan, the 2007 top 20 list was much more diverse, including contracts from Korea, the United States, Germany, Brazil, the United Kingdom (or Paris, if you consider the headquarters of Euronext), Mexico, and India.
- Six (30%) of the top 20 contracts in 2007 were options contracts, whereas options did not make the 1955 list, because stock and futures exchanges had not yet begun to list options. The world's first stand-alone options exchange was the Chicago Board Options Exchange in 1973.
- The Chicago Board of Trade, for many years considered the global king of futures trading, appeared five times in 1955 but only once in 2007. Only its 10-year Treasury Note contract was big enough to make the list, and because it had been acquired by the CME in the summer of 2007, it appears only as a division of the CME Group.
- The CME has five of the top 20 contracts in 2007 but appeared only twice in the earlier 1955 list, for eggs and onions, both of which had vanished by 2007. The egg industry changed in such a way that production seasonality and storage disappeared, and without inventories of eggs, there was no longer much need to manage risk with egg futures, so they just slowly faded away. The CME onion contract was actually banned by Congress in 1958 and is the only U.S. contract to ever have been banned by the federal government.
- Representing a trend toward consolidation and concentration, the top 20 contracts in 2005 were distributed among 12 exchanges, whereas the top 20 contracts in 2007 were distributed among only nine exchanges—25% fewer.

So, starting with these 61 contracts that existed in 1955, over the next 50 years another 842 futures contracts were added in the United States. That's about 17 new contracts a year. Outside the United States, the pace was even faster, since during the shorter 25-year period from 1980 to 2005, international exchanges created 887 new futures contracts, or about 35 new futures contracts per year. Over half of these contracts (both U.S. and global) died within a few years, but some of the surviving ones contributed significantly to the growth of the world's futures exchanges. In the United States, the contracts driving exchange growth were mostly launched in the 1980s (e.g., Eurodollars in 1981 and the S&P 500[2] in 1982, both at the CME).

In the rest of the world, where exchanges were created more recently, the blockbuster contracts that contributed significantly to the growth of these exchanges were created in the late 1990s and into the new millennium. For example, the one-day interest rate contract at the Brazilian BM&F accounts for 55% of all futures trading at the giant exchange, yet was started only in 2004 (see Table 7.3). Or at the extreme case, the dollar/peso contract traded at ROFEX in Rosario, Argentina, represents 99% of all trading volume on

Table 7.3 Top Futures Product at Selected International Exchanges, 1Q2008

Exchange	Top Product	Top Product Volume (millions)	Total Exchange Volume (millions)	Share	Start
Dalian Commodity Exchange	No. 1 Soybeans	26.8	79.1	34%	2002
BM&F (Brazil)	One-Day Interbank Deposit	46.4	84.8	55%	2004
BSE (Hungary)	Budapest Stock Index	1.2	4.7	26%	1995
EUREX	DJ Euro STOXX 50	112.2	338.4	33%	1997
LIFFE UK	Three-Month Euribor	72.9	149.1	49%	1998
Korea Exchange	KOSPI 200	12.6	18.4	68%	1996
ROFEX (Argentina)	Dollar/Peso	7.1	7.2	99%	2002
MEXDER	TIIE 28	20	21.5	93%	2002
NSE (India)	S&P CNX Nifty	45.9	100.3	46%	2001
RTS (Russia)	RTS Index	20.6	45.4	45%	2005
SIMEX	Nikkei 225	5.7	14.7	39%	1986
Taiwan Futures Exchange	Taiex	4.2	7.4	57%	1998
Osaka Securities Exchange	Nikkei 225 Mini	20.2	29.4	69%	2006
Total		395.8	900.4	44%	

Source: FIA Volume Reports.

the exchange, yet the contract was started as recently as 2002. In Japan, at the Osaka Securities Exchange, which has been in the derivatives business since 1987, its largest contract is the Nikkei 225 Mini, which started in 2006. So the strategy of organic growth from product innovation has been quite important.

Global data on the equity exchanges is not readily available as far back as the derivatives data, but according to the records kept by the World Federation of Exchanges, the value of global share trading increased from $9.7 trillion in 1994 to $200.8 trillion in 2007.[3] This 1970% increase in trading value was attributable mainly to more trading in existing products, since the number of listed companies increased only 37% over that same period, from 30,186 listed companies in 1994 to 41,351 listed companies in 2007. So again there was a significant amount of organic growth among stock exchanges, but little of it came from a net increase in company listings. As discussed in the later chapter on product innovation, stock exchanges in some countries have benefited from the recent rapid growth in the number of, and trading in, exchange-traded funds (ETFs).

Organic Growth: New Users

In other cases, the exchanges have grown significantly from either the entry of new users or the growth of one of those groups of users. For example, the CME's Eurodollar contract has benefited greatly from the rapid and sustained growth of the interest rate swaps market. Swaps dealers entering into agreements to swap fixed for floating interest rate payments (or vice versa) would hedge their net risk in Eurodollar futures. In the case of energy derivatives, the rise of energy merchandisers and marketers in the 1990s has significantly driven increased volumes in crude oil and natural gas. And of course the rise of managed futures and hedge funds, which often make extensive use of derivative markets, has contributed significantly to increased volumes at many different exchanges.

One other serendipitous source of volume gains, at least at those exchanges that are or have become electronic, is the rise of algorithmic trading.[4] Algorithmic traders are often making tens or even hundreds of trades per second and contributing significantly to volume growth at exchanges. And whether they utilize algorithmic trading systems or are staffed by somewhat old-fashioned point-and-click electronic traders, proprietary trading shops have popped up in a number of places and also have contributed to volume growth. Of course, electronic markets, especially those with direct access, make these markets accessible to anyone with a computer and money to trade and should significantly expand the customer base in the future.

There are limits to what organic growth can do for an exchange. We have established that exchanges worldwide have added many new futures contracts over the past few decades. We also noted that most of these contracts are simply not successful. In countries where derivatives markets are newer, there have been some recent contributors to significant volume growth, as pointed out earlier. But in the more mature markets, it is much more difficult to do this. First, in mature markets, the best fruit has been picked long back. The blockbuster contracts were those that were created in the 1970s or 1980s (thus most of the trading volume at the CME comes from contracts created in 1981 and 1982). So it is difficult today to find brand-new ideas that translate into futures contracts with high volumes. Attempts to create clones of successful contracts at other exchanges generally do not work either, because of the liquidity-driven monopoly problem. What this means is that once an exchange has established a reasonable degree of liquidity, typically with a relatively large number of buyers and sellers who are always ready to deal and therefore create relatively tight bid-ask spreads, no one will trade the same product at a new exchange that decides to list it, because there are few buyers and sellers to trade with. So attempts to establish clones of successful contracts usually fail. This results in a monopoly in that product for the exchange that lists first and develops a reasonable degree of liquidity.

There may be more room at newer international exchanges to grow organically. As shown in Table 7.3, the top products at these exchanges were typically started much more recently; the average age of the blockbuster contracts is about 10 years. In China, the top product is soybeans because the government has not, as of late 2008, given the go-ahead for the new financial exchange to start trading. Once it does, there will be a huge opportunity for growth in financial products, and it will be only a few years before the top product is a stock index or government bond rate rather than soybeans. Note also that the top product on average accounts for over half of total exchange volume in these markets. But this is not much different than the United States. Before the mergers with the CBOT and NYMEX, the CME's top product, Eurodollars, accounted for about half of total volume, and the top two, Eurodollars and the E-Mini S&P 500, accounted for about 75% of total CME volume. One does worry a bit, however, about MexDer (Mexico) and ROFEX (Argentina), where a single product accounts for 93–99% of total volume.

Growth via Mergers and Acquisitions

We started this chapter by saying that there were two ways for an exchange to grow. The first was to grow organically by either adding new products or adding customers to existing contracts. The second way to grow is to add products to an exchange's portfolio by simply buying those products indirectly through the purchase of another exchange that has contracts that are different from those at the acquiring exchange. And different exchanges almost always have different products because the liquidity-driven monopoly tendency leaves most exchanges with a unique set of products. For example, when the CME and CBOT merged in the summer of 2007, there was not a single duplicate active contract between the two exchanges. Not a single one of the CME's 88 contracts was actively traded at the CBOT. So the CME acquired a solid set of new product lines in this acquisition, including futures and options on U.S. Treasuries and grains. Likewise, when the CME bought NYMEX, it acquired new product lines in derivatives on energy and metals.

Though there have been mergers throughout the history of futures and stock exchanges, they were relatively rare. The CME, for example, experienced spectacular growth until 2007 based only on creating new futures and options contracts and developing their customer base, without ever participating in a merger. The CBOT, during its almost 150-year history, has absorbed only two other exchanges, both incredibly tiny.[5] The Kansas City Board of Trade and the Minneapolis Grain Exchange have had long histories without any merger or acquisition. On the stock side, the New York Stock Exchange and the London Stock Exchange trace their histories back over 200 and 300 years, respectively, but neither participated in a merger till 2005 (NYSE with Archipelago) and 2007 (LSE with Borsa Italiana). There have, of course, been mergers of exchanges, especially when one of the two exchanges is beginning to have trouble surviving on its own and needs to be folded into another exchange to consolidate the administration of the two.

There was an earlier wave of exchange consolidation driven by the first round of technological change in communications—the telegraph, ticker tape, and telephone.[6] Before the development of these early communications devices, exchanges were established in multiple commercial centers throughout a number of countries. For example, the United States once had 250 different stock exchanges. India had 23. England had 20. Information had to be delivered by foot or horseback, so every significant urban center needed its own market. With the development of the telegraph, the telephone, and the ticker tape, it became much easier to both know the almost real-time prices at distant exchanges and to trade on those exchanges. So distance began to matter much less, and traders began to seek out the exchanges with the greatest liquidity for the stocks in which they were interested. This resulted in a tendency toward consolidation and the elimination of duplicate products at multiple exchanges spread all over the country. Of course, the regional exchanges that went into decline would sometimes fight the trend by getting the state to intervene. For example, there was a rule in India that required each company to list itself on the exchange closest to its headquarters, even if it was listed on the country's major exchange at the time, the Bombay Stock Exchange. So firms based in Calcutta (today called Kolkata) would generally list at the BSE but would be required to also list and pay listing fees to the Calcutta Stock Exchange. After the screen-based National Stock Exchange (NSE) was created in 1994 and the BSE shifted from floor to screen to survive, virtually all trading shifted to the NSE and BSE, and the 20 or so regional exchanges were left with no trading activity, though they still earned listing fees because of this rule. The rule was finally dropped early in the new millennium, and then the regional exchanges really did die.[7]

Though the Indian consolidation took place with very little merger activity, the case has been just the opposite in Japan. In fact, we know of no country in which there was such a rapid period of consolidation as there was in Japan during the 1990s and early 2000s (see Figure 7.1). Japan has long had a large number of physical commodity exchanges in commercial centers of various sizes spread throughout the country.[8] In 1991 there were 17 Japanese derivatives exchanges based on physical commodities. By 2007 those 17 exchanges

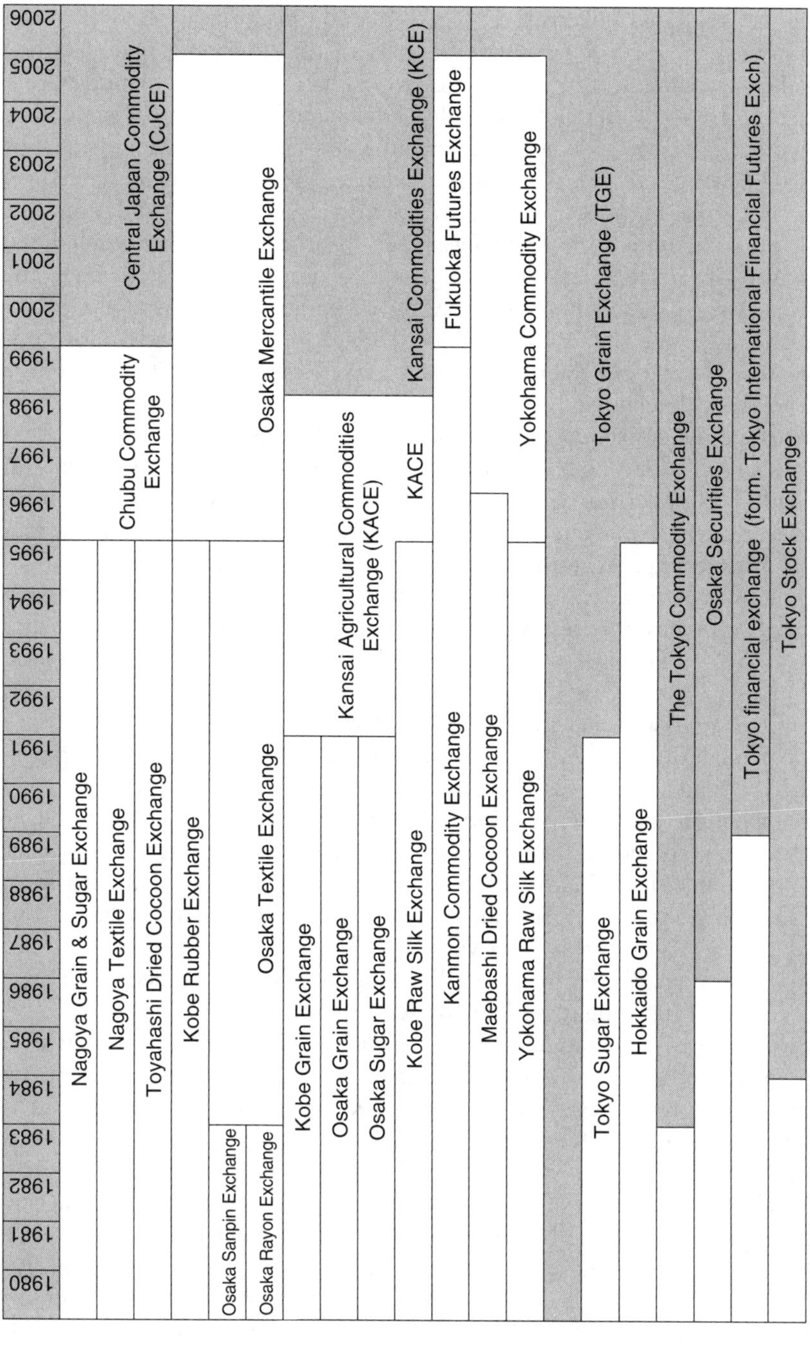

Figure 7.1 Mergers of Japanese exchanges, 1980–2008.

had been consolidated into four, a 75% reduction in the number of physical commodity exchanges. For example, the Tokyo Grain Exchange had absorbed three other exchanges: the Tokyo Sugar Exchange, the Hokkaido Grain Exchange, and the Yokohama Commodity Exchange. The Kansai Commodities Exchange had absorbed five exchanges: the Kobe Grain Exchange, the Kobe Raw Silk Exchange, the Osaka Grain Exchange, the Osaka Sugar Exchange, and the Fukuoka Futures Exchange. And in the largest consolidation, the Central Japan Commodity Exchange had absorbed six other exchanges: the Nagoya Grain and Sugar Exchange, the Nagoya Textile Exchange, the Toyahashi Dried Cocoon Exchange, the Kobe Rubber Exchange, the Osaka Sanpin Exchange, and the Osaka Rayon Exchange.[9] In fact, by the end of these 21 mergers, only one old exchange name survived from the 1980s and that is the Tokyo Grain Exchange.

What drove the consolidation was the fact that some of the more regional exchanges simply could not compete with the larger, more liquid exchanges in Tokyo and Osaka and thus were not able to continue to operate a viable business. These Japanese mergers often involved government coaxing and were a mix of government guidance and exchange strategy. Remember, these exchanges are still member owned, so mergers are a bit more complicated. So it was the Ministry of Agriculture, Forestry, and Fisheries (MAFF) that recommended that the Tokyo Sugar Exchange merge into the Tokyo Grain Exchange. However, the Yokahama Commodity Exchange found itself in a very difficult financial situation and requested that the TGE take them over.[10]

The consolidation in Japan was driven by changes in technology—specifically, falling communication costs, as mentioned earlier—and it involved weaker exchanges that were losing volume being taken over by stronger exchanges that were gaining volume. And this was the way things went worldwide. For example, in 1979 the Cocoa Exchange in New York had been for a decade shrinking about 3% per year, while the Coffee and Sugar Exchange had been expanding 8% per year. In a very logical move, the much stronger and more rapidly growing Coffee and Sugar Exchange took over the Cocoa Exchange to become the Coffee, Sugar, and Cocoa Exchange.[11]

This principle of a dynamic, growing exchange absorbing an exchange in decline was played out in an important U.S. merger that took place before the exchanges began to switch to screens and become public companies, and it illustrates the difficulty of executing a merger between two member-owned exchanges. Until its merger with the CME in 2008, which is part of the new age of exchange mergers, NYMEX had experienced a single merger, the one with COMEX in 1994. The NYMEX and COMEX merger is a great example of how difficult it can be to execute a merger between two not-for-profit, member-owned exchanges. For years, the two exchanges had talked about the possibility of merging. In the autumn of 1987, consulting company Arthur D. Little, Inc., recommended that the two exchanges merge their boards, their administrative staffs, and their clearing mechanisms. COMEX officials had supported the merger for some time, but it now appeared that NYMEX officials were also ready to buy into the Arthur D. Little recommendations. So it was not surprising that in the summer of 1988 industry publication headlines trumpeted, "New York exchanges edge towards merger" and reported that NYMEX officials had finally reached a decision to go ahead with a merger plan.[12] Two weeks later, the merger was off, supposedly because of pushback from NYMEX members. Feelings and rivalries between exchange memberships run deep, and the summer 1988 merger of COMEX and NYMEX proved to be just another false alarm. Then in early 1990, the two exchanges announced that they were exploring a merger and that they would form a joint governing board that would oversee any merged exchange.[13] After a year of discussion, on February 19, 1991, COMEX announced that it had rejected a NYMEX proposal and NYMEX announced, "Having reconciled all differences over material terms, including a generous offer to allow trading privileges, we are saddened by the failure of our colleagues to accept the proposal."[14]

Finally, three years later, in the spring of 1994, came the real deal. The two exchanges announced that they were, in fact, going to finally merge. On the evening of April 25, 1994, the members of the two exchanges had an opportunity to cast their votes. The NYMEX required a simple majority vote to pass the resolution and 83% of the members voted in favor of the merger. COMEX had a stricter standard, requiring a two thirds majority. They barely made it, with 72% of the COMEX members voting yes.

Why were so many COMEX members still opposed? What is important to understand is that COMEX had once been the big exchange based largely on gold trading and NYMEX the much smaller one. As gold fell out of favor and investors turned to other assets (such as U.S. Treasury securities) as a safe haven in uncertain times, and as the importance of crude oil increased, not only were there the normal jealousies over losing rank, but COMEX members began to worry about their future. Seat prices are a good measure of the health of an exchange. The COMEX seat price, which had been $325,000 in 1974, had fallen by two thirds, to $100,000, shortly before the 1994 vote. This was the result of falling volume and revenues, including a 1992 volume drop of 27% and a net revenue decline of 80%.

But in the months leading up to the vote, volume and revenue began to increase. So, the Exchange's improving fortunes made many COMEX members feel that they no longer needed to merge with the larger NYMEX to have a viable exchange. Right before the vote, COMEX members began circulating letters among themselves arguing that the proposed NYMEX payment was too small and the loss of control was too great. In fact, one COMEX director wrote that "the merger will transform COMEX into an essentially colonial backwater of NYMEX."[15] On March 1, one group of COMEX members took the legal route and sued both NYMEX and COMEX in a class action suit to block the proposed merger. But when the vote finally came on April 25, 1994, 72% of the members, 5 percentage points above the required 67%, was enough to approve the merger. On July 22, 1994, the CFTC gave its approval, and the merger became a reality. The deal itself made COMEX a wholly owned subsidiary of NYMEX and gave COMEX members $62 million—$42 million at the close of the deal and $20 million spread over the next four years. It should be noted that in contrast to the mergers of the new millennium, this was not a full merger, since each market retained its own memberships and trading rights.

The only U.S. exchange that is the result of multiple mergers involving a number of exchanges is the New York Board of Trade (NYBOT), which in 1997 was purchased by ICE and recently renamed ICE Futures US. The final merger to form NYBOT involved combining the New York Cotton Exchange (NYCE) with the Coffee, Sugar, and Cocoa Exchange (CSCE) in 1998. But the NYCE had already acquired the almost dormant New York Futures Exchange from the NYSE in 1995. And the CSCE was itself a 1979 merger of the Coffee and Sugar Exchange and the Cocoa exchange. The roots of these components go back to 1870 for the NY Cotton Exchange, 1882 for the Coffee Exchange (renamed the Coffee and Sugar Exchange in 1916), and 1925 for the NY Cocoa Exchange.

From Coffee to NYBOT to ICE Futures

1870	New York Cotton Exchange founded
1882	Coffee Exchange founded
1914	Coffee Exchange adds Sugar as new product
1916	Name changed to New York Coffee and Sugar Exchange
1925	New York Cocoa Exchange founded
1979	New York Futures Exchange founded (NYSE subsidiary)
1979	NY Cocoa merges with NY Coffee and Sugar to create New York Coffee, Sugar, & Cocoa Exchange
1985	New York Cotton Exchange creates its FINEX division to list currencies
1995	New York Cotton Exchange acquires New York Futures Exchange
1998	New York Cotton Exchange merges with New York Coffee, Sugar, & Cocoa Exchange to create the New York Board of Trade (NYBOT)
2007	Intercontinental Exchange (ICE) buys NYBOT for $1 billion ($400 million cash plus rest in ICE shares) and renames exchange ICE Futures US

The New Era of Exchange M&A

Beginning in the new millennium, M&A activity no longer was something that occurred occasionally because there was a weak exchange that needed to be acquired by a stronger exchange; it occurred out of necessity, because of the fundamental transformation of exchanges away from floors and onto screens.

When exchanges became electronic, economic cost curves shifted, and there were very, very strong economies of scale to be gained from processing an increasingly greater number of trades on an exchange. In a floor-based world, adding new products involved incurring significant costs to earn the new revenues that would accrue from increased trading. New floor space had to be found to build the pits for the new contracts, and new bodies had to be put into those pits to make markets and trade. In a screen-based environment, all one needed was more server space to match orders and disseminate prices for the new contracts.

So, exchanges that could expand trading in their existing contracts or could add product lines (whether by launching new products or acquiring them via an acquisition) would significantly lower their average costs per contract traded and therefore increase their profits. Electronic exchanges left behind with a small number of products and a small level of trading activity would experience much higher average costs per contract traded and much poorer profits. To survive and prosper, exchanges had to get bigger by increasing the number of contracts traded on their electronic platforms. This need to get larger resulted in a frantic quest to merge with other exchanges.

This significant ramping up of the economies of scale factor created by the shift to screens drove exchanges to want to merge, but it was another transformation we've discussed that made it easier for them to merge. That of course was the shift from private clubs to public companies. To create a merger between two public companies, you have to convince the shareholders that it's a good idea. For many public companies, a large number of shareholders hold small ownership positions in the company, and these shareholders rarely get in the way of a merger proposed by management and the Board. Even the large shareholders generally view their stock as a financial asset, and they are looking for a good return on their investment. So when a merger makes sense, shareholders rarely get in the way. Not-for-profit member-owned exchanges are a different animal altogether. Exchange members often have a strong emotional view of their exchange, and their exchange membership generally represents a much larger part of their net worth than does a stockholder's shares in any given company. The exchange is the place they go to work every day. They have a bond with other exchange members, not dissimilar to the bonds shared among classmates at the same high school or college. For exchanges in the same city (like the CME and CBOT, or the NYMEX and COMEX), there are often rivalries, as there would be between two football teams. So when members are making a decision regarding whether to merge with another exchange, especially a cross-town rival, it is not a cold, steely-eyed business decision but instead one infused with a significant degree of emotion.

In addition, though there are clear rules for managing mergers and acquisitions among public companies, this is much less the case for nonprofit, member-owned institutions. So it should have been no surprise that the merger between the two not-for-profit exchanges, COMEX and NYMEX, took over six years of on and off and on again negotiations, whereas the CME/CBOT merger of two publicly traded companies took less than two years.[16]

Once an exchange becomes screen-based, it has a strong need to merge to lower average costs and pump up profits, and if it also becomes a publicly traded company it becomes much easier to merge and it almost has to engage in the merger game. Let's take a look at a few mergers that have been part of this new age of exchange M&A. The first is the story of two mergers entered into by the New York Stock Exchange. The first merger, with Archipelago, actually brought the NYSE into the modern era of electronic, publicly traded exchanges. The second merger, with Euronext, was a new age merger, with the special characteristic that it was the first trans-Atlantic exchange merger.

The Merger-Driven Transformation of the NYSE

The NYSE has done a lot of things in its 200-plus-year history. It has created stock indexes, listed ADRs, listed ETFs, opened the trading floor to women in 1943 and to foreign brokers in 1977, but never in its history until 2006 did it participate in a merger. It has now done three mergers, and it is the first two of these three mergers that have completely transformed the exchange and clearly set its path for the future. The three mergers were with an important electronic equities market, called Archipelago, with the pan-European stock exchange called Euronext, and with the NYSE's 150-year-old rival, the American Stock Exchange. We discuss each of these mergers in turn.

The first merger was the NYSE's merger with a Chicago-based electronic exchange called Archipelago. It was this merger that gave the NYSE a solid electronic matching engine, and because Archipelago was already a listed company, it gave the NYSE a listing.

After considerable negotiation and discussion, on April 20, 2005, the NYSE and Archipelago Exchange announced that their boards had approved a definitive merger agreement that would lead to the creation of a new publicly held company called NYSE Group Inc. It was noted that if the agreement was consummated, it would result in the world's largest-ever merger between two securities exchanges. The deal still had to be approved by the members of the NYSE, because the NYSE was still a member-owned entity, and the shareholders of Archipelago, because Archipelago was a publicly traded company. It also, of course, required the approval of the SEC.

The votes were no problem, since the members knew that the NYSE needed to become electronic to compete, and neither was the SEC approval, though it took seven months to obtain the latter. The approval came on November 3, 2005, and on that day the two exchanges announced that the NYSE members and the Archipelago stockholders would be voting on the merger approximately one month later, on December 6. The NYSE rules required that the merger be approved by two thirds of the votes cast by a quorum of NYSE members. The NYSE had 1366 members. Over 90% of those members participated in the vote, and over 95% of the members voting approved the merger. This was nothing like the merger of NYMEX and COMEX back in the mid-1990s, when the votes were much closer. However, not everyone was happy with the merger.

On May 9, William Higgins, an NYSE member for many years, filed a class-action suit against the NYSE directors, trying to stop the merger between the two exchanges on the terms that had been agreed to. Mr. Higgins argued that the NYSE members were being sold short. And though he was not against the merger per se, he felt that it should not go forward under current terms. For one thing, he argued that it made no sense that the proposed merger was valuing the NYSE at less than $3 billion, whereas the Chicago Mercantile Exchange was at the time valued at $7 billion. The lawsuit pointed out that an exchange expert, Benn Steil of the Council on Foreign Relations, had written that the NYSE seat holders should receive as much as 90% of the combined company, not the 70% contained in the current merger agreement. It further argued that though the majority of Archipelago shareholders were free to immediately sell the shares they received in the new merged entity, NYSE members who received such shares were subject to sale restrictions of up to five years. Finally, the suit complained that under the terms of the merger agreement, the NYSE could retain up to 5% of the shares in the company and allocate them to NYSE executive employees who structured the merger agreement.[17]

Whether it paid too much or just the right amount, this first merger made the NYSE into a for-profit, stockholder-owned, publicly listed exchange with serious screen-based capabilities and thus brought it into the new emerging model for exchanges. It was the second merger that made the NYSE truly international and gave it a serious stake in derivatives. In fact, this second merger between the largest U.S. stock exchange and the second largest European stock exchange was the most significant merger of exchanges that has taken place in recent times. The merger between the NYSE and Euronext was significant because it represented not only a merger of two exchanges in different countries but also two exchanges on different continents. It was also the largest merger in value terms of two exchanges to date.

In promoting the merger, NYSE CEO John Thain promised $375 million in merger benefits, $275 million of which came from reduced costs, especially in technology, because the plan was to reduce the number of trading systems at the exchanges from the current six platforms down to two platforms.[18]

In the deal itself, NYSE had to beat out Deutsche Börse, and it did so by offering $10.2 billion in cash and shares. This took place on May 22, 2006. Even though the German exchange came back the next day with a higher bid, Euronext still took the NYSE Group's offer and struck a deal, subject of course to the vote of shareholders and the approval of regulators on both sides of the Atlantic. The European regulators approved the merger on December 5, 2006, causing the Euronext share price to rise 3%. The SEC approval came shortly thereafter. This paved the way for the shareholder votes, which took place on

December 19, 2006, for Euronext shareholders and December 20, 2006, for NYSE shareholders. Both groups enthusiastically approved the merger. Ultimately, the deal was valued at $14.2 billion, and Euronext shareholders received .98 shares in the new merged company's stock plus $21.32 cash for each Euronext share.

Before the merger with Euronext, the NYSE Group Inc. operated two separate securities exchanges. One of them was the traditional New York Stock Exchange. The second was NYSE Arca, the electronic exchange that the NYSE had earlier acquired. In addition to the exchange listed securities, NYSE Arca listed exchange-traded funds and stock options. At the time of the merger, both NYSE and Euronext were publicly traded, for-profit companies. The new company became effective and began trading on April 4, 2007, and was listed on both the exchanges. So it began trading in Paris at 9:00 a.m. Paris time and in New York at 9:30 a.m. New York time.

The third merger, with the NYSE's 166-year-old rival, the American Stock Exchange (AMEX), was really a combination of the old type of merger and the new type. It was an old-type merger in the sense that it involved a stronger dynamic exchange merging with one that was considerably weaker and in some degree of decline. The AMEX had historically been a much stronger innovator than the NYSE. It was the AMEX that had pioneered the U.S. listing of exchange-traded funds (ETFs) in 1993 with the S&P 500-based SPDR ETF. However, due to its tiny size, representing only about 1% of all U.S. equity trading, the AMEX was unable to consolidate its leading ETF position, and in recent years, even though it held the lead in the number of ETFs listed, it had fallen behind the NYSE in terms of the value of turnover in ETFs.

The merger was a classic new-age merger in the sense that it took advantage of the huge economies of scale of NYSE ARCA, the electronic trading engine on the U.S. side of the NYSE Euronext family. By transferring the 381 ETFs that were traded on the AMEX floor to trade alongside the 240 ETFs that were already being traded on the NYSE Arca platform, the NYSE was able to significantly reduce the cost per trade on NYSE Arca. At the same time, this move converted the ETF business in the United States from something like a duopoly to something more like a monopoly. After the merger, NYSE Arca had 96% of the ETFs listed in the United States. The only other ETFs traded in the United States were the 25 at the Nasdaq and one at the CBOE.

There was little trouble getting the merger passed by either the NYSE shareholders or the AMEX members. On June 17, 2008, the members of the AMEX voted 695 to seven in favor of being acquired by the NYSE Euronext. Since not everyone voted, the 695 voting in favor of the merger represented 84% of the total memberships outstanding at the AMEX.[19] What the deal meant financially was that the AMEX would receive $260 million in NYSE Euronext common stock and, following the expected sale of the old AMEX headquarters, members would receive additional NYSE Euronext stock equal in value to the net proceeds from that sale.[20]

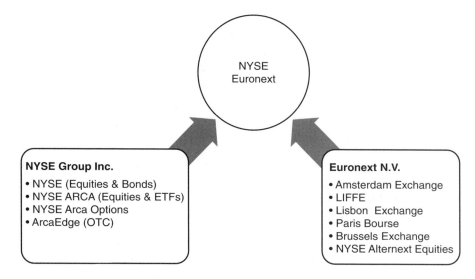

Figure 7.2 NYSE Euronext merger.

As this is written, there has been no public announcement as to how AMEX will be integrated into this increasingly big family of exchanges. It is clear that the AMEX ETFs are being shifted to NYSE Arca's electronic platform to join the ETFs that are already there. The AMEX options will move from the AMEX floor to either the NYSE floor or the Arca Options floor in San Francisco. And it is likely that the listed AMEX stocks would go to a new AMEX-branded entity similar to the Alternext platform in Europe, which was created by Euronext for listing small and medium-sized companies that couldn't meet the listing standards of the five Euronext exchanges.

The structure of the exchange after the mergers looked something like Figure 7.2.

First, there are still two main subsidiaries, one in the United States and one in Europe. The two exchanges do have about 40 members in common, but there is not yet direct seamless access to all products for most investors, though the Exchange is working on a Common Customer Gateway. The chart shows four subsidiary entities to NYSE Group Inc. and six subsidiary groups to Euronext N.V. The NYSE is really the old New York Stock Exchange and includes the old floor as well as the new electronic bond platform. NYSE Arca is the electronic platform for NYSE listed stocks and ETFs as well as AMEX and Nasdaq listed stocks and ETFs. NYSE Arca Options includes electronic and San Francisco floor-trading of all options. Finally, ArcaEdge is the platform for small, unlisted, OTC traded stocks.

On the European side there are the four underlying Euronext stock exchanges, in Amsterdam, Brussels, Paris, and Lisbon, and each of these exchanges lists both stocks and derivatives. Then there is the big London derivatives exchange called LIFFE (for London International Financial Futures Exchange), which is still the fourth largest derivatives exchange in the world (after the CME, the Korea Exchange, and Eurex). Finally, there is NYSE Alternext, which is a more lightly regulated trading platform for small and medium-sized companies from three Euronext countries—France, Belgium and the Netherlands.

The LSE: The Exchange That Couldn't Say Yes

It seemed like everybody wanted to buy the London Stock Exchange, the biggest stock exchange in Europe. The frantic pursuit of mergers was driven by the need to spread the relatively fixed costs of electronic trading over lots of transactions to get average costs down and profits up. The bigger the merger partner, the bigger the effect, especially if redundancies (in staff and facilities) can be quickly eliminated. Deutsche Börse was one of the first and went after the LSE in 2000. Private discussions had been going on for some time, but before the merger was publicly announced, the LSE got some egg on its face by accidentally faxing out the wrong document to the British media. The LSE had just hired a new chief executive, and they were set to send out a press release on the new guy. Someone grabbed the wrong document, a secret memo for dealing with the media should the German-British merger fail to become reality. Specifically, the plan called for LSE representatives to make "statesmen like expressions of regret," should the merger discussions get derailed, but because the British press would be looking for someone to blame, the idea was to informally let the press know that the fault was that of the Germans because of their intransigence and lack of a shared vision with the LSE.[21] The LSE leaders were to come off looking appropriately patrician, while the Germans would take the heat.

Despite the gaffe the talks continued, and in fact, *The Wall Street Journal* ran a headline on May 1, 2000, which read, "UK, German exchanges likely to announce merger this week." It would have created the single European stock market that many securities firms had called for since the creation of the Euro Zone, would have facilitated sector-based investing as opposed to country-based and would have been twice the size of Euronext. When the article was published, the Deutsche Börse Board had just met and approved the deal, and the LSE board was expected to do likewise, and then the shareholders of both exchanges would have to vote. The LSE board did approve the merger, and the shareholder votes were scheduled for September 14.

Then three weeks before the shareholder votes, OM Gruppen of Sweden approached the LSE about a friendly takeover, was rejected, and came back the following week with a hostile $1.19 billion takeover bid. A week and a half later, on September 12, 2000, the LSE decided that it needed to pull out of the merger discussions with Deutsche Börse so that it could focus on the defeat of the hostile bid from OM. The LSE was also getting pushback from a number of its members who felt the proposed merger with the Germans undervalued the LSE, would not achieve the savings promised, was too vague in parts, and involved management risk, given the management style of Deutsche Börse Chief Executive Weiner Seifert, who was slated to become chief executive of the merged organization.[22] The LSE also said that there were still too many issues raised by a cross-border consolidation that had not yet been resolved.[23] By November, the OM hostile bid had been defeated, but not before OM Chief Executive Per Larsson claimed that, "After the shambles of iX (the attempted merger with Deutsche Börse), the LSE is now trying to stake a claim to maximizing shareholder value: yet it is obvious that the LSE has no strategy, no management and no vision."

But nobody was more persistent than Nasdaq Chief Executive Bob Greifeld. In 2002, Nasdaq attempted to purchase the LSE. One of the big concerns was whether the LSE could get a concession from the U.S. Securities and Exchange Commission that a merger with Nasdaq could be done without the SEC seeking to supervise the LSE part of the merged entity. The LSE did not want to be regulated by the SEC.[24] But the merger fell apart after regulators in the United States and the United Kingdom could not agree on precisely how they would oversee the combined market. Every merger involves some degree of regulatory risk, a risk that can be greater if the two entities have different regulators. Following that failed attempt, the LSE was pursued by both Deutsche Börse (again) in 2004 and Macquarie Bank, and both made offers and both were rejected by the LSE. Euronext attempted to merge with the LSE, but those talks failed as well and in 2006, the two failed suitors, Euronext and Deutsche Börse, began talking about hooking up with each other.

Then in March 2006, Nasdaq came back with a new £2.4 billion offer, which was again rejected by the LSE. Not taking no for an answer, Greifeld then embarked on a different path and began buying up shares from other large holders of LSE stock. On April 11, 2006, Nasdaq purchased all the stock held by the Ameriprise Financial's Threadneedle Asset Management unit, the LSE's largest shareholder. Threadneedle transferred its 35.4 million shares to Nasdaq for £11.75 per share. NASDAQ then purchased another 2.69 million LSE shares from an undisclosed seller, most likely the Scottish Widows fund. This increased Nasdaq's ownership stake in the LSE to 15%. Follow-on purchases pushed Nasdaq's share of LSE to 29%.

While rejecting all the publicly known suitors, the LSE likely held informal, private talks with others. One of those was Borsa Italiana, with which it held several talks during 2006, but as usual said it was not interested. Borsa Italiana, the Milan-based stock exchange, after being rejected by the LSE, began discussions with Deutsche Börse and Euronext regarding a three-way merger. The chief executive of Borsa Italiana was Massimo Capuano, a former senior partner to the giant consulting company McKinsey, and a man with a big vision.[25] He wanted to create a major pan-European exchange by merging Euronext, Deutsche Börse, and Borsa Italiana, and he wanted to block the transatlantic merger that was being discussed between Euronext and the NYSE. If he could put this deal together, he would have the largest stock exchange globally. In doing this he would be able to create a significant challenge to the current European giant, the London Stock Exchange. He certainly had political support in this effort from European leaders, who much preferred to see a pan-European stock exchange as opposed to a transatlantic one created with the Americans. However, Euronext went ahead with the merger with NYSE, and Deutsche Börse was never too interested in a merger in which they would not be the senior partner.

On June 22, 2007, the board of directors of Borsa Italiana approved a merger with the London Stock Exchange in which the LSE paid in stock worth £1.1 billion. The LSE has trading in more than 3000 companies; the Borsa Italiana has trading in 322, though it remains the fourth largest exchange in Europe based on trading volume. One of the things driving the LSE's interest in Borsa Italiana was its control of the European bond-trading platform (MTS). The LSE's chief executive, Clara Furse, will become chief executive of the merged entity; Borsa Italiana chief executive Massimo Capuano will be number two. The LSE will own 78% of the new company, and Borsa Italiana will hold the remaining 22%.[26] The shareholder votes were scheduled to take place July 8. One of the major obstacles to the merger was getting the support of Nasdaq, which had tried several times to buy the LSE and had accumulated a 29% stake by buying shares from other major stockholders. LSE executives feared that Nasdaq would try to block the deal.[27] After much internal deliberation, Nasdaq supported the deal, and when the votes came on August 8, almost 100% of the votes cast by shareholders in both exchanges said yes to the merger.[28]

Nasdaq and the Scandinavians

Having both failed in their attempts to take over the London Stock exchange, Nasdaq and OMX began talks, and on May 25, 2007, Nasdaq agreed to buy OMX for $3.7 billion, which was a 19% premium to the closing price of OMX. The two sitting CEOs, Robert Greifeld at Nasdaq and Magnus Bocker at OMX, would respectively become CEO and president of the merged entity. Nothing during this frenzied M&A period was easy, so it should be no surprise that a competitive bidder entered the scene. Börse Dubai, the parent company for both the domestic and international exchanges in Dubai (the Dubai Financial Exchange and the Dubai International Financial Exchange, respectively), came in with a 10% higher bid of $4 billion. However, Nasdaq and Börse Dubai were introduced through a mutual acquaintance, met and talked, and found that their interests were complementary, not competitive. Nasdaq wanted OMX for the European access it provided; Börse Dubai wanted it for its technology. So they came up with a plan that gave them both what they wanted without having to engage in a bidding war. On September 20, 2007, Börse

Dubai agreed to stop competing with Nasdaq over OMX, and both parties agreed to the following deal:[29]

- Börse Dubai pays $4 billion cash to OMX stockholders for 97.2% of OMX shares.
- Börse Dubai gives the OMX shares to Nasdaq.
- Nasdaq, in exchange, gives 20% of the shares in the new entity Nasdaq OMX plus some cash to Börse Dubai (though Börse Dubai's voting rights are limited to 5%).
- Nasdaq becomes the principal strategic partner as well as a strategic shareholder in the Dubai International Financial Exchange (DIFX), which will be rebranded with the Nasdaq name and will use trading technology from both Nasdaq and OMX.
- Nasdaq sells Börse Dubai its 28% stake in the London Stock Exchange for $1.6 billion.

Dubai's huge presence in this deal shows how the Gulf States have moved quickly onto the exchange scene. Between Dubai's 27% stake and the Qatar Investment Authority's 20% stake in the LSE, Gulf States at that moment owned almost half the London Stock Exchange. However, once the merger took place, with the dilution caused by the 40% increase in the number of shares, the two holdings fell to 20% and 15%, respectively, giving the two Gulf States just over a third of the LSE.

Every exchange is looking for an edge. Nasdaq OMX Group positions itself as the largest global exchange company, the first one to actually have operations on six continents. Over 3900 companies in 39 countries listed are listed on Nasdaq OMX. One of the things that distinguishes the company on its OMX side is its long history of providing technical exchange services to exchanges all over the world. According to Nasdaq OMX it now provides technology to over 60 exchanges on six continents.

The CME and the CBOT

As far back as anyone can remember, there was a very strong, sometimes friendly, sometimes bitter rivalry between the two big Chicago exchanges. Their cultures were different. The CBOT was founded by Irish grain traders, and the CME was founded by Jewish butter and egg traders. The CBOT had always been the number-one exchange in Chicago, in the United States, and in the world. The CME had always been number two. People called it scrappy. It really did try harder. Both exchanges were highly successful and were able to develop benchmark, blockbuster contracts early on. The CME actually started the revolution in derivatives on financial products by launching a family of foreign exchange futures contracts back in 1972. A couple of years later, the CBOT launched the first interest rate futures contract in the form of a mortgage-backed security contract. However, its first interest rate contracts did poorly, and the CBOT went on to create the Treasury bond contract that became the anchor of a family of U.S. Treasury futures and options that drove the CBOT's growth. The CME went on in 1981 and 1982 to develop contracts in Eurodollar deposits and S&P stock indexes. These contracts and a few others allowed both exchanges to experience an incredible period of organic growth.

But the two exchanges were fiercely competitive. Whenever one of the two would start a new contract, the other exchange would start an identical or closely related copy of the first, though as we've explained earlier, only one of the two would succeed. Once back in the 1980s, both exchanges spent over $1 million each developing and promoting stock index products that were based on over-the-counter securities, even though both failed. The CBOT went so far during that campaign as to lease from the city of Chicago the lampposts in front of the CME and hung banners touting the CBOT's new product. But the exchanges could cooperate when necessary, most often when they were faced with a political threat from Washington, and occasionally they would cooperate on an administrative level; for example, at one point in the early 1990s, they created a joint CME-CBOT office in Tokyo as a way of keeping down the extraordinarily high costs of maintaining a presence in Japan. And though there were discussions from time to time about cooperation in clearing or even the possibility of merging, few believed that that could really ever happen.

Though there were many objective reasons for the CME and the CBOT to join forces, what really got the job done was the energy and trust between the chairmen of the two exchanges. CME Chairman Terry Duffy and CBOT Chairman Charlie Carey first met in 1983, when they were both trading in the hog pit at the CME. Over the years they remained friends, even as they rose in their respective organizations. During the phone call that changed everything in early August 2006, Charlie Carey had called Terry Duffy to discuss the renewal of the CME-CBOT clearing agreement under which the CME had cleared all CBOT contracts since 2003. Carey was the one who said, "It's time to look at the whole enchilada."[30] Over the next two months Duffy and Kerry, along with their senior staff, met many times; what kept the discussions on track and allowed this massive transaction to reach fruition was the innate trust that these two men had in one another.

When the two exchanges announced the merger agreement on October 17, 2006, they noted the following:

- CBOT members would receive the equivalent in shares of $151.28 per share for a total consideration of $8 billion.
- CME shareholders would end up owning at least 69% of the new merged entity, and CBOT shareholders would own up to 31% of the value of the new company.
- The composition of the board would be 20 directors from the CME and 9 directors from the CBOT.
- Exchange management would consist of Terry Duffy as chairman, Charles Carey as vice chairman, Craig Donohue as CEO, and Bernie Dan as special adviser.
- Chicago would again have the largest derivatives exchange in the world, a title held over the past decade by Eurex.
- Core trading rights of both the CME and CBOT members would be preserved.

- The deal was expected to close in mid-2007 subject to regulatory and shareholder approvals.
- The combination of the two exchanges would create a more diversified entity than either of the two exchanges standing alone.

Despite the logic, the CME-CBOT merger was not going to be an easy thing. On March 15, the Intercontinental Exchange (ICE) made an unsolicited bid for the CBOT. According to the ICE CEO Jeffrey Sprecher, the value of races bid to the CBOT was $1 billion greater than that of the CME. In addition, he claimed that the CBOT would save a significant amount money by using the old NYBOT clearinghouse, which ICE obtained as a result of its acquisition of NYBOT. This offer took place approximately one month before the April 14 scheduled vote of CME and CBOT shareholders.

The first thing that the CME did was to schedule, one week after the ICE offer, a special meeting of the CBOT shareholders. The CME executives devoted the meeting to explaining why the ICE proposal was "significantly inferior ... financially, strategically and operationally."[31]

On June 14, the CME and CBOT revised the merger agreement to give extra benefits to CBOT shareholders. First, all CBOT shareholders will receive a one-time cash dividend of $9.14 per CBOT share, for a total of $485 million. The dividend would be declared before the close of the merger and would be paid immediately prior to the merger, after all merger conditions had been met.

On July 6, 2007, the CME and the CBOT announced that they had agreed to a revised definitive merger agreement, whereby the revision was to increase the number of CME Holdings shares that would be received by each CBOT shareholder. In the original agreement, each CBOT shareholder would receive .350 shares in CME holdings for each CBOT share. That number was increased to .375 shares of CME holdings for each CBOT share. The sweetened offer induced the CBOT's biggest shareholder, Caledonia, and investments PYT Ltd. to announce that it would endorse the revised merger agreement.[32] On July 9, 2007, the shareholders of both the CME and CBOT approved the merger of those two organizations. The CME was again the biggest exchange in the world.

The Future

Whether the exchange lists derivatives or stocks, screen-based trading by exchanges that had become public companies created a situation where every exchange had to get bigger to take advantage of the new screen-driven economies of scale. Exchanges had to absorb or be absorbed, and this has led to a frenzied period of M&A among exchanges. Most exchanges do only one or two mergers, but they discussed potential mergers with many more exchanges than those with whom they ultimately tied up. The period of active M&A is not over yet. There are hypothetically economies of scale to exploit until there is only one exchange left in the world. We don't believe that the entire world will converge to a single exchange, but we do believe that these strong economic forces will continue to propel mergers for some time to come.

Endnotes

1. Data was available only through June 2008 at the time this was written in midsummer 2008. We have projected the full 2008 volumes by doubling the January through June numbers of 20 million contracts for soybeans, 11 million for wheat, and 33 million for corn.
2. The blockbuster equity index contract in recent years has actually been the E-mini S&P 500, a sort of Mini Me clone which is identical, but only one-fifth the size of the regular S&P 500. While the original S&P 500 started in 1982, the E-mini was launched in 1997.
3. www.world-exchanges.org/WFE/home.asp?menu=191&document=535.
4. *Algorithmic trading* means trades executed by a computer software program with little or no human intervention, generally based on price and volume information fed real time into the program. Black-box trading has no real human intervention once the program is written; gray-box trading has some human intervention. This topic is discussed more extensively in a later chapter.
5. One was the MidAmerica Commodity Exchange, which acted as a training ground for traders by listing smaller clones of contracts traded on the big exchanges, like grain contracts that were one-fifth the size of CBOT grain contracts. The other was the Chicago Rice and Cotton Exchange (formerly the New Orleans Commodity Exchange, which moved to Chicago and changed its name). Technically, the MidAm absorbed the Chicago Rice and Cotton Exchange just before merging into the CBOT.
6. The first telegraph was developed in 1844, and until the 1877 development of the telephone, all long distance communication was via telegraph. The first ticker-tape machine, which was essentially a printer to print out stock symbols and their price changes sent by telegraph, was developed in 1867 by Ed Callahan of the American Telegraph Company. Two years later Thomas Edison came out with the Universal Stock Ticker, which could print at the blazing speed of one character per second. The ticker tape was used until the 1960s, when it was supplanted by the computer. But even at its most efficient, stock quotes via ticker tape were typically delayed by 15 to 20 minutes.
7. Thanks to Ajay Shah for pointing out this example of resistance to consolidation.
8. In 1897, there were roughly 130 commodity exchanges, according to Zensaku Sano and Sentaro Iura, "Commodity Exchanges in Japan," *Annals of the American Academy of Political and Social Science*, Vol. 155, Part 1: Organized Commodity Markets (May 1931), pp. 223–233.
9. These last two were actually merged into the Osaka Textile Exchange in 1984, but all the other mergers took place in 1992 or later.
10. So far, however, all the consolidation has been on the side of the physical commodities. There has been no consolidation among Japan's three financial exchanges, the Tokyo Stock Exchange, the Osaka Securities Exchange, and the Tokyo Financial Exchange, which used to be referred to as TIFFE. However, there has been some discussion of the Tokyo Stock Exchange taking over the commodity exchanges.
11. Coffee, Sugar, and Cocoa would later merge with the New York Cotton Exchange to become NYBOT, and NYBOT would later be taken over by ICE to become ICE Futures US. The early history of these combinations can be found in Allen B. Paul, "The Past and Future of the Commodities Exchanges," *Agricultural History*, Vol. 56, No. 1, Symposium on the History of Agricultural Trade and Marketing, (Jan. 1982), pp. 287–305.
12. World Commodity Report, June 22, 1988.

13. "2 Exchanges Might Merge," *New York Times*, January 25, 1990, section D, p. 8.

14. Sean Maloney, "Nymex/Comex Tie Up Off," *Lloyd s List*, February 20, 1991, p. 2.

15. Adam Ryan, "Membership's Vote to Merge 2 New York Futures Markets," *New York Times*, April 26, 1994, Section D, p. 1.

16. Thanks to Michael Frankel, Senior Vice President, Business Development and M&A at LexisNexis, and author of several books on M&A, for helpful conversations on this issue.

17. "NYSE Seat Holder Brings Class Action Against Exchange Directors Seeking to Block the Proposed Billion-dollar Merger with Archipelago," P. R. Newswire US, May 9, 2005, 7:37 p.m. GMT.

18. *National Posts Financial Post and F. P. Investing*, June 8, 2006, p. 10.

19. SEC form 425 filed by AMEX on June 17, 2008.

20. In the summer of 2008, as the merger was being finalized, AMEX had received notice that the New York City Landmarks Preservation Commission was considering whether the M. X. headquarters at 86 Trinity Place should be designated a landmark property. If it does become so designated, this will restrict the uses to which the property can be put and the changes that could be made in the property, and therefore negatively affect the price that any buyer would be willing to pay. In addition, New York City, like other U.S. urban markets, had been suffering downward pressure on property prices due to the fallout of the subprime crisis. All of this was disclosed to the AMEX members prior to their vote on the merger in a special letter to members on June 6, 2008, from the chairman and CEO of the exchange as well as the chairman of the AMEX membership committee.

21. "LSE Plan Would Blame Germans If Bourse Linkup Fails," *Irish Independent*, April 22, 2000.

22. Mary Canniffe, "Challenging Times ahead for London Stock Exchange as Rivals Press Claims," *Irish Times*, September 8, 2000.

23. *Chicago Tribune*, September 12, 2000.

24. Grant Ringshaw, "LSE and NASDAQ Seek Merger Concessions," *The Sunday Telegraph*, June 2, 2002.

25. Robert Galbraith, "The Great Pan-European Stock Exchange Merger," *The Business*, September 24, 2006.

26. "LSE Agrees to GBP 1 Bn Deal for Borsa Italiana," *Irish Independent*, June 25, 2007.

27. "NASDAQ Threat to LSE on Borsa," *The Statesman* (India), June 26, 2007.

28. LSE said that almost 100% of the votes cast said yes to the merger, and those votes represented 78% of issued share capital. Only a simple majority was required to execute the merger. On the Italian side, 99.92% of the votes supported the merger. Jane Wardell, "London Stock Exchange and Borsa Italiana Shareholders Vote in Favor of Takeover," Associated Press Worldstream, August 8, 2007.

29. Stanley Reed, "Nasdaq, Dubai, OMX in Global Tieup," Business Week Online, September 21, 2007.

30. Jim Kharouf, "The Deal of the Year," *SFO*, Vol. 5, No 12, December 2006, p. 16–22.

31. "Chicago Mercantile Exchange Holdings Inc. Announces Meeting with Members and Shareholders of Chicago Board of Trade," P. R. Newswire US, March 20, 2007.

32. "CME and CBOT Agree to Increase Merger Offer," M2 Presswire, July 6, 2007.

Part Two

Implications of the Four Basic Transformations

8 A New Wave of Product Innovation

Executive Summary

Product innovation is crucial to the growth of exchanges. Stock exchanges continually list new stocks, but it has been their venture into other equity-related products such as exchange-traded funds that has created growth. Equity options exchanges have expanded via a number of new equity indexes. The shift to electronic trading has significantly reduced the cost of starting a new product. It used to be that new products required floor space and traders. Today electronic exchanges require just a little more server space. And the pace of product innovation has increased significantly.

In this and the next four chapters, we discuss the implications of the four basic transformations we explored in the first part of the book: floors to screens, private clubs to public companies, national to global competition, and smaller to larger. In this chapter we delve into the implications of the tremendous surge in product innovation that we outlined in Chapter 7. The creation of new products is one of the most important activities that occurs at exchanges. New products, if successful, can translate within a short period of time into new business. Sometimes product innovation can mean the difference between life and death. For example, NYMEX almost disappeared in 1976, after a very serious default on its largest contract, Maine potatoes. The contract was destroyed, and NYMEX was reduced to a mere sliver of an exchange; it might well have disappeared if it had not turned its creative efforts into the area of energy futures contracts. The Chicago Mercantile Exchange today would be only 1% of its current size had it stopped innovating in 1972. Because it created currency, interest rate, and stock index products, it grew to be a giant. But if it had taken a breather after having created successful pork belly and live cattle contracts, it either wouldn't be here today or it would so small, no one would notice it.

We've spoken of several major transformations of exchanges, big fundamental changes in the way exchanges are organized. Have any of these changes affected the way product innovation is carried out today? Of all the transformations, the one that most affects the process of product innovation is the switch from floors to screens, a switch that significantly reduces the cost of listing new products. You don't need floor space. You don't need floor traders and brokers. All you need is a little more space on the server to accommodate new products. In other words, you don't need to find a new specialist and a new post on the floor to list additional stocks. To list new derivative products, you don't need to create new pit space in futures and options markets and fill those pits with humans. This shift to screens has had the remarkable effect on the pace at which new products have been brought to market. This shift is not the only driver, but it is the major driver. If it's cheaper to list new products, we ought to see more products being listed.

What exactly do we mean by innovation? Product innovation means different things in the derivatives exchanges and the equity exchanges. In the case of a stock exchange, a new product is most often the listing of the shares of a new company. These listings, whatever class and type of shares they may be (Class A or Class B, preferred or common), are driven more by the companies than by the exchanges. The exchange may try to induce companies to list on its system as opposed to another exchange (e.g., Nasdaq rather than the NYSE), but until companies are really ready to go public they are not going to list anywhere. The exchange is reactive. The listing process is driven not by the exchanges but rather by entrepreneurial activity and company formation. We doubt that many people would say that the relatively mechanical listing of a new company's stock on an exchange is innovation. The innovations in the equity market have been relatively slow in coming. We had closed-end funds in the form of U.K. investment trusts beginning in the 1860s, American depository receipts (ADRs) debuting in 1927, and exchange-traded funds (ETFs) starting in Canada in 1989. In recent history, most innovation in things traded on stock exchanges has involved new types of ETFs, including a variant called the exchange-traded note (ETN), and new types of equity-related options.[1] We will touch on these developments in a moment.

But the real thrust of innovative activity has been toward the derivative side of the street. To a certain extent each new futures contract is an innovation, unless it is an exact replica of a contract already traded on another exchange.[2] There are so many aspects that must be specified in a futures contract that there is a lot of room for creative thought. Options on futures or options on equities are a little easier and more standardized.[3]

Let's first look at innovation in futures, but before looking at the recent past let's look at the broad sweep of major innovations in modern futures markets by examining Table 8.1. Futures markets began in agricultural products shortly after the American Civil War, when grain futures were introduced at the Chicago Board of Trade. It took 68 years before the next wave of innovation, and that was in the case of metal futures. The first metal futures contract was listed at the Commodity Exchange (COMEX) in 1933. The pace of innovation then sped up; it took only 34 years for the next major innovation in futures markets, and that was adding an energy product in the form of a propane contract at COMEX. The innovation that dramatically changed what could be listed on futures exchanges was the 1972 unveiling of a set of eight currency contracts at the Chicago Mercantile Exchange. This was the first time a futures contract had been listed on something financial, something that was not a physical commodity. Only three years later, the CBOT introduced a mortgage-

Table 8.1 Major Waves of Innovation in Futures Markets

Date	Category	Original Innovation		Dominant Futures Contract in 2007		
		Product	Exchange	Product	Exchange	Volume*
1865	Agricultural	Grains	CBOT	Soymeal	DCE	64.7
1933	Metals	Silver	COMEX	Aluminum	LME	40.2
1967	Energy	Propane	COMEX	Light Sweet Crude	CME	121.5
1972	FX	Eight Currencies	CME	USD/Euro	CME	43.0
1975	Debt	GNMA	CBOT	Eurodollar	CME	621.5
1982	Stock Indexes	Value Line	KCBOT	E-Mini S&P 500**	CME	415.3

*In millions of futures contracts traded.
**The largest equity options contract was Kospi 200 Options.
Source: Exchanges and FIA Monthly Volume Reports, December 2007.

backed debt instrument called the Ginnie Mae, or GNMA, contract. Finally, rounding out a basic set of financial contracts was stock index futures, which started in 1982 with the Value Line contract at the Kansas City Board of Trade.

Note that not a single one of these initial innovative contracts survives as the dominant contract in its class today. What they did was create the foundation on which further contracts in that particular category could be developed. For example, the Ginnie Mae contract at the CBOT was the first of about eight different attempts to create a mortgage-backed futures contract. Every one of them failed. But what initially established itself as the dominant debt futures contract was the U.S. Treasury bond contract. Later the Eurodollar contract at the CME would take and hold the dominant position.

Now, many other innovations in futures came after this, but these were the categories that resulted in large, blockbuster contracts. Weather is an innovation, catastrophic insurance is an innovation, credit default swaps are an innovation, but not one of these has resulted in a large, highly liquid futures contract.

Innovation Acceleration in Futures Products

Let's do the numbers.[4] According to the regulator of the futures markets, the Commodity Futures Trading Commission (CFTC; see Figure 8.1), the number of new futures and options products filed annually with the CFTC has been

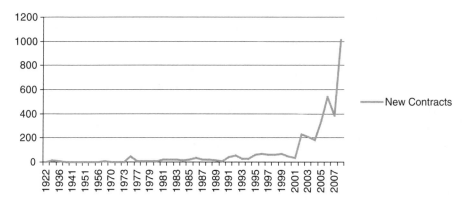

Figure 8.1 Number of U.S. futures and options contracts filed annually with the CFTC, 1922–2008.*
*2008 projected, based on first five months.
Source: Commodity Futures Trading Commission Web site.

moving up at a healthy pace ever since they started keeping records in 1922, and it has exploded in the last six years. Specifically, futures exchanges averaged five new contracts each year in the 1970s, 20 per year in the 1980s, and 48 per year in the 1990s. This is quite respectable growth, with the number of new futures and options contracts more than doubling each decade. But the growth that began in 2000 dwarfed all prior increases. After the period in which 5, 20, or 48 contracts were added in the United States each year, the three years from 2002 to 2004 saw an average of 207 new contracts per year. And during the three years following that, 2005 to 2007, exchanges launched an average of 422 futures and options contracts launched in each of those years.

The Old World: Launching New Products on Trading Floors

So what is going on here to generate such a rapidly increasing rate of innovation? Let's explore this a bit more deeply. On a floor-based exchange, the capacity to list new products, or to trade greater volumes in existing products, for that matter, was a direct function of the size of the trading floor and the number of traders on that floor. Every customer order to buy or sell futures contracts had to be executed by an exchange member acting as a floor broker. And every order had to have the other side taken by either another customer who happened to be putting in an opposite order at the same time and who also had to be represented by another exchange member acting as a floor broker or, more likely, by another member acting as a scalper on the trading floor.

There were two major roles exchange members could take on the trading floor. They could be a floor broker executing customer orders, or they could be a local (or scalper) who traded for their own account. These scalpers would take the opposite side of incoming orders, hold the position for a few seconds or minutes, and then offset these positions by taking the opposite side of a new customer order in the opposite direction, hopefully at a price difference that gave them a small profit. Even though the scalpers had no obligation to make a market, as does a specialist on some stock exchanges, as a group they did just that. There would always be a bid and offer available in the pit because either scalpers would be shouting them out or at least they were prepared to do so if a request for a quote came in. Scalpers made the market and created the liquidity for customer orders. In other words, the crowd on the floor in a particular pit was always bidding at some price and offering at some price and that bid and offer was essentially the market. But this crowd was made up of people, and these people needed a few square feet of trading floor in which to stand.

To list a new product, the exchange needed to build a new trading pit and populate that trading pit with exchange members who would serve as both brokers and locals. Many of the floor-based exchanges had to either engage in physical expansion or renovation programs or literally move to new buildings to accommodate the surge in trading that took place at various times in their histories. The Chicago Board of Trade, for example, created in 1848, moved five times during its first 37 years. While it spent many years at its iconic home at Jackson and LaSalle, it could accommodate the volume boom of the 1970s and 1980s only by building a large annex behind the exchange. The Chicago Mercantile Exchange has also had five different homes during its history. When it moved into its fourth home, at 444 W. Jackson, in 1972, it had the largest trading floor in the world, which was designed to accommodate the Exchange for two decades. Within only five years, the CME was running out of room and had to increase its floor space 30% by purchasing air rights and building out over the sidewalk. Despite the expansion, the building that was planned to accommodate the exchange for 20 years grew too small after only 10 years, and the CME made another move for more space to 10 South Wacker Drive in 1983.[5]

What about people? What about increasing the manpower on the trading floor to accommodate new trades? Initially when exchanges launch new products, they don't know whether they're going to succeed or not, and therefore they do not want to expand the number of members and potentially dilute the value of existing seats until it's clear that the new product will be a success and will contribute significantly to the exchange's business and therefore require an increased number of traders. One of the best examples of temporarily increasing trading capacity occurred in 1982, when the Chicago Mercantile Exchange launched the S&P 500 futures contract. Of course, the exchange did all the right things to promote the use of these new contracts. It put on seminars, it took out ads in the newspapers, and it had the opening bell rung by one of the most famous TV commentators on equity markets at the time, a guy named Louis Rukeyser, the host of the immensely popular program called *Wall Street Week*.

But to succeed, the exchange had to offer liquidity to all the orders that might come in. To build this liquidity in its new stock index product, the exchange essentially borrowed traders from other pits. The exchange leadership[6] organized meetings of all the exchange members in which they strongly urged the members, for the sake of their children and for the sake of the future of the exchange, to support this new contract. This was especially important since they expected to have stock index competition from the CBOT, from the Kansas City Board of Trade (which was actually the first exchange out of the box with its Value Line contract), and most important, from a new futures subsidiary of the New York Stock Exchange that was listing a futures contract on the NYSE Composite index.[7]

Specifically, they asked each member to leave their own pit in which they were making a good living and stand in the S&P 500 pit for 15 minutes a day. Throughout the trading day, there was a voice over the loudspeaker that would remind traders of their commitment with the words "Fifteen minutes, please." It was only three words, repeated twice, but everyone knew what they meant. And to further reinforce pushing a sufficient number of traders into the S&P pit to make a liquid market, the exchange leaders would actually go onto the floor, grab traders in pork bellies or cattle or T-bills by the elbows and escort them over to the S&P pit so that they could fulfill their 15-minute commitment.

Now, while these kinds of efforts did a reasonable job of creating liquidity back in those days, once the new market was established and growing, exchanges often had to resort to the more permanent solution of membership expansion programs. This was done in one of two ways. One was through the creation of new seats that were issued in such a fashion so as to minimize the dilution effect on existing members. The other was to issue "trading permits" with no ownership rights embedded in them.

The new-seat creation technique was used by the CME five times to accommodate waves of new products. In 1972, when the CME became the first exchange to list financial futures,[8] it created a separate exchange called the International Monetary Market (IMM), which, three years later, was merged back into the CME as a major division with 650 new memberships, growing the exchange from 500 to 1150 members. In 1976, the CME sold 300 Associate Mercantile Market (AMM) seats to try to breathe liquidity into the ailing non-livestock agricultural markets, bringing the total memberships to 1450. In 1981, the exchange increased its floor trader capacity 25% by giving each existing member a fractional one-quarter seat. The members could sell, lease out, or combine the fraction with three other quarters they bought in the market to create a new seat and had four years to do so.[9]

Then in 1982, to accommodate new markets in stock indexes and options, the CME created the 1287-member division known as the Index and Options Market (IOM). Finally, in 1994, the exchange added the Growth and Emerging Markets (GEM) division with 413 seats to accommodate a new initiative to list a government bond, a stock index, and a currency for each of the major emerging markets such as Mexico, Brazil, Argentina, South Africa, Taiwan, Russia, and others. In both these cases, some seats were sold to existing members at a deep discount and to outsiders at full price. The fact that existing members had the right to trade all products listed in the new divisions helped mollify concerns over seat value dilution.

The New World: Launching New Products on Electronic Exchanges

Contrast that with life in an electronic exchange. With screen-based trading, new products require simply making additional space on existing servers or installing new servers to handle the flow of orders and price quotes and accommodate the matching of trades. The lower cost and simplicity of creating new trading capacity should encourage the more rapid development and listing of new products.

Because the cost of maintaining a product on the server is trivial (compared to maintaining it on the floor, with traders standing in a pit waiting for orders), products that might not have justified the cost in a floor world are kept in the electronic world. For example, the weather futures contracts traded at the CME really trades on an episodic pattern. There will be several days of no trading; then suddenly two parties will find one another and execute a trade. As long as the contract is sitting on an electronic market and potential customers can request a quote, it's much easier to maintain a market like this than it is to do so in a floor-based system.[10]

The other thing that is absolutely remarkable is the shift in the willingness of exchanges to fragment liquidity into a large number of contracts. In the past, the trend had always been to try to concentrate liquidity into a small number of futures contracts and into a relatively small number of months for each contract. For example, the typical listing cycle for futures contracts on financial instruments has been the March quarterly cycle, meaning that the only contract months listed for Eurodollars, Treasury notes, and the German bund would be March, June, September, and December. The idea was to concentrate liquidity into those four months. The thought was that having contracts every single month and letting people use the month in which they wanted futures exposure would result in lots of contract months, each month having little liquidity. But if you had only a few months, everyone would be forced to use those few months and there would be greater liquidity in those few months. Hedgers might be put off a bit, but they could always take a position further out than they needed and then get out of their futures position when the need for the position disappeared, and they would benefit by finding more buyers and sellers operating in those few months.

The same logic held with slicing up a commodity geographically. You could have four cattle contracts based in different market centers around the country to accommodate people who are interested in the prices of Midwest, Texas panhandle, Southeast, or West Coast cattle. But it was always thought better to have only one cattle contract based in the most important delivery area, to concentrate buyers and sellers in that single contract.

In the new electronic world, this seems to be much less a concern, and, in fact, exchanges have embraced fragmentation of liquidity in a plethora of similar contracts. Take the CME weather contracts. In the past, in order to concentrate liquidity, there might be weather contracts based in one or just a handful of cities. Admittedly, weather varies geographically more than cattle prices, and it would be virtually impossible for a trader to hedge Los Angeles weather on a Boston weather futures contract. Still, the principle of concentrating speculative liquidity dictates keeping the number of such contracts small. Or it used to. So how many weather contracts does the CME have in its stable? To be specific, during the period 1999 to 2008, the CME has registered with the CFTC, either via certification or request for approval, 314 different futures and options contracts based on weather (see Table 8.2). These cover temperature, snowfall, frost, wind, and hurricanes in various European, Asian, and North American cities.

The same is true for energy contracts at NYMEX, as is evident, in Figure 8.2. To date, 387 energy contracts[11] have been processed by the CFTC. Of these, 340 (88%) have been submitted by NYMEX, which is no surprise since it was the pioneer in energy, having started heating oil and industrial fuel oil contracts back in 1975. But back in those days, futures exchanges didn't come out with new products all that often. After the two energy contracts in 1975, it took NYMEX six years before it came up with some more energy contracts, and in fact, of the 26 years between 1975 and 2000, there were 14 years in which there were no energy contracts launched at all. And when contracts were launched, they were typically done one, two, or three at a time.

But everything changed beginning in 2002, when we began to see 20 or 30 or 40 or more contracts launched every year. Many of these are contracts on the difference between two prices, such as Rotterdam vs. Singapore gas oil or Henry Hub vs. New York natural gas. And because there are many locations at which energy products are priced, there are many, many differences that can be calculated. Even though NYMEX has been in the energy business since 1975, 90% of all NYMEX energy contracts filed with the CFTC were filed between 2002 and May 2008.

Table 8.2 U.S. Futures Contracts by Subcategory, 1922–2008

	Subcategory	Contracts
1	Accounting Data	24
2	ADR—American Depository Receipt	33
3	Binary Option	27
4	Credit Event	4
5	Crop Yield	20
6	Currency	294
7	Electricity	81
8	Emissions	66
9	Energy	387
10	Equity Index	201
11	Exchange-Traded Fund (ETF)	48
12	Fertilizer	10
13	Fiber	9
14	Foodstuff/Soft	68
15	Grain	47
16	Hybrid Index	1
17	Insurance	36
18	Interest Rate	226
19	Livestock/Meat Product	35
20	Metal	72
21	Miscellaneous	106
22	Narrow-Based Index (NBI)	34
23	Non-Equity Index	84
24	Oil Seed Product	24
25	Other Agriculture	4
26	Other Natural Resource	4
27	Single-Stock Future (SSF)	919
28	Weather	314
29	Wood Product	20
	Total	3198

*2008 projected based on first five months.
Source: CFTC Web site.

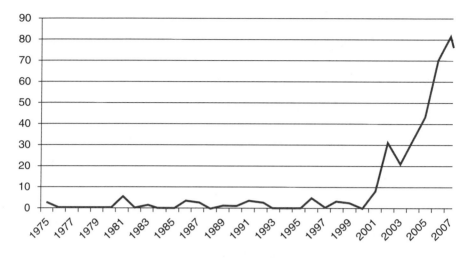

Figure 8.2 Energy contracts filed annually with CFTC by NYMEX, 1975–2008.*
*2008 projected based on first five months.

Some Things Haven't Changed

Make no mistake; there are other aspects of the product development process that have not been affected by these fundamental transformations of modern derivatives exchanges. For example, it still takes a reasonable amount of time to create the terms and conditions for a new futures contract. The usual process for developing a new futures contract involves first having the research economists learn as much as they can about the way the commodity or asset is typically traded and transferred from one party to another in the underlying cash market. They work very closely with industry representatives and frequently will create advisory committees of knowledgeable industry participants to advise on the structure and specifications of a particular contract.

Physical commodities are the toughest to do. There are many characteristics of a physical commodity that must be specified in the contract. For example, for a crude oil contract, will the oil be sweet or sour (which indicates the amount of sulfur in the oil—the more sulfur, the more sour)? Will it be light, intermediate, or heavy (which indicates the density of the oil)? Light, sweet crude fetches higher prices than sour, heavy crude, because it yields more high-value products like gasoline and there is less sulfur to remove. Where will the oil be delivered? How will the oil be delivered—by tanker or by pipeline or in-tank transfer? How big should the crude oil contract be? Pipelines have minimums on the amount of oil that can be shipped through them in a single delivery (typically 25,000 barrels). And when should it be delivered? Should delivery be scheduled for a specific day of the month, or perhaps prorated over the entire month? All of this takes considerable research and time to sort out. The research economists must spend a significant amount of time speaking with people in the industry involved in actual deliveries.[12]

One way to reduce this amount of time is to design a contract to be cash or financially settled. What this means is that there are no actual deliveries, and the final settlement price on the last day of trading is not the price determined during the close in the trading pit but rather some other readily available benchmark price.[13] This system of cash settlement is used for the world's biggest contract, Eurodollars, for all stock index contracts, and for many of the energy contracts traded at NYMEX and ICE Futures. In fact, ICE, a competitor of NYMEX, actually used NYMEX prices to settle a number of its own contracts. NYMEX sued ICE claiming that ICE was appropriating NYMEX's intellectual property, but the court found in ICE's favor and ICE continues to cash-settle contracts based on the NYMEX prices.

In the days before demutualization, when exchanges were owned and run by their members, there were product committees, composed of exchange members and supported by professional staff, that would get involved in the process. Typically the product committee, with the assistance of research staff, would design the new futures contract and then would recommend the adoption of this contract to the Board of Directors. Sometimes there was even another committee between the product committee and the Board of Directors. At the CME, there was an oversight committee for financial products and another one for agricultural products. The members of these product and oversight committees, with their experience in trading other products and sometimes with experience in the underlying cash market, were able to contribute to the quality of the design process. However, this did add a layer of humans, among whom a consensus had to be built. And sometimes, because there were large egos involved, it was difficult to reach that consensus, or at least it took time to do so. One advantage of demutualization is that it took a layer out of the contract design process and thus reduced the time to market for a new product. Some exchanges will still make use of members in the design process; in fact, it would be wasting a valuable resource not to do so. But the members no longer have the same power over either insisting a product be done when it possibly shouldn't or vetoing a product that should be launched.

Regulatory Change Drives Product Innovation

Aside from the switch to electronic trading, there was another very important driver of product innovation, at least in the United States, and that was a huge reduction in regulatory burden as manifested in the Commodity Futures Modernization Act of 2000.

In the old world before 2000, exchanges had to develop a relatively thick document that would explain and justify every single term and condition in the futures contract. In other words, why was a particular delivery point chosen? Why was a particular grade of commodity chosen, or why was a particular time of the month selected for delivery?

In addition, the exchange had to explain why the contract had an economic justification, explaining why the futures contract was good for the world. Naturally, it took a considerable amount of time to put this document together, though a substantial portion of this information would have been needed even without the regulator—just to assure the exchange the product was designed properly. The exchange needed to do the research to find out what the practices were in trading and transferring the commodity from one party to the other in typical cash market transactions. However, the document sent to the CFTC took considerably more time than would have been the case if the exchange were simply making a business decision as to whether to launch a contract.

There were two reasons for this. First, exchanges would not by themselves feel obligated to develop an economic justification for the contract. These justifications required by the CFTC basically amounted to demonstrating that there were risks out in the economy that this new contract would help mitigate. This involved giving specific hedging examples and getting comments from industry participants, who would be interested in using the contract to manage risk. From an exchange's point of view, the ultimate test of whether a contract should be launched was whether or not traders would come. In other words, the exchanges are businesses, or more accurately, exchanges back then were not-for-profit institutions that housed their members and the members were conducting business. The members benefited if orders to buy or sell the new product came onto the floor. If the orders came in, that meant money for the members: commissions for executing orders, the bid-ask spread for scalpers who were making markets, and more opportunities to take a position in the opposite direction as the incoming orders for members who took longer-term positions. The members and the exchange didn't really care whether the orders were coming from hedgers or speculators. Commissions were the same from both.

To be fair, the conventional wisdom was that a successful market was possible only by the interaction of hedgers and speculators. If you didn't have the participation of those involved in the underlying industry (producers, merchants, processors, etc.), the market would not work. It wouldn't work because the idea was that you had industry participants coming in largely on one side of the market (e.g., feedlots coming in with short positions to hedge inventories of cattle) and speculative capital coming in on the other side to take the risk that the industry wanted to lay off. In addition, to have a contract in which physical delivery occurred, you had to have commercial participants who knew the ropes and would be able to make or take delivery of the commodity in question.

The second reason that the exchanges spent excess time and money to produce this document to the CFTC is that they had to explain things in a much more detailed fashion, in a way that could be understood by people who were not necessarily familiar with the underlying market. If they were simply producing an internal document to help them decide what the terms and conditions of the contract should be and to record the rationale for their various decisions, the document would have been much smaller. The bottom line is that if this document could be eliminated, it would save a considerable amount of time and manpower, something that can be critical in a competitive situation, especially when the competitor is from overseas and is regulated in a much lighter fashion and could get the product to market much more quickly.

Once this document had been submitted to the CFTC, the agency had up to one year to either approve or deny the exchange's right to list a contract for trading. Naturally, the exchanges protested the onerous burden of creating this document and waiting for up to a year for approval. So, in the Commodity Futures Modernization Act of 2000, there was a provision that said exchanges need only to certify that listed contracts complied with all the regulations of the CFTC and all the provisions of the Commodity Exchange Act. On top of this, the exchange only had to give a one-day notice to the Commission that it was going to start this new contract. So, on the day prior to launch, at the latest, the exchange would give the Commission a copy of the futures contract along with a one-page letter certifying that the contract complied with all aspects of CFTC regulations and all aspects of the Commodity Exchange Act.

It's also worthwhile to take a look at a number of contracts actually listed on U.S. exchanges over the past 50 years. This is taken from a presentation for which data ends in 2005, but it still sheds light on the points that we are making in this chapter. From Figure 8.3, we see the number of futures contracts that had some amount of trading activity every decade starting in 1955 and ending in 2005, and we notice a couple of things. First, agricultural contracts absolutely dominated the futures landscape in 1955, 1965, and even in 1975. They continued to play an important role up to the present but were gradually swamped by futures contracts in other categories. The second thing we notice is that in both 1955 and 1965 there were only about 50 futures contracts in the entire country that had any activity. But starting in 1975, the total number of futures contracts with activity began to rise, with the increase between 1995 and 2005 swamping all earlier growth experiences. In fact, the number of futures contracts with some trading activity in 2005 was three times the number of futures contracts that had some activity in 1995.

What was responsible for this increase? While the number of agricultural contracts and precious metal contracts dropped, virtually everything else rose, but nothing grew like energy. NYMEX was very aggressive in creating new futures contracts in energy, and thus energy represented two to three times or more the number of contracts in any other category.

Figure 8.4 gives us the number of contracts newly created each year beginning in 1956. As we can see, during the 1950s and 1960s the entire U.S. industry generated anywhere from two to 10 contracts in any given year. And

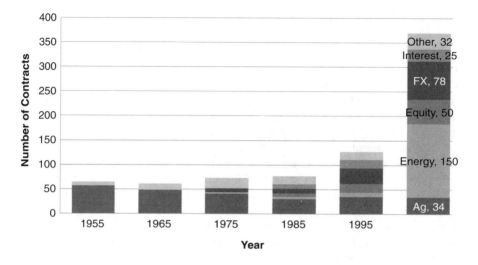

Figure 8.3 Number of futures contracts by product type, 1955–2005.
Source: Calculated from data in selected *FIA Monthly Volume Reports*.

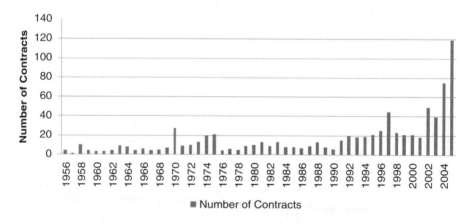

Figure 8.4 New contracts launched (innovations, imitations, and product extension), 1956–2004.
Source: Calculated from FIA Volume Reports.

during the entire period from 1956 to 2001, the number of new contracts launched by U.S. exchanges exceeded 20 only a few times. Then in 2002, it was 50, and the next year 40, and the next year almost 80, and in 2005 the number reached 120.

One interesting question is, how successful are these contracts launches? In Figure 8.5 we explore the question of contract success. Success here is defined

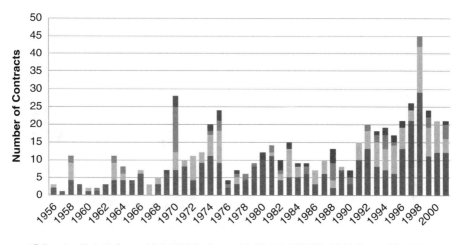

Figure 8.5 Success of new futures contracts by volume in their fifth year, 1956–2000.
Source: Calculated from FIA Volume Reports.

by the volume of trading in the fifth year of trading. The idea is that five years should be sufficient to discriminate between those contracts that are going to succeed and those that will not. As you can see, on average about half of all futures contracts had zero volume in their fifth year of trading, a pretty clear indication of failure. At the other extreme, the number of contracts that were highly successful—that is, experienced trading volumes of over 1 million contracts per year in the fifth year of life—was small. Most years did not produce even one highly successful contract from any exchange. When they came, it was usually one or two, and occasionally three in a given year.

The Rest of the World

So far our focus has been on the United States. Let's now turn to the rest of the world. In 1980, if we had looked at the top 10 futures contracts on exchanges outside the United States, we would've found that eight of the most active futures contracts were based in Japan, and they were all agricultural contracts—soybeans, red beans, rubber, and even raw silk. The other two top 10 contracts were rapeseed and flaxseed traded in Canada on the Winnipeg Commodity Exchange. Fast-forward 25 years to 2005 and again take a look at the top 10 futures contracts outside the United States. First, not a single one of the 1985 contracts found their way onto the 2005 list; in addition, not a single Japanese contract or Canadian contract found

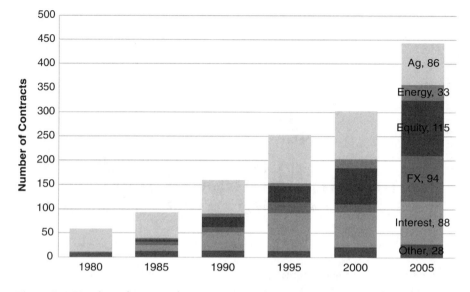

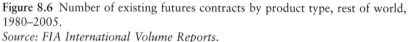

Figure 8.6 Number of existing futures contracts by product type, rest of world, 1980–2005.
Source: FIA International Volume Reports.

its way onto the list. The 1985 list was completely agricultural. The 2005 list was almost completely financial except for two very actively traded agricultural contracts at the Dalian Commodity Exchange in China. The 2005 list was also more geographically diverse. Half of the top 10 contracts were traded in Europe, 20% in China, and 10% each in Brazil, India, and Australia. The point is that the same kind of dynamic changes that have taken place in product development in the United States have also taken place in the rest of the world.

Does the growth curve of new contracts show the same pattern as it did in the United States? If we look at Figure 8.6, we see a pattern of aggressive growth going back all the way to the 1980s. Every five years beginning in 1980 the number of futures contracts[14] with some level of activity grew at rates of 60–70% through 1995. The rate of growth then dropped over the next five years to only 20% but picked up to almost 50% between 2000 and 2005. So the recent rate of growth was actually a bit slower than during the first 15 years of this quarter century. Part of this can be explained by the fact that the rest of the world was growing not only in the number of futures contracts started by each exchange but also by a proliferation of exchanges. Countries that never had a derivatives exchange established one.

Despite the fact that more exchanges were being created in the rest of the world, U.S. exchanges have continued to be the most active in terms of generating new futures contracts. During the period 1981 to 2005, 631

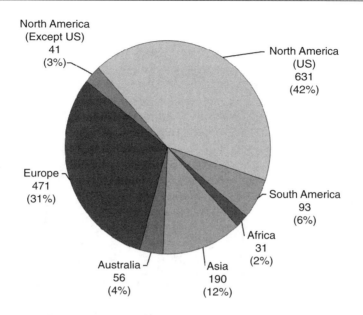

Figure 8.7 New futures contracts started, by continent, 1981–2005.
Source: FIA Volume Reports and *International Volume Reports.*

new futures contracts were established in the United States, as can be seen in Figure 8.7. This represents 41% of new futures contracts created globally. Europe was number two with a 31% share, and Asia was number three with a 13% share.

The fact that this new wave of innovation was not experienced as extensively in the rest of the world as in the United States is evident from Figure 8.8, where we see that innovative activity actually fell in 2003 and 2004 at the same time that such innovation was accelerating in the United States. So, although new futures contracts have continued to be created in the rest of the world, it seems as though the expansion of products has taken on a curve of a different shape. If we carefully compare the rest-of-the-world Figure 8.8 with the U.S. Figure 8.4, we see that during the 1980s the United States and the rest of the world each contributed in the range of 10 to 20 new futures contracts per year. However, once we move into the 1990s, the U.S. average contribution was around 20 per year, whereas the rest of the world contributed something closer to 30 new contracts per year. However, once we approach 2000, the level of innovation in the rest of the world, at least episodically, peaked at 70 and 80 contracts in a single year, whereas the United States peaked at 120 contracts in 2005.

The fact that the rest of the world began increasing its rate of product innovation over a decade earlier than occurred in the United States is in part attributable to the fact that the rest of the world began to adopt some of the big changes a decade earlier than the United States did. Virtually all the

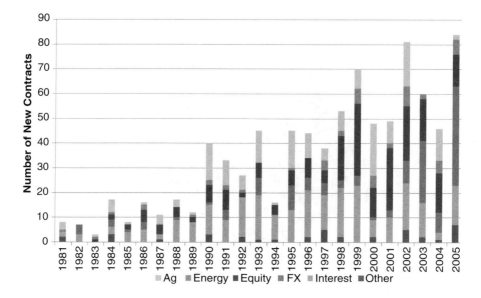

Figure 8.8 New futures contracts introduced by product type, rest of world, 1981–2005.
Source: FIA International Volume Reports.

new exchanges built worldwide since 1990 were electronic, whereas most of the U.S. exchanges were still stuck in a floor-based system until around 2003. In addition, the U.S. exchanges remained not-for-profit and member owned until the early 2000s, whereas a number of exchanges worldwide were actually created as stockholder-owned, for-profit entities. One final dimension is that, as mentioned earlier, the United States did experience a significant regulatory change in 2000, making it much easier to create and launch new futures contracts. So the combination of the late move into demutualization and screen-based trading, combined with regulatory liberalization, accounts for the more dramatic increase in product innovation that we see in U.S. derivatives.

A Note on Innovations in Equities

We have spent much more time on derivatives because that is where the real innovation has taken place. But let's take a quick look at the equity exchanges. By far the most innovative part of the equity world is the continual development of exchange-traded funds (ETFs). ETFs are baskets of something, usually stocks, that are similar to mutual funds but that trade continuously on exchanges. They are superior to mutual funds in that they can be traded at any time

Table 8.3 Number of ETFs by Geographic Area, 2006 and 2007

	2006	2007	Change (%)	Market Share (%)*
United States	340	641	189	32
Other Americas	95	175	184	9
Asia/Pacific	75	108	144	5
Europe	509	898	176	45
Middle East	106	172	162	9
Africa	9	13	144	1
Total world	1134	2007	177	100

*2007 share of global market in number of ETFs.
Source: Calculated from World Federation of Exchanges data.

exchanges are open, can be sold short, and have certain tax advantages (at least in the United States) compared to mutual funds. The first successful ETF was launched on the Toronto Stock Exchange in 1990. Three years later, in 1993, the American Stock Exchange listed the first U.S. ETF, called Spiders, or SPDRs, short for Standard and Poor Depository Receipt. It represented a basket of all the shares in the S&P 500 and was designed by Nathan Most, a 73-year-old employee of the American Stock Exchange. The American Stock Exchange became the real early innovator of exchange-traded funds, though today there are more ETFs listed on the NYSE.

From their original launch in the 1990s, ETFs have grown in number, in diversity, in total assets under management, and in geographical reach. As of the end of 2007 there were, coincidentally, 2007 ETFs worldwide (see Table 8.3). Even though ETFs started in the Americas, Europe has more than caught up and has a commanding lead with a 45% share. The United States is second with 31%, but the product has done less well in Asia, which has only 5% of all ETFs listed. And the 177% growth in the worldwide number of ETFs in a single year, 2006 to 2007, is astounding. Figure 8.9 makes it clear that ETFs were growing slowly in 2003 and 2004 but then took off with growth rates of 40–80% since then. This is consistent with the argument that the lower cost of listing resulting from the shift to electronic markets results in more listings.

The largest of the sponsors of these funds is Barclays Global Investment, which, as of the summer of 2008, had 159 different ETFs available. Along with the normal stock indexes, Barclays has ETFs or ETNs that cover grains, metals (including specific metals such as gold, silver, copper, and nickel), livestock, natural gas, and 22 specific country funds (including Brazil, Malaysia, Mexico, and Taiwan). The oldest sponsor of ETFs is the State Street Global advisors, which has the oldest ETF, the SPDR, still the biggest ETF in

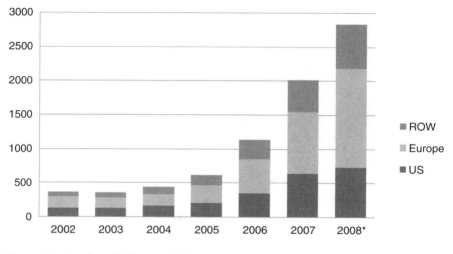

Figure 8.9 Number of ETFs globally, 2002–2008.*
*2008 April data.
Source: Data from World Federation of Exchange.

existence, with assets of about $77 billion during the summer of 2008. There are also leveraged ETFs. For example, Rydex has a fund called 2X S&P 500 and another called Inverse 2X S&P 500, which represents a short position in the S&P 500.

Conclusion

Even though futures contracts have been around for over 150 years, it is clear that we have entered a sort of golden age of product innovation. The pace of innovation has increased substantially beyond what it was in the recent past. This increase has been driven by two factors. First is the shift from floors to screens, which has significantly lowered the cost of adding products to the exchanges' portfolios. The second is the new ease with which new products can be created following the 2002 enactment of the Commodity Futures Modernization Act.

Equity exchanges have been traditionally a little less innovative than the derivatives exchanges. It doesn't take a lot of thought to simply add new stocks for trading on a stock exchange. The one area in which stock exchanges have stood out has been the area of EFTs. There has been a huge increase in the number, the diversity, and the geographical spread of these new products; the number of new ETFs increased 177% in a single year. But though the pace of innovation has accelerated, the success of these new products is something that remains to be seen. There are wonderful new creations of hurricane futures, credit default swap futures, and catastrophe insurance futures, but none has gained any real traction.

At some point, the Ph.D. economists who sit in the research departments of the exchanges will simply run out of new ideas. There are only so many different spread relationships among energy prices in different parts of the United States. Once those are all listed, and most of them don't trade very much anyway, what does NYMEX have left to do? With the increase in the number of new contracts launched every year, there has been a similar increase in the percentage of contracts that have zero trading five years after launch. With a lower cost of listing, more failures can be tolerated, but at some point, this frenzied pace of innovation will lock horns with the reality that the number of traders interested in increasingly obscure products will fall, and the pace will slow considerably. And with the loss of many trading jobs associated with the financial crisis that took hold in 2007 and 2008, that time could be sooner rather than later.

Endnotes

1. ETFs seem universally to be traded on stock exchanges, but options are found both on stock exchanges and on specialized options exchanges such as the Chicago Board Options Exchange, the European Options Exchange, the International Securities Exchange (taken over by Eurex in 2007), and the Boston Options Exchange.
2. Some groups of futures contracts are almost clones of one another. For example, every currency contract at the CME is identical except for the name of the currency to be delivered (Euro, Japanese yen, British pound, Mexican peso, etc.) and the position limit (which is a much smaller number of contracts for the Mexican peso than for the Euro). So each new currency is mainly a matter of just picking another country and making arrangements with settlement banks.
3. For example, it does not take much work to list a new stock option. The design of any new individual stock option is virtually the same as every stock option that preceded it; the only thing that changes is the name of the company. So, though options as a product class certainly represent an innovation, the addition of one more equity option is not much different than the stock of one more company.
4. There are two sources of data on new futures products. The Futures Industry Association (FIA) has published volume data for all U.S. futures contracts since 1955 and international futures contracts since 1980 in its *Monthly Volume Report*. More recently, it has been publishing data on securities options as well. And the CFTC has made available on its Web site a list of every new product registered with the CFTC between 1922 and the present. We rely on both sources for information presented in this chapter.
5. Its 2007 merger with the CBOT and shift to largely electronic trading resulted in the CME selling its trading floors in 2008 and moving the remaining floor traders a few blocks away to the CBOT's sparsely populated floor.
6. While there were many board members involved, this effort was led by Executive Committee Chairman Leo Melamed and Board Chairman Jack Sandner, both energetic, enthusiastic, and charismatic leaders and speakers. They both could stimulate action by virtue of their personalities.

7. Despite the fear the NYSE's entry into the market struck in the CME's heart, the NYSE Composite futures contract and the NYSE's whole futures subsidiary were not successful and were later sold to the New York Cotton Exchange, which was itself merged into the New York Board of Trade, which later became ICE Futures US.

8. On May 16, 1972, the CME opened trading in seven foreign currencies (the British pound, German mark, Swiss franc, Italian lira, Japanese yen, Canadian dollar, and Mexican peso) within a separate exchange called the IMM, to build a separate brand image not associated with pork bellies, cattle, hogs, and other agricultural products.

9. To make the seat fractions useful even before assembling four of them into a full seat, the range of products one could trade expanded with each additional fraction one held. Though specific products varied across the membership divisions (CME, IMM, and AMM), the idea was that a person holding one-quarter seat could trade product A, with two quarters trade products A and B, with three quarters trade products A, B, and C, and with four quarters, which was a full seat, trade all products allowed to members in that division.

10. In fact, the CME does list both floor and Globex hours for most of its 18 weather contracts, so if traders wish to trade weather contracts on the floor, they can do so.

11. Not including the 81 electricity contracts that the CFTC classifies separately.

12. When one of the authors of this book was a research economist at the Chicago Mercantile Exchange, he spent almost a year researching and designing crude oil, gasoline, and heating oil futures contracts.

13. There's often confusion about exactly what cash settlement or financial settlement is. First, the terms mean the same thing. Second, cash settlement does not mean that there is a special delivery of the cash value of the contract, as some people seem to believe. It's easiest to think of cash settlement as simply one additional marking to market. Futures contracts are marked to market and every day, based on the price established during the close. For this reason the closing price in futures markets is actually called the *settlement* price. So every day, all buyers and sellers have their accounts debited or credited based on the settlement price established in the pit or in the electronic market during the closing. And in traditional futures contracts, anyone holding a position in a contract after the final bell on the last day of trading of that contract must, depending on the position, either deliver or take delivery of the underlying commodity. In cash-settled contracts there is no delivery, but there is one last settlement, one last transfer of funds from losers to winners, based not on the price established in the pit or in the electronic futures market but rather on a price that's established external to the exchange, typically in the cash market. The S&P 500 contract, for example, has a final settlement price based on the prices of the 500 stocks on the New York Stock Exchange. The Eurodollar contract has a final settlement price based on a survey that the British Bankers Association does of major banks in London that are involved in the Eurodollar market.

14. Throughout these charts, we include only futures contracts that have had some trading in them. Exchanges will often list contracts that attract no trading, but those are excluded from this analysis.

9 Building Modular Exchanges via Partnerships and Outsourcing

Executive Summary

In this chapter we explore the radical transformation in the structure of financial markets, from monolithic exchanges that served all functions to smaller components that can be snapped together like Lego blocks to quickly build new exchanges. We provide several in-depth case studies that illustrate how various players adapted their business models to electronic exchanges.

Before the shift to screens, exchanges were built to be self-sufficient entities that supported all the functions of the trade cycle. Each exchange had dedicated groups of employees supporting the numerous functions of the trade cycle. Each exchange had its own product development group to create new products that the members of the exchanges could trade. Every exchange had an established clearing group to process trades. Each exchange also had a regulatory group to define and enforce trading rules. In essence, the exchange and its members established and supported the trading model and all the functions associated with it. Over the years, these exchanges with their simple self-sufficient model established themselves as an integral part of the global economy.

Exchanges remain a crucial part of our economy, but their organization and structure have changed tremendously. Today, the shift to electronic trading and vigorous competition among exchanges resulted in a new, more complex electronic trading model that relies on other vendors and even other exchanges to complete the trade cycle. To compete effectively and get to market quickly, exchanges no longer have the time to build all exchange functions themselves. They needed to outsource to vendors that will give them a competitive edge. The exchanges took slightly different paths to adopt the electronic trading model. The one common theme was to take advantage of the technology built by the early adopters and the new players entering the financial markets with applications for the various components of the trade cycle. Every component could be developed by different players and the components could then be connected to complete the trading platform. For new exchanges such as EurexUS entering the derivatives market, time was of the essence. And they were able to start quickly by outsourcing major components such as exchange technology as well as trading screens and regulatory and clearing functions. For the floor-based exchange the needs were different; they had the regulatory and clearing functions, but they needed the technology to migrate off the floor.

The early adopters of electronic exchanges had to build most of their infrastructure internally. They supported and maintained all the functions of the trade cycle. The rest of the market, sometimes reluctantly, soon followed the early adopters. The followers were under pressure to catch up to the success of the early adopters. They needed to embrace technology and find creative ways to enter the electronic trading markets quickly. They took advantage of the componentized architecture of the electronic trading model. By that time the electronic infrastructure had matured, and there were many new players in the market to provide various components of the trade *cycle*. The migration toward a modular exchange and modular financial market began blurring the boundaries between the functions and components of trading. The electronic trading model opened up the global marketplace for exchanges to not only compete but to license technology from each other.

Modular Exchange: Building Blocks

Unlike the early adopters, the followers now had numerous choices available to build their exchange infrastructures. They were reshaping their organization using components built and supported by software vendors as well as early adopters of the electronic trading model. There were partnerships and collaborations between the exchanges. They could build their entire infrastructure by piecing components together from different players instead of building everything from scratch. The time and cost of building the entire infrastructure themselves could jeopardize their chances of survival in this fast-changing market; therefore, the modular exchange allowed them to transform quickly.

Many new players entered the market and established themselves as an integral part of the new model. The new players and their applications provided followers with the modular exchange model, allowing them to build their infrastructure in collaboration and partnership with financial market players to compete in the new global financial market model. There were over 25 software vendors providing front-end trading systems and gateways to the exchanges. More than 200 vendors offered various components, from matching engines for the exchanges to automated trading applications (black box) for traders. A number of hosting facilities provided infrastructure support and maintenance for trading firms that lacked their own technology staff. We can credit early adopters with defining the electronic trading model, but the trend to adopt the modular exchange model began with the followers, who took advantage of this competition to pick components that best suited their needs.

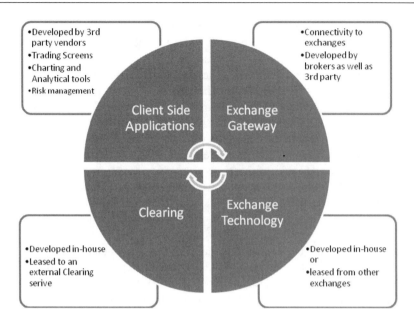

Figure 9.1 Modular exchange model.

The modular exchange model extended beyond the use of technology components as the exchanges began to outsource entire functions of the trade cycle, such as clearing, settlement, and regulatory functions. The success of an exchange depends on solid services provided by all the components of the trade cycle. In the self-sufficient model, the exchanges built and maintained these components based on the needs of their members. However, the new model brought new complexity and new requirements in the trading model. To keep up with these changes, financial markets had no choice but to utilize the modular model. The modular model allowed companies to specialize in specific components to fulfill the demands of the changing model. It was far easier to keep up with the changes in a particular area than the entire trade cycle. The modular exchange model has made exchanges around the world a complex network of partnerships with dependencies on each other, far greater than in the floor-trading model. The exchanges today are a tangled web, utilizing each others' services and technology as well as now depending on new players in the markets to serve as the gateway to their markets. To conduct trading in the new electronic trading model, a trade now goes through numerous components that could be residing in numerous locations around the globe and supported by multiple players in the marketplace (see Figure 9.1).

Exchanges no longer have to build and support every component of the trade cycle as they previously did in the floor-trading model. Instead, they now have choices available for both technology and services through numerous service providers in the financial markets. Early adopters of the electronic model who built their technology from scratch could now provide their technology components to the followers coming into the marketplace, further establishing their leadership in defining and improving the electronic trading model.

The modular exchange has in part brought competition and innovation to financial markets, and it continues to shape the electronic trading model into the 21st century. Independent software vendors (ISVs) continue to innovate in the front-end trading space. Others developing risk management tools continue to adapt and improve their applications to provide real-time risk management, and players in the back office continue to improve and innovate to provide faster and efficient clearing and settlement services for financial markets. Competition and collaboration in financial markets has flourished at an unprecedented speed in the last two decades. Exchanges today rely on these new players to build their exchange infrastructure and to expand their market base. The success of an exchange in today's model no longer depends solely on liquidity and exclusive product listing; it also depends on software and service providers. Picking the best technology and partners to build the infrastructure is an integral part of an electronic exchange.

CBOT: Cautious Migration by Outsourcing Technology

At 160 years old, CBOT is the world's oldest futures and options exchange. CBOT's transformation from the old floor-trading model to an electronic exchange provides a perfect view of the modular exchange model. CBOT, like other U.S. derivatives markets, took the first step toward electronic trading only by extending its floor-trading to after hours to capture volume in the Far East. CBOT built its own application called Project A, a second[1] step toward adapting technological changes in the financial market. Project A was launched in 1994 and allowed CBOT members to trade their products after hours. The connection to CBOT markets through Project A was available via CBOT dedicated terminals scattered in numerous locations, including Asia. Traders in Japan, Australia, and Taiwan used these terminals to place orders for various CBOT products. The success of Project A initially was sporadic at best. Traders primarily used the application to hedge their positions rather than for active trading. In other words, traders who no longer wanted their current exposure overnight could cover their position. Liquidity remained low on Project A due to numerous concerns by traders in Asia, including the potential inability of Project A to process large orders and the concern of moving the market due to thin volume. For example, grain buyers in Taiwan generally traded 400 lots (54,000 tons) per order, which was considered too large to process through Project A. The volumes were far lower than that on the floor. For example, on December 1, 1998, Project A's overnight volume for agriculture futures and options was 75 wheat, 610 corn, and 413 soybean contracts compared to the next-day volume of 35,000 wheat, 54,000 corn, and 40,000 soybean.[2] However, Project A continued to serve as an electronic platform available for traders after hours. It operated every hour the CBOT floor was closed, but the volume on the exchange didn't begin to pick up until 1998, when it finally turned a profit. It saw an increase of more than 120% in volume in the first half of 1998 compared to the year before.[3]

The exchange, however, was still not positioned to compete in the global marketplace. It was facing competition from new players such as BrokerTec, which was planning to launch an electronic trading platform for bond trading; the National Association of Securities Dealers (NASD) in 1999 was also planning to launch an electronic trading platform to trade U.S. Treasury futures, CBOT's flagship products.[4] CBOT was aware of the fate of LIFFE's Bund product and did not want history to repeat itself, especially if they would now be the victim. The exchange knew it could not compete against the other electronic trading platforms with its Project A technology. Project A was a closed platform. If a trader wanted to trade electronically on CBOT, he needed to install the Project A dedicated terminals to access the exchange. This would be a slow process for CBOT and cumbersome and expensive for trading firms. CBOT would have to continue to roll out the Project A terminals instead of providing an open electronic platform such as that for Eurex, which was available to trading firms through a number of ISVs. Trading firms that wanted to trade CBOT products electronically would need to rely on two different screens: one Project A terminal for CBOT and another for other electronic exchanges. The exchange knew it needed to either revamp and upgrade its Project A technology or form a partnership with an existing player.

Partnership with Eurex: First Alliance

The exchange took its first step toward electronic trading by forming a partnership with Eurex to outsource its trading platform module. The members of CBOT who had narrowly rejected the partnership deal with Eurex in January 1999 bowed to competitive pressure and voted overwhelmingly for the Eurex partnership six months later, on June 24, 1999. The partnership would cost the CBOT $50 million, compared to the projected $47 million cost to upgrade the Project A technology. For $3 million extra the CBOT would gain a new trading platform with global access, with Eurex's 5000 screens in 16 countries, compared to only 700 Project A terminal available in only four countries.[5]

The alliance with Eurex served as CBOT's first venture into a modular exchange. CBOT and Eurex agreed to form an alliance in the hopes of increasing their global market share and consolidating the selection of products across the two exchanges. They agreed to provide each other's products on the new electronic trading platform called a/c/e, named after the Alliance between

CBOT and Eurex. The partnership was one of the first transatlantic ventures in electronic trading, which would give customers on both sides trading opportunities on both markets simultaneously. Users could now trade the world's benchmark products, such as U.S. Treasuries and the German bund, through a single screen. The launch proved successful and, after the launch of a/c/e in 2000, volume on the platform grew steadily, reaching over 408,000 contracts per day by 2002.[6]

Partnership with LIFFE

The 162-year-old exchange's resistance to electronic trading was beginning to show. CBOT had lost its number-one spot in futures trading to Eurex, the all-electronic German exchange, and was even falling behind its longtime rival, CME. The alliance with Eurex was successful but short lived. After a number of heated public disputes between the two exchanges over product listing rules, technology fees, and the like, the two exchanges agreed to part ways by January 2004. Once again, the CBOT needed to find a partner to provide the exchange with an electronic platform if it was going to survive in the new world of electronic trading.

The separation led to some significant strategic moves by both exchanges. Eurex announced the launch of EurexUS to compete directly with CBOT, which we will discuss shortly. The CBOT continued its migration toward electronic trading and announced its decision to lease the electronic platform from Euronext.liffe. Euronext.liffe was formed through the merger of Euronext, a conglomerate of European equities markets (Paris, Amsterdam, Lisbon, Portugal, and Brussels), and LIFFE, a derivatives market. The alliance between the two exchanges would be similar to the partnership between the CBOT and Eurex. The CBOT would list its products on LIFFE Connect, the electronic trading platform of Euronext.liffe, and Euronext.liffe would provide support and maintenance of the technology infrastructure for the CBOT. In return, Euronext.liffe customers would now have access to the CBOT products. The partnership would also offer Euronext.liffe access to the CBOT's agriculture products, which had not been successfully created by the European exchanges. The LIFFE Connect platform provided CBOT access to the large European trading community that traded with Euronext.liffe. It allowed the CBOT to take advantage of the enhanced functionality offered by the LIFFE Connect platform. LIFFE Connect was considered the most advanced platform for spread trading and options trading.

The decision to pick LIFFE Connect was met with a significant amount of skepticism. LIFFE Connect technology was significantly different from the earlier a/c/e platform developed with Eurex. For example, stop orders were supported by Eurex but not by LIFFE Connect. LIFFE Connect supported decimal pricing but not the fractional prices supported by the a/c/e platform.

The two exchanges depended heavily on third-party vendors to fill the gaps in functionality to ensure that traders saw minimal impact during the transition. There were some major architectural differences that would impact the trading community when they moved to this new system. The LIFFE Connect architecture stored a trader's order book [7] in local memory on the trader's computer or server. The Eurex system, by contrast, saved the order book on the hard drive of the trader's computer or server. This major architectural difference means that if the trading system lost its connection to Eurex, the orders were restored when connectivity was regained. The LIFFE Connect system, on the other hand, would lose the order book when disconnected and it could not be restored.[8] Another major difference between the two systems was the location of the exchange matching engine. The a/c/e matching engine was in Chicago; however, the LIFFE Connect matching engine was initially located in London, home of Euronext.liffe, which was bad for Chicago traders and good for London-based traders.[9] The distance between the trading front end and matching engine impacts the speed at which orders reach the exchange. This was increasingly important to trading firms, which were increasingly using automated trading systems to implement their trading strategies.

The decision to pick LIFFE Connect also gave the CBOT its first glimpse of a truly open electronic platform and the importance of collaborating with third-party vendors, especially ISVs that were increasingly becoming the primary provider of front-end trading software. The technology was significantly different from Eurex, and trading firms needing access to CBOT would need to connect to LIFFE Connect to develop and test their software. Due to its open architecture, plenty of ISVs were already connected to LIFFE Connect, making it easier for them to provide connectivity to CBOT. These third-party vendors filled the functionality gaps by supporting stop-order functionality and fractional prices and storing the order book within their trading system. The two exchanges had only a year to complete the migration from Eurex's a/c/e platform to LIFFE Connect. The two exchanges worked tirelessly throughout the year to ensure that the transition went smoothly. During the development and testing phase, CBOT and LIFFE worked with over 50 ISVs, providing front-end trading application or black boxes for automated trading, to ensure that they were ready for the CBOT launch on LIFFE Connect by January 2004. Without a successful integration between these new players and the exchanges, the launch would not have been successful, because these vendors provided the single-screen trading concept for the exchange's customers.

The alliance with LIFFE proved successful, and CBOT saw tremendous growth in its electronic trading volume. It was now fully embracing electronic trading. By early 2004, over 60% of financial futures were trading electronically. The CBOT adapted and transformed to meet the growing demands of its users. The exchange fought the competitive battle with EurexUS by using not only its political power to lobby in Washington, but also by switching to the new technology platform, cutting costs, and slashing fees. The CBOT partnered with CME to build a common clearing link between the two exchanges, saving its customers over \$1.7 billion annually through reductions in margin requirements and other clearing-related fees. The CBOT slashed its trading fees on U.S. Treasury futures almost 75%, bringing down trading fees for nonmembers from \$1.25 to a mere 30 cents per contract.[10] The exchange finally saw its business turn around. It posted record volumes and successfully beat its potential competitor, EurexUS. The CBOT posted an average of 41.4 million trades for Treasury contracts, compared to a paltry 110,055 contracts at EurexUS,[11] for the months of March, April, and May 2004.

The Final Move

The exchange has not looked back since its remarkable transformation. Although slow to adopt electronic trading as the new model, the CBOT made strategic moves to slowly adopt technology and transform its 162-year-old business model from a nonprofit member-owned exchange to a for-profit exchange. It made the right decision to adopt the electronic trading model while gently easing its members into electronic trading. Since its launch as a public company, the CBOT migrated all its products to its electronic platform and began discussions of a possible merger with CME. After shaking off two takeover moves by ICE, CBOT merged with CME to form an all-Chicago exchange, making it the largest futures exchange in the world. The takeover by CME brought yet another change in CBOT's technology platform. All CBOT products would now be listed on CME's Globex platform, the third electronic home of these products.

The journey of CBOT toward electronic trading shows the true benefits of a modular exchange. In the electronic trading model, exchanges can switch the underlying technology components to meet changing market needs. In less than 10 years, CBOT moved from an in-house built Project A, to Eurex's a/c/e platform, to LIFFE Connect, and, finally, to CME's Globex. It transitioned its customers smoothly to each new platform while maintaining steady growth in its volume (see Figure 9.2).

The Rise and Fall of Eurex Us: Outsourcing Technology and Services

After severing its ties with CBOT, Eurex announced the launch of EurexUS, one of the most unique launches in the new electronic trading world. Eurex planned to launch EurexUS in Chicago to compete directly with CBOT and CME, the two largest derivatives exchanges in the United States. The Chicago exchanges were still lagging behind Eurex in technology and were still strug-

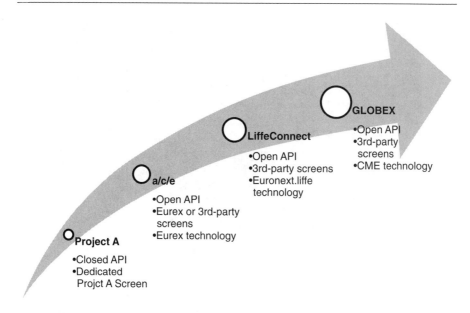

Figure 9.2 CBOT's path to electronic trading.

gling to move their exchanges toward electronic trading, primarily due to resistance from their own members. The move by Eurex to compete with the Chicago exchanges on their own turf forced them, especially the CBOT,[12] to make some bold moves to reposition themselves in electronic trading. EurexUS hoped to repeat history by stealing volume from CBOT's flagship product, just as it did with LIFFE. And so the competition began.

EurexUS fought through heavy political lobbying from the Chicago exchanges to establish itself as an exchange in the United States. It already had a presence there since its launch in Europe. Eurex provided remote terminals to allow U.S. traders to trade product on the Eurex platform. It had 20–25% of its trade volume coming from the United States. However, Eurex wanted to establish a U.S.-regulated exchange to gain additional market share, including the growing number of proprietary traders in the derivatives market. Soon after it announced its intention to launch a new exchange, EurexUS began to put together its building blocks by partnering with a number of financial market players to establish a fully electronic market in the United States.

EurexUS took full advantage of the modular exchange model (see Figure 9.3). EurexUS utilized the technology of its parent company, Eurex. It also adopted the Eurex market model that proved to be so successful in Europe. By partnering or purchasing products from financial market players that had already established themselves in the U.S. derivatives markets, EurexUS managed to keep its staff lean and organization efficient. By outsourcing essentially every

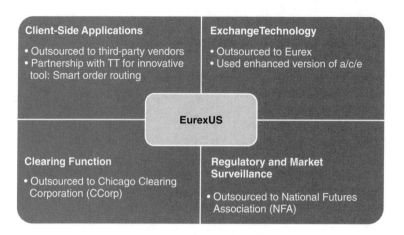

Figure 9.3 Eurex US: Built through partnership and outsourcing.

function, EurexUS managed to run a lean shop with only 35 people on its staff, which was primarily focused on sales, marketing, and customer service.[13] EurexUS passed these savings on to its customers by offering lower fees for trading. It used the updated version of the a/c/e platform, the same platform once used by CBOT, its former partner and current competitor. It formed a partnership with the Clearing Corporation to provide clearing services for its products. It outsourced its regulatory and surveillance functions to the National Futures Association (NFA).

In addition, EurexUS formed a partnership with front-end trading system provider Trading Technologies to provide products such as TT Navigator and a smart order router. TT Navigator allows traders to view the same product from different exchanges side by side, and route orders to the best available market. This gave traders access to the Treasury products, which were listed on both CBOT and EurexUS. Traders using TT Navigator could place orders wherever they saw the best price. After a long battle to gain approval, EurexUS was approved by the CFTC to open for business in the United States. EurexUS was officially launched on February 8, 2004. The launch was successful and first-day trading topped over 15,000 contracts. However, EurexUS struggled to gain significant market share. Only four months after opening, it offered several incentive programs to entice traders to trade on EurexUS. The program worked briefly, and, in July 2004, EurexUS volume reached 40,000 contracts per day.

However, the growth in volume slowly fizzled, and EurexUS never gained traction against the bigger exchanges. A year after its launch, EurexUS managed to gain only about 5% of the U.S. derivatives volume. The exchange was eventually bought by Man Financial group in October 2006 and relaunched as the U.S. Futures Exchange.

Although EurexUS was never able to capture significant volume from the CBOT, it brought much needed competition and innovation to the futures industry. The competitive threat from Eurex forced the CBOT to upgrade its electronic trading system and provide enhanced functionality to the trading community. To keep EurexUS off its turf, the CBOT slashed its fees to match those offered by EurexUS. For example, EurexUS charged a trading fee of 20 cents, forcing CBOT to slash its prices to 30 cents for nonmembers and temporarily waiving fees for its members.[14] By shifting its clearing to the CME, the CBOT could use cross-margining[15] to reduce the clearing costs for many of its customers. So even though Eurex was not able to repeat the success it had in stealing LIFFE's Bund, it managed to jolt the two monopolies in Chicago and brought much needed efficiency, innovation, and lower rates to the trading community.

More important, the development of EurexUS also showed how the modular exchange model allows one to build an exchange quickly. Eurex's technology helped establish the EurexUS exchange infrastructure. Partnerships with ISVs such as TT helped EurexUS tap into the local trading community, which was already using TT's front-end trading applications. The EurexUS launch also opened the door to the global expansion of exchanges. All one needs is to partner and collaborate with various players in the financial markets. As EurexUS proved, launching a new exchange using the modular model is easy. Gaining liquidity and regulatory approval, however, remains difficult.

Battle in the Energy Markets

Energy markets had two major powerhouses: NYMEX in the United States and IPE in Europe. Both exchanges offered similar products such as Brent Crude and West Texas Intermediate (WTI). The competition between these two exchanges is very different today than in the past. As floor-based exchanges, they considered a partnership with each other a few times. In the late 1980s, when IPE failed to successfully launch its own Brent contract,[16] it approached NYMEX to form a partnership and provide NYMEX's WTI contract on their London floor prior to NYMEX opening. The proposal was rejected by the NYMEX board. The defeat prompted a relaunch of the contract in 1988. The product received strong backing by the London traders in response to the blow dealt by NYMEX. The product took off and put IPE on the competitive landscape with NYMEX. Both exchanges spent the next few years attempting to expand their territory through links with exchanges in other regions and new product launches. IPE attempted to link with SIMEX, the Singapore exchange, and NYMEX tried to expand by launching Middle East Sour Crude. Both attempts failed to gain any traction, and the volumes at the exchanges were reaching a plateau.

In the meantime, electronic trading in energy markets was picking up. Enron launched EnronOnline on November 29, 1999, and for the first time allowed energy traders to buy and sell energy contracts online.[17] The trading platform had a short life. The scandals and financial misreporting at Enron led the firm into bankruptcy, and EnronOnline shut down two years later, on November 28, 2001. Another electronic trading provider, IntercontinentalExchange (ICE), fared better. It had a slightly different business plan. The trading firms using the ICE platform were required to sign bilateral counterparty agreements.[18] A trader can see all the posted prices in the market. The ICE electronic platform had two different prices on its electronic platform: white prices and red prices. A white price means it was posted by an eligible counterparty and can be traded. A red price, on the other hand, means the trader is not allowed to trade with this counterparty. If a trader signs up for an optional clearing account, many more prices turn white.

Although ICE was successful in its short history, with over 6000 screens already available by August 2000, it knew that the lack of a proper clearing process would impact its future growth and its potential competition with regulated exchanges such as NYMEX and IPE. NYMEX was already positioning itself to take advantage of the lack of clearing on the ICE platform by listing OTC products with the exchanges clearing services. In early 2001, NYMEX announced its plan to cut margins for OTC products to compete with ICE and launched Brent futures contracts to compete with IPE. The struggling IPE and ICE decided to join forces to compete with NYMEX. On April 30, 2001, ICE and IPE announced their decision to merge.[19]

The merger would give both exchanges the tools needed to compete effectively in the energy markets. ICE was able to form a partnership with the London Clearing House (LCH), which was the clearing house for IPE. IPE instantly got access to ICE's electronic platform, and both exchanges could now merge their large trading community to compete with NYMEX. In addition, ICE also took advantage of third-party vendors and their access to proprietary trading firms. It formed a partnership with Trading Technologies, an ISV for the global derivatives market. ICE granted exclusive access to its OTC products to TT's front-end trading screens. Prior to the partnership, ICE's OTC products could only be traded with ICE's proprietary Web-based application, WebICE. By offering its OTC products via TT, ICE was now available to proprietary traders who were already using TT's application to trade other markets.

The IPE floor was eventually shut down in 2004. Orders traded on either exchange were matched by the electronic trading infrastructure based in Atlanta, ICE's headquarters, and cleared in London, LCH.Clearnet's home. ICE has been fiercely competitive in the energy markets and forced NYMEX to rethink its floor-based model. Today, ICE has its own clearinghouse, which it acquired with the purchase of NYBOT. This acquisition also provided the ICE with soft commodities. ICE recently terminated its partnership with LCH to establish ICE Clearing Europe as its primary clearinghouse. Its recent decision to partner with CCorp will certainly position the exchange to gain the clearing business for products such as credit default swaps (CDS).[20]

NYMEX: Outsourcing New Product Listing

NYMEX, a dominant energy exchange, was one of the strongest resistors of the electronic trading model. Like other followers, NYMEX didn't completely ignore the electronic trading model. It took advantage of the modular exchange model in 2002 when it partnered with CME to list "e-mini" versions of NYMEX's key energy futures. These products would be available for trading via CME's electronic trading platform, Globex. The product would be cleared through NYMEX's clearinghouse. The partnership gave customers of both exchanges access to products from both markets.[21] The collaboration allowed NYMEX to use CME's infrastructure and global network for its mini-products and gave CME's customers new products to trade. NYMEX and CME also worked on a joint clearing platform, CLEARING21, to provide real-time clearing and risk management for mini-products.[22]

Leasing Technology

As the migration to the electronic trading model grew, so too did the adoption of the modular exchange model. The exchanges used numerous technology providers to build their infrastructure and outsourced services to established clearinghouses, regulatory services, and the like, to ensure a quick migration to electronic trading. Partnerships and collaborations within the financial industry became the norm. It is now not uncommon to see two competing exchanges cooperate to use each other's technology or services to meet the fast-changing needs of the financial marketplace.

Technology is by far the most important component of the modular exchange. Electronic trading allows the trade-cycle model to be built as components, which can be pieced together like Lego blocks. New ideas inspire competition, and electronic trading is no different. Every component of the trade cycle saw numerous players. Technology also allowed financial markets to integrate and switch between these components easily and quickly. Components from front-end trading applications to matching engines could now simply be licensed by exchanges and others to build their own electronic trading infrastructure.

European markets began the migration to electronic trading very early on. Innovative technologies such as the OM platform brought the concept of leasing technology to build the electronic exchange infrastructure to markets in Europe. As the organization and structure of the European Union solidified, the need increased to provide a financial market model accessible to all the EU nations. Exchanges in the EU nations used the modular exchange model to build an electronic trading infrastructure. Collaborations and partnerships flourished within financial markets. Today it would be hard to point to a single exchange that is based on a self-sufficient model.

Early Pioneers: Technology Providers

OMX

OMX was among the early pioneers to provide technology services to other financial firms. OMX exchanges consisted of eight Nordic and Baltic exchanges. The technology arm of OMX provided the electronic exchange platform for close to 50 exchanges around the world, across all asset classes. Prominent exchanges such as Singapore Exchange (SGX), International Securities Exchange, Bombay Stock Exchange, and Tokyo Commodities Exchange formed partnerships with OM Technology to use its electronic trading platform. These exchanges utilized the technology developed and supported by OM Technology to build their electronic infrastructure. In early 2008, OMX was acquired by Nasdaq to form Nasdaq OMX. Nasdaq OMX combines the technology and distribution network of the two giants to form the largest equities exchanges in the world, with a presence in over 50 countries.

LIFFE

LIFFE has come a long way after losing the German Bund to Eurex. The loss of the German Bund served as a wakeup call for LIFFE, which realized the electronic trading model was here to stay. It took drastic steps to transform itself by replacing its 18-year-old trading pit with electronic trading in less than two years. After the migration to electronic trading, it never looked back. LIFFE built its own technology platform, called LIFFE Connect, which it provided to exchanges around the world. It licensed its platform to the CBOT, which abandoned Eurex's platform in favor of LIFFE Connect. It is also used by the Tokyo Financial Exchange (TFX). With its merger with Euronext, LIFFE Connect became the technology platform for a number of smaller markets in Paris, Amsterdam, Brussels, Lisbon, and Portugal. With the recent transatlantic merger of Euronext with NYSE, LIFFE Connect became the technology platform for the equity giant NYSE.

Collaboration: Blurring the Lines between Exchanges

Many of the exchanges that resisted change did not necessarily fare badly. The technological innovations that they initially resisted actually helped expedite their migration toward electronic trading. Exchanges around the world began licensing technology platforms from other exchanges or technology providers. They had choices available to them that the early adopters did not. They could pick the best provider for each component to build a solid electronic infrastructure. Followers could also switch their platform to use different components, another advantage of the modular exchange model that allows them to upgrade their technology to suit their market needs.

There are numerous examples of exchanges large and small that depend on each other and other technology providers to complete the trade cycle. These exchanges have adopted the modular exchange model that has allowed them to abandon one platform and pick another to increase market share in the global financial markets. Through partnerships, outsourcing, and mergers and acquisition, exchanges today rely on each other more than they did in the days of the floor-trading model:

- MexDer licensed MEFF's electronic platform to build Mexico's options market.
- Chicago Climate Exchange (CCX) licensed technology from ICE.[23] All traded CCX products are supported via the ICE electronic platform.[24]
- The partnership between Dubai and NYMEX allows Dubai to utilize NYMEX's electronic trading platform and clearing services.
- Singapore Exchange (SGX) partnered with OMX and Orc Software[25] to increase its market base. Prior to the partnership, SGX provided its own front-end trading application. By opening access to its platform and utilizing third-party software, SGX hopes to increase user participation on its exchange.[26]
- With its partnership with Montreal, Boston Options Exchange replaced its existing NSC-based platform from Atos Euronext with Montreal trading platform Sola.

These collaborations between exchanges are growing at an unprecedented speed as the exchanges position themselves in the global financial markets. In addition to partnerships between themselves, exchanges also partnered with ISVs that developed software to connect to multiple exchanges and provide a single-screen trading option for traders around the world. As exchanges launched new products to gain more volume or smaller exchanges hoped to increase market participation on their exchange, they forged relationships with ISVs such as Orc, TT, and more. These relationships allowed ISVs to build new features within their applications that encouraged their users to trade the newly launched products. The relationship with these ISVs also provided exchanges another marketing avenue because the ISVs, hoping to capture more market share among them, would provide users training in electronic trading and new trading styles introduced to take advantage of single-screen trading across multiple markets. Due to the technological innovations in the new model, new exchanges in today's financial markets can be built quickly. Exchanges choose and fit together components like Lego blocks, as we saw with the launch of EurexUS.

Table 9.1 Central Clearinghouses Used by Multiple Exchanges

Clearinghouse*	Exchanges Cleared
OCC	AMEX, BOX, CBOE, ISE, PCX, PHLX, CFE, Onechicago
CCORP	U.S. Futures Exchange (EurexUS), Chicago Climate Exchange, Financial and Energy Exchange
CME Clearing	CME, CBOT, NYMEX*
LCH.Clearnet	Euronext.Liffe, LME, APE, ECX, Hong Kong Mercantile Exchange
JCCH	Common clearing platform for all seven Japanese commodity exchanges
ICE Clear	ICE, NYBOT, IPE, Winnepeg**

*CBOT and NYMEX both are now part of CME Group. Both exchanges were using CME Clearing prior to their merger.
**Winnipeg is now ICE Futures Canada, NYBOT is now ICE Futures US, and IPE is now ICE Futures Europe.

Leasing Clearing Services

The clearing function is an integral part of the trade cycle. Exchanges in the floor-trading days generally had their own clearinghouses that played the role of central clearing for the products traded on the exchanges. However, the trend toward outsourcing the clearing function is not entirely new. The Options Clearing Corporation, for example, was the government-mandated exclusive clearinghouse for all the U.S. equity options exchanges. As the exchanges migrated to the electronic trading model, the clearing service became one of the modules that could be outsourced. Exchanges such as the ICE took advantage of this outsourcing when they acquired IPE. However, because clearing generates revenue, some exchanges, including ICE, are moving to build the clearing services in-house.

Technology allowed more exchanges to list competitive products and form partnerships with exchanges around the world. Both of these moves provided a wider selection of products available for trading. By outsourcing the clearing service, these exchanges provided their customers with a central clearinghouse service. The mergers and acquisitions of exchanges, the cross-listing of products across multiple exchanges, and the listing of multiple-asset classes and OTC products have all spurred competition in clearing services. Today, as exchanges around the globe merge, the use of a common clearing service has increased, as shown in Table 9.1.

Clearing services have also seen a number of changes spurred by the transformation of exchanges. As the exchanges changed from nonprofit to for-profit companies, they had to constantly find new revenue streams to remain competitive in financial markets. To increase their revenues, global exchanges have seen tremendous growth in their product listings due to mergers and acquisitions. Technology provided tools for customers to begin trading products on multiple exchanges around the globe. These integrated exchanges and global marketplaces created demand for independent clearinghouses to clear across exchanges. Having a centralized clearinghouse allows risk management systems to consider trades across products and, therefore, customers can receive better overall margin.

However, exchanges have recently started initiatives to break away from their partnerships with independent clearinghouses to develop their own, primarily to gain the revenue from clearing. ICE recently launched its own clearing service for both the U.S. and European markets. Similarly, LIFFE announced the development of its own clearing service, leaving behind the clearing services of LCH.Clearnet. Even with these recent moves of exchanges starting their own clearinghouses, competition in clearing remains strong. There are a number of new players entering the market, such as Swapstream, which was launched as a swaps trading platform in 2003. In 2006, Swapstream was acquired by CME, which provided its clearing functions for Swapstream.

Collocation

In the floor-trading model, the pit served as a gathering place for traders to stand next to each other and trade. Being taller and louder mattered. It also mattered how physically close you were to the specialist or to the buyer or seller in the pit to ensure that your trade was executed before others. The world of electronic trading changed all that. Traders now only interact with their computer screens. Electronic trading gives the trading community the flexibility to trade from anywhere in the world. Exchanges such as Eurex and CME built their electronic success by providing remote connectivity. However, some things in trading never change. Getting a trade in before anyone else still remains important. To achieve this goal, traders now have to worry about the speed, connectivity, and proximity to the exchanges they trade on. Even if the orders traveled at the speed of light, an order submitted from 100 miles away would take slightly longer than an order from only 10 miles away. In the new trading model, having the most powerful computer or fastest connection to the exchange is a crucial criterion for successful trading.

Being close to the exchanges still matters, but the exchange infrastructure could span multiple locations. In addition, traders are now scattered all over the world. The distance between the trader and the exchange impacts the order's latency—the amount of time it takes for a message to arrive at its destination. Being first in the queue to get the order executed means having the fastest machines close to the exchange. However, traders do not want to move back to the pits. The need to achieve low latency for order submission has prompted yet another wave of infrastructure improvements.

Since traders today are not limited to a single market, the solution is not as easy as simply moving traders closer to the exchange. Instead, traders trade across multiple markets around the globe, and they want their trades to reach all the exchanges quickly. To achieve low latency across all markets, firms started moving their servers closer to the exchanges. When the CBOT began using LIFFE Connect technology, which was located in London, it potentially put its Chicago traders at a disadvantage to the traders in Europe, forcing some of their customers to move their operations to London to be closer to the LIFFE matching engine. Similarly, when IPE shut its trading floor and moved to electronic trading, IPE orders had to travel all the way to Atlanta, ICE's headquarters, and IPE traders noticed higher latency for their orders compared to traders in the United States. Firms around the world would find venues close to the exchange infrastructure to ensure that they achieved low latency. However, for firms trading across multiple markets, simply moving their offices was not enough. To achieve the same speed and low latency across all markets, companies began using hosting facilities and collocation.

Hosting facilities offered to support the technology infrastructure required to trade in the electronic trading world. They were the technology administrators for trading firms. Hosting facilities provide support and management responsibilities for network administration, hardware and software configuration, data line management, security, and backup services. This ensured that trading firms had a stable electronic infrastructure. Hosting facilities also established themselves as the solution to achieve low latency. For example, Trading Technologies' TTNET touted its vast network, with TTNET hub computers close to the exchanges. TTNET used a global network of dedicated lines connected to gateways close to the exchange location, thus providing faster roundtrip times for orders. Other hosting facilities and large investment banks offered customers similar services: a low-latency electronic trading network. These hosting facilities allowed trading firms to distribute trading screens around the world connected through these hosting facility hubs, strategically located near exchanges.

Traders are driven to compete. In the electronic trading world, traders compete with speed. As the trading community embraced electronic trading, it began to use new applications such as black-box trading applications. Black boxes allow traders to trade larger orders automatically. They allow traders to build complex strategies and let the computer execute them on their behalf. Increased automation in trading increases the need for speed. Recent research from Tabb Group estimates that to improve speed by just a microsecond costs firms approximately $250. Therefore, a six-millisecond reduction costs approximately $1.5 million.[27] The cost to achieve speed in trading has continued to increase as more players enter the market to offer ultra-low-latency solutions for financial markets. Exchanges in recent years have entered the market to provide access to their electronic platforms at low latency by offering collocation services to customers. Collocation allows trading firms to install their servers within an exchange's firewall—to have the servers right next to the exchange's matching engine in the same data center. Collocation basically allows trading firms to install their servers within the exchange's electronic infrastructure. It is the virtual trading pit. Instead of loud, sweaty traders standing shoulder to shoulder in a pit, only their servers hum softly next to each other in a cold data center.

Today, exchanges around the world offer collocation services to their customers and ISVs. The London Stock Exchange recently worked with a number of brokers to host their algorithmic trading engine inside their exchange's firewall.[28] The Australian Stock Exchange, in mid-2008, collocated its trading platform and gateway within the same facility as its matching engine, to provide submillisecond access.[29] Major derivatives exchanges in the United States and Europe have established collocation services for their customers, both to attract clients by offering low round-trip times and to earn additional revenue.

CME and LNET

CME began offering its Local Network (LNET) to customers and ISV partners, who would have direct access to CME's electronic platform. A number of trading firms and hosting facilities have taken advantage of this offer and moved their infrastructure within CME's collocation facility. In return, CME charges $6000 per connection per month, in addition to collocation facility charges. The latency with this collocation setup offers order processing time as low as 31 milliseconds for futures and 11 milliseconds for options.[30]

Similarly, other, larger derivatives exchanges such as ICE and Eurex have established and offered collocation services to customers since 2006. The demand for this service has been tremendous. In a year and a half, 36 firms signed up with Eurex's collocation service, and traders saw a tremendous decrease in latency. The round-trip times went down to approximately 10 milliseconds, compared to 29 milliseconds through a connection in London.[31] Firms such as Nico Trading, based in Chicago, saw a reduction in latency from 130 milliseconds to less than 30 milliseconds when they moved their servers within Eurex's collocation facilities.

Collocation has proved crucial for market makers, trading firms using black-box trading software, and ISVs. Market makers providing bid-ask spreads for trades can get their orders in as quickly as possible, making it possible for them to beat out a market maker in another city or country. For automated trading systems, submitting large orders quickly means getting first in the queue for execution. For ISVs, it serves as a competitive advantage to attract and retain their customers. ISVs with a stable and reliable hosting facility located within an exchange infrastructure could be an attractive option for firms looking for higher speeds.

The Modern Modular Exchange

Exchanges were once large physical spaces with monolithic systems that provided all the services required for trading. The modular exchange, on the other hand, is a platform on which other companies, big and small, can specialize and innovate to build better components. Now an exchange can be cobbled together quickly by leasing technologies from or outsourcing services to vendors, which can sometimes be direct competitors. Technology quickly forced traditional exchanges to transform into electronic exchanges, and it just as quickly became a commodity that enables small exchanges to compete with their larger competitors. Exchanges can be built as though from Lego blocks—interchangeable pieces chosen based on cost, features, partnerships, speed, and reliability.

The main beneficiaries of this competition have been trading firms. Healthy competition between exchanges improves services and reduces costs. More important, a vibrant market for client technologies, such as front-end trading screens and risk management tools, allows trading firms to gain an edge on their competition. Rather than being bigger and louder, as on the floor, firms now succeed by being faster and smarter. The modular exchange model allows all market participants to excel in their niche, from the exchanges to clearers, brokers, and traders.

Endnotes

1. CBOT's first step into electronic trading was to develop Aurora, a joint venture with Apple, Tandem, and Texas Instrument. The project never went live. Project A was the first electronic platform to go live.
2. Moriyama, Ayumi, "Asian Traders Hope for CBOT Project Growth," www.expressindia.com/news/fe/daily/19981204/33855054.html (December 4, 1998).
3. Kharouf, Jim, "Project A Spins Off," http://findarticles.com/p/articles/mi_qa5282/is_/ai_n24336071 (August 1998).
4. Moser, Mike, "CBOT Sees Edge with Eurex," www.allbusiness.com/business-finance/equity-funding-stock/295465-1.html (August 1, 1999).
5. Moser, Mike, "CBOT Sees Edge with Eurex," www.allbusiness.com/business-finance/equity-funding-stock/295465-1.html (August 1, 1999).
6. "CBOT and Eurex Hammer out New a/c/e Agreement," www.finextra.com/fullstory.asp?id=6133 (July 11, 2002).
7. Trader's order book contains orders specifically for that individual trader. It consists of all the orders submitted to the exchange by the trader.
8. CBOT required all the third-party vendors to store the order book locally on their trading system, which would allow traders to access the order book when the connection is regained.

9. North American Trading Host (NATH), the LIFFE Connect matching engine, was not launched until October, 2005, almost two years after the CBOT launch on the LIFFE Connect platform, www.euronext.com/fic/000/010/645/106457.ppt.

10. Weber, Joseph, "Chicago Takes on Europe, A Newly Revitalized Chicago Board of Trade Is Fending off Eurex—for now," www.businessweek.com/magazine/content/04_27/b3890096_mz020.htm (July 5, 2004).

11. Weber, Joseph, "Chicago Takes on Europe, A Newly Revitalized Chicago Board of Trade Is Fending off Eurex—for now," www.businessweek.com/magazine/content/04_27/b3890096_mz020.htm (July 5, 2004).

12. EurexUS was planning to list U.S. Treasuries, CBOT's bread and butter for its initial launch.

13. Speech by EurexUS CEO Satish Nandapurkar at the FIA luncheon.

14. Weber, Joseph, "Eurex Blows into Chicago," www.businessweek.com/bwdaily/dnflash/feb2004/nf2004025_6306_db016.htm (February 5, 2004).

15. Cross-margining is an agreement between two different markets or clearing organizations to set a lower net margin for a customer with positions at the two entities, which, when taken together, are less risky than either position in isolation.

16. IPE tried to launch a physically settled Brent contract in 1981 and tried to relaunch it as cash-settled in 1987. Both attempts failed to generate any significant liquidity.

17. Prior to EnronOnline, energy traders either traded on the floors of NYMEX and IPE or called each other to buy or sell energy contracts.

18. Bilateral agreements were required to handle the credit risk associated with trading OTC products. OTC products are unregulated products without a CCP the traders could turn to in case of default.

19. "Irresistible Force Meets Immovable Object," www.petroleum-economist.com/default.asp?page=14&PubID=46&ISS=8674&SID=325717 (Oct 2001).

20. "CCorp Unveils ICE Alliance as Fed Mulls CDS Clearing Proposals," www.sibosonline.com/fullstory.asp?id=19117 (October 10, 2008).

21. The partnership allowed CME members to trade NYMEX products via the NYMEX ACCESS system and NYMEX members to trade on CME's GLOBEX system.

22. "NYMEX Sets Daily Volume Records for Natural Gas Futures on CME GlobexÂ(®)," http://nymex.mediaroom.com/index.php?s=43&item=890&printable (January 31, 2007).

23. Under the agreement, CCX pays a licensing fee of $725,000 and service fee of $500,000 annually. In addition, CCX also pays ICE for technology development cost required for CCX.

24. "An Excerpt from a DEF 14A SEC Filing, Filed by INTERCONTINENTALEXCHANGE INC on 3/30/2007," http://sec.edgar-online.com/2007/03/30/0000950144-07-002932/Section17.asp.

25. Orc Software is an independent software vendor that connects to global exchanges to provide a front-end trading application.

26. By limiting access by providing connectivity only through its own front end, SGX would lose market share because users trading through a single screen across multiple markets would not trade on SGX, since it would not provide them an integrated market view across multiple exchanges on a single screen.

27. Clark, Joel, "Co-location Services Grow While Exchanges Seek to Streamline Operations and Drive Down Latency," http://db.riskwaters.com/public/showPage.html?page=788665 (April 1, 2008).

28. "Feature: Colocation: A Game Worth the Candle?" www.automatedtrader.net/feature-36.xhtm.

29. "ASX goes sub-millisecond with new co-location service," www.finextra.com/fullstory.asp?id=18684 (July 4, 2008).

30. Voyles, Bennett, "Co-Location Catches On," www.futuresindustry.org/fi-magazine-home.asp?v=p&a=1190.

31. Voyles, Bennett, "Co-Location Catches On," www.futuresindustry.org/fi-magazine-home.asp?v=p&a=1190.

10 Regulators: Leadership and Reaction

Andrea M. Corcoran

Principal, Align International, LLC
Former Division Director of the CFTC

Executive Summary

Regulators had to react to fundamental changes in the nature of exchanges, but they also at times were leaders of market change. For example, the response to the push for principles-based regulation granted exchanges more flexibility to design markets and products in thoughtful, cost-effective ways. The U.S. CFTC crafted a creative answer to the desire of foreign markets to place their terminals in the United States, an approach that permitted foreign competition but in a fashion that still protected U.S. customers and other public interests.

In the past turbulent decade, exchanges triumphed economically, providing efficient markets for price discovery, risk shifting, capital formation, and investment by bringing together buying and selling interests and making these transparent. The accelerating allure of the exchange model flowed from a long tradition of commodity and share trading that originated in the 1600s (or before) and occurred at diverse market centers: coffeehouses in London, under the buttonwood tree (and the eponymous agreement) on Wall Street, and elsewhere, where brokers and dealers in lavish bourses, wheat and rice traders in Japan, gold merchants in India, or multinational spice conglomerates or diamond brokers in Amsterdam and Antwerp took and shifted risks.[1] But 21st-century exchanges, though serving traditional functions, are also different. Today's exchanges transform themselves from:

- Floor to screen trading venues
- Private clubs[2] to profit-seeking listed companies
- National to global contenders
- Unitary, sole-purpose marketplaces to global consortiums

Their new incarnations challenge the time-honored regulatory conventions designed for a different age and a different marketplace. In response, their regulators struggle to adapt. Such tremendous change could not help but affect the optimal structure, governance, resources, expertise, philosophy, geographic scope, and trade and competition approaches of regulatory authorities.

Regulatory adaptations, in their turn, prompted market changes that could go to the very heart of their structure and competitive tactics.

This chapter addresses ways in which electronic markets have changed both the regulatory and the business dynamics and attempts to articulate when regulation is the driver of market change and when it is a mere reactor.

Introduction

Though some might quibble, the primary or first cause of the dramatic evolution of markets at the *macro* level was the advent of the electronic marketplace (the movement from floors to screens). With that advent came the capacity (barring national opposition) to exponentially expand and multiply trading venues, products, and direct participants, formerly circumscribed by geography, masonry, and limits on physical access. Some consequences were:

- *Increase in scope.* Virtual exchanges can reach across national boundaries and time zones to permit 24/7 trading activity by—and 24/7 delivery of real-time trading information to—remote end users. Technology makes it practicable for exchange designers to envision the electronic pooling of liquidity across national borders or the virtual passing of an exchange book across time zones.[3]
- *Uncertainty as to domicile.* Absent an internationally agreed paradigm as to what factors make a market domestic, electronic technology (which disperses central servers and access mechanisms geographically) renders it difficult for national regulators to reliably agree on where an electronic exchange is located. How should regulators or legislators decide which IT-assisted operations, when taken together, do—or should—constitute an exchange and when that exchange is—or should be—within a particular national regulator's perimeter? By facilitating user-originated transactions, electronic markets compromise the tried-and-true premise that solicitation of customers and orders is the nexus to which national regulatory jurisdiction attaches.[4] Not least, technology enables exchange governance and ownership arrangements that are outside the exchange's jurisdiction of authorization and possibly even unrelated to the business of finance, thereby altering the basis for, and the relationships among, the regulator and exchange owners and management.
- *Scope of competition.* Technology also permits new kinds of competition. In theory, electronic market operators can compete with broker intermediaries for business by offering access directly to subscribing end users, like managed funds, subject only to financing arrangements appropriate to the interest traded. The abandonment by electronic markets of a member governance and rewards structure to deliver displaced floor traders and market makers the value of their franchise through transferable shares assumes ultimately the transfer of shares to outsiders whose interest is in their own return, not that of market users. Electronic, Internet-based markets, also permit boutiques and niche markets to flourish, for which startup costs formerly would have been prohibitive. Technology, then, is a great leveler. In essence, electronic startups (BATs, ELX, MCX),[5] with no track record but also no legacy (IT, governance, regulatory) costs, can challenge the giants of the financial world[6] with a new, better, and cheaper idea. Electronic technology potentially allows any market

developer from any location to challenge any other market developer, in any other location, however entrenched, by seeking to draw away its liquidity with better software or hardware.

- *Intellectual property.* Markets that are really, at bottom, technology companies may consequently use competitive tactics more characteristic of intellectual property giants than financial services companies. An early example was the purchase by eSpeed of the so-called Wagner patent (reputedly a time/price priority algorithm) to extract royalties from multiple exchange operators. Other examples followed suit. Among these were the attempts to patent various exchange business processes, such as the unsuccessful attempt by the New York Mercantile Exchange (NYMEX) to protect its settlement price in the WTI Crude Oil contract from use by the Intercontinental Exchange (ICE) to settle ICE look-alike contracts. Defensive legal actions to protect one market's algorithms or products from another's competitive depredations, and offensive legal actions to question the rights of a particular exchange or clearing organization to use an algorithm, business process, or contract design[7], increasingly have been a byproduct of the metamorphosis of exchange from public welfare bricks-and-mortar institutions to electronic entrepreneurs. So far, financial regulators have resisted addressing these contests by taking positions on patentability or otherwise.

All these changes stress the regulatory model that evolved around the floor-bound, private-club, unitary, and national and nationalistic exchanges of the past. There is no doubt that the impact of technological innovations on exchange markets is immense and ongoing; how, then, have these changes implicated actual regulatory frameworks and the delivery of regulation?

At the outset, one must recognize that it is quite difficult, if not impossible, to disentangle the elements of precisely how electronic market developments have affected regulation, since each impact is integrated with every other. For example, the change in the nature of exchange ownership from club to shares in turn challenged regulators to reexamine the precise nature of the public interest served by markets and to question whether share-held, profit-driven markets were consistent with the public good, especially if operated under private contractual or self-regulatory models. Exchange technology (such as multiple communication hubs and the Internet) that was unconstrained by national boundaries forced national regulators to (1) think how best to address the extraterritorial reach of electronic screen trading venues, (2) struggle to precisely define what it is they were regulating, and (3) arm themselves to face the prospects of global as well as national competition and causes of price instability. Related changes tested regulators' capacity (without picking winners or losers, but also without losing regulatory focus) to mediate or balance the interests of various market players (wholesale and retail; sell side and buy side), to assess the value of central markets or consolidated order flows against systems that permit trade outside the central market and national location, and to determine the proper treatment of systems that have the capacity to treat the different classes of traders, types of products, and order sizes. Nonetheless, despite the difficulty of unbundling the various individual impacts, it may be possible to look more closely at the objectives regulators have expressed and the way the electronic revolution prompted changes in how these are being achieved.

The Electronic Driver and Overall Regulatory Design

At a high level, for both securities and derivatives (which, if based on financial instruments or equities, are also in many jurisdictions considered securities[8]), regulators have three objectives:

- Protection of investors/customers
- Maintenance of fair, efficient, and transparent markets
- Mitigation of systemic risk[9]

At an even higher level, regulators or related governmental entities often are mandated, at least locally, to assure fair competition and to prevent accumulation of market power from adversely affecting market access, efficiency, pricing integrity, or the real economy.[10]

Though changing the media of trading does not change the message of the regulator, the techniques of regulation and the focus of regulatory interest nonetheless must adapt. Simply put, regulators must refine their processes because electronic markets *are* different. Moving to the *micro* level, electronic markets may:

- Include many of the rules of the market within the trading algorithm itself, thus precluding certain rule violations or floor-based subterfuges but rendering in-depth understanding of the algorithm logic critical
- Eliminate the execution and sales intermediary, thus precluding certain sales misconduct and customer abuses
- Permit types of manipulation or gaming that are not possible in floor markets
- Increase the extent to which the instrument of execution is directly in the hands of remote users or customers, subject to electronic (pre- and post-trade) capacity to track or automatically limit risks, increasing the need for financial guarantors' awareness of customer knowledge of rules and maintenance of risk controls
- Allow liquidity failures or price aberrations that would be correctable or corrected by the etiquette of floor-trading where pit committees, ward heelers, arbitration policies, and business conduct committees stand guard or where market-making activities are typical
- Improve oversight data through cost-efficient, enhanced, real-time electronic audit trails, exposure aggregation, targeted surveillance, and sophisticated exception reporting
- Render sufficient oversight more difficult by:
  - Affording access to a broader class (from the perspective of financial capacity and geography) of direct users
  - Permitting more products and iterations of products, including products with limited liquidity

- Eliminating witnesses to trading activities
- Fueling political suspicion that computer models might cause a headless cascade or escalation in prices (overshooting fundamentals) because of order imbalances or "excessive" speculation
- Rendering validation of the security of the system and the capacity to reliably identify electronic users—especially vital[11]

Indeed, the capabilities of electronic markets for integrated supervision and maximum trading benefit may sometimes be in conflict. Technology potentially can assemble detail on individual positions, aggregate positions in multiple markets, and tailor filters that target risk precisely so as to identify and halt market abuses more readily, immediately, and definitively than in the floor environment. These regulatory advantages may, however, remain unrealized because market participants may prioritize speed of execution over prevention of error risk, or individual advantage over group protection.[12] The volume players expect the current technology to deliver ever more capacity and ever more immediate response times. Ironically, the demand to reduce latency (response time lag due to electronic order queuing) has led to collocated trading rooms, where latency is at a minimum and momentum (and the potential for collusion) is gained by proximity to other traders, as on the floor.

Now that we have articulated a multitude of macro and micro issues raised by the movement from floor to screen, let's examine ways in which these issues have affected regulatory actions.

Screen-Based Trading and the Concept of Regulation by Principle

Interestingly, one of the first responses to the advent of electronic market proposals was international. At the regulatory (and political) level, the global ambitions of screen-based trading systems were evident from the outset. In the late 1980s international concern developed about the global ambitions of Globex, the Chicago Mercantile Exchange's (CME) flagship venture, which had been in development for some time. Some jurisdictions viewed Globex as a threat and worried that the CME had imperialistic ambitions that would outpace and foreclose nascent developments in their own markets. At the time, many jurisdictions did not have specific provisions for authorizing nondomestic markets, because none of these had global reach. Before the promotion of Globex, electronic market initiatives had not yet credibly demonstrated the ability to implement their cross-border aspirations. To correct any authorization gap posed by the Globex challenge, the International Organization of Securities Commissions (IOSCO) in 1990 articulated 10 nonexclusive principles affecting authorization of cross-border derivatives markets (which may have been the first set of such high-level principles at the international level).[13] These remain to this day an excellent example of how a principles-type regime can facilitate common regulatory understandings across borders and cultures.

The core principles effectively set forth an internationally agreed template for admitting electronic screens affecting derivatives markets (both options and futures) within the participating jurisdictions, subject to application by individual national regulators. These principles, developed by a CFTC-led committee, were endorsed by the full complement of IOSCO members (then some 67 countries), a significant achievement in itself at that time. The same principles were subsequently re-endorsed in 2004, when four additional principles were added, and related specifically to cross-border cooperation, in recognition of the potential geographic reach of screen trading systems.[14] Until the recent reopening of U.S.-based discussions (and Congressional interest) in how to best define a "foreign" board of trade (discussed in a moment), the IOSCO Screen-Based Trading (SBT) Principles remained an undisputed benchmark against which:

- Non-U.S. futures markets seeking relief from full application of U.S. regulatory requirements in deference to home-based regulation were evaluated
- U.S. futures markets seeking to locate screens likewise could be tested by non-U.S. authorities[15]

As such, these principles not only assisted admission to multiple jurisdictions but also provided an agreed international template for individual jurisdictions to inquire in greater detail about individual screen-placement applications.

In essence, the principles sought to benchmark the capability of particular screen markets to deliver equitable executions, prevent market abuses, and be responsive to the surveillance and market integrity needs of affected government authorities—in a word, to measure the extent to which applicant markets achieved the consensus, high-level objectives of regulation. Among other things, the principles require that the system sponsor (or market operator) demonstrate to the relevant regulatory authorities that the system:

- Meets regulatory and legal standards and operates equitably to all market participants of the same class (specifically as to response times and capacity)
- Provides equitable availability to timely trade and quotation information
- Uses a reliable execution algorithm that appropriately prioritizes orders
- Assures proper and objective risk assessment of vulnerabilities before implementation and on an ongoing basis
- Ensures the competence, integrity, and authority of system users
- Assures that appropriate mechanisms are in place to conduct adequate surveillance for supervisory and enforcement purposes
- Addresses whether additional risk management exposures result from interaction with related systems

- Provides relevant disclosures as to significant risks of the system and limitations on the scope of liability of the sponsor
- Develops and implements procedures to assure that the system is responsive to the directives (interventions) and concerns of all relevant regulatory authorities.

In 1998 (as further explained in the IOSCO Assessment Methodology of 2003, updated and reissued in May 2008) the IOSCO Objectives and Principles of Security Regulation added, as a general goal for all IOSCO members, six more generic principles on secondary markets, relating to authorization and oversight, fair and equitable rules, deterrence of unfair trading practices, management of large exposures and default risk, and clearing and settlement integrity. Nonetheless, the SBT Principles remain the relevant international statement on the regulatory treatment of cross-border, electronic options and futures markets.[16] Of the generic principles, Principle 25 acknowledges the change in structure of markets wrought by the migration from floor to PC. That principle specifically provides for regulation of system (electronic venue) operators, broadly defined, and their accountability for the ongoing operation of the market consistent with regulatory standards, whether or not they are members or owners.

Ironically, CFTC-regulated markets, which were among the first to take the idea of global electronic trading systems abroad, were among the last to abandon floor-trading systems at home. Ironically, the CME, having led the way in both:

- Electronic trading systems and linked clearing (the SIMEX, predecessor to SGX, CME Mutual Offset system begun in 1984) as a means of greater access to global liquidity[17] and
- Developing criteria relative to the international regulation of electronic markets, which not only secured international buy-in but also facilitated the phenomenal growth of U.S. markets (SBT Principles, Boca Declaration[18])

became ambivalent about the virtues of open markets.

The last major non-U.S. market, Singapore's SGX, converted fully to electronic trading in 2007; the MATIF in France had converted in one day almost a decade before. Of course, many emerging markets (India, China, Russia, and Poland) elected electronic trading systems, especially for equities and bonds, from the outset. In contrast, electronic trading on U.S. markets did not attain a majority share of trading activity or gain a full head of steam, even after demutualization of the largest exchanges. Only when the CME and the CBOT felt threatened by Eurex's establishment of a Chicago-based subsidiary (U.S. Futures Exchange) and intended to be fully compliant with U.S. rules, did electronic trading begin to accelerate. Even so, more than 50% of trading did not become electronic until the Intercontinental Exchange (ICE) challenged the primacy of the New York Mercantile Exchange (NYMEX) in energy contracts (especially WTI crude oil), and its purchase of the New York Board of Trade (now ICE Futures US) in 2006 and 2007, respectively.[19]

The ICE's challenge, through increased enthusiasm for electronic trading, lessened U.S. exchange enthusiasm for universal open access. ICE's success demonstrated the competitive power of newly formed electronic interlopers. It also precipitated a thorough and continuing discussion of how to define, with more specificity, what the respective regulatory interests of dual regulators of the same listed commodity derivative market might be. (ICE's EU entity, a successor to the International Petroleum Exchange, was regulated in the United Kingdom; ICE had an exempt market that used the NYMEX settlement price for WTI in the United States, a back office in New York, and servers in Atlanta). These issues became embroiled in the August 2008 Congressional attempt to address oil price escalation through more robust regulation of the U.S. futures markets[20] and resulted in the CFTC applying more conditionality to its approvals of cross-border screen placement. Many continued to recognize the futility, and likely unintended consequences, of trying to stem the global growth of listed derivatives markets (in the name of dampening speculation) and to value the benefits of open access at home. The predominant U.S. contract for many years, the Eurodollar contract, is arguably a non-U.S. contract, and the value of futures exchanges has to date exceeded that of equity markets, which have taken a more nationalistic approach. Indeed, the greatest spurt in exchange trading in history has occurred in the last decade.[21] On the other hand, bad facts can make bad law. Some now say that the global repercussions of the subprime crisis and the relative insulation from closed markets may lead to ever more revisionist thinking on open markets. Still, others have said that national regulators' attitudes to screen placement are just a red herring since the unrestricted flow of funds and persons across borders makes most markets global in any event.

Concern about which "competent authority" or national regulator using which regulatory framework should be responsible for authorizing and overseeing trading activities on nondomestic market screens placed in its jurisdiction drove the initial regulatory conclusions on screen-based trading systems reached in IOSCO and the EU. The interplay between business developments (Globex, Eurex US, NYSE-Euronext, ICE) and regulatory developments is evident. But do regulatory developments also drive business strategy?

Regulation and the Evolving Architecture of Markets

As regulators provisionally distinguished what constellation of activities constituted an exchange and what activities did not—Automated Order Routing Systems (AORs) operated by brokers, Automated Trading Systems (ATSs) with the election to operate as brokers, dealers, electronic communication networks (ECNs), multilateral trading facilities (MTFs), exempt commercial markets— business paid attention. As regulators established the bases for recognition of one market by another, business decisions about the relative advantage of various market structures and where to establish ("home jurisdiction") and to offer services ("host jurisdiction") had to take account of whether there were differences that made one location or structure more favorable than another. One might locate in London to take advantage of the EU passport for financial instruments to subscriber/participants throughout the EU. One might locate in Portugal to trade a U.S. security using U.S. GAAP (in the interim, before the U.S. converges with the EU to International Financial Reporting Standards) or the EU limits national admissions to trading of issues on non-regulated markets.

Proliferation of Platforms

"Which came first, the regulation or the market?" is a typical chicken-and-egg question, but the business impact of differentiating regulatory consequences by structure and licensing jurisdiction was profound. For example, in the United States, a national market system (NMS)—which some said should lead to a single black box—has been "mandated" since 1975,[22] but its recent moves to fulfill that mandate have both responded to and generated new entrants. Indeed, the dramatic escalation in the electronic challenge to traditional securities markets in the United States grew out of changes by the U.S. Securities and Exchange Commission (SEC) in the late 1990s. These changes, intended to complete the vision of a national market, began partly in response to the emergence of new equity trading venues. The order-handling (or national best bid and offer, NBBO) rules in 1997 and consequent demise of NYSE rule 390 (or NYSE first rule) put a new premium on electronic capacity and competitive pricing at non-NYSE exchanges. The concomitant development of SEC-lite or ATS rules permitted ECNs to proliferate under regulatory conditions different from those applied to exchanges—resulting, in the view of some, in ECNs gaining an unwarranted competitive advantage.[23]

Though there remain legacy aspects of the floor system in equity trading in the United States, the incursions by ECNs (BATs and Instinet) and ATSs have accelerated automation by traditional exchanges. In some cases, they have purchased their own ECNs or enhanced electronic capacity (such as NYSE's Archipelago, a totally electronic market, or the resuscitation from near death of LIFFE via technology) or changed the profile of their leadership teams.[24] Decimalization (trading in pennies rather than in fractions), implemented in Canada in 1996 and in response to exchanges and Nasdaq in 2001, the resulting demands on market capacity[25] also favored enhanced electronic systems and expertise. Regulation NMS explicitly supports the principles of competition among markets, competition among orders, and serving the interests of long-term investors, notwithstanding the existence of multiple trading venues, by further refining rules to assure that investors receive fair access and the best price. The NMS requirements for "order protection," "data dissemination" "access fee limitations," and "best execution" (loosely speaking, subject to many exceptions, the best price among venues),[26] adopted in 2005 to be fully implemented in 2007, supports these goals.

In Europe, the adoption of a quartet of new EU directives (market abuse, prospectus, transparency, and the MiFID, or markets in financial instruments) addressed the same efficient market issues being grappled with by the U.S. SEC. The directives replaced national concentration rules that required all orders to come to a central regulated, national market, with new requirements that clarified free access across borders to EU exchanges by EU denizens. The directives added specific post-trade reporting requirements for systematic internalizers (brokers or mechanisms executing issues traded on regulated markets from their own inventory at above a specified threshold of frequency)[27] and intensified best execution requirements to promote assurance that investors continued to receive the best price, notwithstanding the abandonment of the concentration requirements. These changes, by recognizing new markets, in turn permitted new systematic internalizers (Turquoise) or exchange competitors to appear. Although enabling more comprehensive market regulation than existed before, and cognizant of the new electronic challengers, the new directives also permitted the operation of markets outside the "regulated market regime" in certain instruments above a certain notional amount and among qualified persons.[28]

These market structure initiatives on both sides of the Atlantic, in addition to increasing new entrants and facilitating competition, have had what some might view as the perverse effect of promoting the emergence of markets intentionally designed to fit outside various portions of the regulatory framework.[29] New arrivals such as Alpha (Canada), Turquoise (UK, which went live September 19, 2008, across 13 European equity markets), BIDs (U.S.), or expanders such as ICAP (U.K.), and others seemed poised, until the recent turmoil, to contest the supremacy of traditional exchanges. In fact, *The Financial Times* in September 2008 reported that in the United Kingdom, Nasdaq OMX, Chi-X, and Turquoise have formed an informal working group with Plus Markets to provide more consolidated information on pricing, similar to the U.S. consolidated tape, not only to facilitate discovery of the best execution price but also to render it easier to place trades on their platforms by removing the need for multiple feeds. They reasoned that the current proliferation of price-reporting systems meant that, when the London Stock Exchange was down, trading should have moved to other potential venues but did not, as LSE still was considered the prime pricing mechanism for shares.

Tiering

Electronic technology, then, made multiple market architectures potentially cost effective. It is not surprising that the tiering of regulation led to a tiering of market structures. It also led to regulatory (and industry) discussion of the differences (and relative value) of quote-driven versus order-driven markets, the virtues of concentration rules (intended to force all trades into a central market) compared to upstairs and over-the-counter trading, and whether certain market structures were more appropriate than others for different products (e.g., debt and equity)[30] and certain customers (institutional and retail). The growth of non-exchange markets in response to such tiering engendered a broader regulatory deconstruction of what orders should be centralized, what is liquidity, and an analysis of the tipping point at which a market should be made subject to comprehensive regulation.

On the futures side in the United States, the CFTC Modernization Act of 2000 (CFMA) was specifically constructed to permit a tiered market structure. Within this structure, certain commercial markets (energy) or markets in so-called nonmanipulable products (interest rates and currencies), and one-to-many (or electronic dealer) markets could operate substantially outside the scope of the Commodity Exchange Act. In the United States, what some called the breathtaking deregulation of 2000 (now likely to be substantially rolled back when the 2008–2009 crisis response team decides who should regulate what) was driven on the listed derivatives market side by the contract approval provisions of the CFTC. U.S. exchanges were concerned that institutional over-the-counter (OTC) markets in swaps and other OTC products that had been exempted from regulation by legislation since 1993, premised on such transactions being based on individual credit judgments and bilateral tailoring, were offering increasingly standardized products and automating their functions. This OTC automation made it increasingly difficult, if not impossible, to differentiate an "exempt" market from a regulated market based on the usual formulas. Further, the competitive challenge from the OTC market—which was growing faster than the listed derivative market— forced the issue of whether it was essential for the government to have its hand in the design of regulated exchange contracts. The drafters thought that exchanges might be made accountable by certifying that their contract designs met federal requirements related to nonmanipulability and integrity (more like the disclosure-based system for approval of listed issues on the equities side) rather than submitting them for pre-approval. The fact that electronic markets could accommodate more products and less liquid products than floor markets was a driver for this change in view, as was the realization that it seemed wrong to apply more requirements to the regulated, transparent venue than the unregulated, opaque OTC venue with respect to product design. In fact, the adoption of the CFMA led to new markets, though most of those chose to be totally exempt or to be fully designated rather than to use any intermediate alternative tiers.

The more conspiracy-oriented observer would say, at least for the energy markets, that the resulting exempt markets within the recently closed "so-called Enron loophole" were the product of nefarious lobbyists and politicians seeking to remove business from regulatory scrutiny.[31] The organized exchange response to the Enron case also demonstrated, however, the value of the 2000 changes with respect to promoting central counterparty clearing—now a specific regulatory and competitive response to the ills of the credit default markets both here and abroad.

NYMEX found that clearing systems common to regulated markets could be sold to certain OTC participants who wanted to mitigate counterparty risk when there was concern about nontransparent OTC interrelationships or credit circumstances that rendered credit judgments difficult. Electronic systems that facilitated uncoupling trading and clearing and delivering the benefits of either to different market participants or to the same participants at different times, without bringing the original negotiations of private parties under regulation, helped deliver OTC clearing business to NYMEX's Clear Port and spawned a whole new post-trade processing business.

This possibility of uncoupling clearing and execution was specifically foreseen by the CFMA. Moreover, the CFMA generously acknowledged that OTC clearing could be brought under one of several regulatory umbrellas, including certain foreign clearing standards.[32] The CFTC did not itself promote complete deregulation of commodities of finite supply. The CFMA basically permitted a market to opt for a more stringent standard and required the most stringent standard if a market wanted to reach the largest (including retail) customer base. Further, CFTC had conducted a multiyear international project with Japan and the United Kingdom looking at what information was necessary for appropriate surveillance of contracts for commodities of finite supply. This was prompted by the Sumitomo copper manipulation—a matter squarely on the table after the July 2008 unprecedented spike and later fall in crude oil prices.

The resulting communiqué that advocated best practices for contract design and surveillance to prevent manipulation in physical commodities was signed by 16 jurisdictions in 1997 and 1998[33] and cited by IOSCO as well.

Suffice it to say that globally, the idea of tiered regulation has drawn its share of criticism, remains under study, and is vulnerable to attack.[34] Nonetheless, the genesis of tiered regulation was the core difficulty of determining how to align the regulatory framework for widely differing products and customers with the basic regulatory interests of customer protection, price efficiency, and market integrity. It was also a product of the desire to prevent the stifling of innovative startups by exchange colossi. Regulators in multiple jurisdictions opted to permit more than one market design to prevail in assessing where their regulatory interest lay. The resulting framework has, perhaps inadvertently, resulted in unexpected arbitrage. Some of this may now be corrected or overcorrected by Congress. The concept of exchange markets also might be wounded unfairly in the coming evaluation of the subprime investment banking crisis.

Electronic Mishaps

While identified as an area of concern from the earliest set of SBT Principles, regulators have not sought directly (other than with respect to the Y2K initiative) to solve issues related to errors or electronic system lapses. The business consequence of inadequate attention to these issues is so dire that for the most part the regulators, with many other matters on their minds, have left the markets to provide guidance on the treatment of "fat finger" and other inadvertent trades and how to prevent error-related abuses.[35] Many know that a quantity error as large as that placed on the MATIF in the early 1990s (100,000 contracts for 100) could (if reversed) have threatened the viability of the market itself. More recently, the Tokyo Stock Exchange's foremost issue is repairing the IT malfunction issues that have plagued its systems for the last two years, and possibly decelerated any move toward a public offer. A respected compliance reporter recently reported that more than 50% of all financial services firms did not have adequate compliance arrangements to address IT failures. In many cases these systems connect to exchange engines. People who use or review systems wonder from time to time if they actually perform as intended and if there are ways that the defenses intended to protect their integrity can be breached without detection. The recent rogue trading by Société Générale's Monsieur Kerviel, which reputedly tricked the computers, and of MF Global's Mr. Dooley and others, who tried to avoid computer limits, is likely to reignite these inquiries at a regulatory level. Similarly, glitches reported in *The Wall Street Journal* on September 25, 2008, led to cancellation of multiple electronic trades that occurred at prices more than 20% above or below the closes on the U.S. exchanges that were affected by the ban on short selling to address the September financial crisis; these also may lead to additional discussions on error causes, effects, and remedies.

Introducing flexibility into regulation to permit realization of some of the benefits of electronic technology has permitted innovation to flourish. Both the regulatory and the business responses indicate that a defining feature of electronic technology is its tremendous capacity to change the conditions of competition and to create new winners and losers in the marketplace.

Private Club to Public Company

Most analysts thought that demutualization of the member-owned exchanges was the linchpin to loosening the hold floor members had on exchange governance, going "electronic," and promoting other innovations essential to maximizing the network effects of exchange businesses. For these, unlocking the value of exchange clubs and confronting the consequences of the more intense competition to be expected in the future were dependent on "governance change." Events seemed to bear out these conclusions. Indeed, the conquest by screens and the change in the ownership structure of markets seemed to proceed hand in glove.

The Nordic exchanges (Stockholm, Helsinki, and Copenhagen) demutualized in the early 1990s; Amsterdam, Italy, and Australia followed suit in 1997 and 1998, Singapore's SIMEX (now SGX) and LIFFE (now NYSE-Euronext) in 1999, and Toronto, Hong Kong, London, and Frankfurt in 2000. Nasdaq was the first U.S. market to demutualize, and the U.S. futures exchanges did not begin to alter their structures until the very end of 2001; only a few still remain mutual companies (Minneapolis Grain Exchange; CBOE; Tokyo Stock Exchange). Going electronic, going public, and self-listing followed. In some jurisdictions (Hong Kong, Singapore, Pakistan, Italy) the government itself determined to revamp exchange ownership structure to increase market efficiency, integrity, or resources, but more typically, these changes were driven by the members acting alone.

Demutualization was the opening gambit to monetizing seats without diminishing trading rights, as Prof. Roberta Karmel eloquently wrote— turning seats into shares.[36] It was also a critical step toward more aggressive competition for market share. One side effect of this consequence of the electronic tsunami was the need for regulators to develop techniques to deal with markets and market participants who might no longer bow to the disdain of a raised eyebrow or peer pressure. For club-like entities, the threat of exile for violating "just and equitable principles of trading" was a major buttress of good conduct for most.[37] But the more removed traders became from the exchange ownership, the governance and discipline process, and from the geographic jurisdiction, the more concern traders had about whether such principles would be applied fairly and the more concern the regulator had that they could be enforced at all.

Ownership and Governance of For-Profit, Demutualized Markets

What then was the regulatory response to these changes? Did regulators conclude that profit-driven, publicly held exchanges could retain the will and capacity to enforce their rules when ownership and trading rights were separated?

The way most regulators became involved in exchange demutualizations and conversion to public, for-profit entities was to weigh in on the possible negative effects, such as:

- The potential for conflicts between the resulting market's responsibilities to its own shareholders and its responsibilities to customers
- The types of disclosure relevant for an exchange as a public company
- The level of independence of the governing board

Regulators' gravest regulatory concern was apparently that exchanges that were public companies could list themselves, monitor themselves for continuing compliance, and refuse to list their competitors. In December 2000, after extensive internal discussion, IOSCO issued a consultation paper (it became final in June 2001) that said just that.[38] To this date, however, regulators do not have a single common approach, not even to the question of self-listing.

Although there is agreement that the listing (or admission-to-trading) function may be the most pressing concern from a conflicts perspective, there is not unanimity as to how to resolve that conflict. There is real worry whether a for-profit exchange will be remiss in its public functions; but there is also no widespread agreement on the extent to which (if any) the regulator should withhold self-regulatory functions. The United Kingdom took the most drastic approach. It moved the London Stock Exchange (LSE) listing function (review and qualification of listings for regulated markets) after an extensive consultation process (which FSA is just this year in the process of revisiting) to the U.K. Listing Authority (UKLA). In effect, UKLA became just another department of the U.K. Financial Services Authority, albeit with a mixed mission (regulation and attracting capital) in recognition of the commercial value of listings. Thus, in the U.K., listing of all companies effectively became a regulatory function. Other major markets took more targeted approaches. For example, Australia, Canada, Singapore, and the United States each went its own unique way, having parsed the conflicts issue differently based on how essential each thought that the listing process was to the business of being an exchange.

In every case, however, the development of demutualized, for-profit, publicly traded exchanges has resulted in changes that went well beyond reducing the power of the floor and compensation for its disappearance. And though the changes to exchange boards may have emanated in the first instance from the exchanges themselves, the impetus was that the regulator might otherwise directly interfere. For example, the Australian Stock Exchange, a self-listed company, currently reviews listings and undertakes market supervision through a separate supervision subsidiary and the Australian Securities Investment Commission approves the rules; nonetheless the recent listing of certain competitors has prompted a new review, this year, of the listing structure and potential attendant conflicts and further insulation of the supervision subsidiary by creation of a separate chair. In New York, a separate regulatory entity of the exchange, NYSE Regulation, which reports to a special board oversight committee, undertakes market regulation including insider trading oversight, approves listings, and monitors continuing compliance with listing standards. The marketing of listings is still accomplished by the exchange commercial operation, NYSE Market, though this structure also continues to evolve. As of July 2007, NYSE member regulation (including capital and margins) is handled by the Financial Instruments Regulatory Authority (FINRA). In August 2008, FINRA and NYSE Market agreed with other

U.S. markets to undertake all insider trading reviews. In Toronto, listing remains an exchange function, but independent assessment is required of competitor listings. Member regulation was performed by the Investment Dealers Association and market regulation, more recently, by Regulatory Services, Inc., two independent self-regulatory/industry associations that were merged during the summer of 2008 into the Investment Industry Regulatory Organization of Canada (IIROC).

More generically, the creation of for-profit exchange companies has again raised the question of whether self-regulatory surveillance, financial integrity, and market oversight powers remain appropriate.

At the bottom, both floor-based and screen-based exchanges adopt and enforce rules and list or design contracts. Both floor- and screen-based exchanges have business and regulatory interests that are aligned in that the value of the exchange depends on confidence in the integrity of the prices it produces and in the ability to settle transactions reliably—indeed, in the effective operation of the exchange as a market. Thus, it is not surprising that both sides, for and against self- or private regulation, have been argued.

Many commentators note that member-owned exchanges were not devoid of conflicts. Indeed, claimants from time to time have charged that futures exchange officials, who were responsible for preserving the integrity of price formation, may have favored the positions of their own members over those of nonmember participants.[39] Promoters of private regulation argue on the other hand that the users of the market, when they are the sole owners, apply a self-correcting, frontier justice against those who do not play by the rules of the game. In their view, market failures are costly and borne by members as a group, so members will not tolerate individual members who put the overall membership at risk. Some purists urge that the fox can never be charged with guarding the chicken coop and cite many cases of self-regulatory failure where regulation seemed to take a back seat to revenues or self-interest, whether the Nasdaq spread-fixing case, the FBI sting affecting the CBOT and the CME, or other dramatic cases, such as the Barings collapse or the Feruzzi soybeans manipulation. Some argue that even if the exchange imposes strict discipline, some exchanges choose to discipline outsiders rather than insiders when making so-called message cases interpreting principles of fair trading.

Similarly, with respect to for-profit markets, some argue that separating the management more fundamentally from the traders may improve the fairness of self-regulation; others fear that shareholders with a stake in revenues and not in trading itself may be unwilling to bear the necessary costs of regulation or are insufficiently expert to manage such oversight. Other stakeholders worry how management can manage if it is excluded from knowledge about exchange regulatory issues. These commentators also find that government regulators might not have adequate resources (either monetary or expertise) to perform regulation of markets directly without frontline sentinels on the watch. On the other hand, others have even suggested that it would be odd to relieve public companies that are exchanges from accountability for their compliance functions while enhancing other public companies' responsibilities in that regard.[40]

The question as to the proper scope of self-regulation, if any, has been answered variously by different jurisdictions. For example, many exchanges cling tightly to private contractual or self-regulatory powers. Hong Kong even managed to claw back certain listing and prospectus powers that had devolved to the Hong Kong Securities and Futures Commission; in Canada, the provincial authorities have constituted independent self-regulators (some might call them private regulators) to provide certain services to the exchanges that regulators can rely on in performing their own duties. In comparison, in Europe many jurisdictions take the position that the exchanges are not, and should not be, self-regulators. Unlike in the United States, European exchanges are not vested with quasi-governmental functions. In fact, in jurisdictions such as France, the development and consolidation of the regulatory authority over the financial markets has been accompanied by the waning and ultimately the disappearance of a self-regulator (the CMT) directly connected to the market.[41] Though the exchanges do enforce their own rules as a contractual matter, the competent authorities view this rule enforcement function as a general compliance or private contractual function and not a regulatory mandate. Outside the United States, some markets have made the structure of their governance arrangements part of their marketing, and they jealously guard their self-regulatory responsibilities from regulatory encroachments.[42]

Perhaps an even more controversial and contentious regulatory issue emerging from the move of markets to public companies is whether the regulator should directly prescribe the governance structure and specifically construe the independence of the Board more narrowly than for other public companies. The idea is that the public purpose of an exchange market requires a different, more public-spirited Board than an ordinary public company. Jurisdictions, in consequence, have struggled with ways to maintain the balance between public function and commercial interests of exchanges without compromising the vigor of either. In the United States, the debate over this issue, which had been in abeyance for several years, still remains open-ended. Meanwhile, most exchanges, in response to moral suasion or in concessions to regulators made to achieve other business goals, have consigned regulatory matters to independent/specialist parts of their boards, meeting specific independence criteria. Some believe that the basic rules related to independent directors of public companies are sufficient to assure that drive for shareholder revenues will not compromise the protection of the public interest in properly functioning markets. For others it seems that some public concerns would be resolved if the rulemaking powers of the exchanges were subject to public comment or regulatory review. For still others, this particular debate is peculiarly parochial to the United States in that many other jurisdictions have additional supervisory boards or other means to protect nonshareholder stakeholder interests at the Board level. In Italy, the regulator even has the authority to vet the fitness and propriety of exchange shareholders above a specified threshold.

The debate continues over governance and how to assure that the oversight of the markets is fair and equitable. Some believe that the oversight structure should be more fundamentally integrated. In the United States, for the equity exchanges, FINRA has been able materially to expand its power and scope partly due to industry desire to avoid the duplication of audits and other reviews that had affected broker members of multiple markets, even though the SEC's required appointment of designated examining authorities, maintenance of a joint audit plan, and special treatment of consolidated supervised entities were intended to avoid such duplication. The so-called Paulson blueprint (which calls for a conduct, a prudential, and a market stability regulator), originally published in June 2008 and resuscitated after the crisis of September 2008 as a structural response, puts into play yet again the question of rationalizing the "multiplicitous" regulators and self-regulators of the U.S. system. In the blueprint, the suggestion is that most regulation should be organized in a different way, that the power to regulate should be reallocated, and that some regulators, such as the CFTC and the OTS, should be eliminated. This structural debate may be "on the table," interminably prompted by the exit of the investment banks in September 2008 as a result of the subprime fallout (mutual funds "breaking the buck," the meltdown of financial stocks, the withholding of credit, the horrific freezing of funds of Lehman for what the administrator predicts will be years in the United Kingdom, the alleged oil market squeeze, and the multiple phases of the massive US$-now trillion-plus bailout proposed by two administrations led by the U.S. Treasury and the Federal Reserve). Notably, even before the Madoff Ponzi revelations, the Paulson blueprint also gave more private regulatory authority to FINRA over certain collective investments, perhaps a hint of what is to come for hedge funds, which could also have market implications.

The debate about governance also reflects that there is increasing competition between exchanges and brokers for the same customer base and that the change in ownership structure wrought by going public did not in and of itself resolve, as some thought it would, the concern that the exchange might favor its self-interests over those of its broker traders and financers of trading activity. That being said, it seems likely that there always will be a tension between entities that compete for the "edge" or market advantage, whether an entity that profits mostly from transactions in the central market or one whose profits derive primarily from off-market (upstairs, privately placed, or over-the-counter) transactions.

Finally, it is under this rubric—exchange governance—that regulators and legislators determine whether they want to impose percentage restrictions on ownership and control by individual persons or entities. The limitations on ownership by a single shareholder are to some extent basic limits on controlling interests that are unrelated to the market but potentially could be applied to restrict various ownership combinations, to maintain national control, or to justify protectionist actions.

Globalization and the Accelerating Effect of Electronic Technology

The history of electronic markets is one of opening access, but the discussion on how regulators should approach entities with global reach continues to rage. There is no doubt that exchange competition has become increasingly global and intense. Global regulatory issues typically fall under one of three categories:

- Access
- Ownership
- Limitations on combinations of market power

Each is an issue in every major market jurisdiction, and each potentially implicates national regulatory programs. The old saw that every market wants access to every other jurisdiction's markets but wants to restrict access to its own is still in ample evidence. The move to electronic markets, nonetheless, has intensified the search for globally agreed regulatory solutions that enhance competition without prejudicing national interests, whether:

- Price stability in the real economy
- The need to service local entrepreneurs' capital formation or trading needs
- The desire *not to* cede volume to other venues or *to* protect national markets' sustainability

As the success of Ireland, London, or Singapore might demonstrate, the ability to draw interests from outside the local jurisdiction may be critical to growing a market. National authorities also are aware that there are risks in taking too isolationistic a view on access to home markets lest there be "informal retributions" when seeking to take that market on the road.

As indicated at the international level, IOSCO made clear that it had no problem with members invoking national jurisdiction where a purchaser in that jurisdiction was being targeted from offshore.[43] Thus if an Internet exchange entrepreneur in Dubai were to solicit persons in Quebec using the French language, Quebec could claim that the Dubai market was acting within Quebec. The conclusion that a regulator would be legally justified to apply local law both in the jurisdiction of the market's establishment (Dubai) and in that of the trader (Quebec), however, does answer how, as a practical matter, that would be done. The regulatory response to placement of trading screens is fundamentally, therefore, an act of implementing jurisdictional powers consistently with the capacity to apply them effectively.

Regulators are well aware that globalization poses a number of regulatory conundrums. Regulators are quintessentially national (and in some cases even provincial) institutions. In contrast, markets, even if located within a domestic location and with domestic management, once public, will have non-domestic customers, may have non-domestic ownership, and typically will aspire to have the broadest possible nondomestic reach. Indeed, it is the very lack of geographic constraints on electronic markets that at once makes them competitive powerhouses and pushes the envelope of regulatory effectiveness. At a minimum, increasingly regulators must share information and cooperate with each other formally, or informally, to address markets, brokers, and investors who cross borders, whatever their approach may be to placement in their individual jurisdiction of foreign screens. An essential pillar of IOSCO's current strategy, as an international standard setter, is to make regulatory (and in some cases judicial) agencies cooperate to address securities fraud and misconduct, originating outside one's own jurisdiction. This is a condition of membership in the global regulatory community,[44] thus assisting regulators in confronting these difficult decisions.

The most difficult issues then, are not to acknowledge that cooperation is essential but to learn how to implement such cooperation. When should a regulator assert its jurisdiction, and when should it rely on a regulatory colleague to do so? These questions are further compounded by the particularly difficult question of where an electronic exchange can say it is located and the legal truism that regulators ordinarily cannot limit their jurisdiction by interpretation. The answers to these questions are nonetheless critical in that national law defines when the full complement of local regulation applies—and if and when it does not.

More than one approach has been taken to this daunting task. Most jurisdictions take the IOSCO guidance to heart—and believe they have both the jurisdiction and international accord to assert their authority where trading occurs on screens located in their airspace. At the same time, most realize that this power needs to be accompanied by the actual capacity to take regulatory actions and have conducted multiple bilateral investigations to try to see if that is the case. For example, the CFTC took a no-action approach initially, in 1996, to "foreign" screen placement. In the case in question, the market (the Deutsche Termineböse or DTB, a predecessor of the Eurex) did not determine U.S. activity was extensive enough to compromise the notion that the offshore market was *bona fidely* located under the principal authority of another jurisdiction (in that case, Germany) and the market met certain international criteria (see the earlier discussion of SBT principles). The no-action approach permitted articulation by the CFTC of conditions customized to the specificities of various markets and to address new issues flexibly as they arose.

In fact, the CFTC specifically rejected adopting a prescriptive, rule-based approach in 2000 with respect to both the placement of non-US based markets screens and brokers. Instead, the U.S. CFTC tried to further parse which regulator was in the best position to exercise direct oversight. For example, where a broker was located and licensed offshore and was offering non-U.S. products to US customers, CFTC used a case-by-case "comparability-substituted compliance information-sharing and reliance model" beginning in 1989 (and now being adapted by the SEC[45]), under which some 140 brokers currently operate and which some markets used to "brand" their regulatory systems. We could take issue with the theory of these approaches, but they worked well for more than a decade, until a British-regulated market (ICE Futures EU) used the process to compete directly for transactions in WTI Crude (a light, sweet oil deliverable in the United States) by using the fully regulated NYMEX settlement price for its exempt cash-settled contracts. In fact, the CFTC could easily have adapted its approach to the unique facts of the ICE situation and imposed conditions to protect the prices drawn from a common deliverable supply. And, after Congressional prodding and then direction in late 2008, the CFTC did just that.

In Australia, brokers and markets licensed in specified jurisdictions may apply for class relief based on reliance on regulation by an appropriate home authority and the agreement to share specified information with the Australian authority; in Canada there are also means to avoid the full application of national law in deference to another regulator for cross-border business; and the United Kingdom has recognition requirements that are calibrated to whether or not the entity can be regarded as an overseas investment exchange or is doing business directly in the country. The SEC is in the process of testing a "mutual recognition" type regime with several jurisdictions, of which Australia is the first and Canada is right behind.

It is likely that the debate as to how to rationalize who should regulate what when more than one jurisdiction has an interest in a market is not likely to end soon, particularly as business combinations that cross borders must try to satisfy regulators in each relevant jurisdiction. Some formulas used in other contexts that could be considered are:

- Recognizing the entity's place of "initial" establishment and principal place of business as the primary authorizing regulator as is the case for business corporations more generally
- Acknowledging that issues related to financial capacity (capital) have to be decided within the company as a whole, whereas liquidity might be decided based on where the entity does business (as is the case in banking)
- Acknowledging that issues related to conduct of trading are relevant to each jurisdiction in which the conduct occurs

• Determining criteria for when products traded in more than one jurisdiction essentially form one market for purposes of price discovery (as enacted for certain products in the 2008 CFTC reauthorization legislation)

Additionally, though there is a lot of interest in the "mutual recognition" concept, there are various views of what that regime would entail outside the EU, where almost 50 years have been spent articulating the basis for such recognition by assuring the free flow of goods, services, and markets based on establishing "equivalent conditions of competition." Assuming that conditionality can be part of any mutual recognition regime, France and the United States *did* adopt such a scheme for futures firms in 1989,[46] though it has not been much used by French firms to access the United States. As a practical matter, there is no doubt that mutual receptivity is likely to be a stated, or unstated, aspect of most access determinations. The European directives explicitly include the notion of reciprocity (mutual recognition), though reciprocity alone, unbuttressed by other public interests, was rejected as a needed trade objective in the broader financial services portions of the Uruguay Round.

In the United States, the SEC and the CFTC approached globalization at different speeds and from different perspectives. These differences might derive from the difference between secondary-only markets that list self-created products and secondary markets that service a primary market in shares whose issuers favor a level playing field approach to the costs of raising capital. Commodity derivatives markets have typically been more global than stock markets because the cash markets that underlie the derivatives are often themselves fundamentally global, whether reflecting prices for oil, grain, sugar, cotton, or interest rates. Often the conventions of the cash market that are mimicked in futures market benchmark contracts also are equally global. In contrast, often equity markets service local issuers that would not be of international interest. National public policy is unlikely to favor regulation or structures that might prefer global business to mechanisms that assure a secondary market for local issues.

Perhaps the slow inroads of electronic trading within the United States prevented exchange leaders from foreseeing the extent of the external electronic challenge and raising the "patriotic" flag for regulatory barriers ("in the public interest"). Instead, they focused their "regulatory" interests on various one-off initiatives. Some opposed the movement of liquidity and open interest without compensation. Some used intellectual property rights to challenge competitors. Others found ways to cross borders within the system: through private placements, private equity deals, offshore affiliates, global institutional money managers, and acquisition of nondomestic markets. Globalization happened both with and without the regulators' blessing—so much so that in the summer of 2007, when the SEC held its hearings on opening up its markets more internationally, many participants questioned the necessity.[47]

Global Competition and Mergers and Acquisitions[48]

Global competition, in particular the competition to use profits made in share offerings to purchase other exchanges and by so doing increase the geographic customer base, may or may not be addressed directly by regulators. In some jurisdictions, there may be express provisions intended to limit the amount of nonlocal ownership (Italy); in others there may be none (United Kingdom).

It is not such a startling observation that markets are growing in ways that transcend national sovereignty. This phenomenon, though speeded by electronic technology that resolves the space and time limitations on physical markets, is not without historical precedent. In other places and times, market entities such as the Dutch East India Company and the Hanseatic League formed powerful cross-border trading combinations. The former was a multinational trading and colonizing company with a military arm that operated under seven different flags between 1600 and 1800. The Hanseatic League—a consortium of 60 city-states at its height—powerfully united cross-border commodity trading and producing guilds under a choice of law (Luebeck), a common language (Middle-Low German), a loose, infrequently convened political organization, or Diet, and two central counter "banks" between the 13th and the 17th centuries. The Hansa cities even had currency arrangements that transcended national boundaries. When these cross-border trading conglomerations reigned, despite cooperative operational mechanisms and political sponsorship, there were arguments about abuse of monopoly power, lack of reciprocity, confusion of lines of authority leading at times to competitive disputes, and outright turf battles. So, in a way, nothing is new. From at least the turn of the 19th century there were telegraphic communications that tied markets together.

That being said, the regulatory model of the national regulator is being severely tested by the business combinations occurring now,[49] and this is raising issues as to what the ultimate regulatory response will be. Will these markets be permitted to achieve their potential, or will regulatory or competition authorities or political sentiment prevent that from happening?

The Attraction of the Federal Model

For the moment, one model that has allowed national (or provincial) regulators to transcend their perimeters has been the federal model. This model of regulation permits multiple markets to operate on a common platform (such as NYSE-Euronext, which combines London, Paris, Amsterdam, Brussels, and Lisbon and potentially the Qatar exchanges) under a single holding company while preserving national regulatory interests and powers.[50] Use of the federal model assumes that a world regulator (and even an agreed lead—or primary—regulator) is not likely to be just around the corner. The federal model is consistent with the customs and practices of international conflicts law, which acknowledge national sovereigns' fundamental interest in protecting their own populations. Federal structures may be interim structures from a business perspective in that they cannot fully achieve the network benefits of market combinations. Federal models also rely on regulatory deference—that is, on regulators interpreting their rules to fit the federal business model—a difficult undertaking. Indeed, the conclusion of the intergovernmental arrangement that supports the NYSE Euronext system was described by one regulator as miraculous.

One can argue that regulatory federalism should be elegantly achievable within Europe, where the regulatory structure is underpinned by a series of federal-like treaties and harmonizing directives that support it, even if the current acceleration of the single-market concept has not fully captured the hearts and minds of the people.[51] There is, however, sentiment that other models might be more efficient and thus preferable. But so far no international (or even national) regulatory consensus has emerged on parameters for what that would be.

Implications of Market Conglomerates for Further Regulatory Integration

Some have argued that at least for conglomerates of markets within the EU, there should be an attempt to move over time toward a more unitary regulatory model.[52]

In fact, some European institutions, notably the Committee of European Securities Regulators (CESR), have themselves followed a trajectory from forums for regulatory discussion and informal coordination to more official consortiums. CESR and its companion committees in the banking and insurance sectors now operate with mandates to provide expert input on implementing harmonizing legislation. These committees address how to handle application and enforcement issues under the Lamfalussy process, which attempts to rationalize how the various European institutions and competent national authorities interface in articulating, transposing, and interpreting the European directives. Nonetheless, it is unlikely that institutions such as CESR could or would take over from the participating college of regulators that covers the national markets united on the NYSE-Euronext platform. This is so even though there are ongoing Europe-wide discussions about the following:

- How best to remove continuing divergences across borders without further mandating uniformity in particular areas
- Whether to provide more girth to the currently consensus-based decision-making powers of the banking, securities, and insurance "level three" committees of the EU[53]
- More generally, how regulation might be coordinated[54]

Outside Europe, integrating regulation across borders is even more difficult. Even within the single country of Canada, despite federal banking regulation and enforcement and the so-called national instrument of common requirements—containing a common registration system, among other things—the 13 provinces have to date clung to their independent regulatory powers. Canada has been creative in developing means to coordinate on nationwide issues by appointing a primary authority and, with the exception of Ontario, agreeing to adhere to a passport system through the Canadian Securities Association by 2009. The recent consolidation of the Toronto Stock Exchange and the Montreal Exchange and of the self-regulatory authorities charged with market and broker oversight might signal a trend for further consolidation. Ottawa has indicated, through convening an expert panel, its interest in a more integrated regulatory system. That being said, if Ontario were to join the common passport regime, doubtless arguments would have to be made as to what the efficiencies of further consolidation would actually be. Indeed, further consolidation is unlikely to come without a fight; some synergies may be precluded by the Canadian constitution, and Canada is a broad, expansive country of many diverse peoples, spanning more than six time zones and operating under both civil and common law principles.

Within Asia, Latin America, the Middle East, and Africa there often is talk of regional markets or platforms, but none has really emerged, though in the Middle East, for example, there are many candidates (Egypt, Abu Dhabi, Dubai, Jordan, Saudi Arabia, Iran). It is likely that developing a regional regulatory framework before there is a regional business framework to support it might be particularly difficult. In such a case, often markets will look to a template that is already tried and true—thus the export of the European model to various aspirants to the Union and beyond and the international work of the exchanges and the self-regulatory institutions that seek to expand their reach beyond national borders by promoting common rules and principles. These tried-and-true templates, however, might not take root for failure to sufficiently account for cultural or local differences. Additionally, regional outreach efforts can fall victim to the internecine rivalries within or between governments exercising new and substantial powers to oversee business activities.

National Interests

While some support exists for moving to a more global regulatory model, the $64,000 question is, whose model would that be? Notably the Balls legislation, adopted in the United Kingdom at the time of the purchase of Euronext-LIFFE by NYSE, bared the U.K.'s nationalistic teeth at potential incursions on their regulatory turf by U.S. ideas, ideals, and personnel. The legislation was intended to make clear that the U.K. would not recognize the "extraterritorial reach" of U.S. regulation (specifically, SEC oversight) or "regime change" if applied to the EU entity located in the U.K. In Germany, an even tougher line was taken. Extreme political distaste surfaced against the non-German-based ownership entities ("locusts of capitalism") that affected the governance, and business decisions, of Deutsche Börse. In many jurisdictions the "fit and proper test" (of propriety, reputation, etc.) applied to market operators is a potential means to "look at" these types of "shareholder issues." The market temperature for external ownership may blow hot and cold depending on the political climate and how well the market is doing. The United States now appears to be, at its peril, revving up politically to define what a so-called futures market "foreign board of trade" is without further discussion in the international community. Interestingly, this is occurring in the futures markets that have long had very open policies to support international trading at just the moment that the U.S. securities regulator is proposing a more open approach. It would be a hard case to demonstrate that more open markets have adversely affected competition.

A separate, regulatory issue potentially raised by mergers and conglomerations is the question of whether—and when—an entity would constitute an improper exercise of market power and share. There have been several competition authorities' shots across the bow of various exchanges based on such exchanges' ambitious takeover policies and whether the integration contemplated is horizontal (such as Euronext markets in Amsterdam, Portugal, France, England, and perhaps Qatar) or vertical (as where settlement is integrated into the market itself). To date, notwithstanding these, the U.S. Justice Department has stood down, as has the Office of Fair Trade in the U.K. The EU also has so far declined, despite some threatening rhetoric, to the dismay of some, to mandate an equities market settlement directive, at least in partial deference to a market-led initiative to adopt a code of conduct that assures transparent pricing and interoperability of such systems. However, the official debate on derivatives clearing structures is just beginning and has been accelerated by the recent banking crisis. It seems that for the moment the regulators may rethink letting the markets themselves sort things out competitively because the end game, though quite unclear, will certainly address the clearing and possible required clearing of certain OTC products. Furthermore, such highly politicized issues as the structure of clearing can find themselves being attached to other legislative and geopolitical reforms in the wake of the subprime, CDS, crisis and response measures.

A Word about Regulatory Structure and Philosophy

Regulation has increasingly become a business in which stakeholders are regulatees, the general public, and the body politic. Increasingly, markets and regulators see that there is an alignment of their individual interests in that the efficient operation of securities and risk management markets fundamentally benefit the economy and wealth production or can have adverse effects that extend beyond pricing of financial instruments into the economy at large. Increasingly, regulators are also making transparent some of the limits of their authority. For example, the Netherlands authority, or AFM, states that: "Supervision of the financial markets is well-organised in the Netherlands, but just as the traffic police cannot prevent every accident, so AFM cannot guarantee that every participant will always exercise due care," a matter hardly in doubt with respect to most regulators now as perceived by the general public. Also, increasingly one hears regulatory slogans or brands, such as "treating customers fairly," "regulatory impact analysis," performance measurement, "principles-based" and "risk-based" approaches, and "regulatory accountability," which are intended to better communicate with the public what the regulator is doing, or trying to do. The theories behind each of these approaches to regulation may evolve and be tested further against events; indeed one can count on this after the 2008–2009 financial market crisis.

For example, the U.K., through Sir Howard Davies, in launching the Financial Supervisory Authority (UKFSA)—a so-called integrated regulator combining banking, securities, and insurance, plus building societies, spread trading, and other financial activities—warned against "regulating the innovative capacities of the cities of London and Edinburgh out of existence." As such, this launch speech advocated the desirability of not applying the same level of regulatory scrutiny to wholesale and retail markets and stated while "perfect protection from risk would be associated with highly imperfect and sclerotic markets, there is a need for continued efforts to raise the understanding among consumers of the nature of the financial products offered to them." In setting the correct balance, Sir Davies noted that, special scrutiny and attention should be paid to retail consumers, "who face ever more complex products and choices, and who need help and protection"—particularly vulnerable groups such as pensioners.

The brief for change in the U.K. was a "vague sense of unease about financial regulation and about the integrity with which financial institutions carry out their business." Today regulators' concerns have progressed well beyond unease, almost to a state of panic. Even so, the two most advocated changes were (and are) increased transparency and an independent, accountable regulatory authority (neither beholden to the exchanges nor to political whim)—as relevant today as at the beginning of this century.[55] Interestingly, in the current crisis, the optimal level of governmental intervention and the means of such intervention now being tested are likely to continue to be the subject of debate for years to come. In this regard, it is hopeful that some attention will be paid to the fact that a licensing authority will be considered accountable for the health of the entities it licenses, whatever the prevailing theory on moral hazard.

What better for risk-based insurance and/or compensation schemes and pro-phylactic, prespecified market crisis/default provisioning to prevent contagion than ad hoc and episodic infusions of government funding at the taxpayers' expense?

Conclusion

What all this history of change and response means is that the implications of recent market developments are as significant for regulators as a group and as national entities as they have been for business. Technology has brought us a whole new generation of markets with a whole new generation of challenges: most particularly, how to find the correct means to address participants, com-binations, and owners outside any single regulator's authority with no assured loyalty to any single jurisdiction or market. In these circumstances, no regulator can be an island. In recognition, a major project of the international regulators' community is to assure sufficient information exchange and cooperation among national regulators to avoid international gaps and to address national prob-lems that originate from across borders. One overriding truism is that technol-ogy is not only making it harder to locate the market, it is also altering the conditions of competition and the competitors in ways that permit no one to predict the final outcome. The point is to keep one's weather eye on the high-level objectives: investor protection; fair, efficient, and transparent markets; and reduction of systemic risk. If we were ever in doubt, the experiences of Sep-tember and October 2008 have made the world at large aware of the stakes (including the real-economy stakes) of getting right the means to achieve these goals.

It was the current fashion to think forward to a fully integrated, single regu-lator approach, but the likelihood is slim that the markets will keep still for this to be effectuated on a global scale. But the future promises to see regulators and markets alike revisit and remake their structures to deliver fair, efficient, and attractive serviceable markets for as many years continuing into the future as in the past. Moreover, the market's performance under duress has demon-strated its receptivity to "lessons learned," and it is likely that the exchange community has some ideas that could be exported to the financial community at large.

Endnotes

One final thought. At this moment, the multiple financial powers-that-be are racing to provide further content to an internationally orchestrated revamping of regulation in time for the reconven-ing of the G-20 summit in April 2009. Rapid intervention, essential as it has been to prevent the downward spiral of the financial system taking the economy—and some have said modern economic theory—with it, may not be the best way to introduce reforms that may effectively redraw customer and prudential protections long in place, some of which worked extremely well during this period of extreme deleveraging and asset revaluation. Also the rush to change the puppeteers and the stage should not obscure the fact that getting the substance right is critical. And the approach to substance should be clear-sighted enough to see for example that the language of procyclicality, currently being drawn on by advocates of reducing required capital reserves, can be used for ill as well as for good. Finally, any review should take into account the resilience of markets and the value of the information they provide and take care not to adopt solutions that bias the competitive landscape.

1. See, e.g., Jerry W. Markham, "For Whom the Bell Tolls: The Demise of Exchange Trading Floors and the Growth of ECNs," ExpressO; available at http://works.bepress.com/jerry_ markham/1 (unpublished works; 2008).
2. Often equity exchanges in particular are referred to as public utilities. In the United States, in fact, the fees charged for data production and dissemination by such exchanges were originally set by regulation and now still have maximum caps applied to them.
3. In 1975, when the U.S. legislature first considered a national market system for equity securities, Junius W. Peake and Morris Mendelsohn argued that a black-box approach to centralizing order flow was the fairest means of addressing customer protection, in particular best execution. See, e.g., Peake and Mendelsohn, "Whose Market Is It, Anyway? Intermediaries or Investors," Wharton School, Rodney L. White Center for Financial Research Working Papers, July 1994. Until 1993, the CFTC exchange-trading (concentration) requirement contained in Section 4(a) was construed to favor the central marketplace, and exceptions were narrowly construed (and various stratagems devised) to permit certain types of over-the-counter trading in swaps and financial forwards to be interpreted not to breach this general requirement. Of course, electronic technology not only made centralization possible, it also made niche markets possible and facilitated automated dealer transactions. The changes in technology that permitted further automation of various types of markets and transactions created a difficulty for regulators seeking to keep pace with innovation, to take sensible positions, and to nonetheless honor the relevant legal constraints.
4. IOSCO Internet Task Force Report on Securities Activities over the Internet, 1998. See especially Part IV: Key Recommendations, at paragraphs 14, 15, and 16, www.iosco.org/library/ pubdocs/pdf/IOSCOPD83.pdf.
5. BATS trading, www.batstrading.com, is an ECN formed in 2006 as a subsidiary of a technology company based in Kansas City, Missouri. BATS is now in the course of establishing BATS Europe. It trades up to 15% of Nasdaq volume. Electronic Liquidity Exchange (ELX) is a new dealer-owned futures exchange, announced in 2008 by Howard Ludnick, who had sponsored Brokertec; MCX is the Multi-CommodityExchange of India.
6. For example, India and China have studied other templates but created their own. This may be why the achievements of the Indian markets are quite substantial in that they tried to put together the needed infrastructure on the business side and to provide by contract what was not there by law, much in the manner of the old markets that preceded today's modern behemoths. See Corcoran, "The Uses of New Capital Markets: Electronic Commerce and the Rules of the Game in the International Marketplace," www.wcl.american.edu/journal/lawrev/49/ corcoran.pdf?rd=1.
7. For example, cases related to the enforcement of the so-called Wagner patent, Trading Technologies business process case, and the NYMEX case against ICE attempting to claim that its settlement price for WTI crude was proprietary. See John Fazzio, "Financial Innovation Patents: The Future of Futures Markets or Old Wine in New Bottles" (14 March 2006).
8. Objectives and Principles of Securities Regulation, IOSCO Library, Public Document (1998) n. 1.
9. Id.

10. Office of Fair Trade (U.K.); Justice Department (U.S.); European Commission Competition Ministry. See also, for example, Core Principle 18 for Designated Contract Markets of the Commodity Futures Modernization Act of 2000 (CFMA).

11. See, for example, Corcoran and Lawton, *The Journal of Futures Markets*, Vol. 13, No. 2, 213–222, John Wiley & Sons (1993).

12. For example, today equities markets are commonly referred to as *commoditized*, that is, traded based on volatility and general market fundamentals to profit from volume and small "alpha" differentials through technical algorithmic trading models rather than specific risks, stock picking, or analysis. Capacity today is at a premium. At the New York Stock Exchange (now NYSE Euronext), the current transaction capacity of billions dwarfs the highest level of trading experienced in the 1987 crash, when the 800,000 shares traded effectively stopped trading; response time is now down to infinitesimal fractions of seconds. See, for a commercial example of the quest to eliminate and measure latency, www.netqos.com/solutions/trade_monitor/index.html?gclid=CMzglvL21pQCFQVfFQodVSGYkA.

13. *Screen Based Trading Systems for Derivative Products*, IOSCO Library, 1990. The report accompanying these principles, though instructive, was distributed by IOSCO but never adopted, since the drafting committee participants could not agree as to the next level of granularity. Note that the original U.K. Financial Services Act of 1986 contained principles of market conduct, as did the first EU passporting directive, known as the Investment Services Directive of 1992.

14. See: *Principles for Oversight of Screen Based Trading Systems for Derivatives Products, Additions*, IOSCO, Library (October 2000). The additional four principles are:

    1. Regulatory authorities with responsibilities arising from the operation of cross-border markets for derivative products ("relevant regulatory authorities") should develop cooperative arrangements and coordinate supervisory responsibilities, consistent with each authority's responsibilities and in a manner that promotes regulatory effectiveness and avoids the imposition of unnecessary regulatory costs.
    2. Each regulatory authority with responsibilities related to a cross-border market for derivatives (whether in respect of the market operator and the market participants) should be prepared to share relevant information in an efficient and timely manner. In developing cooperative arrangements, regulators should attempt to identify in advance the information needed, the sources of that information, the manner in which the information can be obtained, and the channels through which it can be shared.
    3. The applicable regulatory requirements in the jurisdiction of each relevant regulatory authority and the framework for regulatory coordination and cooperation should be transparent.
    4. In considering their approach to cross-border markets for derivatives, access jurisdictions should take into account whether the initial jurisdiction authorizing the market operator applies the IOSCO Objectives and Principles of Securities Regulation (September 1998) and the 1990 Principles as supplemented above.

15. CFTC Screen No-Action Policy Statement, November, 2006; But see: July 8, 2008 amendments to no action position accorded to the Dubai Mercantile Exchange and to ICE UK.

16. These set forth basic high-level objectives of oversight of securities markets and market operators more generally, irrespective of medium of trading, including appropriate conditions of authorization, transparency, prevention of market abuses—such as manipulation and insider trading, assurance of financial integrity of participant, and clearing and settlement standards addressing finality and protection of customer funds.

17. CME-SIMEX mutual offset clearing system, initiated in 1984.

18. www.cftc.gov; CME manages accessions to the companion agreement among exchanges to share relevant information about exposures and the like in various types of market events sufficient to determine the whole position (on multiple markets) of a particular trader.

19. The transition to electronic trading in the United States has been a long, drawn-out process, whereas in France and London, for example, the floor disappeared in almost a blink of an eye—in London, the dominant but floor-operated LIFFE folded to the Deutsche Börse's attempt to retrieve the bund contract in less than six months, and the floor of the MATIF disappeared overnight. Many of the current developments are the same on both sides of the Atlantic.

20. See the Petersen antispeculation bill (Commodity Markets Transparency and Accountability Act of 2008), a version of which was reintroduced in 1997—and Senator Harkin's sponsored amendments to the CFMA. HR 6604 passed in the House on September 18, 2008, and was sent to the Senate on September 23, 2008.

21. See FIA volume figures, which reflect an exponential increase.

22. See n.3 above.

23. 17 CFR Sec. 242.300.SEC Rule 11 Ac1-1, 17 CFR Sec. 240.11Ac1-5 and 11Ac1-6; for an international view, see: *Report on Issues in the Regulation of Cross Border Proprietary Screen Based Trading Systems,* IOSCO Library (1994).

24. Note, for example, the purchase by NYSE of Pacific Board of Trade's Archipelago and the choice of CEOs with IT expertise.

25. Volume in options was expected to materially increase.

26. Rules 600 to 612: 17 CFR 242-600 to 612.

27. The MiFID defines *systematic internalizer* as "an investment firm dealing on its own account to execute client orders outside a regulated market or a multilateral trading facility." It requires firm quotes on liquid shares when the firm is dealing in retail quantities. However, CESR guidance suggests a materiality threshold as to when internalizing orders is part of the commercial business model that is rather high.

28. See, e.g., Prospectus Directive.

29. These markets might appeal to third countries (non-EU participants) by permitting, for example, listing of non-International Financial Reporting Standards or nonprospectus directive-compliant products, or might be structured to avoid other aspects of the regulated regime.

30. See: Corporation of the City of London, "European Corporate Bond Markets, Transparency, Liquidity, and Efficiency" (May 2006), www.cepr.org/PRESS/TT_CorporateFULL.pdf; Toni Gravelle, Banque de Canada (2002); Ian Domowitz and Benn Steil, "Automation, Trading Costs, and the Structure of the Securities Trading Industry," Department of Economics and Institute for Policy Research, Northwestern University, 1997.

31. The CFTC was reauthorized in legislation known as CFTC Reauthorization Act of 2007. HR2419 eliminated the Enron loophole with respect to certain products and became law May 22, 2008.

32. See Section 409 of the Federal Deposit Insurance Corporation Act of 1991 as amended, which effectively permits a clearing agency registered under the U.S. securities laws, the CFMA, or is a foreign financial futures regulator that the U.S. Comptroller of the Currency, the Board of Governors of the Federal Reserve System, the Federal Deposit Insurance Corporation, the SEC, or the CFTC determine has satisfied appropriate standards.

33. Tokyo Communiqué, www.cftc.org.

34. *Report on the Permanent Subcommittee on Investigations,* 2007, and the recent spate of legislation before Congress on energy and speculation (July 2008).

35. Policies on Error Trades, IOSCO Library (October 2005).

36. Roberta S. Karmel, "Turning Seats into Shares: Causes and Implications of Demutualization of Stock and Futures Exchanges," 53 *Hastings, L. J.* 367 (2002). For a comprehensive discussion of case studies, see: Akhtar, ed., "Demutualization of Stock Exchanges, Problems, Solutions and Case Studies," Asian Development Bank (2002).

37. Indeed, looking at this phenomenon another way, the club culture in some places was so dominant that, even today, the regulators must use "mercenary regulators" from other jurisdictions because of the difficulty of reintegrating regulatory enforcers after their government service into the business/exchange club.

38. The key regulatory issue is whether these changes will undermine the commitment of resources and capabilities by a stock exchange to effectively fulfill its regulatory and public interest responsibilities at an appropriate standard. The identified regulatory questions and concerns fall into three areas:

    a. What conflicts of interest are created or increased where a for-profit entity also performs the regulatory functions that an exchange might have regarding:
       i)   Primary market regulation (listing and admission of companies, self-listing)
       ii) Secondary market regulation (trading rules)
       iii) Member regulation
    b. A fair and efficient capital market is a public good. A well-run exchange is a key part of the capital market. Is there a need to impose a special regime on exchanges to protect the public interest, such as particular corporate governance arrangements or rules regarding share ownership?
    c. Will a for-profit exchange be run with due regard for its financial viability? Will adequate funding be allocated to regulatory functions, including arrangements designed to manage defaults?

    The Committee acknowledges that many of these are not new issues for either stock exchanges or their regulators, but the effect of demutualization and increased competition warrants a reexamination of both the issues and available regulatory responses.
39. See, for example, the Hunt silver case and the Feruzzi soybean case, which had international repercussions.
40. See Corcoran, "Autorégulation et contrôles opérationnels: réflexions sur la surveillance des produits dérivés négociés sur les marchés réglementés," *Revue d'economie financiere*, no. 82 (2006); See also, Corcoran, "Self-Regulation and Derivatives Markets Governance: The U.S. Experience, Parts 1 and 2," *Futures & Derivatives Law Report*, Vol. 27, Issues 10 and 11 (November and December, 2007).
41. See French, AFM Web site.
42. See, for example, the Tokyo Stock Exchange Web site. Interestingly, as reported in *The Wall Street Journal*, the move from private club to public company has had one possible business advantage: In the recent lawsuit in the United States over the compensation of Richard Grasso, former president and CEO of the New York Stock Exchange, the court found that the fact that the NYSE had become a public company before the pay package was implemented was a factor that prevented it from attack.
43. IOSCO Internet Task Force report (see above fn).
44. IOSCO strategy calls for the Multi-lateral Memorandum of Understanding on Cooperation and Mutual Assistance (MMOU) to be executed or committed to as a condition of membership by 2010.
45. Cite SEC initiative.
46. One of the first examples of a mutual recognition was the MRMOU (mutual recognition memorandum of understanding) negotiated under Article 175 authority of the U.S. State Department and a binding arrangement for the United States and the French, then COB, for which certain staff received the *Legion d'honneur*.
47. Prof. Eric J. Pan, "Why the World No Longer Puts Its Stock in Us," December 13, 2006, Cardozo Legal Studies Research Paper No. 175, http://ssrn.com/abstract=951705.
48. See, e.g., *Banque de Canada Financial Stability Report*, 2007, at p. 45, www.bank-banque-canada.ca/en/fsr/2007/fsr_1207.pdf.
49. CME (with CBOT and with the NYMEX); Nasdaq and OMX, NYSE-Euronext, TSE and Quebec, Winnipeg and ICE US, the Nordic Circle, Dubai/Doha interests in London, and so forth.
50. Corcoran, "Regulating Futures Markets, the Evolving Federalist Model," *Futures Industry Association Magazine*, May/June 2007, http://www.futuresindustry.org/fi-magazine-home.asp?a=1188.

51. Failure of France, the Netherlands, and now Ireland (the only EU member for which a referendum was required) in the second round of processes to confirm the EU Constitution. Moreover, within Europe there are niche players (Luxembourg, Ireland, Austria). See: Ambassador Bruton, What Next? The Lisbon Treaty, the Irish Referendum and the Implications for the European Union, www.eurunion.org/eu/index.php?option=com_content&task=view&id=2042

52. Eddy Wymeersch, "The Future of Financial Regulation and Supervision in Europe," *Common Market Law Review,* January 2005.

53. See Chapters 4, 6, and 7, Davies and Green, *Global Financial Regulation, The Essential Guide*, Polity Press, 2008.

54. See article by Carmine di Noia, 20 October 2008, which argues that regulation should be organized under four peaks at both the national and the European levels. These would be under a coordinator: the central bank, a prudential regulator, an investor protection regulator, and an antitrust authority. http://voxeu.org/index.php?9=node12462.

55. See Speech by Sir Howard Davies, then Chairman of the FSA, 28 October 1997.

11 Electronic Exchanges and Trading: Benefits

Executive Summary

Electronic exchanges offer many benefits to every constituent, from traders to regulators. Globalization, more tradable products, and a vast ocean of real-time data, along with global networks and powerful computers, have led to fundamental changes in the way markets function. Buy-side firms can now execute complex order types and route them to exchanges through broker-neutral platforms.

It has been a busy few decades for financial markets globally. The transformation to electronic trading has allowed exchanges to fundamentally change their structure and their business model. Today most exchanges are for-profit global companies based on the electronic trading model. One of the biggest drivers of this change has been the adoption of technology by the financial markets.

Today technology is the primary engine for every component of the trade cycle. The exchange infrastructure is mostly electronic and is connected to the global trading community through computer networks. The exchanges have significantly benefited from this new model. Globalization has allowed the exchanges to expand their market share and significantly increase volume. As public companies, the exchanges today have the flexibility to merge with or acquire other exchanges around the world. Their electronic architecture allows them to complete these mergers and acquisitions quickly and smoothly. For example, it took over seven years for NYMEX and COMEX, both member-owned exchanges at the time, to complete their merger. By contrast, the merger between the CME and CBOT as stockholder-owned company took less than two years. There has been a frenzy of mergers and acquisitions between exchanges, allowing them to grow market share and acquire new products. Today the exchanges view technology as an integral part of their business, giving them a new revenue stream and helping them grow their business at an unprecedented speed.

The changes within exchanges have also fueled competition across financial markets. Today they are flooded with new players offering products to the trading community to help them access global exchanges more cheaply and quickly. The financial markets have seen new levels of transparency, speed, and anonymity in the trade cycle that would not have been possible in the floor-trading days. Traders have access to more markets and more data in real time than they ever did in the past. A new wave of innovative applications is helping the trading community use the flood of data to develop new strategies and new order types. Automated trading applications are helping traders trade a larger suite of products and manage greater volume. Transparency in the marketplace has also helped regulators and risk managers track markets and trading activity more efficiently and accurately. The benefits of the new model have been significant and, as exchanges continue to grow, the financial markets will continue to find creative ways to reap the rewards.

Globalization: Bringing the World Closer Together

The physical boundaries of exchanges limited their growth and market share. Although traders could trade by telephone, customers off the floor were at a disadvantage to the traders on the floor. Any significant growth for an exchange would require a bigger physical floor, which is costly to build and maintain. The only way to significantly increase market share would be to eliminate the physical boundaries of the exchanges. And the new model provided exchanges just that. The computers and networks allowed exchanges to connect to the trading community virtually. The globalization of exchanges through the use of technology has allowed them to expand by connecting with exchanges around the world. They are now able to list new products (created or acquired) quickly and with very little up-front cost. This global expansion has led to a significant surge in the volume across exchanges and across asset classes.

Pioneers chose cyberspace instead of a physical floor to build their exchanges. Some of the early followers took the risk of migrating their products off the physical floor and onto the electronic platform. These exchanges began seeing the benefits of the electronic trading model as they moved their operations off the floor. They saw their market share increase and exchange volume surge. We saw CME establish Globex to capture market share in Asia, and we saw Eurex build remote connections to reach traders in continental Europe and the United States. With the help of this expanded market, Eurex was able to capture LIFFE's flagship product. This infamous steal was a wakeup call for other derivatives exchanges. As these upstarts grew, the financial markets saw the power of the electronic trading model. As more exchanges began adopting electronic trading, the market share and trading volume at those exchanges increased. Whether it was the battle between the ICE (electronic energy market) and NYMEX (floor based) in the futures world or ISE (electronic options market) and CBOE (floor based), the story was the same: Electronic trading won.

As the exchanges converted from the floor-trading model to the electronic trading model, they began their journey toward globalization. They established their global footprint by transforming their business model through partnerships, mergers, and acquisitions. The open exchange API served as a bridge between the exchanges and the trading community. The new players in the market, such as trading screen providers, market data providers, and other software developers, jumped at the opportunity to take advantage of the open exchange connectivity. The technology vendors helped exchanges and other financial players reduce their trading costs. For example, NYSE's purchase of ARCA has saved them over $200 million in technology expenses.[1] Technology providers such as OM and AEMS[2] license their software to exchanges around the world. AEMS alone sells its software to over 20 exchanges, responsible for 17% of Euronext's revenue.[3]

Mergers and acquisitions within financial markets have further increased the interconnectivity between players. As we saw in earlier chapters, the mergers and acquisitions between exchanges have increased significantly in the past decade as the physical barriers were broken and the migration toward electronic trading picked up. The pioneers who had a head start in establishing their position in electronic trading saw their volume pick up as they expanded their market share. The increase in volume provided the exchanges with increased revenue, which in turn allowed them to further bolster their product offerings by forming partnerships with more exchanges.

Table 11.1 shows some of the major exchange groups and their volume increase between 2006 and 2007. These exchange groups are collections of exchanges that are formed through mergers as well their own subsidiary creation to trade new asset classes. For example, CBOE group is composed of the Chicago Board of Options Exchange (CBOE) as well as the CBOE Futures Exchange. The CBOE Futures Exchange was created by the CBOE to begin futures trading. As the table shows, the exchange group has seen healthy growth in its volume from 2006 to 2007, even when one of the exchanges or electronic trading platforms had slower growth, such as LIFFE-Paris, which is part of NYSE Euronext, or even negative growth, as with Clearport, which is part of the NYMEX group.[4]

CME: Expansion through Global Marketplace and Acquisition

CME has come a long way from its humble beginnings as a regional exchange in Chicago, where it was once the Egg and Butter Exchange. Today it controls approximately 98% of the U.S. futures market and is one of the leading derivatives exchanges in the world. CME entered the world of electronic trading very early by first launching the Globex platform in 1992. Globex was offered in conjunction with floor-trading to allow trading after hours—the first step in capturing global market share. On the first day of its launch, Globex traded 2,063 contracts.[5] Today over 80% of the volume on CME goes through its electronic platform. The growth in volume at CME has been phenomenal, with over eight consecutive years of double-digit growth. In September 2008, CME averaged 13.9 million trades per day.[6] CME achieved this tremendous growth by both opening its electronic trading platform to the global marketplace and through mergers and acquisition. The partnership between CME and Reuters

Table 11.1 Exchange Groups, 2006 and 2007

	2007	2006	Change (%)
Australian Stock Exchange	24,969,811	22,452,328	11.21
Sydney Futures Exchange	91,121,162	78,120,106	16.64
Australian Securities Exchange Total	116,090,973	100,572,434	15.43
Chicago Board of Options Exchange	944,471,924	674,735,348	39.98
CBOE Futures Exchange	1,136,295	478,424	137.51
CBOE Total	945,608,219	675,213,772	40.05
Chicago Board of Trade	1,029,568,853	805,884,413	27.76
Chicago Mercantile Exchange	1,775,429,438	1,403,264,034	26.52
CME Group Total	2,804,998,291	2,209,148,447	26.97
Eurex	1,899,861,926	1,526,751,902	24.44
International Securities Exchange	804,347,677	591,961,518	35.88
Eurex Total	2,704,209,603	2,118,713,420	27.63
ICE Futures Europe	138,470,956	92,721,050	49.34
ICE Futures US	53,782,919	44,667,169	20.41
ICE Futures Canada	3,452,165	2,896,536	19.18
Intercontinental Exchange Total	195,706,040	140,284,755	39.51
Liffe–UK	695,974,929	515,478,934	35.02
Liffe–Amsterdam	159,827,511	126,833,753	26.01
Liffe–Paris	90,868,890	86,016,916	5.64
Liffe–Brussels	1,348,884	1,300,009	3.76
Liffe–Lisbon	1,005,238	673,514	49.25
NYSE Arca Options	335,838,547	196,586,356	70.84
NYSE Euronext Total*	1,284,863,999	926,889,482	38.62
New York Mercantile Exchange	304,994,104	233,397,571	30.68
Comex	40,468,298	30,072,043	34.57
Clearport	7,923,010	12,682,712	−37.53
Dubai Mercantile Exchange**	223,174		
NYMEX Total	353,608,586	276,152,326	28.05

*Excludes OTC contracts.
**DME was launched in 2007.
Source: FIA.

created the FX Market platform.[7] The 50/50 joint venture would provide access to currency products, a nice complement to CME's currency futures products.[8] The recent acquisition of CBOT allowed CME to offer financial futures such as 2-, 10-, and 30-year U.S. Treasury futures as well as agricultural products. CME's recent merger with NYMEX added energy products to its product suite.

LIFFE: Using Technology to Make a Comeback

After losing significant market share to Eurex, LIFFE found its footing by putting itself on the fast track toward electronic trading. It ordered a complete shutdown of its floor within one year. It was a bold move that risked losing traders and liquidity, the lifeblood of an exchange. For LIFFE, the risk paid off. After closing its floor in 2000, the exchange has seen steady growth. With its merger with Euronext, the exchange became a conglomerate covering markets in several European countries. It also took advantage of the modular exchange model to provide its electronic trading platform to other exchanges. The CBOT, until its recent merger with CME, used the LIFFE Connect platform for its trading platform. TFX in Japan still uses LIFFE Connect for its trading needs. Finally, with its recent merger with NYSE, LIFFE has established itself as part of a major transatlantic exchange conglomerate. Through mergers, acquisitions, and partnerships and its migration toward electronic trading, it now boasts a product suite across asset classes and a presence in the United States, Europe, and Asia. Similarly, exchanges around the world jumped on the bandwagon of partnerships, mergers, and acquisitions to gain market share. Whether it's the pioneers solidifying their positions in the electronic trading world or the followers playing catch-up, technology provided exchanges and financial markets the flexibility to expand and capture market share around the world.

Surge in Volume

Trading on the floor was fun and chaotic. It was a unique work environment cherished by the financial community for over a century. However, the growth in financial markets in recent years would be unthinkable in the floor-trading environment. Manual trading, clearing, and settlement could never be able to keep up with the volume growth seen in the last decade. The trading community used computer screens and automated trading applications to trade more products across multiple exchanges, fueling the surge in volume across them. The cycle of growth continued. The exchanges expanded, the traders traded more, and the exchanges beat their volume record year after year. For example, in the U.S. equities market a normal day of volume today is almost twice as much as the record set in the 1987 crash, and the volume for a given stock on a busy day equals the volume of the entire market in the past.[9] The derivatives markets

Table 11.2 Global Exchange-Traded Derivatives Volume by Region, 2006 and 2007

Region	2007	2006	Change (%)
Asia/Pacific	4,186,511,897	3,511,548,425	19.22
Europe	3,355,222,878	2,674,329,578	25.46
North America	6,137,204,364	4,616,725,727	32.93
Latin America	1,048,627,318	864,665,702	21.28
Other	459,104,373	194,943,593	135.51
Global Total	15,186,670,830	11,862,213,025	28.03

Source: FIA.

have been flourishing as well, and the growth has been remarkable in every region of the world (see Table 11.2) from 2006 to 2007.

The electronic infrastructure has allowed exchanges to process this growing volume with the speed and degree of accuracy that could not have been achieved with floor-trading. In the floor-trading days, spikes in volume would certainly introduce significant delays in trade processing. But the ability to handle increasing volume today is far better than in the past. The surge in volume has continued to put a burden on the electronic infrastructure of the exchanges, but it is easier to upgrade a machine to handle this surge. And the exchanges have largely been keeping up with the growing volumes.[10] They continue to take advantage of new technologies and new computer hardware, which has given them the capacity to handle more trades. The CME, for example, has expanded significantly in recent years. It successfully completed the merger with the CBOT in 2007 and, with the recent acquisition of NYMEX, has significantly increased its product suite and market share. The exchange upgraded its Globex system to handle the additional load. It added additional hardware to support order entry, market data, and the matching engine, which would process CBOT trading.[11] CME also adopted FAST (FIX Adopted for Streaming[12]) to transmit market data for both the CME and the CBOT. This reduced the bandwidth requirement for CME customers by over 50%.[13,14] The electronic trading model gave exchanges the flexibility to scale their infrastructure to support the growing volume by adopting newer technologies, upgrading hardware, and scaling their architecture.

The early adopters proved the viability of the electronic trading model, and the growing volume has changed the minds of even the strongest opponents of the new model. The exchanges with an electronic trading platform saw tremendous volume growth and threatened the exchanges still doing business on the floor. The pioneers solidified their position as the electronic trading leaders by improving their electronic infrastructure. In the end, however, most followers didn't fare so badly, either. They jumped on the electronic trading bandwagon by making use of the modular exchange model, which allowed them to pick the best players for each component of the trade cycle. As these exchanges moved toward electronic trading, they saw a significant boost in their trading volume. For example, when the CBOT unveiled side-by-side trading for grain futures in August 2006, within five months migration to screen for corn, wheat, and soybeans reached the halfway point. The CBOT's open-outcry volume for agricultural product grew 23% year-over-year, but adding in the electronic trading pushed the growth rate to 40%.[15]

It was clear evidence that electronic trading would provide a significant boost to overall volume for the exchange, whether it was the fight between ICE, an upcoming electronic trading exchange, versus NYMEX,[16] an established energy exchange, or the upstart in equity options ISE taking on CBOE, a leading established options exchange. Exchanges across asset classes saw a tremendous surge in volume. The volume in global futures and options markets grew from 6.2 billion contracts in 2002 to 15 billion in 2007[17] across 54 exchanges globally, an increase of over 58%. The story was the same in equities and equity options. The NYSE[18] and Nasdaq[19] saw their volumes increase as they forged ahead with the adoption of electronic trading platforms. The NYSE saw a 16.7% increase in 2007 and Euronext saw another spectacular year, with its volume going up 47% in Europe. Similarly, the Nasdaq OMX saw a 30% increase in market share. The U.S. options markets also saw significant growth. According to the Options Clearing Corporation (OCC), the equity options turnover jumped 40%, to 2.8 billion contracts, in 2007 compared to 2006.[20]

Volume Growth around the World

Trading was once dominated by U.S. and European exchanges. Although the established markets, such as CME, Eurex, NYSE, and CBOE, continue to be the leaders in today's financial markets, the overall landscape has certainly changed. There have been new players in the United States and Europe in all asset classes. The Boston Options Exchange (BOX) was launched in February 2004 and captured almost 5% of the options market within the first 20 months of trading.[21] ICE, founded in 2000, took over IPE to compete with NYMEX for its flagship product, Brent Crude. These markets challenged the established markets in the United States and Europe. More important, the financial community began seeing the emergence of new markets around the world in countries with no established exchanges. And many of these markets came under the spotlight as they saw a significant surge in their trading volumes.

As shown in Table 11.3, the ranks of the global derivatives exchanges have plenty of new players. For example, China and India have seen tremendous growth in their markets. The National Stock Exchange of India ranked ninth on the top exchange list. Similarly, markets in Hong Kong saw their volumes

Table 11.3 Top Derivatives Exchange Ranking, 2006 and 2007

Rank	Exchange	2007	2006	Change (%)
1	CME Group	2,804,998,291	2,209,148,447	26.97
2	Korea Exchange	2,709,140,423	2,474,593,261	9.48
3	Eurex	1,899,861,928	1,528,751,902	24.28
4	LIFFE	949,025,452	730,303,126	29.95
5	CBOE	945,608,219	675,213,772	40.05
6	International Securities Exchange	804,347,677	591,961,518	35.88
7	Bolsa de Mercadorias & Futuros	426,363,492	283,570,241	50.36
8	Philadelphia Stock Exchange	407,972,525	273,093,003	49.39
9	National Stock Exchange of India	379,874,850	194,488,403	95.32
10	Bolsa de Valores de Sao Paulo	367,690,283	287,518,574	27.88
11	New York Mercantile Exchange	353,385,412	276,152,326	27.97
12	NYSE Arca Options	335,838,547	196,586,356	70.84
13	JSE (South Africa)	329,642,403	105,047,524	213.80
14	American Stock Exchange	240,383,466	197,045,745	21.99
15	Mexican Derivatives Exchange	228,972,029	275,217,670	−16.80
16	Intercontinental Exchange	195,706,040	140,284,755	39.51
17	Dalian Commodity Exchange	185,614,913	120,349,998	54.23
18	OMX Group	142,510,375	123,167,736	15.70
19	Boston Options Exchange	129,797,339	94,390,602	37.51
20	Australian Securities Exchange	116,090,973	100,572,434	15.43
21	Taiwan Futures Exchange	115,150,375	114,603,379	0.48
22	Osaka Securities Exchange	108,916,811	60,646,437	79.59
23	Tel-Aviv Stock Exchange	104,371,763	83,047,982	25.68
24	Zhengzhou Commodity Exchange	93,052,714	46,298,117	100.99
25	London Metal Exchange	92,914,728	86,940,189	6.87
26	Hong Kong Exchanges & Clearing	87,985,688	42,906,915	105.06
27	Shanghai Futures Exchange	85,563,833	58,106,001	47.25

Table 11.3 (*Continued*)

Rank	Exchange	2007	2006	Change (%)
28	Multi Commodity Exchange of India	68,945,925	45,635,538	51.08
29	Mercado Espanol de Opciones y Futuros	51,859,591	46,973,675	10.40
30	Tokyo Commodity Exchange	47,070,169	63,686,701	−26.09
31	Singapore exchange	44,206,826	36,597,743	20.79
32	Montreal exchange	42,742,210	40,540,837	5.43
33	Tokyo Financial Exchange	42,613,726	35,485,461	20.09
34	Italian Derivatives Exchange	37,124,922	31,606,263	17.46
35	National Commodity and Derivatives Exchange	34,947,873	53,266,249	−34.39
36	Tokyo Stock Exchange	33,093,785	29,227,556	13.23
37	Mercado a Termino Rosario	25,423,960	18,212,072	39.60
38	Turkish Derivatives Exchange	24,867,033	6,848,087	263.12
39	Tokyo Grain Exchange	19,674,883	19,144,010	2.77
40	Budapest Stock Exchange	18,828,228	14,682,949	28.23
41	Oslo Stock Exchange	13,967,847	12,156,960	14.90
42	Warsaw Stock Exchange	9,341,968	6,714,205	39.14
43	OneChicago	8,105,963	7,922,465	2.32
44	Central Japan Commodity Exchange	6,549,417	9,635,688	−32.03
45	Malaysia Derivatives Exchange	6,202,686	4,161,024	49.07
46	Kansas City Board of Trade	4,670,965	5,287,190	−11.66
47	Minneapolis Grain Exchange	1,826,807	1,655,034	10.38
48	New Zealand Futures Exchange	1,651,038	1,826,027	−9.58
49	Wiener Bourse	1,316,896	1,311,543	0.41
50	Chicago Climate Exchange	283,758	28,924	881.05
51	Dubai Mercantile Exchange	223,174		
52	Mercado a Termino de Buenos Aires	177,564	147,145	20.67
53	Kansai Commodities Exchange	164,743	318,483	−48.27
54	U.S. Futures Exchange	8,111	135,803	−94.03

double in 2007. Technology also helped bring smaller markets such as Johannesburg and Dubai into the global financial spotlight, with Johannesburg taking 10th place in the top exchange list with an astonishing increase of 214% in its exchange volume.[22] Whether it is the 263% increase in the Turkish Derivatives Exchange or Brazil's BM&F posting a gain of 28% or Rosario Exchange of Argentina logging an increase of 40%, the world of derivatives exchanges has seen astonishing growth in recent years.

Innovative Products Increasing Growth

The electronic trading model has also helped exchanges launch new products.[23] It is far easier to list a new product today than it was in the floor-trading days. The exchange no longer has to worry about the physical space needed for the new product nor find market makers and/or specialists to encourage liquidity. Technology has allowed exchanges to experiment with innovative products and see what works without adding significant cost. And the innovations in new products have certainly paid off. Exchanges in recent years have launched a number of new products that have helped them capture market share around the globe. Exchanges have listed new products such as a 10-year interest rate swap or E-Mini S&P contracts that are small enough in size[24] to allow a greater number of market participants to trade them. These products have helped exchanges increase their volume in the new competitive landscape. For example, the Mexican Derivatives Exchange (MexDer) increased its volumes when it listed a 10-year interest rate swap that offered better hedging opportunity for traders; however, the TIIF 28, a short-term interest futures contract, saw a decline in volume in 2007. So, even though MexDer saw declining volumes on one product, it was offset by the increase in volume on the new product. Similarly, exchanges around the world have seen a significant increase in new product launches, such as CBOE's Volatility Option (VIX) and ETFs on equities exchanges. The exchanges have certainly listed some products that have failed, but with the low cost of launching new products, they can easily afford to experiment. Overall, the increase in product choices has helped exchanges grow their overall volume tremendously in the last few years.

Data, Data, and More Data

Trading is a numbers game. Whether trading on the floor or electronically, traders always make their decisions based on numbers. Traders base their decisions on numerous criteria, such as the exchange volume, price of the product, volume of a particular product they are looking to trade, and the last price at which a product was traded. They also look at external data describing the market fundamentals, such as unemployment numbers, interest rates, and productivity numbers. The list goes on and on. With more information about the market and other events at hand, traders can make better decisions. As the markets moved toward electronic trading, the financial community saw the availability of financial data increase tremendously. More important, the traders were able to access this data in real time, allowing them to adjust their trading strategies or positions instantaneously.

Computers allow the financial markets to store and process tremendous amounts of information that would have been impossible before. In the floor-trading days, these tasks were manual. In a frantic trading day it would be impossible for any trader on the floor to capture all the information that is available through a trading screen today. The technology advancements have provided financial markets significant amounts of storage capacity. The storage capacity allows exchanges to store detailed information about trades. Every trade today has information such as details about the traders, their account information, purchase price, trade quantity, and time of trade. Exchanges have also taken advantage of improvements in telecommunications. The connection between the exchange and the trading firm can be large enough for the market data to flow between the two parties in real time. Established vendors such as Bloomberg and Reuters provide real-time market data to the trading community. Software vendors such as Trading Technologies built their reputations not only by providing innovative tools such as MD Trader but also by building high-speed exchange gateways that allow traders to access market data from multiple exchanges in milliseconds.

One Screen: So Much Data

Figure 11.1 shows a screen shot of Trading Technologies' MD Trader. It illustrates the amount of information a trader has at hand to analyze the markets. It is an order-entry screen that allows traders to view an array of market data information for that particular product. In Figure 11.1, MD Trader allows you to view the depth of the market, which is a list of all pending bid and ask orders at different prices. The depth of the market could range from five to over 20 levels deep. Traders use this information to judge how prices might move. The screen also displays other basic information:

- Last traded price: Price at which the last trade occurred
- Last traded quantity: The trade size of the last transaction
- Total volume traded: Volume for the day for the contract
- Total volume traded in the market: Total volume for the exchange
- Volume at price: Total volume traded for the day at a specific price

In the MD Trader screen, the left column allows the trader to select and change the order size and allows the trader to cancel orders already sent to the markets, all with just one click. A trader using trading screens or tools similar to MD Trader has a tremendous amount of information available about a

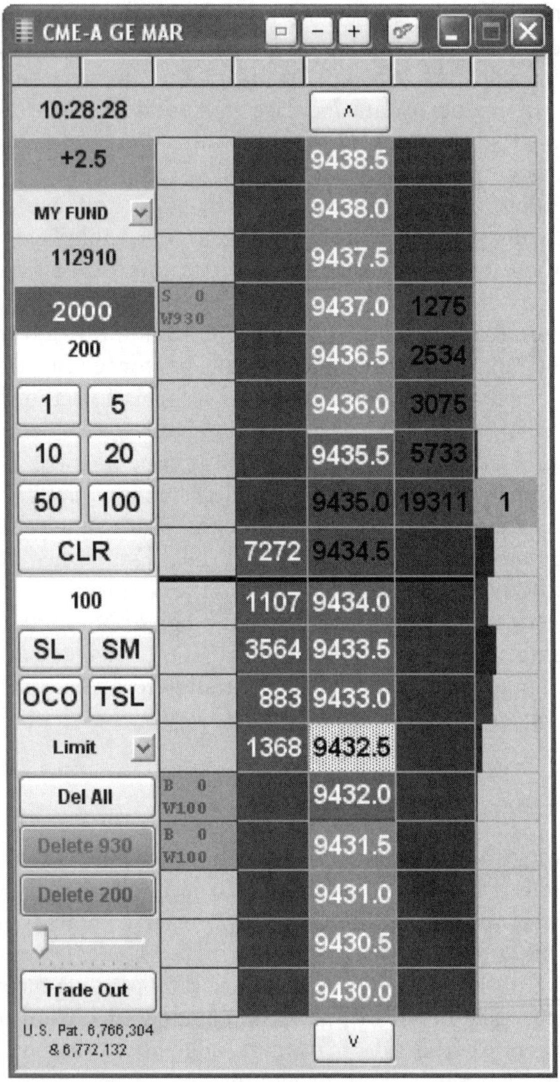

Figure 11.1 TT MD Trader.

specific product and the exchange, which can help him make a better trading decision. With the ability to enter the order directly from the screen that displays the market information, traders can monitor market movements in real time and quickly move in and out of positions throughout the day.

Trading on the floor was primarily conducted through gut feeling. Traders would have to remember past trades or the last price at which a trade was bought or sold. Electronic trading, on the other hand, provides all that information and much more instantaneously. The information is updated on the screen at all times. Today, traders need to be computer savvy. They need to understand how to use the many features available in complex trading applications to effectively act on the information available at their fingertips. They must analyze the information to find new trading styles or strategies or order type to get an edge in the market.

Similarly, ECNs in equities markets began disseminating market data, which was once accessible to a select few in the wider trading community. ECNs began providing Level 2 quotes in real time. Similar to market depth, Level 2 allowed users to view all public quotes for buys and sells. It also provides information on recently executed orders—for example, the last order size that was executed and the price at which the order was executed.

Transparency

The financial markets are much more transparent than ever before. Exchanges provided an open application programming interface (API), which allowed the trading community and technology firms to directly connect to the exchanges. Anyone with a computer and Internet connection can access real-time market data from exchanges around the world. Technology has brought transparency to a financial market that was once opaque in the floor-trading days. It has also leveled the playing field. Market information today is disseminated to computers around the world in real time. In floor-trading days, the closer you were to the pit, the better your chances of getting your order executed. People stood next to each other and traded. It was not uncommon for people to not trade with someone simply because of a grudge, or to trade with someone else because they were friends. In electronic trading, the computers simply enqueue the orders and match them using a matching algorithm. Similarly, all the prices are published on the computer screen. Trading firms, ISVs and other technology players in the market build innovative applications using the wealth of information available, arming the trading community with tools to create new strategies, allowing traders to react to market events faster, and providing risk managers with better monitoring tools. And the information is available in real time to the global financial community. There is no longer an advantage for a market maker or a trader on the floor.

Greater Oversight of Trading Activity

The regulators, risk managers, and exchanges prefer the electronic trading model because they rely on accurate and timely information on trading activity. More information on each trader allows for better monitoring and risk controls. In the electronic trading model, there is an audit trail of virtually every mouse or keyboard click a trader makes. Every trade today captures myriad information about the trade and the trader. Whether it is the time the order was submitted, the account information, the fill time, or the number of changes made to the order, every single event is recorded and stored. Trading platforms are flexible, and any new rules or required information simply need to be programmed once and the trading tools will capture, store, and disseminate that information.

Regulators

Regulators can now track all trading activities to analyze trading patterns and discover any violations of rules. Regulatory mandates such as those established by MiFID[25] would not have been possible to capture in the floor-trading era. Regulation existed for floor-trading as well, but it was hard to monitor and capture trading violations, especially in real time. There were floor managers who tried to enforce major rules, but on a chaotic, crowded trading floor, monitoring for violations would always be challenging. For example, there were no audit trails to help resolve disputes. The trading activity was captured manually, with very little information stored for historical review. To capture a larger trade violation, one had to actively monitor trading activity for days, weeks, and sometimes months to uncover violations. In electronic trading, every trade, along with the details, is captured and stored. For example, many front-end applications provide tools to display audit trails with built-in alerts to notify the compliance officer. This data can be stored and analyzed further to identify suspicious trading trends and violations. The rules can simply be programmed to ensure that trades are executed correctly.

The electronic trading model has allowed regulators to react to market conditions much faster and implement or modify rules at a pace unimaginable in the floor-trading days. Recently on Wall Street, short selling and its potential impact on financial firms came under the spotlight. Regulators had to implement a short selling ban overnight. In floor-trading days, they would simply rely on the floor managers and specialists to ensure that short sales were not conducted. With electronic trading, the short sales features were disabled on the trading screens so that no new short sales could be executed. Furthermore, if the feature accidentally remained on, further controls in different components of the trade cycle could catch and prevent the execution of short sales. Overnight rule mandates were implemented quickly.

Regulatory bodies around the world have worked on revamping the requirements for trade oversight to keep up with changes in financial markets. Similar to MiFID, the SEC in the United States passed Regulation NMS, which included an updated list of requirements to ensure transparency and fairness in the equities markets. Technology has allowed the financial markets to enhance and modify their trading systems to meet these new requirements. For example, firms must comply with numerous mandates for storing trade data. Fortunately, technology allows firms to store this data with ease. Applications are developed to capture, store, and archive the required information. Today, a majority of firms store trade-related data between 5 and 10 years. Electronic storage also allows firms to analyze the data or search for specific information. It would be almost impossible to sift through five years worth of data to find a particular trade(s) in floor-trading, but it is very quick to accomplish that task with electronic trading.

Markets in Financial Instruments Directive (MiFID)[26]

MiFID is the regulatory directive created by the European Union (EU) to cover markets across all 30 EU countries. Launched on November 1, 2007, it was created to foster competition and protect consumers. Some of the highlights of MiFID are:

- *Client category.* MiFID requires firms to categorize clients as counterparties, professional clients, or retail clients, to ensure that proper procedures are implemented based on the client category. These categories must be verified before investment authority is given to clients.
- *Client orders.* Regulation requires firms to collect information that would ensure a client's best interest takes priority.
- *Transparency.* Both pre- and post-trade transparency rules were enhanced significantly to foster competition. For example:
  - All order-matching systems (exchanges and nonexchange) are required to display five best price levels for bid and offer.
  - Firms are required to publish price, volume, and time of all trades in listed products, even if executed outside a regulated market.
  - All internal systems are treated as mini-exchanges and are subjected to rules similar to those for established exchanges. Internal systems are used by firms to match clients' orders against their internal liquidity pool.

Risk Management

Trading is a risky business, and it is a common saying that the higher the risk, the higher the reward. Every day trillions of dollars in securities change hands. Exchanges, brokers, and risk managers within the trading firms spend a significant amount of time and money building risk models to manage trading activity and control risk. Risk management plays a significant role in the trade cycle. It allows exchanges and brokers to control the trading activity, to limit a trader's exposure to risk. The risk management landscape has changed significantly in the electronic trading world. Just like other tasks in floor-trading, risk management was also a manual task seldom followed actively. Manually managing risk for daily trading activity is not ideal. It is difficult to manage traders' risks in real time on the floor. Transparency in the electronic trading model has changed all that. The abundance of data available for trading provides risk managers better visibility into the daily dealings by their traders. Just as traders can view multiple products across asset classes on one screen, risk managers can view the entire portfolio for a trader or the entire firm on one screen. The availability of detailed information on trading activity has allowed firms to build sophisticated risk management models. Firms such as Rolfe & Nolan and AIM-TO have built sophisticated applications for risk management. For example, Rolfe & Nolan's Alerts Direct application allows risk managers to monitor margin exposure throughout the day to control the firm's exposure to risk. Their Margin Direct application allows risk managers to revalue portfolios throughout the day to adjust for volatility in the markets.[27] Similarly, AIM-TO's VerusHedge product allows firms to analyze their entire portfolios using risk models such as Value at Risk (VaR).[28]

In addition, risk management tools can be integrated with the trading systems to proactively prevent trades from reaching the exchange for execution. Almost all the front-end applications support basic risk management parameters. The front-end technology providers such as Trading Technologies (TT), RTS, and ORC all have pre-risk capabilities built into their applications. These applications allow risk managers to view real-time P&L (profit and loss) and view all orders from traders in the firm. The firms can customize the application to alert risk managers whenever the risk parameters are triggered. For example, a risk manager can set up limits on the size of an order a trader can trade at once or in one day. Let's say that the risk manager limits the trader's maximum trade size per contract to 500. This means that if the trader submits an order for 501 or higher, the risk management system will automatically reject the order and alert the risk manager. These pretrade rules can be configured to meet specific needs for the firm and its risk tolerance.

Competition

The electronic trading model brought flexibility and speed to financial markets. Technology players allowed financial markets to adopt electronic markets with creative new applications at rapid speed. Competition flourished for every component of the trade cycle. As the floor-based exchanges faced tough competition from electronic exchanges, the struggle for survival became the top priority. Gone were the days when exchanges were mostly regional. Today exchanges are competing across asset classes around the world. Similarly, the trading community in the past relied on brokers for execution, clearing, and settlement of their trades. The physical boundaries and manual trading limited the number of products a trader could trade. Market information was opaque, and the majority of trading was conducted over the phone. Things are very different today. Exchanges are competing with each other. There is a growing amount of product innovation. Trading screens with access to global markets have allowed firms, such as hedge funds, pension funds, day traders, and large proprietary traders, to trade more markets and more volume.

As the adoption of electronic trading increased, the number of players offering electronic trading components and tools for the financial community increased tremendously. Numerous independent software vendors (ISVs) emerged to provide services such as trading screens, market data, news feeds, risk management tools, and analytical tools. Software firms have become a major player in the financial markets. They grew their business by providing technology for exchanges and trading tools for the financial community. Financial markets today have numerous choices in every component of the trade cycle to build a low-cost, fast, reliable trading infrastructure.

Direct Market Access (DMA)

In the floor-trading days, direct access to the markets was limited to the privileged few who owned or leased exchange memberships to trade on the floor. The rest of the financial market users relied on middlemen—brokers—to trade. These middlemen were the "gateway" connecting the exchanges to the financial customers. They provided information, such as the bids and offers for products, submitted the buy and sell orders to the exchanges on behalf of their clients, provided market-related information, and often served as advisors to help clients make decisions to buy or sell a product. The market data available through these brokers was generally limited and certainly delayed. Clients relied mostly on the relationship with the broker to get a good deal on their trades. The users outside the floor were essentially missing the pulse of the market.

Electronic trading brought a level playing field for all users in the marketplace. As the exchanges moved toward electronic trading, connectivity to exchanges was accomplished through their APIs. These APIs allowed users to receive market information and send their orders to the exchange. They served as a gateway to the virtual trading floor. For the first time, access to exchanges was not limited to the privileged few on the trading floor. An open API allowed third-party vendors and trading firms to connect directly to the exchange. Users were no longer dependent on their brokers to provide them with trading information. In the new world of electronic trading, one did not need to have a membership to gain access to the pulse of the marketplace. For the first time traders could directly access the exchanges they wanted to trade without brokers as their middlemen.

It is always good to have the upper hand in negotiations. In electronic trading, direct market access (DMA) has given the upper hand to trading firms. Buy-side firms that generally relied on brokers for their trade execution can now directly connect to the exchanges. As we discussed in the previous chapter, the exchange API introduced DMA, which gives firms the flexibility to pick their trading infrastructure instead of relying solely on their brokers. DMA allows firms to reduce their trading costs and provides better control over their trades and the speed with which they can trade. More importantly, it allows trading firms to take control of their execution flow.

DMA takes the modular exchange model to the next level. Trading firms today have many more choices for exchange connectivity. Trading firms can choose the connectivity options based on cost and trading features. They can customize their trading infrastructure by picking the best option available to suit their trading style. They can build connectivity on their own. They can use one of the ISVs to provide them with exchange connectivity. They can lease the technology from brokers. All three options are widely used by trading firms today. For example, a trading firm can use an ISV for both trading screens and connectivity. Firms such as GL Trade, Trading Technologies, Pats Systems, Portware, and Lava Trading all offer trading services and exchange connectivity for trading firms. These software companies compete with each other based on trading applications and services. GL Trade, for example, offers its customers connectivity to over 150 exchanges worldwide.[29] The exchange connectivity and the innovative features offered by these software companies allow trading firms, large and small, to focus on trading and let the ISVs maintain the technical infrastructure.

Using DMA through ISVs, trading firms can also maintain their anonymity. They can use customized tools to build trading strategies to suit their trading style. They no longer have to depend on their brokers for execution. To keep trading firms as their clients, brokers in the last decade have spent significant amounts of time and money to build their technical infrastructure and electronic exchange connectivity. To compete, a number of brokers have acquired ISVs that already had the technical infrastructure for exchange connectivity. For example, Bank of America, Bank of New York, and Citigroup bought Direct Access Trading, Sonic Trading Management, and Lava Trading, respectively.[30] Other banks, such as Barclays, chose to build their own technology. Large banks acquired ISVs to instantly capture ISVs clients. Through acquisitions they could now have the buy-side firms as their clients and continue to offer DMA for the exchanges. Buy-side firms can maintain control over their execution flow. Sell-side firms can no longer rely on revenue from execution flow alone. They must offer new services and trading features to gain clients' execution business.

Shifting the Balance of Power

In the past, trading firms generally relied on a single broker for their execution needs. As proven by DMA, the exchange API allowed the financial community to connect to exchanges directly without going through middlemen. It brought flexibility and innovation to the electronic trading model and has changed the landscape of financial markets. ISVs took the opportunity to build single screens

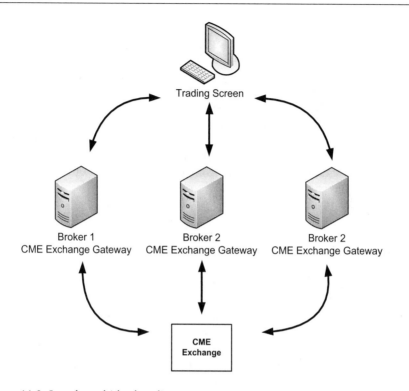

Figure 11.2 Sample multi-broker diagram.

connecting to multiple exchanges. As electronic trading grew, trading firms began using electronic platforms through ISVs; however, brokers rushed to acquire these ISVs to capture the execution business, and the trading firms once again were limited to using closed platforms offered by brokers. The remaining ISVs fighting to gain market share developed the multi-broker platform. Buy-side firms can now set up their trading infrastructures to allow them to access the same market through multiple brokers. The ability to pick their broker(s) has allowed these firms to take control of their order flow. The multi-broker platform has changed the relationship between brokers and trading firms. A broker-agnostic platform shifted power back to the trading firms.

Brokers are not entirely out of the picture in the world of execution. As the big players in the markets, they have the capital to build infrastructure to connect to multiple markets around the globe. With DMA, trading firms can now execute their business through different brokers, yet still maintain control of their order execution. A single trading screen can access exchanges through multiple brokers.

Figure 11.2 shows a sample multi-broker setup. As shown, through the multi-broker setup the trader can access the CME exchange through the different brokers. The front-end screen displays the market information through each of the brokers. Front-end screens are designed to recognize the connection from each broker so that when the trader submits the order for CME, the order is routed to CME based on the broker picked by the trader at the time of order submission. The multi-broker model provides traders with access to pick brokers for order routing based on the fees or trading features offered. Brokers today must compete with each other to capture the execution business by providing added services that attract trading firms. They must provide services that are unique and that enable traders to trade faster and better. Brokers have spent significant amounts of time and money to build services such as automated trading, smart order routing, new order types, alerts for market events, and the flexibility of reaching multiple exchanges. For trading firms the choices today are endless.

Automated Trading: Replacing Humans

The electronic trading model dramatically changed the landscape of trading. The migration from floor to electronic trading caused the disappearance of many jobs unique to floor-trading. Computers replaced or eliminated jobs such as runners, clerks, and manual order matching. Traders today use computers instead of "trade cards" to submit their trades. Throughout financial markets, technology now plays a vital role in keeping markets running. Traders today face tough competition. They have access to markets around the globe and a much larger selection of products than they ever had on the floor.

Traders today can trade more products across more asset classes around the globe through a single screen. To succeed in electronic trading, traders have to be fast and creative. Traders increasingly rely on technology and innovative tools offered by new players. These tools help them move beyond simple market and limit orders. They help them analyze market events and historical trends to make better trading decisions. In recent years, traders have relied on technology to actually trade for them. The use of computers as trading tools has moved from simple point-and-click to automated program trading.

Black boxes are another phenomenon of electronic trading that has further transformed financial markets. Black boxes are automated trading tools programmed to submit trades to exchange(s). Financial market users have increased the use of computers for trading. As the product choices and exchange access increased competition, trading manually became more difficult. It would be difficult for humans to watch hundreds of products around the globe. Computers, on the other hand, make it look easy. To watch additional markets, all one needs is a bigger machine. However, these black boxes will not necessarily lead to the total extinction of human traders.

Computers are good at following orders, but these orders must still be given by traders. Computers provide the trading data, but it is still the trader's responsibility to analyze the data and determine the right strategies to follow.

These automated trading tools allow traders to focus their attention on analyzing and developing these new strategies, reducing the time wasted manually submitting these orders.

Every ISV and broker today spends significant amounts of time and money building these automated trading applications. Brokers and ISVs in recent years have focused on developing algorithmic engines to attract execution business. These automated trading tools are a crucial part of decision making for trading firms when picking their electronic trading platforms. Brokers and ISVs develop these automated tools to provide the flexibility and creativity needed in the world of electronic trading.

Abundant Choices of Order Types

In floor-trading, traders were limited to just a few order types such as market, limit, stop, stop limit, and a few other simple orders. The world of electronic trading is no longer limited to a world of just a few simple order types. Instead, there are countless order types that traders use. Order types are constructed to time the market, to hide the order size, and to execute orders at a better average price. Simple order types such as limit or stop orders are still used by traders, but the list of sophisticated orders has grown significantly in recent years. Software vendors and sell-side firms have designed new innovative order types to gain traders' business.

In the world of electronic trading, where screens are becoming a commodity and exchange connectivity is becoming easier to acquire, trading firms are looking for an edge. Sophisticated order types with names such as Trailing Stop, OCO, Sniper, Iceberg, and Growlers are created by software vendors and sell-side firms to provide traders with an edge. Table 11.4 provides a brief overview of the types of orders that are available to trading firms today. For example, traders interested in preserving the anonymity of their orders are more likely to use order types such as Iceberg or Growlers, whereas a trading firm that is trying to improve the prices of its orders is more likely to use Limit or Pegged-to-Midpoint.

The variety of order types allows traders to submit multiple orders for various products. It also allows them to better control the price and order size while maintaining anonymity in the marketplace. ISVs such as Portware, Flex-Trade, and Strategy Runner, as well as sell-side firms, have constructed creative order types to support new trading strategies and styles used by traders. Trading firms have many choices available in both order types and vendors that can implement them.

New Trading Styles

The single-screen access provided traders a much broader view of the markets. Through one screen they can view market information on multiple exchanges

Table 11.4 Order Types to Achieve Trading Objectives

Objective	Sample Order Types and Algorithms[31,32]
Limit risk	Bracket, Market-to-Limit, Market-with Protection, Stop, Stop Limit, Trailing Stop, Trailing Stop Limit, OCO
Speed of execution	At Auction, Discretionary, Market, Market-if-Touched, Market-on-Close, Market-on-Open, Midpoint Match, Pegged-to-Market, Pegged-to-stock, Relative/Pegged-to-Primary, Sweep-to-Fill
Price improvement	Auction, Block, Box-Top, Limit, Limit-on-Close, Limit-on-Open, Limit-if-Touched, Pegged-to-Midpoint
Privacy	Arrival Price, Balance Impact and Risk, Hidden, Iceberg/Reserve, Minimize Impact, Percent of/Growler, Scale, Guaranteed VWAP, Best Efforts VWAP
Time to market	All-or-None, Fill-or-Kill, GAT (Good after date/time), GTD (Good till Date/Time), GTC (Good till canceled), Immediate-or-Cancel
Advanced trading	Basket, Conditional, OCA, Spreads, Volatility

as well other market fundamentals. A trader on the floor could probably trade three or four products[33] at once because the trading process was entirely manual. Traders had to be in a pit for that particular product. It would be difficult for a single trader to go from pit to pit to trade in different products; it would be unmanageable for traders to keep up with the market activity on more products and trade effectively. As we have seen, in electronic trading product information is available on trading screens. An average trader today has three or more computer screens blasting market information for hundreds of products. It is now realistic for one trader to monitor and trade 20 to 30 products at a time.

Access to products across exchanges, automated trading tools, and new creative order types have allowed traders to create new trading strategies. In equities markets, for example, firms such as Lava Trading and Portware allow traders to use basket trading. Basket trading allows traders to construct a portfolio of multiple stocks that can be traded as one stock. Traders select a set of stocks based on a particular industry, investment style, or market capitalization. They define the number of shares for each stock that they want to purchase and the prices for each of these stocks they want to pay. Trader can create these baskets and let the system trade all the stocks within the basket automatically based on the predefined rules.

Similarly, options markets benefited from the growing innovation in electronic trading. Options markets have seen tremendous growth in their short history. With fully electronic markets, such as ISE and BOX, electronic options execution has grown significantly. Today over 70% of options are executed off the floor. Options trading has always been known for its complex strategies. Words such as *strangles, straddles*, and *butterflies* are common vocabulary in the world of options trading. Although options traders used these strategies on the floor, the number of strategies used by traders was limited. Firms such as RTS, Brass MicroHedge,[34] and Actant specializing in options trading have brought a new level of sophistication to an already complex trading environment. These new players built tools that today allow traders to create countless numbers of strategies. These vendors provide a portfolio of over 30 to 40 trading strategies already constructed. Traders can simply select the strategy, define the number of contracts they want to purchase, and submit them to the exchange. The system automatically submits the strategy if it is natively supported by the exchange or the put and call orders to synthetically implement the strategy.[35]

Finally, the futures world is no different. The exchanges once known for trading pigs, cattle, corn, and other physical commodities have transformed themselves to become a crucial part of the global financial markets. The migration of futures exchanges toward electronic trading significantly increased the number of users. Today, growing numbers of traders from other asset classes have entered the world of futures trading. The front-end trading systems, such as Trading Technologies, Ecco Trade, and Pats, were specialized for futures trading. Trading Technologies, for example, focused on exchange connectivity to futures exchanges around the world. Its initial focus was on the "big four": CME, CBOT, Eurex, and LIFFE. These firms provided innovative tools to allow futures traders to analyze products across exchanges. Firms such as TT and Ecco brought automation to strategies such as spread trading. TT screens, for example, allowed traders to create intramarket and intermarket spreads and have the system automatically trade spreads. For proprietary trading firms, spread trading became one of the most common techniques used to hedge risk, especially in derivatives markets. Spread trading allows traders to reduce their risk by trading long and short contracts. A common strategy used by traders in derivatives markets got a facelift in the world of electronic trading. The intramarket spread trade is constructed with contracts combining two or more products on the same exchange, whereas intermarket spread trades are constructed with contracts combining two or more products on different exchanges. Traders using front-end systems could now construct spreads on any product available to them on the screen. The trading applications allowed them to synthetically create spread strategies. This means that a trader can construct a spread between two products by defining parameters on the trading screen. The trading application then automatically submits each leg of the contract individually to the exchange. These trading applications allow traders to use automated trading tools to create multilegged spreads on futures products.

Smart Order Routing

Electronic trading is all about flexibility. As we discussed, the exchanges today offer DMA access. Exchanges have been competing with each other to capture market share by listing new products and cross-listing products. Over the last decade, many exchanges have cross-listed products to expand market share. EurexUS entered the U.S. market by listing Treasuries, a flagship product on CBOT. ICE listed crude oil contracts, a popular product on NYMEX. LIFFE listed sugar contracts to compete against the NYBOT. These cross-listings have also brought fragmentation in the liquidity of these products. The cross-listing product may not always succeed, but during the competition, there is the issue of which liquidity pool an order should be directed to. To ensure that traders continue to receive the best price in the midst of competition and fragmentation, software vendors and sell-side firms offer specialized services to gain client business. TT Navigator, for example, was built when EurexUS launched U.S. Treasuries to compete with the CBOT. TT Navigator offered traders smart order routing to ensure that traders get the best execution for the same product listed in multiple markets.

Smart order routing allows traders to make intelligent decisions to route their orders to markets that have the best prices or to a broker that offers the lowest execution cost. Smart order routing has been a growing phenomenon in the financial markets. Smart order routers provide a consolidated view of the markets and allow traders to execute orders through a single screen across exchanges and brokers. Smart order routers serve as the bridge that consolidates and distributes data between exchanges. Traders can use the smart order routers with their multibroker platform to pick brokers and to route their orders based on a number of factors, such as speed, execution cost, and exchange availability.

Conclusion

Electronic trading allows more traders to get more data on more products in more markets. A click of the mouse from anywhere in the world can instantly send a variety of exotic order types to multiple brokers and exchanges around the world. Risk managers and regulators can monitor the flow of market information and orders in real time for violations or undue risk taking. The constant pressure of competition forces prices down and inspires improvements in every component of the trade cycle, from automated trading applications to matching engines to clearing services. Every aspect of the century-old floor-trading model has been transformed, unrecognizable even to those who have spent a lifetime in the business. The loud and chaotic fraternity of floor traders has been replaced by the cold efficiency of computers humming softly in a data center.

Endnotes

1. Finneran, John, "Technology Takes over NYSE," July 31, 2006, www.fool.com/investing/high-growth/2006/07/31/technology-takes-over-the-nyse.aspx.
2. AEMS is a joint venture between Euronext and French integration company Atos Origin.
3. Finneran, John, "Technology Takes over NYSE," July 31, 2006, www.fool.com/investing/high-growth/2006/07/31/technology-takes-over-the-nyse.aspx.
4. As of August 22, 2008, NYMEX is part of CME Group.
5. "History of CME Globex," www.cme.com/trading/get/abt/welcome/history.html.
6. "History of CME Globex," www.cme.com/trading/get/abt/welcome/history.html.
7. "Reuters and Forex to Launch the Global FX Marketplace," 4 May 2006, www.finextra.com/fullstory.asp?id=15267.
8. CME had currency futures. By offering currency products available on Reuters, it provided new trading opportunities for the trading community.
9. Salcedo, Yesenia, "Can You Handle It." Futures, May 2004, http://findarticles.com/p/articles/mi_qa5282/is_/ai_n24278530.
10. We will discuss the technology issues exchanges face in the next chapter.
11. CME essentially added separate hardware to run the Globex system for CBOT. So there is one set of hardware processing CME trading and another set of hardware for CBOT.
12. FIX is the standard protocol. FAST optimizes FIX to handle market data more efficiently.
13. CME already has pretty large bandwidth requirements. It requires its active traders to install a T3 line to connect to the exchange. Adding additional CBOT products and message traffic would have significantly increased the bandwidth requirements without FAST.
14. Salcedo, Yesenia, "Can You Handle It?" Futures, May 2004, http://findarticles.com/p/articles/mi_qa5282/is_/ai_n24278530.
15. www.futuresindustry.org/fi-magazine-home.asp?a=1171#volumetables.
16. Leising, Matthew. "NYMEX Spent up to $20 Mln on London Trading Floor," www.bauer.uh.edu/spirrong/ATT00359.txt (March 8, 2006d).
17. "Surge in Volume," FIA article.
18. NYSE acquired its electronic trading platform when it purchased ARCA and expanded its market share as well as electronic trading infrastructure through its recent merger with Euronext.
19. Nasdaq has been an electronic marketplace for quite some time but has grown significantly in recent years. Its latest merger was with the OMX Group, the Nordic exchange conglomerate.
20. "U.S. Equity Options Volume to Double by 2010-Study," http://uk.reuters.com/article/marketsNewsUS/idUKN212562012008022 (Feb. 21, 2008).
21. "U.S. Equity Options—Exchange Update," www.futuresindustry.org/fi-magazine-home.asp?a=1077.
22. "Surge in Volume," FIA article.
23. We will discuss product growth and innovation in the new product innovation chapter of this book.
24. E-mini S&P 500 is 1/5th the size of CME's S&P 500 futures contract. It closely tracks the price movement of the S&P 500 Index. "CME Expands Quarterly Month Listings of Equity Index Futures Products," www.cme.com/trading/prd/equity/emini-sp500.html (June 24, 2007).
25. Markets in Financial Instrument Directive (MiFID) is the set of new regulatory mandates implemented by the European Union and designed to foster competition and protect consumers.
26. http://www.mifidirective.com/
27. Innovators in Automatic trading, www.rolfeandnolan.com.
28. Alternative Investment Management–Technology Outsourcing, www.aim-to.com.
29. "Trading on Emerging and Frontier Markets.," www.gltrade.com.

30. Safarik Dan. "Direct Market Access—The Next Frontier," www.wallstreetandtech.com/advancedtrading/showArticle.jhtml?articleID=60404150 (Feb. 28, 2005).
31. "Order Types and Algos," Interactive Brokers, www.interactivebrokers.com/en/p.php?f=orderTypes&ib_entity=llc.
32. "Futures Algorithms Directory," Advanced Trading, http://advancedtrading.thewallstreetwiki.com/directories/directory-futures-algorithms.php.
33. In futures markets, a trader generally traded a single product and often a single month of that product.
34. Subsidiary of Sungard.
35. Not all strategies are natively recognized by the exchange. For example, an exchange may not support a more exotic options strategy.

12 Electronic Exchanges and Trading: Challenges

Executive Summary

As with any innovations, challenges are introduced or exacerbated by electronic exchanges. Greater speed and globalization mean that there is less room for error and problems can instantly spread around the world. For all its advantages, technology is still rather fragile and unreliable. People are still prone to error and bursts of panic. The result can be greater volatility and, sometimes, ad hoc resolutions to glitches in the electronic infrastructure.

Change is never without challenges. The transformation of financial markets has had its share of bumps and hurdles. An emotional attachment to floor-trading has been difficult for the exchanges and the financial community to overcome. The move to electronic trading meant that it was losing a way of trading that has defined global financial markets for over a century. In addition, there have been challenges such as losing some of the jobs that were unique to financial markets and learning to adapt to new technologies to make a living in the new trading world. There have also been challenges unique to the world of technology that would never have occurred in the floor-trading model. Exchanges continue to upgrade their systems to keep up with growing volumes. Exchanges new to electronic trading continue to struggle with the speed and reliability of their electronic infrastructure.

The exchanges have dealt with numerous technology hurdles as they migrated from the floor-trading model to the electronic trading model. The ease of listing products has allowed exchanges to compete with each other for liquidity. Multiple listings of the same products on different exchanges have raised concerns of fragmentation. The transparency and speed of electronic trading have brought new levels of volatility in the marketplace. New trading styles have brought new challenges, some of which have been large enough to bring trading to a standstill or to jeopardize the survival of a firm. As the dependence on technology increases, the markets will continue to face these challenges.

Although the electronic trading model prevailed, the new world is far from perfect. The financial markets have weathered some major issues throughout the transformation phase. The exchanges have faced severe technology failures, bringing down the entire exchange for hours at a time. As the financial community transitions toward electronic trading, it has made some costly errors that have impacted entire trading firms and, at times, the wider trading community. There have been some memorable glitches by both exchanges and trading firms. Some of these have been isolated to just a few players; others have brought down an entire exchange. And in a market that has fought change for so long, any mistake, big or small, is put under the microscope. Any slip gives the skeptics new ammunition to challenge the electronic trading model and its viability. Markets today are far more competitive, and in this competitive world one cannot afford to make mistakes. As the financial community continues to transform its business model to adopt electronic trading, it will continue to face new issues. The exchanges will need to continue to enhance their technology to meet the challenges of growing volumes and increasing market share. The financial community will need to adapt to the new risks it faces in the world of electronic trading.

Dependency on Each Other

The world of electronic trading brought the speed, reliability, efficiency, and growth to financial market that would have been unimaginable in floor-trading. The new model, as we have seen, is far more complex and interdependent than its predecessor. Modular exchanges made it easy for the exchanges and the trading community to pick and choose components for the trading infrastructure offered by software application providers and other exchanges. The exchanges and trading community rely on technology providers for connectivity to the financial markets. Trading firms rely on vendors and brokers for their electronic platforms. Brokers rely on vendors to provide exchange connectivity. The exchanges, trading firms, vendors, and brokers all rely on telecommunications players such as MCI and AT&T, which provide the telecommunications infrastructure between these industry players. All these participants rely on disaster recovery and hosting solutions providers such as Equinox and BT Radianz. The financial markets are truly interconnected. The shared dependencies have brought many advantages for financial market players, such as cost savings, messaging standardization, and trading speed, to name just a few. This dependency has also introduced new challenges. Technology glitches at these external vendors can potentially have widespread impact on the overall financial markets. Outages at a single firm, technology provider, or exchange can bring down numerous other players.

Technology Glitches

As we have seen, technology is now an integral part of financial markets. Today every step of the trade cycle passes through computers and networks. All technology can fail. Computers and networks are hardware devices that do not have infinite lifespans. They will fail at any time without notice. The electronic trading architecture is built on software programs that communicate with each other. These software programs will have bugs that cause applications to behave abnormally or to fail. The network connections between computers and companies can be overloaded with message traffic. Whether it is a machine failure, a bug in a software application, or a capacity issue in the system, these glitches can have a significant impact on the financial markets. In its short history, electronic trading has seen systems fail, bringing down exchanges for anywhere from a few minutes to several hours and exasperating traders around the world. Exchanges with systems unable to cope with growing volume can add significant latency to order execution and market updates. As we will see, the financial markets have seen the widespread impact that a glitch in one single application can cause. Technology glitches in software applications have caused significant swings in the markets. Software bugs have caused erroneous trade execution and incorrect market updates, bringing a new era of out-trades. Over the last few years we have seen technology issues that have virtually disconnected individual trading firms from the trading world. These failures have caused both financial and reputational harm to the individual players suffering from these technology glitches.

Exchanges today spend significant amounts of time and money to build a robust trading infrastructure that can support the growing volume and growing number of traders. The software players spend tremendous amounts in research and development to build innovative tools and to provide robust and reliable applications to their customers. The trading community today measures exchanges not only by the product suite offered but also by the stability of its systems.

Exchange Outages

Since the exchanges began their journey of transformation, they have faced many challenges in building a reliable infrastructure. For exchanges today, their technology has to work seamlessly. Any outage has a direct impact on the trading volume on the exchanges. An unreliable exchange could literally lose liquidity and significant market share. In addition, due to the modular exchange model and interdependence between vendors, a failure on one exchange could have an impact on other exchanges halfway around the world. Over the last two decades, a number of exchanges have faced outages lasting from a few minutes to a full day. For example, Euronext's Paris-based exchange suffered over 10 trading suspensions in 2002 alone. By comparison, DTB suffered only one outage on April 16, 2002.[1] And in today's competitive world, these outages can be dreadful.

Some Major Exchange Outages Around the World[2]

Nasdaq, December 9, 1987

Nasdaq's systems in its data center in Connecticut were brought down when a squirrel climbed into the main electrical power line with a piece of aluminum foil. It was not a happy end for either the exchange or the squirrel. The exchange was down for almost the entire day and the squirrel was electrocuted.

Nasdaq, Summer of 1994

Nasdaq suffered several problems with its trading system in the summer of 1994. The system was down once again when a different squirrel chewed through the power line in Nasdaq's data center in Connecticut.

LSE, April 5, 2000

A severe computer malfunction brought the entire exchange to a halt. The exchange remained closed for approximately eight hours, preventing traders from bailing out of one of the busiest trading days. It was the end of the financial year, when many traders adjust their trades for year-end profits and losses.

NYSE, June 1, 2005

The NYSE shut down its trading operations at 3:56 p.m., four minutes prior to the scheduled closing time, due to a communication problem. Trading did not resume for the rest of the evening, and all crossing sessions[3] were canceled.[4]

TSE, January 18, 2006

The exchange suffered its first closure in its 57-year history. Although it had suffered technical issues since going electronic, this was the first time the entire exchange was shut down. The Tokyo Stock Exchange was closed during the peak afternoon trading session. But this was certainly not the last time. The most recent closure was in July 2008, when a software bug caused the exchange to suspend trading between 9:21 and 11:00 in the morning session and 12:30 to 1:45 in the afternoon.[5]

LIFFE and Its System Issues

As one of the early entrants in electronic trading, LIFFE has had time to improve its electronic trading infrastructure. With any new launch, people expect problems to occur. Therefore, the technical issues in the early stages were easier to tolerate. There were few competitors and even fewer people in electronic trading. However, even in those early days, any outages were noticed since traders made their living trading these markets. And traders are not very patient people. So an outage of even a few minutes is bound to create many unhappy traders. In 2001 alone, LIFFE suffered more than six different outages that brought its entire trading system to a screeching halt. For example, the system was down due to technical issues on August 23, and the exchange was forced to halt trading in Gilt futures, sterling interest rate futures, Euro interest rate futures, swap futures, and U.S. stock index futures.[6] In December 2006 it suffered an hour-long outage that once again brought down its trading system.

In June 2007, LIFFE suffered one of its biggest outages since 1997, the year when it launched LIFFE Connect and completed its transition to electronic trading.[7] The exchange was forced to shut down its operations from 7:00 a.m. to 11:00 a.m. when the exchange monitoring systems broke down. The exchange officials noticed an issue with the Connect tools that it used to monitor and control the markets. The markets are automatically opened at 7:00 a.m. When the issue was identified, the exchange moved to delay the opening of the exchange; however, by the time the system halt was implemented, some trading had already occurred for some of its big products, such as Euribor,[8] UK Gilt, and CAC 40 Index. Trading in Euribor and UK Gilt[9] was open for 21 seconds and almost 20 minutes for CAC 40 Index.[10] All the orders submitted for these products were canceled by the exchange. The exchange system was fully operational at 11:30 a.m. (London Time), almost four and a half hours later than its usual opening hour.

LIFFE has had a history of outages and system failures. Although the exchange issued an apology and moved to reassure its customers that the issue was identified and resolved, the exchange's reputation for system stability and reliability suffered significantly compared to LSE, which had not suffered a single outage in its seven-year-old technology, SETS. Of course, as we will now discuss, with its move to a new-generation technology platform, LSE suffered one of the worst outages in the financial markets as well.

Seven-Hour Outage at LSE

On September 8, 2008, London traders were bracing for one of the biggest rallies in a market that had been in a downward spiral for quite some time due to the mortgage crisis, which had almost brought the global financial system to its knees. The U.S. government had stepped in to rescue Freddie

Mac and Fannie Mae to help ease the tension in the financial markets. London traders were ready for a busy day. They got a glimpse of the busy trading when over 270 million shares exchanged hands in only the first hour of trading, compared to 617 million traded in the previous day.[11] At approximately 9:00 a.m., LSE announced it was shutting down its trading system when it noticed connectivity failure between the exchange and several brokers. The traders were unable to connect to LSE's 15-month-old trading system, TradeElect, a proprietary trading system that promised to provide faster round-trip order execution and expanded capacity to handle the growing volume. Trading was not resumed until 4:00 p.m., 30 minutes before the official close. It left hundreds of traders on LSE out of the trading activity for almost the entire day.

On a day that would have seen some significant trading, the LSE system came to a complete standstill. For the next seven hours the traders could not trade a single product on LSE, and the exchange volume took quite a hit. Shares of bank stocks such as Barclay, HBOS, and Lloyds TSB listed on the LSE traded 30%, 31%, and 21% less than their past three-month daily average. By comparison, bank stocks listed on other markets such as UBS AG and Deutsche Bank AG saw their volume double that day compared to their past daily average volumes. The LSE traded a total of $7.5 billion worth of shares, which was only about half of its usual volume.[12] The FTSE-100 was trading 200 points up an hour into trading when suddenly the traders could not route orders through the LSE trading platform. And for the next seven hours thousands of screens connected to the LSE trading platform were frozen with the FTSE 100 stuck at 5440.2, up 199.5.[13]

For the LSE this was only the second major incident since 2000 that kept traders out of the market for over eight hours. The occasional system glitches are expected and reluctantly tolerated by traders, but this recent outage could not have come at a worse time. The LSE had been fighting to remain independent while other exchanges were merging to increase their market share. And new alternative trading systems such as Chi-X and Turquoise were arriving. Only a year old, these two trading platforms offered high-speed trading platforms at low cost, something the trading community, which had been increasing its use of automated trading, gravitated toward. If these system reliability issues continued on the LSE, trading platforms such as Chi-X, which already claimed to have 13% of FTSE 100 volume,[14] would most certainly pose a more formidable competitor to the LSE. Although this particular outage did not provide a significant boost to the trading volume on these other two electronic trading platforms, it was primarily due to both systems being fairly new, and few trading firms had signed on to trade on these platforms. Outages such as these made the new electronic trading platforms a possible alternative for trading firms that were virtually idle for most of this trading day.

LSE Outage Impacting JSE

Exchanges today utilize each other's technology for various trade cycle components. Problems on one exchange can impact another exchange if they are sharing technology. And that's exactly what happened on September 8, 2008. The connectivity issues at the LSE, which brought the entire LSE trading system to a halt for most of the day, also shut down the JSE in Johannesburg, South Africa, for most of its trading day. The JSE uses the LSE electronic platform, TradeElect, for its trading activities. The platform is hosted in London at the LSE data center. So the computer glitch in the LSE impacted JSE. Traders on JSE were also left out of the busy trading day, since JSE depended on LSE's platform and infrastructure.

CBOE: Floor-Trading Continues Amid System Issues[15]

One of the leading U.S. options exchanges, the CBOE has been late to the electronic trading party. Just like NYSE, the CBOE took a cautious approach to electronic trading. It still maintains its floor operations for options trading; however, the majority of its trading now flows through its hybrid trading system, launched in 2003. As described in a previous chapter, this system allows CBOE customers to route trades through the CBOE's hybrid system, CBOE*direct*, or to continue to trade on the floor. The intention of the hybrid system is to provide an integrated market, which includes both the floor-trading quotes and electronic trading. Today over 92% of the CBOE's orders flow through the electronic system; however, 45% of the trading volume still occurs on the floor. Nevertheless, the impact on trading volume was certainly apparent on November 10, 2006, when the CBOE's electronic system suffered technical issues. The system was unavailable to the trading community from approximately 12:00 p.m. EST until the end of the trading day[16] on Friday. The CBOE Futures Exchange (CFE),[17] which is fully electronic, was also unavailable for the remainder of the day. Trading for the CBOE was only available on the floor, which remained open for the entire day. Although floor-trading was available, the CBOE volumes were lower than the previous day. Approximately 1.8 million options were traded, compared to 2.8 million on the previous day. The trading firms for the U.S. options markets have alternatives. The firms using electronic trading platforms can route orders to exchanges such as the ISE or Philadelphia Options Exchange. And the competitor exchanges saw an increase in their volumes as a result of the system outage at the CBOE. However, the trading firms had no alternatives for contracts such as S&P 500, which is exclusively listed on the CBOE. Trading of the S&P 500 was significantly lower than the daily average volume. On Friday, approximately 225,000 contracts exchanged hands compared to daily average volume of 430,000. The lighter volume is certainly an indication of the increasing reliance on electronic

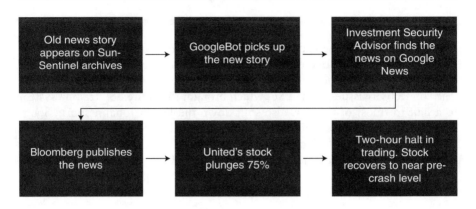

Figure 12.1 Events leading to United Airlines' stock price plunge and recovery.

trading by the financial community. So even though the floor was open for trading, the exchanges logged lower trading volume.

The Impact of Real-Time Data Availability

Data on trading activity, market events, and company news is available in real time to anyone with a computer and Internet connectivity. Firms such as Bloomberg and Reuters built their business by consolidating financial data across financial markets and providing it to traders in real time. Not only does Bloomberg, for example, provide traders with the prices and volumes of all trades for global exchanges, it also collects and displays economic news and company-specific news. Traders rely on this information to make their trading decisions. Technology has made it easier and faster for users to receive this information, helping them react to market events faster and adjust their strategy, thus minimizing potential trading losses.

As we saw earlier in this chapter, computers are not perfect, and failures in systems can have a significant impact on trading. Today trading firms rely on technology to get market data and other financial news throughout the trading day. Incorrect or missing information can be costly. The recent plunge in United Airlines' stock was a prime example of such a glitch.

On September 8, 2008, United Airlines' stock plummeted almost 75% in just a few minutes until trading was manually halted by the exchange. The series of events leading to this plunge was astonishing and shows how information flow can have dire impacts on trading (see Figure 12.1). It started when Google News[18] grabbed a story from the South Florida *Sun-Sentinel* about United Airlines' bankruptcy filings. The story grabbed by Google News was, unfortunately, an old link to a story on United's bankruptcy that was originally published in 2002. The article had no publication date, so Google News applied

United Airlines stock price move, 2008.

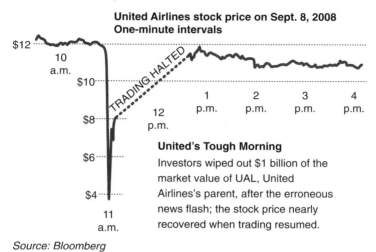

United Airlines stock price on Sept. 8, 2008
One-minute intervals

Source: Bloomberg

Figure 12.2 United Airlines stock price move, 2008.

the search date to the publication when it posted the story. This old link was picked up by the *Income Securities Advisor*, which scours the Web to find stories about distressed companies. The news story was then distributed to Bloomberg. The news instantly reached every computer that subscribed to the Bloomberg newsfeed.[19] All of a sudden an old bankruptcy story from 2002 emerged six years later as a breaking news story in 2008. When an 11:02 a.m. Bloomberg headline was posted: "UAL Corp., United Airlines, Files for Chapter 11 to Cut Costs," the airline's shares plunged from $12 to $3. A minute later, at 11:03 a.m., another update on Bloomberg: "Shares Fall Following Headline of Chapter 11."[20] Trading was halted by the exchange to investigate the sudden drop. Though the stock eventually recovered and closed that day at $10.92, it was not without significant losses for some traders and reputational harm for United Airlines and the numerous parties involved in this chain of events.

Although the stock recovered as fast as it fell (see Figure 12.2[21]), these glitches remind the trading community that the impact of such mishaps in electronic trading, where news travels fast and is accessible to the entire financial community, can be costly for company stock as well as the traders who reacted to the news event.

Market Volatility

Exchanges around the world are completing their migration toward electronic trading. The trading community is getting accustomed to the availability of real-time data and the trading applications used to route orders. So far we have seen technology glitches that cause system outages and halt trading on an exchange. And we have seen the impact incorrect data has in a real-time trading environment. One of the other major impacts of technology is the potential volatility in the market that can be caused by system latency and capacity issues. As we will see, these issues are not due to actual failures in the system or inaccurate information. Instead, it's a potential delay in data dissemination that can make the market appear to be far more volatile than it is. In the automated trading world, traders build algorithms and strategies specifically to react to large volatility swings in the markets. If the volatility in the markets is caused abruptly due to capacity issues, it can trigger unwanted orders that can be costly to the trading community.

Sell-Off due to System Issues

The Dow suffered significant losses on February 27, 2007. Market events, such as the uncertainty about the U.S. economy and declining global stock markets, caused traders to be on edge. The NYSE saw a significant increase in the total volume traded on the exchange. Their computer systems were unable to keep up with the increased volume. As trading increased throughout the day, the NYSE messaging system began slowing down. Trades began queuing in their computer system, which means that it was taking longer to post messages. In other words, the market data on the traders' computers screens was delayed without them realizing it.

When the exchange noticed the system performance issues, it switched to its backup system. Once online, the message traffic caught up and within a minute the Dow saw a plunge of 178, and over 240 in less than three minutes.[22] Traders panicked, which triggered a larger sell-off. Although the over-400-point decline was accurate, it actually occurred over the course of an hour, not in just three minutes, as reported when the systems caught up. A sudden market plunge is never good in a volatile market. A 178-point drop over the course of an hour is different than if it happened in a minute. The market has time to react and time to absorb the reasons for the drop. A sudden drop leads to rumor, panic, and fear. The trading decisions are usually very different for markets with a sudden drop versus a gradual drop.

The market volatility in the months of September and October 2008 is something most people in the financial market will not forget for quite some time. It had been a painful time that tested the patience of even the toughest traders. The mortgage crisis brought the U.S. economy almost to a standstill and required a massive bailout from the U.S. government. Plenty of records were broken. The U.S. equities markets saw one of the biggest point drops when the Dow dropped 777.68 on September 29, 2008, wiping out almost $1.5 trillion in market value. The following two days saw a 600-point reversal. These wild swings in the market caused by the large volume of trades tested the computer systems of the NYSE.

Short Selling[23]

Although no companies were spared in the tremendous sell-off in September 2008, the financial sector was the major victim. Almost every bank stock suffered significant declines. Financial stocks were in a downward spiral for a few weeks, and some thought the cause was short sellers. To prevent further declines in these stocks, regulators implemented a temporary ban on short selling on 799 financial companies,[24] which went in to effect on September 19, 2008.[25] The changes were implemented in the electronic systems and enabled the financial markets to comply with the new rules overnight. At the beginning of trading on Friday, the exchanges noticed trades executing at very odd prices. Some of the trades were executed at more than double their closing price; others were as low as a penny. Almost every electronic trading system saw orders executed at these odd prices, causing the exchanges to cancel thousands of orders and leaving some traders with unexplained losses.

The electronic exchange systems are set up to accept a wide range of bids and offers. These trades are executed when the bids and offers are matched. On the surface there doesn't seem to be an issue; however, the exchanges noticed the unusually wide range in bids and offers[26] that were being submitted by electronic trading systems. The exchanges blamed the issue on the initial confusion about the rules surrounding the ban as well as on high trading volumes. The exchanges moved to cancel all trades that traded 20% above or below Thursday's closing prices. Thousands of trades, a much larger number than usual, executed on the NYSE ARCA, Nasdaq, BATs Trading, and Direct-Edge were canceled. NYSE Arca alone canceled approximately 30,000 trades. As we will discuss later in the chapter, if the exchanges notice an incorrect or invalid trade, they can automatically cancel it. However, in this situation, not all trades were clear cut, and many trades were deemed valid by the exchanges and left traders with some significant losses.

Another Erroneous Trade, Another Volatile Trading Session

September 30, 2008, will be remembered by many traders who traded Google stock. A data glitch caused an erroneous trade from another exchange to flow into the Nasdaq trading system.[27] Shares of Google stock were trading in the range of $395–420 for most of the day until the close of the market, when suddenly the stock dropped almost 93% in the final minutes of trading. The stock price swung wildly, reaching prices as low as $25. The price bounced back quickly, but the price fluctuations continued. The stock traded in the range of $320–488 for the remaining five minutes until the closing bell. The exchange quickly announced that it was investigating the erroneous trade that caused the unexpected price drop. After a review, it was determined that an erroneous transaction was submitted and drove down the price, causing artificially low bid and offer prices. Nasdaq canceled all trades above $425.29 and below $400.52 that were executed between 3:57 and 4:04 p.m. EST. The exchange adjusted the closing price for Google shares to $400.52, updating the inaccurate original settlement price of $341.43.[28,29]

Inefficiency: Out-Trades in the Electronic Trading World

As we saw in our examples, errors in trading can be costly. The financial markets have worked hard to reduce these errors. In the floor-trading model, a majority of trade operations were conducted manually. The trades were recorded on paper or trade cards and manually entered by an army of clerks. Things are bound to get lost in translation, and they often were. Traders misspoke or misheard or miswrote information on the order or trading card. Clerks mistyped. Every morning traders would review the "out-trades," trades that could not be matched. Let's say that there were two traders who traded 500 lots of IBM. They recorded this information on a paper or trade card, which was then entered by a clerk for matching. There are a number of ways a matching error could occur. The two traders might not have recorded the information correctly. The clerk could enter incorrect trade information that did not match what the traders entered. These trades were reviewed by traders the next day, and disputes were usually settled among traders and their firms.

For example, the CME used to have over 25% of its trades recorded as out-trades. As the financial markets adopted technology, it began reducing its dependency on error-prone humans for most components of the trade cycle. So it would only be logical to think that the era of out-trades would be over in electronic trading, now that trading is conducted through computer screens and every trade is transmitted electronically. There are no manual entries and no middlemen. The trade information is always recorded properly, and there is an audit trail for every trade, as discussed in a previous chapter. And though it is true that electronic trading certainly helped to reduce out-trades caused by human errors, new issues such as technology glitches still cause trade execution that at times must be canceled by the exchanges. The world of electronic trading might have gotten rid of trade cards and the crowded floors, but it has not entirely eliminated trading errors. Trading still relies on humans. Whether it is a trader entering trades on a computer screen or creating rules for automated trading systems, humans are still the key element in the trade cycle, and thus the trading errors continue.

In the world of electronic trading, speed rules trading, so when errors occur they are significant and extremely costly for the financial markets. The past 20 years of electronic trading are filled with examples of trading errors that have jolted traders and the markets time and time again. To cope with these trading errors, exchanges around the world have policies to handle erroneous trades. Out-trades are replaced by terms such as *busted trades*, which are erroneous orders that are canceled by the exchange. The reasons for errors in electronic trading can be in two main areas: system glitches and "fat-finger mistakes." The system glitches can occur in any of the components in the trade cycle. Fat-finger mistakes are simple human errors that occur when a trader unintentionally enters the wrong trade information. In that sense, fat-finger errors are similar to the old out-trades from the floor-based systems.

In the floor-trading days, out-trades were generally handled and resolved by the brokers and trading firms. Any losses or adjustments were simply handled outside the exchanges. In electronic trading, things are different. Every trade is recorded as it occurs and can't simply be erased by the trading parties, thus requiring the exchange to determine when to bust a trade. Every erroneous trade is costly, but some costs are confined to a particular trading firm, whereas others can have widespread impact on the market.

"Fat Fingers": A $331 Million Mistake[30]

On December 13, 2005, a simple human error led to an instant $331 million loss for Mizuho Securities Company. A trader at Mizuho was preparing to sell one share of J-Com at a price of 610,000 yen. The actual order submitted was 610,000 shares of J-Com at 1 Yen! News of the bargain price traveled fast, and buyers quickly bought shares of J-Com. It was an early Christmas present for day traders, who were the most active buyers, but they were not alone. By the end of the trading day, Morgan Stanley, a large investment bank, owned 31.5% of J-Com. Although the trades were not busted, there was substantial criticism of the exchange for failing to stop the trade even after the trader realized his mistake and tried to cancel the trade. A simple human error led to frenzied trading on the Tokyo market, contributing to an almost 300-point drop on the Japanese index, the Nikkei 225, which closed down 2%.[31] In the end, six of the trading firms agreed to repay $141 million. Mizuho is expecting to recoup the remaining amount from the exchange due to the lack of controls on the exchange to stop erroneous trades.

Similarly, one of the traders at the former Lehman Brothers erased almost $50 billion (30 billion pounds) off the FTSE index in 2001 when he accidentally submitted £300 million for a trade instead of £3 million. The erroneous trade caused the FTSE 100 to drop almost 120 points. Another fat-finger mistake caused an almost 100-point drop in the Dow Jones Industrial Average when a trader at Bear Stearns entered a $4 billion sell order instead of $4 million.[32] These mistakes, although caused by a single firm, have widespread impact on the markets and require exchanges to deal with these trades and the potential losses and adjustments, which at times can take weeks.

The fat-finger mistakes are still likely to occur in the electronic trading world. The trading firms and exchanges continue to implement controls to catch orders that might be caused by a fat-finger mistake. For example, CME has price banding limitations, which restricts its trading platform from accepting orders outside a specified trading range for products. The front-end trading systems have a number of checks built in to control a potential incorrect order from flowing to the exchanges. These applications can set controls to limit the size and price of orders submitted by traders. For example, if a trader sets a limit for order size at 1000, an alert would pop up on his screen to confirm a trade larger than 1000. Although these controls are likely to reduce the number of fat-finger mistakes, they are still likely to occur.

Some of the Memorable Fat-Finger Mistakes Around the World[33]

UBS's £80 Order (January 1999)

A careless trader entered a sell order for 10 million shares on the Swiss exchange for a Swiss pharmaceutical company, Roche. The total number of shares issued for the company was 7 million shares. The order remained in the order book for over two minutes until the trader realized his mistake and entered a buy order to execute against his sell order.

Blame the Keyboard (October 1998)

A trader, leaning his elbow on his keyboard, triggered a 14,500 contract sell order for a 10-year French government bond on MATIF; 10,000 contracts were executed. The keyboard for electronic trading applications is designed with some "hotkeys" for fast execution. In this case, the F12 key was programmed for "instant sell," meaning that if a trader enters a quantity and presses F12, an instant market order is submitted to the exchange. The firm suffered several million dollars in losses.

LSE's Biggest Order (February 2001)

An erroneous order for a U.K. software company, Autonomy, was entered by a trading firm for £8.1 billion, over four times the total capital of the firm. The order was canceled almost immediately by the exchange when it noticed the anomaly.

Mixing the Order Size with Company Code (September 1997)

LSE received three orders within an hour for 989,529 shares of Zeneca. Each order, valued at £21 million, was three times the normal volume for that day. When the exchange called the firm to inquire about the order, the firm realized that the trader entered Zeneca's Sedol number, the code used by the exchange to identify the stock, as the order size. If the order had been executed, it would have cost the firm £60 million.

£300 Million Instead of £3 Million (May 2001)

A trader at Lehman Brothers caused a 120-point drop in the FTSE 100 and wiped out £30 billion of value from the index when he sold shares of BP and AstraZeneca. He keyed in £300 million instead of £3 million. The firm was fined £20,000.

2000 Instead of 2 Shares (January 2006)

A Citigroup trader intended to purchase two shares of Nippon Paper at ¥502,000. The trader accidentally entered a buy order of 2000 shares instead. Furthermore, the firm's compliance department approved the trade, thinking the shares were worth ¥500 instead of ¥502,000. The firm's CEO, Charles Prince, flew to Japan to apologize for the mistake.

$4 Billion vs. $4 Million (October 2002)

The Dow Jones Industrial Average fell 100 points when a trader at Bear Stearns entered a sell order for $4 billion instead of the intended $4 million. More than $600 million of the stock exchanged hands before the mistake was identified. The mistake was blamed for much of the 183-point drop in the market.

Rugby Executing $50 Million Trade (September 2006)

At Bank of America, a trader's keyboard was set up to execute trades by simply pressing the Enter key whenever the senior trader gave the go-ahead. The trader missed a rugby ball thrown his way, which landed on the keyboard and trigged a $50 million trade ahead of schedule. The ball thrower was reprimanded, but no additional actions were taken. As one of the traders put it lightly: "Rugby balls are a regular danger on any trading floor, so the victim trader ought to have hedged against this possibility."

Oh, the Zeros on the ¥ Again (December 2001)

A UBS trader intending to sell 16 shares of Dentsu at ¥600,000 instead sold 610,000 at ¥6. This was hours before UBS was getting ready to take Dentsu public in the year's biggest IPO. By the time the mistake was discovered, 64,915 shares, almost half of the 135,000 in the Tokyo listing, were already sold. Dentsu's bid was set at ¥600,000 for the open, but fell to ¥405,000. UBS lost over $100 million when it was forced to buy the shares it sold.

The electronic trading system is credited with bringing competition, faster order execution, transparency, and anonymity to the financial markets. The exchanges as well as the financial community have reaped the rewards of the new model. Though electronic trading is transforming the financial industry, there still remain some challenges that must be recognized and, hopefully, overcome. The most significant issue is the inevitable unreliability of computer technology. Both the hardware and software are prone to failure. In particular, the software is terribly complicated and difficult to verify as correct. As the financial community gains more experience with electronic trading systems, it will learn to build more reliable systems that can mask and work around these failures. Since exchanges are using the modular exchange model, every component by every vendor must be built with the same devotion to quality for the entire system to remain bug free. The exchange is only as good as the weakest component in the trade cycle.

As long as humans are involved in any process, there will be human error. These errors can range from simple mistakes to rogue trading—activity by a trader who gets around limitations to put a firm at grave risk. Again, these mistakes can be mitigated by having better error detection on anything that requires manual interaction. It could be as simple as raising a warning whenever a trader inputs a trade beyond some value or banning flying objects in a trading room. When mistakes are made, exchanges will need to develop better resolution procedures than ad hoc decisions to cancel trades. A more difficult issue is dealing with panic. Electronic trading brings markets closer to the economic ideal of "perfect information," but when the information is imperfect, traders panic and markets swing wildly. In a fast-moving market, it will be near impossible to tame fear and greed. Despite these issues, electronic trading solves far more problems than it creates.

Endnotes

1. Moore, James, "Euronext Hit by System Faults," www.telegraph.co.uk/finance/2852140/Euronext-hit-by-system-faults.html (May 17, 2003).
2. "London Exchange Paralyzed by Glitch Blow to a Market Facing New Rivals; Huge Trading Day," http://online.wsj.com/article/SB122088611707510173.html?mod=hpp_us_pageone (Sept. 9, 2008).
3. Sessions after regular closing hours where trading can occur.
4. "History of New York Stock Exchange Holidays," www.nyse.com/pdfs/closings.pdf (Nov. 2008).
5. "Software Bug Caused Tuesday's TSE Outage," www.thetradenews.com/trading/exchange-traded-derivatives/2136 (July 23, 2008).
6. "LIFFE Suffers Sixth Connect System Outage This Year," http://64.233.169.132/search?q=cache:SxcjWqKJfhEJ:findarticles.com/p/articles/mi_hb5555/is_/ai_n21937801+liffe+system+outage&hl=en&ct=clnk&cd=1&gl=us (Sept. 2001).
7. Moore, James, "System Fault Forces LIFFE to Shut Down," http://findarticles.com/p/articles/mi_qn4158/is_/ai_n19199066 (July 5, 2007).
8. Euro Interbank Offered Rate (Euribor) are interest rate contracts.

9. U.K. government bonds.

10. Moore, James, "System Fault Forces Liffe to Shut Down," www.independent.co.uk/news/ business/news/system-fault-forces-liffe-to-shut-down-451780.html (June 5, 2007).

11. Waller, Martin, "London Stock Exchange Glitch Costs millions," http://business.timesonline. co.uk/tol/business/markets/article4710793.ece (Sept. 9, 2008).

12. Shah, Neil, "London Exchange Paralyzed by Glitch Blow to a Market Facing New Rivals; Huge Trading Day," http://online.wsj.com/article/SB122088611707510173.html?mod=hpp_ us_pageone (Sept. 9, 2008).

13. Wearden, Graeme, and Tryhorn, Chris. "Seven-Hour Outage Creates City Chaos," www. guardian.co.uk/business/2008/sep/08/freddiemacandfanniemae.creditcrunch (Sept. 8, 2008).

14. Sakoui, Anousha, "Trading Halted on London Stock Exchange," http://us.ft.com/ftgateway/ superpage.ft?news_id=fto090820080742439122&page=2 (Sept. 8, 2008).

15. "Electronic Trading at CBOE Interrupted," http://money.cnn.com/news/newsfeeds/articles/ newstex/AFX-0013-11945248.htm (Nov. 10, 2006).

16. The cause of the system issues was not provided by the exchange. However, the issues were resolved, and the electronic trading system was available on Monday.

17. CBOE Futures Exchange lists some of the proprietary index, including the CBOE Volatility Index.

18. Automated news grabber that scours the Internet to grab news article and displays them when a user searches on a Google search engine.

19. Baer, Justin, "United shares plunge on old news story," www.ft.com/cms/s/0/b843a240-7ddd-11dd-bdbd-000077b07658.html?nclick_check=1 (Sept. 8, 2008).

20. Brown, Jeffery, "United Airlines Tallies Damage from False Stock Report," www.pbs.org/ newshour/bb/media/july-dec08/unitedstock_09-09.html.

21. Helft, Miguel, "How a Series of Mistakes Hurt Shares of United," www.nytimes. com/2008/09/15/technology/15google.html (Sept. 14, 2008).

22. Regan, Keith, "Computer Glitches Heaped Fuel on Stock Sell-Off," www.ecommercetimes. com/story/56032.html?wlc=1222521986&wlc=1222648420 (March 1, 2007).

23. Salisbury, Ian, and Rogow, Geoffery. "Glitches Cancel Electronic Trades," *Wall Street Journal*, www.marketwatch.com/news/story/glitches-cancel-electronic-trades/story. aspx?guid=%7B76F833E8-6A8E-4C57-9865-7B418F9DCFC7%7D (Sept. 24, 2008).

24. Goldman, David, "SEC Bans Short-selling. Agency puts temporary halt to trading practice that 'threatens investors and capital markets' for 799 financial companies," http://money.cnn. com/2008/09/19/news/economy/sec_short_selling/?postversion=2008091907 (Sept. 19, 2008).

25. The ban ended on October 8, 2008.

26. The exact reason for the price fluctuation was not disclosed by the exchange.

27. The exchange did not disclose details of the glitch or the exchange it received the order from.

28. "Erroneous Orders Routed to NASDAQ Result in Cancelled Trades," www.nasdaq. com/newsroom/news/newsroomnewsStory.aspx?textpath=pr2008\ ACQPMZ200809301844PRIMZONEFULLFEED151328.htm&cdtime=09%2f30% 2f2008%20+6%3a44PM&title=Erroneous%20Orders%20Routed%20to%20 NASDAQ%20Result%20in%20Cancelled%20Trades (New York, Sep. 30, 2008).

29. Rooney, Ben, "Google Price Corrected After Trading Snafu. Closing price adjusted after shares of the tech giant plummet due to erroneous trade. Change to final Nasdaq value to follow," http://money.cnn.com/2008/09/30/news/companies/google_nasdaq/index.htm (Sept. 30, 2008).

30. Wallace, Bruce, "Trading Blunder Raises Concerns about the Tokyo Stock Exchange," http://articles.latimes.com/2005/dec/14/business/fi-nikkei14 (Dec. 14, 2005).

31. McCurry, Justin, "Too Fat, Too Fast. The £1.6bn Finger," www.guardian.co.uk/business/2005/ dec/09/japan.internationalnews (Dec. 9, 2005).

32. McCurry, Justin, "Too Fat, Too Fast. The £1.6bn Finger," www.guardian.co.uk/business/2005/ dec/09/japan.internationalnews (Dec. 9, 2005).

33. Wilkinson, Tara Loader. "The fat finger points to trouble for traders," www.efinancialnews. com/usedition/index/content/2447370453 (Mar. 14, 2007).

13 The Future of Financial Markets

Executive Summary

The transformation to global electronic exchanges is still a work in progress. This chapter explores several trends and their impact on financial markets. Globalization could lead to monopolies, but it is now easier to assemble new competitive exchanges. Automated trading will make trading even faster, forcing exchanges to continue to innovate technologically. And other components of the trade cycle are still in the process of adapting to these changes.

The last two decades have been a busy time for financial markets around the world. Technological advances have allowed exchanges to replace the century-old floor-trading model with the electronic trading model. Markets today are far more complex, with new market structures, new trading strategies, and new trading models. The adoption of electronic trading is transforming the global landscape of financial markets, redefining not only the concept of an exchange but also the roles of nearly every player in the financial markets. Trading firms, market makers, buy-side firms, sell-side firms, clearing organizations, and regulators have undergone significant changes. The market function of all these players will undergo a dramatic transformation as they adapt to the new market structure, new products, new trading models, and increasing regulations. The balance of power will tilt as trading firms take greater control over their trades and brokers find different sources of revenue to make up for the diminishing margins for trade execution. The new financial markets will be dominated by concerns over transparency and speed. Intense competition in the coming years will help shape the global financial markets for the next century.

Exchange Consolidation

Exchanges are no longer private clubs with privileged access to a select few. Today exchanges around the world and across asset classes are restructuring their businesses to become for-profit global enterprises. Operating as public companies, exchanges are looking to expand their business franchise globally to find new growth opportunities and to increase revenue. Exchanges earn a majority of their revenue from the volume of trades on their platform. Exchanges can simultaneously increase volumes and reduce average costs by adding new products. In the new world, adding new product lines is fairly inexpensive—a few new servers and a little programming. So any new volume from the new products contributes directly to the exchange's bottom line. With exchanges being increasingly stockholder owned and publicly traded, an easy way to add products is by simply acquiring or merging with other exchanges. We expect these mergers to continue and for exchanges to get larger. Mergers between publicly traded companies are much easier than between member-owned organizations.

Exchanges across all asset classes have been merging with other exchanges to capture more market share and to expand product offerings, including new asset types. In 2007 there was approximately $39 billion worth of mergers and acquisitions.[1] Some long-established exchanges, in different asset classes and even different countries, have joined forces to compete with other exchanges and the new electronic trading platform. These transatlantic mergers include such venerable names as Nasdaq-OMX, NYSE-Euronext, and ISE-Eurex. The largest derivatives merger was the CME-CBOT-NYMEX merger during 2007 and 2008. The past few years have been pretty busy for exchange consolidation, and the trend is likely to continue. A majority of the mergers in recent years have been in North America and Europe. The rest of the world is just beginning to enter the global markets. As the financial markets continue their journey toward globalization, exchanges will continue their trend toward further consolidation. Consolidation allows exchanges to combine their product suites onto a single technology platform, thus reducing their infrastructure costs. The financial community will see further consolidation among exchanges to gain market share in different countries.

The financial community will merge multiple asset classes together to capture additional volume and market share. The trend of consolidation across asset classes has already begun with Nasdaq's acquisition of the third largest option exchange, the Philadelphia Stock Exchange (PHLX), in November 2007.[2] The acquisition of PHLX will allow Nasdaq to compete in the options market, which has grown more than 30% annually since 2003.[3] Established exchanges will find partners in other areas with fast-growing volume. With the growing popularity of OTC markets and the competitive threat they pose to exchanges, there will be a number of acquisitions of these OTC platforms by the established exchanges. CME's purchase of SwapStream in 2005 to capture the market for credit swaps and ICE's purchase of Chatham Partners to expand into the market for natural gas options are recent signs of established exchanges expanding outside their standard exchange-listed products.[4]

There are significant opportunities for further consolidation in global financial markets, including in North America and Europe, where consolidation has already been under way for several years. Australian markets had undergone some consolidation with the Australian Securities Exchange's (ASX) merger with the New Zealand Stock Exchange and the Sydney Futures Exchange. Established markets in Asia will need to consolidate to compete with larger exchanges such as NYSE and CME, which have several acquisitions already under their belt. The Tokyo Stock Exchange bought an almost 5% share of the

Singapore Exchange, the most allowed without the approval of the Monetary Authority of Singapore.[5] NYSE Euronext invested 5% in the National Stock Exchange of India, and Deutsche Börse invested 5% in the Bombay Stock Exchange.[6] Asia, by and large, has not seen a large number of mergers and acquisitions due to stricter regulation and closed financial market policies.

As the established markets in countries such as Hong Kong, Singapore, and Japan look to expand their territories, there will be a growing convergence between the East and West. In addition, markets in India and China are growing quickly and will likely use partnerships to expand into markets beyond their countries. Similarly, markets around the globe such as Brazil, Dubai, and South Africa have seen double- and triple-digit growth in recent years. As the world of financial markets becomes more flat and more open, these growth rates will further fuel mergers and acquisitions around the world. Exchanges will no longer be a single asset class isolated within one region. Instead, they will be multi-asset markets spanning multiple continents.

In Response to Exchange Consolidation

The consolidation of exchanges always raises concerns of exchanges becoming a monopoly, which could lead to stagnation in innovation and potential increases in trading cost. However, the recent emergence of new upstarts tells us that the established exchanges will continue to face pressures from new electronic platforms that will keep the overall trading cost low and innovation healthy. There are a growing number of electronic platforms, called multilateral trading facility (MTF), that are already challenging large exchanges in both the equities and the derivatives world. Chi-X, now owned by Nomura, has brought fierce competition to Europe. As of October 2008, it already owned 22% of FTSE 100 trading and 15–18% Dutch AEX, French CAC 40, and German DAX 30.[7] Chi-X claims to provide order execution 10 times faster than major European exchanges and to offer trading services significantly cheaper. The annual license fees associated with market data redistribution are zero at Chi-X compared to £44,000 at LSE and €36,750 at Euronext. The trading fees are considerably lower as well, with Chi-X charging only 0.05 basis points for DMA trade volume. By comparison, Euronext, the LSE, and Deutsche Börse charge 0.50, 0.51, and 0.57 basis points.[8]

Of course, the competition doesn't end with Chi-X. A number of other players have already launched or are planning to launch MTFs to compete with the established exchanges. Turquoise, another MTF, was also launched in the last year. Turquoise, backed by large global banks, has also made inroads and captured almost 5% of the FTSE 100. A more recent entrant has been BATS Trading, which will also compete with established exchanges such as the LSE as well as other MTFs. Plenty of other MTFs are already under development, such as Equiduct, majority owned by Börse Berlin; Burgundy, a Nordic venture backed by banks in the region; and Nasdaq OMX Europe, backed by Nasdaq OMX.[9] Whether all of them will be successful or not is yet to be seen, but one thing is for certain: Competition will remain healthy in coming years. The established exchanges have already begun responding to the threats of emerging MTFs by cutting fees and upgrading their technology to match the ultra-fast platforms offered by these upstarts.

Transparency and Speed

Trading on the floor was loud and chaotic. Physical stature mattered. The louder and taller you were, the better your chances of getting your orders filled. Electronic trading changed all that. Today traders are accessing markets around the globe through a single screen. Orders for an exchange come from around the globe electronically. The financial community can access all the information it needs to make trading decisions directly on computers. Players around the world can access the same information in real time. Electronic trading puts the focus on accessing information and submitting orders as quickly as possible. The focus has been shifted from physical stature to the stability, reliability, and speed of the trading infrastructure. These are the criteria that financial players use when developing or purchasing components to implement the trade cycle. Already in its short lifetime, electronic trading has seen significant adoption within the financial markets. According to TowerGroup, over 38% of buy-side order flow in 2008 will be pushed through algorithmic trading.[10] An IBM study estimates that over 40% of LSE trades are generated through black boxes around the world.[11] It is predicted that over 80% of equity market flow in the U.S. and Europe will be generated through automated trading applications.[12]

The rise of automated trading as well as the globalization of financial markets has produced a tremendous surge in volume across all asset classes. The increase in volume and the number of new listed products have also increased the amount of electronic information sent to and from the exchanges. Exchanges around the world have been updating their electronic trading platforms to provide fast and reliable systems to clients. The connectivity requirements at the exchanges have been increasing year after year to handle the growing message traffic. To maintain a low-latency connection to CME, the bandwidth requirement is 40 mbps,[13] which is four times faster than a typical cable modem. NYSE recommends a bandwidth of 20 mbps for optimal performance.[14] These bandwidth requirements have been steadily increasing as the exchanges' message traffic increases. TABB group predicts an increase of 140% in market data, rising from 4 billion messages per day in 2006 to 130 billion messages per day in 2010 in global equity and options markets.[15] Exchanges have been spending a significant amount of time and resources to continually upgrade their systems to efficiently support the electronic trading models and to gain a competitive advantage. The LSE spent £40 million and four years to launch its upgraded trading platform to handle and process the increasing volume.[16] The upgraded platform improved execution speed from six to three milliseconds, and it processes 20,000 messages per second, well above the previous 10,000 messages per second.[17] After suffering a number of failures due to its unstable technology platform, the Tokyo Stock Exchange spent over $500 million to upgrade its infrastructure to improve its reputation as well as prevent market share loss to competitors such as the Osaka Securities Exchange.[18]

Other financial players such as trading firms, brokers, market data vendors, and other technology providers have also been focused on improving their technology to gain a competitive edge in this rapidly changing marketplace. As the exchanges improve their technology to handle and process more data, the financial players continue to push the limits of their trading systems to trade more and trade faster. Technology players used the open exchange APIs to develop direct exchange connections to provide their clients with real-time market access. Market data providers such as Wombat and Hyperfeed gained market share by providing fast market data feeds to their clients, forcing established market data vendors such as Reuters and Bloomberg to follow a similar path to remain competitive.[19] Brokers are investing in technology to develop and improve their trading infrastructure to provide their clients with the speed and transparency that has become the cornerstone of electronic trading. They are focused on developing and acquiring technology to provide innovative and customized applications to their clients. For example, Credit Suisse is positioning itself as a full-service broker offering clients its proprietary algorithmic engine, CrossFire,[20] as well as the trading infrastructure required to get direct market access.

Transparency and speed will continue to dominate the trading world. In the coming years these two factors will reshape the financial markets and change the business models of many players. Trading firms will need to adjust their strategies and invent new trading styles to compete in a transparent world. They will build or buy applications that provide direct and fast connections to the exchanges to compete in electronic trading markets where a millisecond advantage could result in a better trade and a better price. Brokers will no longer have the advantage of privileged information and will need to reinvent their model to compete for trade execution business through value-added services, such as automated trading or a trading infrastructure that is faster than their competition. They will need to find new revenue sources by entering new markets and establishing their technology arm. Exchanges will need to provide a solid and scalable trading platform that can handle the increasing growth in volume. Technology players will need to continue to develop innovative products. More specialized technology players will emerge with innovative products that promise to provide a competitive advantage in a world where everyone has equal information. For example, Vhayu specializes in providing quality tick-by-tick information that is crucial for automated trading. Automated trading systems rely on massive, detailed market data information for markets to analyze, which help trading firms find and take advantage of new strategies and anomalies.[21]

Partnership and Alliances

To gain an edge in a fast, transparent world, technology will continue to play a crucial role in the coming years as financial markets develop the trading platforms for the next century. Exchanges have been pursuing partnerships in recent years to capture additional market share and reduce expenses. Similarly, significant numbers of vendors have emerged, offering applications to support various functions of the trade cycle. These vendors are all trying to increase market share and increase growth. We will see them develop specialized applications to differentiate themselves in the marketplace. They will forge strategic partnerships to gain a competitive advantage while reducing their technology expense. We will see strategic partnerships between these vendors and brokers as both continue to attract the trading community of hedge funds, proprietary trading funds, and other trading players.

Trading firms are building complex trading strategies covering all asset classes. With the increasing use of smart order routing, technical analysis, new order types, and new trading strategies, firms are demanding more services from brokers and vendors alike. To earn business from these trading firms, brokers and vendors will need to align themselves to provide unique services. Alliances between these two players will be increasingly important to meet the complex demands of trading firms. We will see brokers depending on vendors such as Cinnober for low-latency solutions for market data dissemination, Tethys Technology for multi-broker platform, Ullink for FIX solutions, and Quanthouse for algorithmic trading solutions. There are plenty of vendors offering specialized solutions in these spaces. The brokers will gravitate toward vendors that offer the most unique application or solutions to the latest problem, and, more important, they will forge alliances with vendors that are favored by the customers.

We will also see increasing dependence on software providers who offer networking solutions such as hosting facilities. As the customers become more computer savvy and adopt more automated trading applications, the need for speed will be increasingly important. To provide a fast, reliable solution to their customers, vendors will look to partner with other vendors such as Trading Technologies, which offers trading applications built for speed along with a high-speed hosting solution. The role of brokers is likely to change in coming years as they move to scour the lists of vendors to offer specialized services to their sophisticated client base. The vendors will continue to invest in research and technology to find new trading solutions and building systems to offer services in every component of the trade cycle. In the end, customers will benefit greatly through these strategic relationships between the brokers and vendors who will continue to offer customized solutions to meet specific needs of their customers.

Clearing: Next Transformation

As we have explored in this book, clearing is an integral part of the trade cycle. Every trade executed on exchanges around the world must be cleared through a central counterparty clearinghouse. The U.S. equities markets have long had one central clearinghouse, DTCC. However, the derivatives markets and the European equities markets have had a number of clearinghouses. The clearing landscape is at the beginning of transformation. We expect to see a new wave of both mergers and competition in the clearing area as the exchanges continue to expand their territory by acquiring exchanges around the globe. The clearinghouses also will see new opportunities as the OTC market such as credit default swaps come under the spotlight.

The clearing space saw the beginning of consolidation in 2003 when the merger between the London Clearing House and Clearnet provided a European clearing counterparty, the common clearing link between Chicago futures exchanges was formed, and a proposal to form a Global Clearing Link was floated around through the partnership between Eurex and the Clearing Corporation (CCorp). The Common Clearing Link provided significant saving to customers through margin efficiencies. It was estimated that approximately $1.7 billion in capital was saved, and free capital means trading firms have more trade, resulting in greater volume at the exchanges. The Global Clearing Link by Eurex and CCorp offers to provide clearing for both U.S. products and Eurex products through one clearing structure. This was originally prompted when Eurex launched its U.S. subsidiary, EurexUS, to compete with Chicago markets.

The clearing landscape today is undergoing a new wave of transformation. The derivatives exchanges, such as ICE, are starting their own clearinghouses to gain added revenue in clearing fees. Following on ICE's footsteps and also due to the threat from MTF, such as Project Rainbow, LIFFE recently announced its intention to leave LCH.Clearnet and move clearing of its products in-house.[22] Whether the derivatives exchanges will continue to maintain their own clearing organizations is still up for debate. Recently the U.S. Department of Justice findings claimed that the exchanges controlling their own clearing and settlement process inhibit competition and called for the separation of the clearing function from the futures exchange.[23] The new upstart MTFs coming into the picture to compete with these exchanges have also complained of challenges they face due to the fragmenting world of clearing in derivatives markets.

The pendulum has been swinging between consolidation and fragmentation in the clearing space. With recent announcements by the exchanges such as

LIFFE and ICE to launch their own clearing service, the derivatives landscape has been leaning toward fragmentation. In addition, the recent emergence of MTF and growing regulatory pressures from initiatives such as MiFID have led to two new clearinghouses, EuroCCP and European Multilateral Clearing Facility (EMCF). EMCF, a subsidiary of Fortis, plans to provide clearing services for many of the MTFs.[24]

As the exchange consolidation continues and new platforms emerge, the clearing landscape will continue to evolve, where partnerships between clearinghouses will be formed to provide links between them. The most recent announcement between DTCC and LCH.Clearnet to form a single clearinghouse perhaps is a sign that the pendulum will be swinging toward consolidation. The DTCC and LCH.Clearnet merger will provide a single clearinghouse for a wide range of asset classes such as equities, fixed income, derivatives, and OTC products such as interest rate swaps, credit default swaps, carbon emission, and freight forwards.[25] The combined group promises to provide the financial community clearing services at cost[26] and enhanced cross-margining among products, which would save users capital similar to the benefits achieved by the common clearing link between CME and CBOT.

The clearing process will see further growth as they look to enter the OTC market. The recent turmoil in the global financial markets was largely attributed to the credit derivatives market. A market with $58 trillion in notional value was traded by the trading community with essentially no central clearing counter party. The risks of this were painfully endured by the financial markets, with large investment banks such as Lehman and Bear Stearns falling and the rest getting significant bailout package from the government. By the time this book goes to print, we are likely to have not one but a couple of clearinghouses providing CCP services for the credit derivatives markets. NYSE Euronext is planning to support the credit derivatives markets on its BClear system that already process over $7.5 trillion of OTC equities derivatives markets.[27] LCH. Clearnet is planned to be the clearing service for the CDS contracts that processes through the BClear system. In addition, Eurex, the first exchange to list CDS on its platform, is also planning to provide clearing services for CDS contracts. Finally, CCorp is also looking to support CDS contracts by building a partnership with DTCC, which currently holds more than 3 million outstanding CDS contracts.[28]

Global Financial Market for the Next Century

We are a long way away from a true global marketplace where every component of the trade cycle is connected seamlessly. There is still a tremendous amount of work to be done to achieve straight-through processing, where the trades pass through front-end trading systems to the settlement process without any manual intervention.

But the past two decades have seen some tremendous changes in the financial markets. Technology has allowed exchanges to shed regional and physical boundaries and move into the global world. They have shed their member-owned model and transformed themselves into stockholder-owned companies. Through mergers, acquisitions, and partnerships, financial players are connected across asset classes and continents. The software vendors are playing an integral role in connecting exchanges, brokers, and the trading community. For example, integration of Bank of New York's proprietary algorithmic engine with Bloomberg's Execution Management System (EMS) reaches 260,000 financial users in 125 countries.[29]

These vendors will continue to develop new applications in all three areas of the trade cycle: the front office, the middle office, and the back office. There has been significant innovation in the front office. Numerous vendors offer trading screen, charting, and analytical tools; pre-trade risk management tools; exchange connectivity; and market data engines. We will continue to see innovation in the front-office to meet the changing needs of the trading community. We also believe that there will be greater innovation, collaboration, and standardization in the middle and back office. Just as FIX has become the standardized protocol for the front office, the vendors are depending on SWIFT as the standard protocol for the back office. There is a tremendous amount of fragmentation in the back-office area where firms are handling multiple interfaces for back-office tasks such as trade reporting, end-of-the-day price reporting, and collateral reporting. The standardization in the back-office area will lead to new applications to move the financial markets another step closer to STP.

Common Platforms

The recent transatlantic mergers such as NYSE-Euronext, ISE-Eurex, and Nasdaq-OMX have certainly given these exchanges greater share of the global financial markets. As we have explored in this book, these mergers have helped capture new products and increase volume. They have also helped achieve economies of scale by merging technology and operating expense between the exchanges. NYSE-Euronext hopes to achieve a $250 million reduction annually in its operating expense and deliver a single trading platform across asset classes. NYSE-Euronext wants to build a single platform to connect its seven options markets between the United States and Europe (Amsterdam, Paris, London, Brussels, and Lisbon in Europe and Arca and AMEX in the United States).

By providing one platform,[30] the exchange hopes to increase volume by having its European customers trade the U.S. markets, and vice versa. To provide a single global platform, NYSE-Euronext knows it has to provide a consolidated market data feed and a solid infrastructure for connectivity. And it is on its way to achieving that in next couple of years. With its recent purchase of Wombat, a company specializing in high-speed delivery of market data, NYSE will provide new market data feeds across all asset classes supported by NYSE-Euronext. To provide global connectivity, NYSE-Euronext has rolled out the Secure Financial Transaction Infrastructure (SFTI), which will allow its members and vendors to connect to all NYSE-Euronext services. The SFTI is already available in the United States and, with access centers in London, Paris, Amsterdam, Brussels, and Lisbon now set up, NYSE-Euronext's European base will be able to connect to all the NYSE-Euronext services.[31]

Similarly, the Eurex and ISE partnership is also looking to build a common trading and clearing platform to provide its global customer base cross-border access to its products. Eurex-ISE plans to provide clearing links through the Options Clearing Corporation. With this link established, Eurex members will have access to the 2000 ISE products and will be able to trade these products through its existing Eurex connectivity. The common clearing link will allow these members to trade ISE products and still be able to clear these products through their existing Eurex Clearing setup.[32] The common trading and clearing platform will be crucial to the success of the exchanges that have merged in recent years and for the financial community to experience a truly global financial market.

Looking Ahead

As in so many other industries, the computer revolution has upended financial markets. Though face-to-face interactions between traders worked for centuries, it was swept away in a few short decades by computers and telecom networks. Where traders once shouted orders on a trading floor, they now tap them into a computer. Where traders were once limited to the suite of products available in their pits, they can now scan products and markets across the globe. Where private regional exchanges once handled local products, profit-seeking exchanges now cross national borders to reach a broad audience of global traders. Vast quantities of data travel at the speed of light around the globe to new markets with new products. The flowering of fresh competition in every component of the trade cycle has led to rapid innovations and radical changes in the markets. All this change and turmoil in financial markets is just a side effect of the computer revolution.

The future of financial markets will surely be as tumultuous as its recent past. The transformation from the floor to the screen is only half the revolution. Most OTC products have yet to move to electronic exchanges. Many back-end operations still rely on ad hoc communications, such as text files, emails, phone calls, and faxes. Until markets agree on an API, these components will be a drag on market efficiency. Regulators will need to catch up to the new realities of a fast-moving global marketplace. Though the leading exchanges will try to dominate different markets, new platforms will pop up quickly to undercut their monopolies. The next wave to hit financial markets will come from new players that invent new business models to help markets move closer to straight-through processing.

Endnotes

1. Edqar Ortega, "Nasdaq and Goldman Set Their Sights on Philadelphia Stock Exchange," www.iht.com/articles/2007/10/21/bloomberg/bxexchange.php (Oct. 22, 2007).
2. "NASDAQ to Acquire Philadelphia Stock Exchange," www.nasdaq.com/newsroom/news/newsroomnewsStory.aspx?textpath=pr2007%5CACQPMZ200711070730PRIMZONEFULLFEED130788.htm.
3. "NASDAQ to Acquire Philadelphia Stock Exchange," www.nasdaq.com/newsroom/news/newsroomnewsStory.aspx?textpath=pr2007%5CACQPMZ200711070730PRIMZONEFULLFEED130788.htm.
4. Dora, James, "The Mating Game: Exchange Consolidation Hits a Fever Pitch," www.futuresindustry.org/fi-magazine-home.asp?a=1219.
5. Dora, James, "The Mating Game: Exchange Consolidation Hits a Fever Pitch," www.futuresindustry.org/fi-magazine-home.asp?a=1219.
6. Scherer, Ivy, "Exchange Consolidation Wave Is Expected to Continue in 2008. U.S. exchanges are seeking mergers overseas and looking to consolidate with U.S. regional exchanges to diversify into multiple asset classes and cut technology costs," www.advancedtrading.com/crossingnetworks/showArticle.jhtml;jsessionid=XBDDMTPQANXHKQSNDLOSKH0CJUNN2JVN?articleID=202800838&_requestid=140313 (October 31, 2007).
7. Kim Jim. "Chi-X Faring Well Still in Europe," www.fiercefinanceit.com/story/chi-x-faring-well-still-europe/2008-10-08 (Oct. 2008).
8. Randal, Peter, "New Super-speed Competition," www.ftmandate.com/news/fullstory.php/aid/1414/New_super-speed_competition.html (April 2007).
9. Grant, Jeremy, "The Fast Bowlers Arrive," www.ft.com/cms/s/0/eea60bbc-7788-11dd-be24-0000779fd18c.html?nclick_check=1 (Aug. 31, 2008).
10. Webster, Paul, "A Need for Speed: The Rise of Algorithmic Trading," www.canadianbusiness.com/innovation/article.jsp?content=20070605_142120_1116 (Canadian business online June 5, 2007).
11. www-03.ibm.com/industries/financialservices/doc/content/bin/fss_latency_arms_race.pdf.
12. "Algorithmic Trading: Behind the trade," www.ibspublishing.com/index.cfm?section=TRP&action=view&id=10831 (June 2007).
13. "Network Access Options," www.cme.com/trading/get/trad/netaccopt.html.
14. NYSE Transact Tools, www.nysetransacttools.com/news/wp-content/uploads/2007/12/sfti_bandwidth_guidelines_tt.pdf.
15. Rabkin Martin, "Investment on High-Speed, Advanced-Trading Infrastructure Value Chain across Asset Classes to Hit $860M in 2007, Rising to $1.3B by 2010, Says TABB Group," www.tabbgroup.com/PageDetail.aspx?PageID=16&ItemID=48.
16. Luke Jeffs, "European Exchanges Focus on Execution Speed," www.efinancialnews.com/usedition/content/2451371489 (July 30, 2008).
17. Luke Jeffs, "European Exchanges Focus on Execution Speed," www.efinancialnews.com/usedition/content/2451371489 (July 30, 2008).
18. www.rblt.com/documents/SIN100807.pdf.
19. Whitney, Tina, "The Need for Speed: Market Data Vendors Ramp Up Offerings," www.wallstreetandtech.com/news/trading/showArticle.jhtml?articleID=21700216 (June 10, 2004).
20. Eugene Grygo, "Brokers in Battle for Algo Market," www.efinancialnews.com/tradingandtechnology/index/content/2450491046 (Apr. 28, 2008).

21. Whitney, Tina, "The Need for Speed: Market Data Vendors Ramp Up Offerings," www.wallstreetandtech.com/news/trading/showArticle.jhtml?articleID=21700216 (June 10, 2004).
22. The proposal is pending approval of both LCH.Clearnet and U.K. regulators
23. "Liffe to Move into Clearing – Bloomberg"; London-based derivatives exchange Liffe is planning to enter the clearing business in a bid to fight off competition from Project Rainbow, the European exchange being set up by investment banks, according to a Bloomberg report, www.finextra.com/fullstory.asp?id=18151 (Feb. 27, 2008).
24. www.ipe.com/articles/print.php?id=29211.
25. Peggy Bresnick Kendler, "DTCC, LCH.Clearnet Announce Plans to Merge and Create Single Clearing House; The merger proposal aims to create the world's leading clearing house," *Bank Systems & Technology*, www.banktech.com/payments-and-cards/showArticle.jhtml?articleID=211600050 (October 22, 2008).
26. Any excess left over after the operating expenses are covered will be returned to the users in the form of rebates.
27. "We're Ahead in CDS Clearing Race, Claims Liffe," www.fointelligence.com/Article/2034529/Were-ahead-in-CDS-clearing-race-claims-Liffe.html (Oct. 23, 2008).
28. Will Acworth, "Clearing the Deck: Credit Derivatives Market Moves Closer to Clearing Solution," www.futuresindustry.org/fi-magazine-home.asp?a=1255.
29. "BNY Brokerage Provides Access to Trading Algorithms through Bloomberg Professional Service," www.bobsguide.com/guide/news/2006/Feb/14/BNY_Brokerage_Provides_Access_to_Trading_Algorithms_through_Bloomberg_Professional_Service.html (February 14, 2006—BNY Brokerage, a subsidiary of The Bank of New York).
30. Currently there are two platforms: NYSE Arca for US Options and LiffeConnect for European options trading.
31. Sherree DeCovny, "Transatlantic Connections: Exchanges Link U.S. and European Options Markets," www.futuresindustry.org/fi-magazine-home.asp?a=1269 (Oct. 2008).
32. The common clearing link is currently under regulatory approval. Eurex, ISE, and the OCC expect to provide the transatlantic link by the second half of 2009.

Appendix A Abbreviations Used

Abbreviation	Exchange
AMEX	American Stock Exchange
a/c/e	alliance/CBOT/Eurex
AMEX	American Stock Exange
API	Application Programming Interface
Arca	Archipelago
ASX	Australian Stock Exchange
ASX	Australian Securities Exchange
ATS	Alternative Trading System
BEC	Bolsa Electrónica de Chile
BISX	Bahamas Intl. Securities Exchange
BM&F	Brazilian Mercantile & Futures Exchange (BM&F)
BMV	Mexican Stock Exchange
BOTCC	Board of Trade Clearing Corporation
BOVESPA	Bolsa de Valores de São Paulo (São Paulo Stock Exchange)
BOX	Boston Options Exchange
BSE	Budapest Stock Exchange
BSE	Bombay Stock Exchange
BSE	Bulgarian Stock Exchange
BSE	Boston Stock Exchange
BVL	Lima Stock Exchange
CASE	Egyptian Exchange
CBOE	Chicago Board Options Exchange
CBOT	Chicago Board of Trade
CCorp	Clearing Corporation (formerly BOTCC)
CCP	Central Clearing Counterparty
CESR	Committee of European Securities Regulators
CFTC	Commodity Futures Trading Commission
CHX	Chicago Stock Exchange
CME	Chicago Mercantile Exchange
COMEX	The Commodity Exchange
CSE	Cyprus Stock Exchange

Abbreviation	Exchange
DCE	Dalian Commodity Exchange
DFM	Dubai Financial Market
DIFX	Dubai International Financial Exchange
DTB	Deutsche Termin Boerse
ECN	Electronic Communications Network
EMS	Execution Management System
ETF	Exchange Traded Fund
Eurex	European exchange
FCM	Futures Commission Merchant
FIA	Futures Industry Association
FIX	Financial Information eXchange
GUI	Graphical User Interface
HKFE	Hong Kong Futures Exchange
ICCH	International Commodities Clearing House
ICE	Intercontinental Exchange
IDX	Indonesia Stock Exchange
INTEX	INTEX
IOSCO	International Organization of Securities Commissions
IPE	International Petroleum Exchange
IPO	initial public offering
ISE	International Securities Exchange
ISE	Istanbul Stock Exchange
ISE	Irish Stock Exchange
ISV	Independent Software Vendor
JSE	Johannesburg Stock Exchange
JSE	Jamaica Stock Exchange
JSE	Johannesburg Securities Exchange
KCBT	Kansas City Board of Trade
KRX	Korea Exchange
KSE	Kuwait Stock Exchange
LIFFE	London International Financial Futures & Options Exchange
LME	London Metal Exchange
LSE	London Stock Exchange
MATba	Mercado A Termino De Buenos Aires
MATIF	Marchéà Terme International de France
ME	Bourse De Montreal

Abbreviation	Exchange
MEXDER	Mexican Derivatives Exchange (MEXDER)
MGE or MGEX	Minneapolis Grain Exchange
NASD	National Association of Securities Dealers
NASDAQ	National Association of Securities Dealers Automated Quotation System
NCDEX	National Commodity an Derivative Exchange
NFA	National Futures Association
NMCE	Multi Commodity Exchange of India
NSE	National Stock Exchange
NSE	National Stock Exchange (former Cincinnati Exch)
NSE	National Stock Exchange of India
NSX	National Stock Exchange of Australia
NYBOT	New York Board of Trade
NYFE	New York Futures Exchange
NYMEX	New York Mercantile Exchange
NYSE	New York Stock Exchange
NZFOE	New Zealand Futures and Options Exchange
NZSE	New Zealand Exchange (NZX)
OCC	Options Clearing Corporation
OMX	OM (Optionsmäklarna) Exchange
OMS	Order Management System
OSE	Oslo Exchange
OSE	Osaka Securities Exchange
PCX	Pacific Exchange
PHLX	Philadelphia Stock Exchange
PSE	Prague Stock Exchange
SAFEX	South African Futures Exchange
SEBI	Securities and Exchange Board of India
SEC	Securities and Exchange Commission
SET	Stock Exchange of Thailand
SFE	Sydney Futures Exchange
SGX	Singapore Exchange
SHFE	Shanghai Futures Exchange
SIMEX	Singapore International Monetary Exchange
SOFFEX	Swiss Options and Financial Futures Exchange
SSE	Shanghai Stock Exchange

Abbreviation	Exchange
SSE	Shenzhen Stock Exchange
SWX Europe	Swiss Exchange Europe (was virt-x)
STP	Straight Through Processing
TADAWUL	Saudi Stock Exchange
TAIFEX	Taiwan Futures Exchange
TASE	Tel-Aviv Stock Exchange
TGE	Tokyo Grain Exchange
TIFFE	Tokyo International Financial Futures Exchange
TOCOM	Tokyo Commodity Exchange
TSE	Tehran Stock Exchange
TSE	Tokyo Stock Exchange
TSX	Toronto Stock Exchange
TWAP	Time Weighted Average Price
USFE	US Futures Exchange
VWAP	Volume Weighted Average Price
WCE	Winnipeg Commodity Exchange
WSE	Warsaw Stock Exchange
ZCE	Zhengzhou Commodity Exchange

Appendix B Technology Terminology

Application Programming Interface (API)	A set of functions, procedures, methods, classes or protocols that is used by a software program to request another software to perform a task.
ECN (Electronic communication network)	A computer system that facilitates trading of financial products electronically.
Exchange Gateway	A bridge between trading screens or automated trading system and the exchange matching engine. Orders routed from any trading terminal first goes through the exchange gateway where they either gets accepted or rejected based on the order structure.
Execution Management system (EMS)	A software application that allows financial community access to multiple trading venues similar to front-end trading systems. EMS generally offers trading community access to exchanges, crossing networks, and brokers' trading network.
Financial Information eXchange (FIX)	The FIX Protocol is an open messaging specification used by the financial industry to standardize electronic communication in the financial markets.
FIXML	FIXML is FIX implemented using XML, a structured validated eXtensible Markup Language that is widely used by the computer industry.
Graphical User Interface (GUI)	A computer screen which allows user to interact with computer program. Front-end trading screen serves as the GUI for traders to trade across exchanges electronically.
Hosting facility	A data center that operates and maintains computers and software systems for other companies for a fee.
Independent Software Vendor (ISV)	Usually small software company that builds products that depend on software platforms built by larger software companies.
Market data	Refers to the bid and ask prices of the financial instrument as well as additional trade related information such as order quantity, last traded price, trade time, and trade volume.
Matching engine	A system at the exchange that pairs all the buy and sell orders that are at the same price based on the matching rules defined by the exchanges.

Order Management System (OMS)	A computer software system used by the financial community to manage order flow between trading systems and exchanges. OMS validates and routes orders received from trading systems to the appropriate trading venue.
Straight through processing (STP)	STP enables the entire trade process and payment transactions to be conducted electronically without any manual intervention by a person.
SWIFT	Society of Worldwide Interbank Financial Telecommunication (SWIFT) is a messaging standard for financial industry. SWIFT messages are used primarily for back-end processing such as transfer of funds between two banks.
TCP/IP	A low level protocol for transferring data between computers.
Trading screen	A popular term used to describe the computer system used by the traders to conduct trading activities.
Time Weighted Average Price (TWAP)	A trading strategy to achieve a specified average price for contracts or shares over a specified time.
Volume Weighted Average Price (VWAP)	A trading strategy toVolume-Weighted Average Price (VWAP) is the ratio of the value traded to total volume traded over a particular time horizon (usually one day). It is a measure of the average price a stock traded at over the trading horizon.

Appendix C Markets Glossary

Ask There are often several resting limit orders to sell in any liquid market. Each of these orders has a price associated with it. These prices associated with offers to sell are called offers or asking prices. The lowest of these asking prices or offers is generally referred as "the ask" or "the offer" or the best offer. In a dealer market, the dealer or market maker will have a single offer or ask at which customers can buy from the dealer.

Basket Trade This is a trade in which a group of securities, currencies or futures contracts is bought or sold with a single order. Fidelity, for example, will take basket orders for 2-50 securities, with a minimum size of $2,000.

Bid There are often several limit orders to buy in any liquid market. Each of these orders has a price associated with it. All of these limit buy orders are bids, but the highest of these prices or bids is generally referred to as the bid or the best bid. In a dealer market, the dealer or market maker will have a single bid at which customers can sell to the dealer.

Bid-Ask spread The difference between the highest bid and the lowest offer is known as the bid ask spread. A small bid-ask spread is generally a sign of a liquid market.

Bond A debt security, issued by a corporation or government entity. The most common is the bullet bond where the issuer agrees to pay the face value of the bond on the bond's maturity date and to pay an annual or semi-annual amount equal to the "coupon interest rate" times the face value of the bond. For example, a $1,000 face value bond with a coupon interest rate of 10% would require the issuer to pay $100 interest each year, typically divided into two equal payments of $50 every six months.

Buy side The "buy side" refers to those who buy exchange services, those who do the investing like pension funds, mutual funds, and hedge funds. This is distinguished from sell side, which are firms that sell exchange services, firms like brokerage firms.

CCP A central counterparty (CCP) is a financial institution that facilitates the trading process between the buyers and sellers. It functions as a buyer to the sellers and as a seller to all buyers.

Dark Pool	Dark pools are markets, generally used by institutional investors, in which large orders can be matched without a big effect on the prices quoted in the public markets. The bids, offers and trades are not publically quoted and participants can remain anonymous until the trade is made. Dark pools are owned by exchanges, broker-dealers but can be independent like Liquidnet.
ETF	ETF's are instruments that hold a basket of assets, usually stocks and bonds, that generally track some index. These instruments are traded on stock exchanges. The value of ETFs are generally quite close to the underlying basket of assets, unlike closed end funds whose value can deviate significantly from the value of the underlying assets, referred to as the net asset value. Available since the early 1990s, ETFs have become very popular.
Futures	A futures contract is a legal contract between two parties to transfer a particular financial instrument or commodity (standardized by the exchange) at a particular time and at a particular price in the future. Beginning in 1981, some futures contracts have been designed to avoid the need for physical delivery by being "cash settled" which means there is one last marking to market to some cash price or index, thus ensuring convergence between cash and futures prices. All stock index futures contracts are cash settled as is the 3-month Eurodollar contract, the world's largest. Marking to market is one of the financial safeguards in futures markets whereby funds are transferred from the accounts of losers to winners on a daily basis based on each day's settlement (closing) price.
Limit order	A limit order is an order to buy or sell a financial instrument or derivative at a price equal to or better than some specified price.
Market Maker	A firm or individual who continuously quotes both a buy and a sell price in the market for a financial instrument or commodity, creating the opportunity for customers to buy and sell when they wish and allows the market maker to make a profit from the bid/offer spread.
Market order	A market order is an order to buy or sell a financial instrument or derivative immediately at the "best" price currently available in the market.

Options	An options contract gives the holder or buyer the right (but not an obligation) to buy some asset (a call option) or sell some asset (a put option) at a specified price (called the strike or exercise price). Options are traded both on exchanges as well as OTC. The most popular exchange traded options are based on individual stocks or stock indexes, though they are also available on debt, foreign exchange and physical commodities. Like futures, exchange-traded options are highly standardized. American options can be exercised at any time on or before the expiration date, whereas European options can be exercised only on the expiration date.
OTC	Financial assets can be traded either on exchanges or over the counter (OTC). An OTC trade is directly between two parties, traditionally over the telephone, but increasingly on electronic platforms. The term comes from early times when stocks and bonds would be purchased over the counter at a bank window. The OTC market is bigger than the exchange traded market and includes stocks, bonds, foreign exchange, commodities and derivatives. The world's largest market, the $3.2 trillion per day foreign exchange market, is over 95% OTC. Unlike exchange traded products, which are highly standardized, the OTC market allows for transactions to be customized to traders needs. The downside is that counterparty risk is much greater, which is why increasingly OTC trades are being moved into exchange clearing houses to reduce that risk.
Sell side	Sell side refers to firms, like broker/dealers and futures commission merchants, that sell securities to buy side firms or investors.
Settlement	Settlement is the process that involves delivering shares, bonds, foreign currency or commodities in return for payment. This is the last step in a trade that fulfils the obligations of both parties. In US equities, for example, settlement occurs on the third business day following the trade, referred to as T+3 (for trade date plus 3 days). Most OTC foreign exchange transactions are settled T+2.
Specialist	Specialists are members of an exchange who oversee the floor and are responsible for maintaining a fair and orderly market. They electronically execute orders that are passed to them by various traders and brokers.

Spread   The spread can refer to the bid-ask spread, the difference
                      between the bid and ask prices in a specific market. Or the
                      difference in prices or rates in two related markets or
                      instruments, such as the interest rate spread between junk
                      bonds and AAA corporate bonds.

Stock   A stock or equity is a financial instrument that denotes an
                      ownership right in a corporation.

Scalper   Scalpers, or locals for local trader on a floor, are traders who
                      trade to benefit from small price movements in the market.
                      In effect they act as market makers by providing liquidity to
                      a market by being ready to buy a little lower and sell a little
                      higher than the last trade. They may only keep their
                      positions only for seconds or minutes.

Index